This is a general study of the development of higher education in Europe from antiquity until the end of the middle ages, set against a background of the social and political history of the period. It shows how the slender traditions of ancient learning, kept alive in the monastic and cathedral schools, was enriched by an enormous influx of knowledge from the Islamic world and how in consequence the schools developed into universities. These early institutions are examined from a variety of points of view, as institutions, as places where ideas spread, and as points of interaction with local and national authority. Special attention is paid to early intellectual history and to the scientific disciplines, and to the everyday life of the students and their teachers.

The book is intended as a broad introduction to the subject for students of the history of education, but it will also attract general readers with only a slight knowledge of the subject.

THE FIRST UNIVERSITIES

THE FIRST UNIVERSITIES

Studium generale *and the origins of university education in Europe*

OLAF PEDERSEN
Aarhus University

English translation by Richard North

CAMBRIDGE UNIVERSITY PRESS
Cambridge, New York, Melbourne, Madrid, Cape Town, Singapore, São Paulo, Delhi

Cambridge University Press
The Edinburgh Building, Cambridge CB2 8RU, UK

Published in the United States of America by Cambridge University Press, New York

www.cambridge.org
Information on this title: www.cambridge.org/9780521105231

© Olaf Pedersen 1997

This publication is in copyright. Subject to statutory exception
and to the provisions of relevant collective licensing agreements,
no reproduction of any part may take place without the written
permission of Cambridge University Press.

First published 1997
Reprinted 2000
This digitally printed version 2009

A catalogue record for this publication is available from the British Library

Library of Congress Cataloguing in Publication data
Pedersen, Olaf.
The first universities: *Studium generale* and the origins of
university education in Europe/Olaf Pedersen.
p. cm.
Includes bibliographical references and index
ISBN 0 521 59431 6 hardback
1. Universities and colleges – Europe – History. 2. Education,
Higher – Europe – History.   I. Title.
LA628.P43   1997
378.4′09′02 – dc21   97–7037 CIP

ISBN 978-0-521-59431-8 hardback
ISBN 978-0-521-10523-1 paperback

Contents

Preface	page ix
Preface to the English edition	xiii
List of abbreviations	xiv
1 The classical inheritance	1
2 From ancient science to monastic learning	29
3 The Carolingian Renaissance	67
4 The schools of the middle ages	92
5 From school to *studium generale*	122
6 The battle for the universities	155
7 Structure and form of government	189
8 The material situation	213
9 The road to degrees	242
10 Curricula and intellectual trends	271
Index of names	302
A. Early period	302
B. Modern authors	307

Preface

Modern study of the earliest history of the universities was begun at the close of the last century. In 1885 Heinrich Denifle published *Die Entstehung der Universitäten des Mittelalters bis 1400*, which was followed ten years later by Hastings Rashdall's *The Universities of Europe in the Middle Ages*. So far no work has superseded these pioneering efforts in matters of accuracy and control of the source material. That this material is of an extremely variegated and impenetrable character has certainly prevented many researchers from attempting to give any summary of corresponding range and quality. However, there are reasons to consider treating the subject again, even if this is in a more modest and popular type of book which claims only to be introductory reading and in no way comparable with the two works mentioned above.

Some reasons are of a personal nature. With many years' experience of the 'internal' history of science, it is easy to understand the growing urge to know its external boundaries – in medieval terms, the schools and universities, which were at that time the only real workshops of science and learning. Other reasons are more general. The universities of our day are in many ways legitimate children of medieval parents, and many of our present difficulties, on closer inspection, appear to have been built into the system right from the beginning. Historical reflections are scarcely any help in solving contemporary problems; but on the other hand a certain acquaintance with the historical development may even contribute to a more relaxed and tolerant attitude to present-day events.

I would also be the last to deny shortcomings and weaknesses in this book. Many important questions have been left out, while others have been very cursorily treated. This is especially true of the extremely important interaction that took place between Arabic and Latin science and was one of the main causes of the reorganisation of higher learning in Europe. I have only hinted at this theme, given that a truly satisfactory treatment would need a book of its own, and one which, for linguistic reasons alone, I would be unable to write.

The main problem with a work of this kind lies in methodology. Since the last century, the range and quality of source material for university history has greatly increased. With the *Chartularium* of the University of Paris as an eminent example, numerous universities have published major and minor collections of their older documents. In addition, numerous monographs and dissertations have appeared on individual universities, specialised periods and problems, which all in all make the history of the university seem like an impenetrable jungle in which it would be a capital offence to tread. In a situation of this kind I have followed a very primitive method – to stay with sources and primary literature long enough to see emerging a picture of the entirety whose main features I can then illustrate with selected examples. This has been done in full awareness of the dangers of an exemplifying approach. The examples chosen might not be true to type, and they might be insufficient, irrelevant, or anecdotal. The extent to which the result is justified by the means is an open question which may be left to the reader's final judgement; but there are certain fundamental points of view that deserve to be brought to light.

In this book the medieval university is consistently regarded as a social organism, in the proper sense of the word. Until now the first universities were often taken to be unworldly debating societies for theological quibbles or the abstractions of philosophy. Today it is possible to regard them as organised structures which evolved from the learned world of the past in a constant attempt to meet pressing social needs, at a time when people were striving to protect their own more narrow interests. This has ensured that no mention is made in the following discussion of the history of science or learning in the narrow sense of the word. The main emphasis is on the correlation between the university as an institution on the one hand, with the external pressures of the society it was meant to serve on the other. This comes out most strongly in the two central chapters of this book. In chapter 5 it is argued that the real impulse for reshaping the schools of the twelfth century into universities was due not only to scholarly motivation within, but also to a political run of events outside that was closely connected to the struggle between emperor and pope, each of whom in his own way courted the favour of the world of learning. In the same way, chapter 6 shows in essence how the structure of the university reached its final form during some thirteenth-century battles for leadership over the new institutions. In all ages university people like to think of themselves as seekers after truth. Here they appear also as people who impatiently fought for power – with each other and with the authorities outside their walls – both to win and to keep as much academic autonomy as possible.

Throughout this work there is much emphasis on the progress of higher learning through history. Late medieval historians often regarded their own universities as identical with the famous schools of antiquity in Athens and Alexandria, which were now supposed to live on in Paris or Oxford. The grain of truth contained in this naive idea was that certain traditions from antiquity exerted an influence from the earliest times on the medieval system of learning as a whole. Some of the more important elements of this tradition are discussed in the first chapter. This is a matter not only of ancient science, the significance of which for posterity has always been obvious, but also of the Roman law which was later to become not only an important university subject but also – through its doctrine of corporations – an established instrument with which the structure of the university itself could be fixed and the battle for independence won. There is naturally reason to apologise if the material in this chapter is so compressed as to irritate the reader already familiar with the face of science in antiquity. Nonetheless, an apology will not do for the two chapters following, even if some find them superfluous or even too circumstantial as accounts of what took place in a period when all progress beyond the established norm had reached a standstill. Seen from within, both the age of monastic learning and the Carolingian Renaissance seem to have been crucial to the later successful placing of the piecemeal legacy of antiquity into a new social and ideological context.

This book attempts to describe the prehistory and origin of the universities. The main part of this material therefore touches on the time towards and during the thirteenth century, even if my last chapters discuss material of a later time in deference to other needs, such as a consistent account of the conditions of scholars, the normal course of their study, and the intellectual progress of the universities themselves. However, this demarcation ensures that many essential questions go unanswered. For example, there is the expansion of the university system all across later medieval Europe to be considered, and the effects of the individual faculties on such important sectors of society as the health service, popular education, the training of priests, and the system of law. There is also the universities' attempt to find their feet in new movements such as humanism, the Reformation, and the new sciences and technology, within a Europe more or less characterised by nationalism, capitalism, and imperialism. It is my hope to be able to conclude my account of the history of the medieval university with yet another volume in which these questions are illuminated.

Here I shall take the opportunity to express my thanks to the friends who in various ways have helped me during my work in the past ten years. In the first instance this means many colleagues and friends both here and abroad whose names are too numerous to mention, but whose knowledge and interest have been of great help to me. This applies to my wife, too – without her constant encouragement, I could scarcely have turned what was originally a brief series of lectures into a book that was fit to publish. I am also indebted to assistants at the Institute of the History of the Exact Sciences at the University of Aarhus and especially to Kate Larsen, Mette Dybdahl, and Else Lehmann, who took much patient care with my manuscript and its many earlier drafts. I am grateful to the fellows of St Edmund's House in Cambridge for the opportunity to steep myself in the source material and discuss the subject of this book with colleagues in a comfortable and rewarding environment.

Preface to the English edition

The English version of this book owes its existence to the initiative of the late Professor Edward Shils to whose memory I feel truly indebted. I am also very grateful to Richard North who made the translation, and to the Danish Research Council which gave it financial support. Finally I wish to thank Jean Field for her meticulous work on making the manuscript ready for the press.

Abbreviations

Aigrain	R. Aigrain, *Histoire des universités*, Paris, 1949
Arts libéraux	*Arts libéraux et philosophie au moyen âge*, Actes du 3e Congrès International de Philosophie Médiévale, Montréal–Paris, 1969
Catto	J. I. Catto (ed.), *The Early Oxford Schools*, Oxford, 1984 (*The History of the University of Oxford*, vol. 1)
Chartularium	*Chartularium Universitatis Parisiensis*, I–IV, ed. H. Denifle and A. Châtelain, Paris, 1889–97
Cobban	A. B. Cobban, *The Medieval Universities, Their Development and Organisation*, London, 1975
Cooper	C. H. Cooper, *Annals of Cambridge*, vol. I, Cambridge, 1842
Decreta	*Corpus Juris Canonici*, I–II, ed. J. H. Boehmer, Leipzig, 1839
Denifle	H. Denifle, *Die Entstehung der Universitäten des Mittelalters bis 1400*, Berlin, 1885 (repr. Graz, 1956)
Digesta	*The Digest of Justinian*, I–II, transl. C. H. Munro, Cambridge, 1904–9
D'Irsay	S. D'Irsay, *Histoire des universités françaises et étrangères des origines à nos jours*, vols. I–II, Paris, 1933–5
DSB	*Dictionary of Scientific Biography*, vols. I–XIV, New York, 1970–8
Dyer	G. Dyer, *The Privileges of the University of Cambridge*, vols. I–II, London, 1824
Gabriel	A. L. Gabriel, *Garlandia. Studies in the History of the Mediaeval University*, Notre Dame, 1969

Gilson	E. Gilson, *La philosophie au moyen âge*, 3rd edn, Paris, 1947
Grabmann	M. Grabmann, *Geschichte der scholastischen Methode*, vols. I–II, Freiburg i.B., 1909–11 (repr. Graz, 1957)
Haskins	C. H. Haskins, *Studies in the History of Mediaeval Science*, Cambridge, Mass., 1924
Jedin	H. Jedin (ed.), *Handbuch der Kirchengeschichte*, vols. I–III, Freiburg, 1963–8
Kibre	P. Kibre, *Scholarly Privileges in the Middle Ages. The Rights, Privileges, and Immunities of Scholars and Universities at Bologna, Padua, Paris, and Oxford*, London, 1961 (Publications of the Medieval Society of America no. 72)
Koch	J. Koch (ed.), *Artes liberales von der antiken Bildung zur Wissenschaft des Mittelalters*, Leiden, 1959 (repr. 1976)
Leach	A. F. Leach, *Educational Charters and Documents A.D. 598–1909*, Cambridge, 1911
Leff	G. Leff, *Paris and Oxford Universities in the Thirteenth and Fourteenth Centuries*, New York, 1968
Le Goff	J. Le Goff, *Les intellectuels au moyen âge*, Paris, 1960
Liber Procuratorum	*Liber Procuratorum Nationis Anglicanae in Universitate Parisiensi*, vol. II, ed. H. Denifle and A. Châtelain, new edn by H. Didier, Paris, 1937
Mallet	C. E. Mallet, *A History of the University of Oxford*, vol. I, Oxford, 1924
Mansi	J. D. Mansi, *Sanctorum Conciliorum Amplissima Collectio*, I–XXXV, Florence–Venice, 1759–98
Marrou	H.-I. Marrou, *Histoire de l'éducation dans l'antiquité*, Paris, 1948
Migne PL	*Patrologiae Cursus Completus: Patrologia Latina* 1–224, Paris, 1844–64
Mullinger	J. Bass Mullinger, *The University of Cambridge*, vol. I, Cambridge, 1873
Rait	R. S. Rait, *Life in the Medieval University*, Cambridge, 1912

Rashdall	H. Rashdall, *The Universities of Europe in the Middle Ages*, vols. I–III, 2nd edn by F. M. Powicke and A. B. Emden, Oxford, 1936
Ridder-Symoens	H. de Ridder-Symoens (ed.), *Universities in the Middle Ages*, Cambridge, 1992 [*A History of the University in Europe*, vol. 1, ed. W. Rüegg]
Salter	H. E. Salter (ed.), *Mediaeval Archives of the University of Oxford*, vols. I–II, Oxford, 1920–1
Sarton	G. Sarton, *Introduction to the History of Science*, vols. I–III, Baltimore–Washington, 1927–47
Sorbelli	A. Sorbelli and L. Simeoni, *Storia della Universita di Bologna*, vol. I, Bologna, 1940
Strickland	Strickland Gibson (ed.), *Statuta Antiqua Universitatis Oxoniensis*, Oxford, 1931
Thorndike	L. Thorndike, *University Records and Life in the Middle Ages*, New York, 1944
Thurot	Ch. Thurot, *De l'organisation de l'enseignement dans l'Université de Paris au Moyen Age*, Paris, 1850
Ullmann	W. Ullmann, *Law and Politics in the Middle Ages*, London, 1975
Waddell	H. Waddell, *The Wandering Scholars*, London, 1927, new edn, 1954
White	Lynn White jr, *Mediaeval Technology and Social Change*, Oxford, 1952
Wise	J. E. Wise, *The Nature of the Liberal Arts*, Milwaukee, 1947

CHAPTER I

The classical inheritance

Today the oldest universities in Europe trace their history back to the middle ages, and they generally date their origin to a time around the end of the twelfth century. However, this has often been difficult to determine precisely, because the sources are sparse and the concept of a university itself was still not clear at that time. In medieval times people were not satisfied with this kind of dating. Historians of the past in England were convinced that the university in Oxford had already been founded in the ninth century by King Alfred the Great, and on the continent people regarded the university in Paris as a direct descendant of Plato's old Academy in Athens, which they thought had been moved to the French capital via Rome. Never mind that such ideas are chiefly evidence of the small critical sense in certain medieval historians – at the time they contained a proper understanding of the fact that the universities had roots in the past which went back as far as the great schools of classical antiquity. Today the prehistory of the universities can be traced back even further, considering that there were schools among the pre-Grecian cultures in the Middle East as well. These schools gave instruction, advanced for the conditions of the time, to select groups of students who could later count on entering particular positions in society in order to apply their special knowledge there.

There is no real knowledge of when human society reached such a stage in its development that the conditions and requirements for real school education existed. Even in the most primitive societies it was of vital importance that certain knowledge and accomplishments could be passed down from one generation to the next, but in spite of this, real school education could have existed only in the first settled urban communities. Strong concentrations of population presupposed a central authority in the form of a town council, or a royal power, equipped with administrative organs to attend to the common tasks of society. Collecting taxes and duties required a class of administrators with specialised knowledge of accounts, no less of writing too, just as there were well-defined systems for weights and measures of various wares. Furthermore, a permanent administration made chronology and a calendar necessary; in most cases the calendar was developed on astronomical principles which were often closely associated with the religious cult of the day. As all these things in the beginning must have been dark mysteries for the ordinary man, skilled specialists probably attended to them. What is immediately clear is the essential interrelationship between school bodies and the bureaucracy, and this is confirmed by what we now know of the best-known urban cultures of the ancient Middle East.[1]

In this way we are relatively well informed about education in ancient Egypt, where boys were normally educated at home, until they began to learn a trade as apprentices at the age of ten. Various Egyptian texts have been preserved, in the form of 'Books of Wisdom' containing a father's advice to his son on the principles of leading a happy life as a useful member of society. This led to the well-to-do classes of society sending their sons to proper schools to learn reading, writing, and counting, something to which numerous *ostraka*, or inscribed potsherds with the exercises and tasks written on them, can testify. Girls seem not to have had access to these schools, in which special emphasis was also placed on literary proficiency; mathematics played a subordinate role, and sport or other physical education was left out altogether.[2]

A more specialised teaching went on nonetheless in the so-called 'houses of life', which had several different functions. Here professional writers were trained and religious texts for use in temples were copied, not to mention the *Book of the Dead*, which was reproduced in thousands of copies. Here too proper theological teaching was carried out, just as the very highly developed Egyptian medicine was associated with these institutions and with the sanatoriums that in the later period could often be found attached to the temples.[3]

---

[1] General works of reference for this chapter are Marrou, and W. F. Albright, *From the Stone Age to Christianity*, 2nd edn, Baltimore, 1946.
[2] On the Books of Wisdom and other Egyptian literature see E. Wallis Budge, *The Literature of the Ancient Egyptians*, London, 1914, and the two works by A. Erman, *Die Literatur der Aegypter*, Leipzig, 1923 and *Die Religion der Aegypter*, Berlin, 1934. See also A. Erman and H. O. Lange, *Papyrus Lansing. Eine aegyptische Schulhandschrift des 20. Dynastie*, Copenhagen, 1925.
[3] The best general introduction to Egyptian and Mesopotamian mathematics and astronomy

One text of great significance for our knowledge of how Egyptians were educated is the *Rhind Papyrus*, which was found near the Ramesseum in Thebes in 1858 and is now kept in the British Museum.[4] This is a papyrus scroll a good 5.5 m long and 33 cm broad, containing about 100 different mathematical texts. It has as its title 'Accurate Arithmetic: Introduction to the Knowledge of All Existing Things and All Dark Secrets', which clearly shows that we are dealing with a textbook. From the preface it appears that the book was finished in the thirty-third year of the reign of A-User-Re (one of the Hyksos kings), by the scribe A'h-Mose, from an exemplar in the form of an older text from the time of King Ne-Ma'et-Re. This man is identical with one of the last pyramid-builders in the twelfth dynasty, Amenemhed III, which means that the text really gives us a glimpse of Egyptian mathematical education about 2,200 years before Christ.

The *Rhind Papyrus*, first of all, contains purely mathematical tables for use with fractions, together with a series of practice examples all worked out. Some of these are of purely abstract character, while the majority are couched as problems of many different kinds. Acreages are worked out, the cubic content of corn silos, the division of bread among labourers, and much besides. The form of the examples itself shows the *Rhind Papyrus* being what could be called a Teacher's Manual. An equivalent volume for the pupil is the *Moscow Papyrus*, which derives from about the same period. This contains exercises of largely the same types, often with the teacher's note 'You have got it right!'

Such texts could only have been interesting to a certain group in society – people learning how to survey land, how to gather in the crops and store them, and how to administer and supply working shifts. In other words it is a matter of the Egyptian administrators or 'scribes' who in this way received a regular training related to their future occupations. The existence of real schools for administrators can therefore be inferred from as early as the third millennium BC, with members as guardians of the 'dark secrets' represented in the *Rhind Papyrus*, in clear contrast to the more literary and elementary education of general schools. These schools for administrators aimed directly at specialised knowledge beyond the horizons of the

---

is O. Neugebauer, *The Exact Sciences in Antiquity*, Copenhagen, 1951, reprinted New York, 1962.

[4] A. B. Chase and R. C. Archibald, *The Rhind Mathematical Papyrys, 1–2*, Oberlin, Ohio, 1927–9.

generally educated. With their practical outlook, such schools were integrated into Egyptian society on one hand and formed a clear basis for class privilege on the other. They gave their pupils qualifications for power and influence in society, and archaeology has uncovered numerous funeral monuments which testify to the high social position of the scribal class. A text from about 1300 BC shows us the scribe Akhtoy in the process of explaining to his son Pepi the high rank of the scribe, which is glorified at the expense of physical labour. Don't be a farmer! Don't be a baker! Don't be a priest! Don't be an officer! Be a civil servant! – this is advice which crops up again and again in these texts as an early example of academic snobbery.

From the ancient Mesopotamian cultural area a huge amount of material survives on clay tablets. The oldest of these date from about 3000 BC and are written in the original pictographic script of the Sumerians. In the course of the following millennium this was developed into the wedge or cuneiform script that was eventually used across large parts of the Middle East by Babylonians and Assyrians, Hittites and Persians. Most of this material is made up either of religious texts or of documents to do with practical life – deeds, accounts, reports from civil servants, laws and statutes, and proclamations and the like. Other known texts deal with mathematics, with the memorisation of procedures for solving problems of largely the same practical kind as those we know from Egypt, even if Babylonian mathematics in time became far more advanced. Among the mathematical texts of the later period (the age of the Persians and Seleucids), there are several with astronomical tables and calculating procedures of importance to the calendar and astrology. In Mesopotamia too, therefore, it is clear that schools existed which gave advanced teaching to different categories of future officials.

Life in such a school is described in a Sumerian text from about 2000 BC, of which many copies were made in later times. It consequently enjoyed a certain popularity and can therefore be taken as typical.[5] The many Akkadianisms in the text show that it was written by an Akkadian student, but in the Old Sumerian language, which enjoyed a status as a language of learning similar to that of Latin later in Europe. The student leaves home in the

---

[5] S. N. Kramer, Schooldays. A Sumerian Composition Relating to the Education of a Scribe, *Journal of the American Oriental Society* 69 (1949), 199–215.

The classical inheritance

morning bringing his lunch which is later eaten in school. The headmaster is a 'school father', and mentioned in the text is also one teacher in Sumerian and another in arithmetic. Lessons take the form of the copying of already existing clay tablets, and the subjects are Sumerian, arithmetic, and book-keeping. A porter, a classroom pedagogue, and a playground superintendent maintain strict discipline – the student is lashed seven times a day for a series of different offences that school pupils would still recognise today: arriving late in the morning, talking in class, getting up without leave, leaving the school grounds without permission, and skimping written work. Only towards evening does the student trudge wearily home, making a report of the day's work to his father (formerly an official himself), eating his supper and going to bed early so as to be fresh the next morning. On one occasion the teacher is invited home when the father wishes to put in a good word for his son who would like to be a perfect scribe and a learned man – cleverer than his schoolmates, even those from the royal house.

It is interesting to note that Jewish society in Israel did not distinguish itself from the neighbouring countries where the existence of an educated scribal class was concerned. This social class has left a literature still partly preserved in the Old Testament as the Book of Proverbs, Ecclesiastes, the Book of Wisdom, and the Wisdom of Jesu Sirach. This class was particularly closely bound to the court and also sought to keep its privileges by running schools and training its own children. Its literary legacies as a whole are quite without any philosophy. For example, the Book of Proverbs can be summarised as a handbook for the perfect functionary, in that it codifies, in aphoristic rules of conduct developed from day-to-day experience of life, the traditional wisdom of life on which the ideology of this class was based. That Israel in this way was an element in the general cultural pattern of the Middle East also appears in the straight borrowing of a passage in Proverbs (22: 17–23: 11) from the Egyptian Book of Wisdom of Amenemopes of *c.* 1100 BC. Clear traces of Hellenistic cultural influence can be found in later Hebrew works. Now and then a clear sign of class-consciousness can be traced in the way the work of the scribe is glorified and manual trades are despised. In connection with religious shallowness, this is surely the background to the polemic that the prophets directed at the scribes. Jeremiah, for example, has little time for their pretended wisdom or for the court circles that made use of them.

Seen from the point of view of education, ancient Middle Eastern societies can be comprehensively labelled scribal cultures.[6] It was the scribe who received the highest education. It was he who mastered the secrets of the arts of writing and arithmetic and thereby had access to high offices bringing power and social position. He was conscious of his class, often looked down on simpler manual workers and sought to pass on the privileges of his rank to his children with the help of special schools of advanced learning with a practical emphasis on the needs of the next generation of administrators, in such a way that a conflict of principle between higher education and the rest of society would have been unthinkable. The integration of education into the state was complete.

If we now turn to the culture of the Greeks, we find a totally different picture with far more details because of more numerous and better-researched sources. It is not hard to point out a series of features which divide Middle Eastern scribal cultures from Greek learning of the sixth century BC onwards. The learning in question is demonstrably that of the more or less loosely knit city states on which the Greek world was built. The ideological backgrounds were significantly different. The scribal training of the Orient had a strongly pragmatic character and was aimed directly at maintaining a status-conscious class of administrators in society. Yet among the Greeks there was an idea of an education that was in principle open to all members of society. This was not carried out consistently, since slaves had no civil rights and got no regular education, and similarly girls usually got a less comprehensive education than boys. But this does not change the fact that the idea of an education as the right and duty of all (free) citizens is first found among the Greeks. This presupposed a view of society according to which each citizen must be ready to take part in the government of the state by appearing in the popular assembly, while the idea of a special class of administrators, by and large, was strange to the Greeks.

With this in mind it is understandable that the term the Greeks used for education – *paideia* – was synonymous for them with culture and civilisation.[7] The Greek *paideia* distinguishes itself from the pragmatism of the East by being far more comprehensive. Where the Egyptians and Babylonians only aimed at skills and accomplish-

---

[6] The term 'scribal culture' was coined by Marrou, p. 19.
[7] On Greek education in general see W. Jaeger, *Paideia. Die Formung des Griechischen Menschen*, vols. I–III, Berlin–Leipzig, 1934-47.

ments that were of direct benefit for an official, the Greeks laid stress on an upbringing that could be measured as much by intellectual as by artistic and physical standards. The whole man was to be shaped, physically through gymnastics and sport, artistically through dance and singing, intellectually through such elementary subjects as reading, writing, arithmetic, and more advanced skills in literature and philosophy. For this reason Cicero was not mistaken when he later Latinised the Greek *paideia* to the Roman *humanitas*. This applies despite the fact that not all Greek states put equal stress on the different elements of their education. In Doric societies such as Sparta and Crete, physical training dominated with strict discipline and overt military aims, while the intellectual and artistic side had far greater meaning in the Ionic cities on the coast of Asia Minor, and later in the Attic society of Athens and elsewhere on the mainland. This also decided the different ways in which schools were run: as state institutions in Sparta, but usually as private schools in Athens and other places.

In the course of the fifth and fourth centuries BC there was a series of important innovations in Greek schools. With the raising of the intellectual level and the growth of knowledge in many areas, special schools grew up here and there which gave advanced education in one particular subject. Famous in this context are the school and hospital associated with the temple of Asclepius in Epidaurus, and the Hippocratic school of medicine on the island of Cos, founded by Hippocrates (469–399), the most famous physician of the Greeks. The greatest mathematician of this period, Eudoxus of Cnidus (c. 408–355), had his own school in Cyzicus, which he moved to Athens in 368 BC. In opposition to this specialisation came the sophists in the fifth century, who tried to deal with the advances made in learning by thrashing out difficult problems with the aid of rhetorical methods but without a sufficient theory of knowledge. This was the context of the critique which Socrates (469–399) made and of his attempt to build a firmer foundation of knowledge. How fine the fruits of traditional learning could also be, can be seen at about the same time in Socrates' younger friend Isocrates (436–338), who gave his pupils in his school of rhetoric in Athens a thorough preparation for a practical life in politics.

The schools in Hellas proper at this time were not the only contribution to a system of education that in relation to the Middle East was new and progressive. In the Greek colonies in Italy and

Sicily we find from about 500 BC 'the so-called Pythagoreans' (the term is Aristotle's), who lived, in any case to start with, in closed societies of a very special character. Their ideology is not known in all its details because it was kept a strict secret to all but initiates. Their societies may be regarded as religious orders or brotherhoods; this was not peculiar, given that Greek schools in Hellas too were frequently constituted as cult communities. But the Pythagoreans marked themselves out from other brotherhoods by making the purification of man the aim of their society's whole existence. Again one thinks of the whole person, with the body purified through various forms of asceticism, the soul through instruction. The initiates divided themselves into two groups, of which the 'acousmaticians' just sat by and listened while the 'mathematicians' got something of the higher mysteries. The latter word comes from the Greek verb *manthanó*, 'I learn'. Thus the derived form indicates those who had learnt something, namely Pythagorean science. The connection with the later meaning of this word is evident from the list of disciplines standing foremost on the list. It is said in a statement of Archytas the Pythagorean (about 400–350 BC) that mathematicians had 'entrusted us with clear knowledge of the speed and motion of the stars and of their rising and setting, and of geometry, arithmetic and spherics, and not least of music; for these studies have proved to be sisters'.[8]

With these we meet subjects for the first time that later under the name of the Pythagorean quadrivium would come to play such a prominent role in the university curriculum. *Quadrivium* means 'the fourfold way'; incidentally the same gloss is first used in Boethius' *Arithmetica*.[9] Diagram 1 shows a scheme of these disciplines.

	in the abstract	in nature
discrete numbers	arithmetic	music
continued dimensions	geometry	spherics (astronomy)

Diagram 1

---

[8] H. Diels, *Die Fragmente der Vorsokratiker*, ed. W. Kranz, vol. 1, p. 429, Dublin–Zurich, 1966. The quotation has survived in Porphyry's commentary on Ptolemy's *Harmonics*. Pythagorean doctrine can be studied in the sources and commentaries in G. S. Kirk and J. E. Raven, *The Pre-Socratic Philosophers*, Cambridge, 1962, chs. 7–9 and 13. See also W. Burkert, *Weisheit und Wissenschaft. Studien zu Pythagoras, Philolaos and Platon*, Nuremberg, 1962.

[9] Boethius, *De Institutione Arithmetica*, I, 1, ed. G. Friedlein, Leipzig, 1867, p. 1.

That these studies are sisters presumably means that certain relations were found to exist between them as shown in the diagram. That together they came to form the nucleus of the secret lore of the Pythagoreans shows how much weight was placed here on the mathematical subjects. This is in harmony with Aristotle's account of the Pythagoreans' faith in an inner, mathematical structure of the universe: the nature of things is in numbers. So it seems that the Pythagoreans wished to cleanse the soul – of its congenital darkness and ignorance – through a concept of nature that according to their first principles had to be 'mathematical'. Thus a new element was added to the Greek ideal of education that would later have the most far-reaching consequences.

The Pythagoreans represented something really new in the field of education. Just as the Egyptians and Babylonians did, they reserved education for a limited circle; but this does not seem to have formed any real class of society with special economic privileges, rather a circle of initiates who sought deliverance through study. Whereas the training of the Orientals had been practical, pragmatic, and directed to the general needs of society, that of the Pythagoreans was theoretical, idealistic, and directed to the spiritual needs of a closed and private group. And while both they and their fellow Hellenes elsewhere in Greece focussed their system of education on the whole man, this took place in Hellas with the aim of giving all citizens equal opportunities in national life, whereas among the Pythagoreans it led to the initiates of the inner circle becoming superior to those excluded from it. The ensuing tension was resolved one way or another at the time when the Pythagorean system became known in Athens.

This happened with Plato (427–347), who was not only a pupil of Socrates and had links through him with the traditional learning of Athens but had also become a friend of Archytas when, after Socrates' execution in 399, he left Hellas to visit Sicily and Egypt.[10] When he returned and in the year 393 founded his Academy in Athens, two traditions were united here in a way that was of epoch-making significance. Plato's Academy was a higher institution of learning that partly required of all its pupils some preparatory special training, partly presumed a common Greek education with

---

[10] Among the innumerable works on Plato it is useful to consult A. E. Taylor, *Plato, the Man and his Work*, 3rd edn, London, 1929, and J. E. Raven, *Plato's Thought in the Making*, Cambridge, 1965.

gymnastics for the body and music for the soul. In addition, a grounding in mathematics was required in accordance with the inscription over the gate of the Academy: 'No man unskilled in geometry enters here.' However, this famous criterion of entry was first mentioned by the Byzantine author John Tzetzes in the twelfth century and is in this way not entirely trustworthy. Certainly the development of mathematics itself had made an overwhelming impression on Plato and was one of the most important prerequisites for his views on metaphysics and the theory of knowledge: for in mathematics the proofs were secure, the doctrines true, so that true knowledge was not an unobtainable ideal as the sophists had claimed. On the other hand, mathematical truths are abstract and never wholly obvious in that material world to which only the senses have access; such truths are accessible only to the reason that is able to contemplate them in a distinct and immaterial world of ideas in which all changeable, visible, and transitory things have their own unchangeable, immaterial, and eternal models.

All this bears witness to the general importance of mathematics for Plato. Concrete Pythagorean tenets turn up, for example, in the *Timaeus*, a dialogue on the making and structure of the world. On the other hand, Plato's literary form in his extant writings, with the consistent application of the dialogue form, is clearly taken from an older Greek tradition and from Socrates himself.

In its external organisation the Academy was constituted as a cult fellowship for the purpose of venerating Apollo and the muses, something that was also in keeping with Greek tradition. Pythagorean was the community life of teachers and pupils, with common meals and ascetic practices, the latter being expected to cleanse the soul and further the understanding. The form of instruction itself was defined in a strongly active way. It consisted not only of lectures but also of discussions between teachers and pupils which in a recurring way regularly culminated in festive symposia on declared themes.

As regards the immediate object of this training, however, Plato was undoubtedly more a Hellene than a Pythagorean. He wished first and foremost to educate his pupils to be good citizens and capable politicians in general society, and many of them did in fact play a role in the public life of Greece. How penetratingly Plato thought of the problems of education can best be seen from two dialogues, *The Republic* and *The Laws*, in which he discusses the possibility of a human society entirely ruled by the laws of reason. In these writings he gives a very prominent place to the debate on the problems of educating the young, in the first known attempt to work out a proper pedagogic theory that was intimately linked with the ideal form of society portrayed in these seminal works.

This theory builds first and foremost on a sharp critique of the existing Greek society, in its democratic, oligarchical, or tyrannical forms. Nowhere does reason rule alone, and the few philosophers there are, moreover, are reckoned to be ineffective. This state of affairs may be changed; 'if the philosophers do not become kings in the state, or those who now bear the name of kings and rulers do not begin to occupy themselves with philosophy in a genuinely satisfactory way, and if this union of power and political philosophy does not succeed, then, my dear Glaucon, there is no chance of evil ever being brought to an end in the cities, nor, I believe, in humanity', says Socrates in *The Republic*.[11] 'No city or government can ever be perfect', it is said further, 'until these philosophers that are so few in number and unspoiled, and yet are called ineffective creatures, are forced by some happy chance (whether they will nor not) to take power in the city, and the city forced to obey them.'[12]

Besides his ruling philosopher class, Plato furthermore imagines the republic as made up of two groups, partly soldiers (guardians), partly citizen tradesmen, of course in addition to slaves. He outlines a very detailed training for all three groups, one of which starts early in childhood where the first skills are inculcated in a sort of nursery pedagogics with play and games. To this the indispensable subjects gymnastics and music are added, with all that this implies, and at some higher stage the pupils receive an adapted form of teaching of a more abstract kind in which the Pythagorean quadrivium, with its mathematics and astronomy, plays a major role. Special significance is attached to these subjects among free people, for they sharpen the reason and at the same time raise the soul from the low, material world to a contemplation of the eternal truths where wisdom begins. Later the most able of all are chosen for a protracted in-service training which prepares them directly for the leading posts in their society. Also the training of teachers is taken into consideration.

By our lights, Plato's ideal society is a rather harsh dictatorship in which all human matters are regulated in the smallest detail and in

---

[11] Plato, *The Republic*, v, 8 (473c).   [12] Ibid. vi, 12 (499b).

which the poets, for example, 'must not compose anything that conflicts with what is law and order in the republic or with what is beautiful and good'[13] – or publish their works before they are approved by special censors. But this did not prevent Plato from putting two new ideas into circulation which meant a complete break with tradition and became a lodestar for the ages to come. In *The Laws* Plato says: 'It shall not be so, that teaching is only sought by those whose fathers wish it, yet is neglected by those whose fathers will not have them taught; but', so he says, 'each man and each boy shall so far as is possible submit to compulsory education, for they belong more to the republic than to their parents. Regarding women, also, my law means of course exactly what it does as regards the male sex: they too shall take part in just as many exercises.' And further: 'Quite foolish is that which goes on in our countries, that not all men and women are agreed on occupying themselves with all their power with the same things.'[14]

These were new thoughts. Quite clearly the principle that education should be public and obligatory had been put into practice in Sparta; but in Athens and most other states it was still private and voluntary. Completely new, however, was the proposition that education and employment should be open to women to the same extent as to men. In both points Plato was therefore ahead of his time – so much so that his idea cannot yet be said to be realised or even recognised everywhere today.

Throughout more than 900 years Plato's Academy stood out as the first example in antiquity of an institution with an education at once socially useful and generally humane as its aim. It has since often been considered the world's first university, and as the hearthstone of the Platonic tradition in philosophy the Academy has also meant more for European thinking than most of the other schools either before or since. Its strength was the acumen and consistency with which fundamental problems of science and humanity were set out in debate. But its weakness was precisely the philosophical dialectic that was the tool of the Academy's method in all areas without being a sufficient basis for a solid expansion of scientific knowledge. In our eyes the Academy therefore needed just the supplementation it got when Plato's former pupil Aristotle (384–322) returned to Athens in 335/334 to set up his own school, the Lykeion

---

[13] Plato, *The Laws* VIII (801c). [14] Ibid. (804d).

or 'peripatetic' school, which he directed for the next thirteen years, until, as a Macedonian, he had to leave Athens on political grounds, to die in Chalcis only a year later.[15]

The Lykeion was formally a typical Greek-Athenian private school and was organised just as the Academy had been, as a cult society, containing a temple with consecrated offerings, and a colonnade with statues of the muses. The statutes worked out by Aristotle prescribed a life of perfect order with common meals, a monthly symposium, and the like. But the spirit was other than that at the Academy: where Plato had sought to educate by teaching, Aristotle wished in addition to train by research. He also saw as his aim the development of a good and harmonious member of society, but the methods were different. The relevant subjects are pursued, in Aristotle's view, not only through theoretical reflections on basic problems of philosophy, but also by direct experience through exploration of both natural phenomena and the structure of society. So he equipped his school as a real research institute with ordered collections of scientific material. In the so-called Museion there was an extensive manuscript library and a collection of teaching materials. In a colonnade there hung maps of the regions that Greek geographers and other travellers had explored, and there frequently came to the Lykeion shipments of hitherto unknown animals from the East; some of them were gifts from Aristotle's former pupil Alexander the Great, who did not forget to send home to his teacher new material for research from his remote military expeditions. All this now meant that for the first time scholarly research appeared as an activity in its own right at an institute of learning. The immediate consequence of this was that while all scientific work had previously been carried out under the common name of philosophy, a series of subjects now broke away as special topics of research with the resulting establishment of a series of independent sciences.

Aristotle personally completed a programme of research with his treatise *On the Natural History of Animals*, in which he classified and described about 540 different species of animal; with this work zoology was founded as a science, just as Aristotle's description of the development of the chicken can be said to be the start of embryology.

---

[15] The most recent general introduction to Aristotle is the article on Aristotle in *DSB*, vol. 1, pp. 250–81. See also W. Jaeger, *Aristoteles*, Berlin, 1923 (English transl. Oxford, 1934); I. Düring, *Aristoteles, Darstellung und Interpretation seines Denkens*, Heidelberg, 1966; G. E. R. Lloyd, *Aristotle, the Growth and Structure of his Thought*, Cambridge, 1968.

Another big project was the compilation of a comparative work on the different constitutions of the Greek city states, material which took a long time to gather together. This task Aristotle never managed to complete, and only a fragment found in our day, *On the Athenian Constitution*, bears witness to this attempt to give the science of government an empirical foundation – in clear opposition to Plato's purely speculative programme of an ideal Utopian state.

Aristotle's work at the Lykeion was continued by his successors: Theophrastus (*c.* 370–*c.* 300 BC), who systematised the theory of music; and Eudemus (end of fourth century BC), who wrote an account of the history of Greek mathematics, a corresponding history of astronomy, and a work on the history of religion, all of which, apart from individual fragments, have unfortunately disappeared. Thus there is a good reason to regard Aristotle as the father of many sciences and his institute in Athens as the first school in antiquity of university character. The union established here between teaching and research proved its efficacy at once and was soon the model for similar efforts elsewhere.

Of course the scientific research that Aristotle established raised many questions to do with method and the theory of knowledge. These he analysed in a long series of writings, which together supplied science with a variety of impulses, many of which can be seen today. These writings were not brilliant dialogues such as Plato's own polished literature, but dry lectures written down by Aristotle himself or by his pupils. We find first of all a series of works on logic, which is often organised together under the common name of *Organon*. The most important work is *Analytica priora*, which with its teaching of the syllogistic form of conclusion established formal logic as an independent discipline, together with *Analytica posteriora*, which presented Aristotle's theory of science and essential elements of his theory of knowledge. Here we meet the fundamental principle of experience that says that all human knowledge begins with the testimony of the senses to the concrete things in our environment. Further, Aristotle illustrates how the reason deals with the immediate impressions of the senses through a constantly more widely ranging process of abstraction.

1. First one can abstract the individual properties of things and study what material things of a certain kind have in common. This results in a number of disciplines that Aristotle puts under the name of physics or natural philosophy.

2 On the next level one must abstract from the material reality of things and study their numbers, size, and geometric forms. This leads to mathematics, which Aristotle therefore takes to be an abstract science of concrete things, whereas Plato had taken it to be a science of mathematical forms in a separate world of ideas.
3 On a third level of abstraction, finally, one can even go further and study the very general properties of concrete things, for example their reality and existence and the causes of their changes. This doctrine Aristotle called metaphysics or theology, because it ends with a proof that all changes in the world, when all is said and done, have their cause in an unchangeable, eternal 'prime mover', or God, as Aristotle calls him.

This doctrine of the three levels of abstraction involves a rational classification of a long series of sciences whose mutual relations are thereby explained. In addition, the *Analytica posteriora* contains an indication of how the results of the scientific research in any given area can be presented in the form of a logical theory. It begins with definitions of applied concepts, continues with the unproved assumptions (axioms or postulates), and finishes with a list of statements (theorems, propositions), which can be inferred (deduced) from definitions and assumptions by logical means. Not least would it be Greek mathematicians who made quick use of this scheme.

Aristotle himself wrote no work on mathematics, even if the many mathematical examples in his work show his knowledge and understanding of it. On the other hand he occupied himself intensely with the sciences on the other two levels of abstraction. Most important here is his *Metaphysics*, which presents the most common principles of things, and by the way defines science as the doctrine of the causes of things, among which Aristotle distinguishes four types – the material, the formal, the effective, and the final cause which, for example where a statue is concerned, describe respectively its material (marble or bronze), its form, the work that must be undertaken to produce it, and the artist's purpose in making it. In a previous treatise called *The Physics* Aristotle had subjected the problem of changes – spatial or 'local' movements in particular – to an equivalent philosophical analysis, so that the work is not a physics textbook in the modern sense of the word.

The physical or natural philosophical sciences on the first

abstract level received Aristotle's special attention, to judge from the many texts concerning this that he left behind. We have already mentioned the great work on *The Natural History of Animals*, to which may be added a book *On the Soul: De Anima*, which is the first extant work on psychology and sense physiology. The treatise *On Heaven* (*De Caelo*) gives a picture of Aristotle's opinions on astronomy, while in the treatise *On Growth and Decay* (*De Generatione et Corruptione*) he occupied himself with changes in matter, on the basis of the doctrine of the four elements and their mutual metamorphoses, which is also the foundation of his *Meteorology* (*Meteorologica*). A long series of shorter scientific treatises normally goes under the name of *Parva Naturalia*.

All the works mentioned above are 'theoretical' in the sense that they concern themselves with sciences whose only goal for Aristotle is knowledge. Yet he also recognised a second group of 'practical' disciplines, whose goal is the analysis of human actions. On these he wrote a series of works on moral philosophy and ethics, of which the most important is the so-called *Nicomachean Ethics*, according to tradition dedicated to Aristotle's son Nicomachus. To this group also belongs the *Politics*, while an equivalent *Economics* is no longer regarded as Aristotle's own work.

Finally mention may be made of two lesser works, with which Aristotle turned his attention to the subjects of the trivium, namely the *Rhetorica* and the *Poetica*. In these we find among other things an interesting theory of the human significance of the art of poetry (the doctrine of catharsis).

Aristotle's works and scientific conclusions immediately became extremely important to Greek culture, not least because of the school in Alexandria which will be described below. Later on Aristotelianism would become one of the main currents in the universities of the middle ages and even a contributory cause of their origin and development, as will be shown in chapter 6.

After the expeditions of Alexander the Great and the expansion of the Greek-Macedonian supremacy in the Orient, Athens lost a crucial part of its political power. The gravitational centre of Greek culture shifted to other regions, where schools were soon set up which could come a close second to the Academy and Lykeion. The most famous of these new institutions was the school in Alexandria, which around the year 300 BC was set up by King Ptolemy I Soter together with Demetrius from Phaleron (*c.* 350–*c.* 290 BC) – one of

Theophrastus' pupils – as an adviser.[16] This initiative on the part of the Egyptian government could look like a fulfilment of Plato's and Aristotle's demands for the state to take education upon itself. Yet Ptolemy's main motive seems to have been the wish to counterbalance the schools in Athens, where strong anti-monarchical tendencies were the rule. Perhaps he also wished to contain the half-socialist movements around him that were raising their heads in protest against the new and economically privileged bourgeoisie. However that may be, the school in Alexandria was not the result of one individual thinker's concern but was a state enterprise right from the start, provided with considerable economic help from the king and his successors.

This institution consisted of several individual foundations, each situated in Alexandria's residential quarter, the Brucheion. The library was here from the first and in time became incredibly rich in books, even though statements as to its contents vary a great deal. What precisely they were cannot be made out with much certainty – figures vary between 100,000 and 700,000 works – but the aim was clearly to gather the whole of Greek literature under one roof.[17] Later significant collections of other literatures, for example the Egyptian and Judaic, were added; it was also in Alexandria that Jewish scholars undertook the first translation of the Old Testament into Greek (the Septuagint). This library existed for several hundred years, even if the contents in the course of time suffered greatly from fire and robbery, as for example when Caesar removed a section of the manuscripts to Rome, following his journey to Egypt. In compensation, significant collections were acquired from time to time from other cities; it was thus that the libraries of both Aristotle and Theophrastus ended up in Alexandria. Apart from the library there was the so-called Museion, founded as a workshop for researchers summoned to Alexandria or coming there to visit of their own accord. There was room for about a hundred scholars, and it is here that we must imagine most of the learned men of the Hellenistic world working for short or long periods. Finally, there was also a smaller library in Alexandria that was attached to the Serapeion, that is, the temple of the Serapis cult introduced by

---

[16] The principal work on the early history of Alexandria is P. M. Fraser, *Ptolemaic Alexandria*, vols. I–III, Oxford, 1972.
[17] See E. A. Parsons, *The Alexandrian Library. Glory of the Hellenic World*, London, 1952. Cf. H. J. de Vleeschauwer, *Les Bibliothèques Ptoléméennes d'Alexandrie* (Mousaion vol. 1), Pretoria, 1955.

Ptolemy I to bind the Greeks and Egyptians together in a common religion. Here there were 42,800 scrolls in 235 BC. Astronomical observations could be made from the temple courtyard, a witness to the fact that the Alexandrians also acknowledged the truth of the empirical foundations of science.

However, with these literary aids in mind, it is no wonder that Alexandrian study was of a markedly bookish character. One major task was the cataloguing of books itself, which resulted among other things in a register of large parts of classical Greek literature worked out by the librarian Callimachus, 'the father of bibliography', who is presumed to have worked around the middle of the third century BC. Besides he is one of the few writers who described the school in a book – *On the Museion* – which has unfortunately disappeared. Also the science of textual criticism was founded in Alexandria, with the final redaction of Homer's *Iliad* and *Odyssey*, among other works. Numerous literary commentaries and grammatical works came to light here. Nor was mathematics neglected in any way in favour of the humanities; and with regard to the exact sciences one can clearly see that tendency to compile complete summary works which was one of the hallmarks of Alexandrian scholarship. This was already true of the mathematician Euclid (who lived shortly after 300 BC), who not only collected nearly all Greek mathematics in his *Elements*, but also bequeathed to us works on optics, astronomy, and the doctrine of harmony. One of the librarians was the mathematician Eratosthenes (c. 275–194 BC), who made a new determination of the earth's circumference and may be regarded as the first scientific geographer; from his comprehensive interests it is evident why he was also the first scholar to describe himself as a philologist. In the first century AD we find a polytechnic seminar in Alexandria led by Hero (about 60 AD), and hardly a century later Alexandria was the home of the greatest authority in applied mathematics in antiquity, Claudius Ptolemy (c. 100–c. 160 AD), who dealt with optics, the doctrine of harmony, cartography, geography, and astronomy in big monographs, from which the main work of astronomy – later circulated under the Arabian name *Almagest* – was the basis for the whole of theoretical astronomy right up to Copernicus.[18]

---

[18] On Alexandrian science see M. Clagett, *Greek Science in Antiquity*, New York, 1956, and O. Pedersen, *Early Physics and Astronomy*, Cambridge, 1993. Also G. Sarton, *Hellenistic Science and Culture in the Last Three Centuries B.C.*, Cambridge, Mass., 1959. On Hellenistic civilisation in general see W. Tarn, *Hellenistic Civilization*, London, 3rd edn, 1952.

Students streamed to Alexandria from the whole known world. Here the classical Greek tradition met currents from Egypt and the East, and significant cultural interactions inevitably took place. The result was a cultural synthesis which is normally termed Hellenism, and which in the centuries immediately before the beginning of our era spread out over the Mediterranean area and also resulted in the founding of schools in many places. An Alexandrian school was founded even in Athens with the name Ptolemy's Gymnasium; later the Emperor Hadrian set up a new library which was still praised by the church father Jerome (348–420) as one of the best in the world.[19] Next to Alexandria in repute for a while was the school in Pergamum, which had a series of collections, a zoological and botanical garden, and a library, which in the year 41 BC held 200,000 scrolls, all catalogued. This was removed by Antony, who gave it to Cleopatra, after which it went into the Alexandrian library. Similar even if lesser centres of learning could be found for example in Antioch, Berytus (Beirut), and on Rhodes.

To Rome came the first Hellenistic schools and the first Greek scholars, presumably shortly after 250 BC, and with this Hellenistic culture began to penetrate into the Latin world. To begin with this movement took the form of a triumphal march for the Greek language. Originally the schools were bilingual with a steadily greater emphasis on Greek, so the ability to read Greek literature in the original language soon became an obvious hallmark of a general education. For a short time this development threatened to go off the rails, when for example a law from the year 92 BC simply prohibited purely Latin rhetorical schools. Eventually, however, this law proved untenable; normally the two languages flourished side by side, with state professorships in both Latin and Greek under Vespasian (69–79 AD). Rome also got libraries of its own, when Caesar assigned the most learned Roman of the age, Marcus Terentius Varro (116–27 BC), to set up public libraries; one of them had the misfortune to be plundered after Varro's death.[20] Even though the Greek language and the familiarity with Greek scholarship blossomed in this way in the Republic and through the whole imperial age, no Roman school ever came close to the standard of the centres of learning in Athens and Alexandria. Old Rome never got its university, a fact that would

---

[19] See Jerome's translation of Eusebius' *Chronica, Migne, PL* 27, 467.
[20] H. J. Vleeschauwer, *Jules César et la Bibliothèque Publique dans la Rome Antique* (Mousaion vol. 28), Pretoria, 1958.

remain of decisive importance for the whole development of culture in western Europe. This is closely bound up with the characteristics of the old Roman city society as much as with those of the later empire.

Already in its age of kings Rome was a very dynamic city state, constantly trying to extend its influence through both warlike and peaceful means and placing constant demands on the most capable members of society. Fighting ability on the battlefield and political know-how in town government became the noblest human qualities, and abstract scholarly speculations had to take second place. For the Romans, nature was no great intellectual problem demanding scientific or philosophical investigation, but rather a medium for the economic development of man – more textbooks on agriculture were written in Rome than treatises on natural philosophy. The meeting with the Hellenistic world, therefore, became an opening up of an intellectual culture that was as glittering as it was unobtainable and as admirable as it was useless – unless it could be taken into the service of Roman society. In Rome therefore Greek culture had a twin purpose: from the first moment it was a status symbol for the wealthy classes, who could keep their distance from the common folk and commonplace Latin with a veneer of Greek culture. Here the Scipios were leading the way already in the third century BC, and later statesmen such as Sulla (138–78 BC) and Lucullus (117–56 BC) wrote their memoirs in Greek. Secondly, it soon became apparent that Greek philosophy and science were exceptional aids for the rhetorical technique, which had to be mastered fully if one was to have any hope of a political career and obtain the offices that gave power, wealth, and influence.

As we could talk of a culture of scribes in Egypt and Babylon, so we meet in Rome what could properly be called a culture of orators. The educated citizen distinguished himself first and foremost in speaking well, commanding the language, and arguing persuasively. So it had also been in Greece, and it was in this field that the Greek system of education proved useful for the orators of Rome. The most famous of them, Marcus Tullius Cicero (106–43 BC), made no secret of his conclusion, in his Platonic-type dialogue *De Oratore*, that knowledge is useful for the rhetor:

> The art of speaking beautifully is greater and composed of more sciences and study than people can imagine ... In my opinion no person can become a speaker accomplished with any laudable capability unless he has

acquired knowledge of all significant subjects and all liberal arts ... for unless there is something beneath the surface that the speaker feels and understands, rhetoric will remain an empty and childish stream of words.[21]

But even though Cicero in this way confined himself to the old ideal of the good citizen as a *vir bonus dicendi peritus* (a good man and skilled in speaking – the expression is Cato's), he clearly realised that the persuasive power of an argument is strengthened when it is supported by factual knowledge and formed with dialectic logic. Both elements could be learnt from the Greeks, and consequently the Roman schools of oratory were filled with Greek rhetors looking for a career abroad.

All the same, in Rome this Greek training was secondary, a support for a political eloquence which had other than scholarly aims. Cicero's ideal of *humanitas* is not scholarly as such. It aims more at wide-ranging knowledge than special study, and more at character-building than the development of the intellect. This is stressed even more clearly by another orator, Marcus Fabius Quintilianus (c. 35–95 AD), whose treatise *De Institutione Oratoria* later played a large role in the debate on education in Europe, not least in the humanistic movement. Here he says:

But I regard it as sufficient for a rhetor not to be wholly ignorant of the subject he is talking about. For he cannot have knowledge of all causes, and yet he must be able to talk about all of them. What, then, is he able to talk about? – those things he has studied. Similarly as far as the arts are concerned, he must study them, if the opportunity offers itself he must talk about them, and then he will be able to talk about the arts that he has studied.[22]

It is obvious that in preparing his speech an orator could not plough through all the Greek literature on the subject. What he needed first and foremost were handbooks in which he could look up and track down the essentials as quickly as possible. Perhaps this is why the Romans did not leave us very many important specialised works of a scholarly kind, but why, on the other hand, they left us a large collection of encyclopedias, in contrast to the Athenians, who had no major predilection for the handbook genre. These Roman encyclopedias were often very comprehensive and as a rule bear

---

[21] Cicero, *De Oratore* I, 4, 6 and I, 6, 19–20. Cf. S. F. Bonnet, *Education in Ancient Rome from the Elder Cato to the Younger Pliny*, London, 1977.

[22] Quintilian, *Institutio Oratoria* II, 21, 15; cf. Wise, ch. 5 and W. H. Smail, *Quintilian on Education*, Oxford, 1938.

witness to the deep and genuine learning of their authors. But seen from the point of view of the history of scholarship, they suffered from the crucial flaws that nearly always affect lexical literature as such: they more or less paraphrased the results of Greek scholarship, giving little or no insight into the methods by which they had been obtained. With such works in front of him, a Roman could learn what Greek research had achieved, but he could not learn how to do research by himself. This state of affairs is also one of the essential premises of cultural development in the west following the collapse of the cultures of antiquity.

In one respect the writers of Latin encyclopedias played a very significant role in this development, namely by ordering and disposing the material of the so-called *artes liberales* or 'liberal arts'. Henceforth this phrase recurs constantly, even if with shifting meanings that clearly reflect characteristic changes in the ideal education. Though the phrase itself is Roman, its content goes back to the Greeks, where Plato had already knit together the concepts of science and freedom in two different ways. In *The Republic* he urges those

> who are to have part in the highest occupation in the state, to go in for the art of arithmetic and cultivate it, not in any dilettante fashion, but until they succeed in contemplating the nature of numbers with thought itself – not so that they exercise themselves in this art for reasons of buying or selling just as merchants or shopkeepers do, but for reasons of war and to make it easy for the soul itself to turn away from things which appear, towards truth and reality [i.e. towards the mathematical world of ideas].[23]

The same applies to geometry, astronomy, and certain other subjects, 'which compel the soul to turn itself around towards that point where the most blissful part of existence is – that point where it may get to see things absolutely'.[24] Aristotle also claims that 'each occupation, art or science that makes free men's body, soul or spirit less suited to virtue, is vulgar ... But there are also certain free arts which it behoves a free man to learn.'[25]

For Greeks, therefore, the liberal arts were firstly the theoretical or intellectual occupations with which it befitted free men to occupy themselves in opposition to shopkeepers, manual workers, or slaves. Apart from this, however, liberal arts can be characterised as

---

[23] Plato, *The Republic*, VII, 8 (525b).   [24] Ibid. 10 (529a).
[25] Aristotle, *The Politics* VIII, 2 (1337b).

disciplines that free the soul by drawing it up out of the material and transient world towards the ideal heights of pure knowledge. This theory never passed completely into oblivion, even if the Romans more readily interpreted *artes liberales* as the theoretical preconditions of the orator when he prepares his speeches.[26] The first and most important handbook in this subject is a (now lost) dissertation, the *Disciplinarum Libri IX* of Varro, who in contrast to the Greeks gave a completely precise definition of the liberal arts (see diagram 2).

I	II	III
grammar	geometry	medicine
rhetoric	arithmetic	architecture
dialectic	astronomy	
	music	

Diagram 2

Group II is here simply the old exact quadrivium of the Pythagoreans, to which Plato had already given a special place in his teaching programme. Group I – later called the trivium by a commentator on Horace in the court of Charlemagne – consists of linguistic and philosophical disciplines which are placed first as being absolutely necessary for an orator.

Finally, in Group III, we find two subjects that have practical aims at the same time as requiring great theoretical insight. As far as medicine is concerned, the Romans made no independent effort of any significance, but by and large committed themselves to Greek physicians, some of whom gained great importance in the later development of science. This was true of Dioscorides, who worked as a doctor in the imperial army under Claudius and Nero (*c*. 40–68). He left behind, among other things, a great systematic description of nearly 600 medicinal herbs and 1,000 preparations, building on careful observations and completely free of magic and superstition. This superseded all the earlier treatises on pharmacology and became the model later in the middle ages for numerous similar productions in *materia medica*. An even bigger name was Galenus of Pergamum (*c*. 130–199), who worked in Rome from 169 to his death. As with many of the scholars of late antiquity, Galen focussed first of all on the comprehensive reproductions of his predecessors' views,

---

[26] On Roman science in general see W. H. Stahl, *Roman Science. Origins, Development and Influence to the Later Middle Ages*, Madison, 1962.

which he supplemented with the results of his own anatomical dissections and experiments in physiology. His numerous works later became the basis for both Arabic and European medieval medicine, and in course of time his authority among physicians became as great as Aristotle's among the philosophers.[27]

It was quite different in architecture. For while the Greeks never left behind them any comprehensive account of the principles and methods of the art of building, the genius of the great engineers of Rome was manifest in the great work *De Architectura* of Vitruvius Pollio, who lived under Augustus (at about the beginning of our era). In ten books all essential problems that any Roman architect or engineer might face are dealt with, from town-planning and architecture to land-surveying and machine-building. This was therefore one of the most original works in Latin scholarly literature, and the master builders of both the middle ages and the Renaissance understood how to exploit it. A rather later work of great historical interest was the book on Rome's water supply, *De Aquis Urbis Romae*, by Sextus Julius Frontinus, who about 100 AD was the *curator aquarum* (director of waterworks) in Rome. It is full of details of aqueducts and their history as well as the legal problems linked to the job of keeping a large town supplied with drinking water.[28]

Yet the attempts made by the practical Romans to involve architecture and medicine in the liberal arts did not succeed. Thus the late Roman encyclopedia on *artes liberales* with the odd title *On the Wedding of Mercury and Philology* (*De Nuptiis Philologiae et Mercurii*) contained only the first seven subjects, which hereafter became the firm canon of these sciences. The author, Martianus Capella (first half of the fifth century), was too affected by the Greek tradition to give place to disciplines that had other than purely theoretical aims; later in the middle ages numerology and the Biblical doctrine of the Seven Pillars of Wisdom (Proverbs 9: 1) also came into play – to the detriment of the respect of the technical subjects.[29]

While Rome played no independent role in the theoretical sciences that the Greeks had lovingly cultivated, a lasting result was gained in the shaping of a discipline that would become important throughout the history of the world. This was theoretical law, a subject that started in Rome, probably on account of the special

---

[27] G. Sarton, *Galen of Pergamon*, Kansas, 1954.
[28] V. Mortet, *Recherches Critiques sur Vitruve*, vols. I–II, Paris, 1902–8.
[29] W. H. Stahl, *Martianus and the Seven Liberal Arts*, vol. I: *The Quadrivium*, New York, 1971.

problems that arose partly as a consequence of Rome's unbroken thousand-year history, partly as a result of the expansion of the Roman empire.[30]

The oldest Roman city state had a customary judiciary, based on an old tradition. The law was already known, and so the task was to find out what the law said in a particular case – a function originally left to members of the patrician class who appeared as the king's representatives. After the introduction of the Republic and the increased power of the plebeians a ten-man panel codified in 451/450 BC a list of the pronouncements of the old law which were published in the famous Twelve Tables of the Forum. They had already been destroyed by 390 BC, when the Gauls burned Rome down, but still in Cicero's time schoolboys learnt the twelve-table law by heart; a wholly satisfactory reconstruction of its content has not been made to this day.

New sources of law appeared in the Republic. The high officials, first of all the *praetor urbanus* (later called *consul*), could issue 'edicts' as long as his period of office lasted; but when these pronouncements were confirmed by his successors, they got a permanent character, with the result that a steadily increasing collection of laws developed (the *ius praetorium*).

In the imperial age the legislation of the emperor led to a series of *constitutiones* that were of a very different kind. As the highest official, the emperor could issue edicts himself which normally applied to questions of general importance for his domain, as for example the famous edict with which Caracalla in 212 AD gave all free-born inhabitants in the empire Roman citizenship. Other examples are the edict with which Diocletian in 303 started the last persecution of Christians and the Milan edict ten years later by which Constantine and Licinius set the church free once more. Other imperial laws were the *decreta*, that is, imperial verdicts in concrete judicial matters; *rescripta* or *epistulae*, which were responses to existing cases of legal doubt; and finally the *mandata* for governors and other relevant management personnel. While the first emperors acted with a veneer of respect for republican institutions and so had their lawgiving ratified by the senate, after Diocletian and Constantine this became more and more a formality to the extent that emperors from then on issued *leges generales* on the basis of their absolute power alone.

---

[30] See H. F. Jolowicz, *Historical Introduction to the Study of Roman Law*, Cambridge, 1961.

In this way, the ever-increasing number of laws heaped up in the course of Rome's long history could only create confusion, and inevitably this led to the desire for more system and clarity. Usually Tiberius Coruncanius is named as the first jurist in Rome, a man who became consul in 280 BC and was the first plebeian *pontifex maximus*. He gave the public access to his consultations and thereby changed the law from an esoteric profession reserved for initiates to a public affair. The first writer on law of any distinction was Quintus Mucius Scaevola (140–82 BC), who devised with his *Iuris Civilis Libri XVIII* a collected statement of the civil law which, together with his *Liber Definitionum*, became the model for numerous later works. A strong impulse for legal study was the Emperor Augustus' foundation of a law library in the temple of Apollo on the Palatine. This quickly became a centre for legal instruction partly undertaken by practising advocates, partly by private theoreticians. One such private teacher in the time of Augustus was Sabinus Masurius, who lived off the honoraria of his pupils until he was taken into the equestrian order at the age of fifty years. He is thought to have been the founder of a school of 'Sabinians', who in competition with another school of 'Proculians' developed Roman law in the next 200 years into an independent discipline with its own methods and literary genres.

In this legal literature we first find the so-called *institutiones*, elementary textbooks for use in school instruction; famous was the *Institutionum Iuris Civilis Commentarii Quattuor* of Gaius from the end of the second century AD. These textbooks were supplemented by handbooks of different kinds, among which the so-called *digesta* were comprehensive collections of laws from all areas of the judiciary. Most of these works were drawn up on private initiative and so had no official character, even if their benefit for judges and advocates was plain to see. Lawyers were involved for the first time in some real codifying when in about 130 the Emperor Hadrian encouraged Salvius Julianus (*c.* 100–*c.* 162) to condense the Praetorian Law into one single work. The result was a *digesta* of ninety books, which was ratified by the senate with the title *Edictum Perpetuum* and given legal effect. With the lawyers Paulus and Ulpian at the beginning of the third century the first creative period in the history of the law came to an end.

Later imperial lawgiving likewise was gathered together for the first time in the *Codex Hermogenianus* and the slightly earlier *Codex Gregorianus* of about 291; both were private works. On the other hand the *Codex Theodosianus* had official status, published by the Emperor Theodosius II in 438 and containing constitutions from the time of Constantine and after. This work was the last late fruit of Roman law, whose development halted soon after that with the final collapse of the western empire.[31]

The establishment and further development of theoretical law was a business that in itself bore witness to the Roman capacity for systematic thinking, which surpassed the Greek in this one area. Later we shall see how Roman justice time after time came to play a significant role in European history long after the imperium had given up the ghost and the last legions had left the provinces. In part the system showed itself applicable in the formation of many later states; in part it was able to serve as an example for work in systematising and codifying legal systems of other origins.

In addition, one single detail in Roman justice would show itself to be of decisive importance in the organisation of higher teaching in the Europe of the middle ages, for which reason it makes sense to discuss it now. This concerns the doctrine of Roman law on unions of people who were bound together in one way or another by a common office or occupation and could therefore form *colleges* or *corporations* outwardly appearing as individual legal persons. Gaius the jurist says about this, that 'when persons are permitted to form a corporation in the form of a guild or company or another combination, they have just as a town society the right to own property in common, to have a common chest, and to have an *actor* or *syndicus* to attend to their transactions and conduct their cases'.[32] Examples of such corporations in Rome were colleges of priests in the individual temples, vestal virgins, augurs (the official soothsayers of the state), and government scribes, as well as various unions of artisans and merchants. That members of such a corporation gathered under one banner were denoted by the word *universitas* is the first presage of the direct significance of Roman law in the history of the university.[33]

So far we have had a brief glimpse of the most striking features of

---

[31] On the great jurists of imperial times see F. Schultz, *History of Roman Legal Science*, Oxford, 1946.

[32] Quoted in *Digesta* III, 4, 1.

[33] On the concept of *universitas* see *Digesta* I, 8, 6 and elsewhere. The study of corporations was founded in Th. Mommsen, *De Collegiis et Sodaliciis Romanorum*, Kiel, 1843. Important later works are J. P. Waltzing, *Étude Historique sur les Corporations Professionelles chez les Romains*, vols. I–iv, Louvain, 1895–1900, and L. Schnorr von Carolsfeld, *Geschichte der juristischen Person. Universitas, corpus, collegium im klassischen römischen Recht*, Munich, 1933.

schools in antiquity in the four chief cultures which more than all others were important for the development which led the way to the universities of Europe. However unsatisfactory this account may be, it still helps to explain the importance and multiplicity of our inheritance from these old civilisations. The Egyptians and Babylonians already knew how schools could be instituted and intellectual disciplines developed to meet the immediate economic and administrative needs of society. The Greeks took a further leap by shaping a series of rationally formed, abstract, and theoretical sciences culminating in Greek mathematics, the development of which must always be regarded as one of the most impressive achievements of the human spirit. At the same time the Greeks were able to develop a philosophical metascience, in the form of a philosophy of science that illuminated many aspects of scientific knowledge so fruitfully that Hellenistic scholars could become familiar with a whole array of different methods of academic research. Even though the word as such first appears in a later stage of development, the various institutions in Alexandria together made up a centre for teaching and research which can with justice be considered the world's first real 'university'. Finally, the Romans knew how even the founding stone of civilisation itself – public law and order – could be codified and analysed within the frame of a theoretical law of astonishing scope and vitality. Together all these gains became the foundations on which the whole later university system was built. Before this could happen, however, the ancient system of teaching and scholarship had to live through a crisis that for a while seemed almost likely to destroy it completely.

CHAPTER 2

From ancient science to monastic learning

Historians of earlier times were fond of talking about the collapse of ancient culture, its slumber during the dark ages, and its resurrection in the Renaissance. Yet the more detailed our knowledge of its historical development has grown, the more this popular and heavy-handed construction has proved to be increasingly meaningless and unsuitable. The sharp distinction between the ancient and medieval worlds is becoming unclear and arbitrary, and the darkness of the middle ages now appears to a certain extent to be due to the weak light by which it used to be seen. Today the picture is far more varied. No-one wishes to deny that the Roman empire perished as a political unity. But whether its fall also involved the annihilation of ancient culture is a far more complicated question. On the one hand it is incontestable that very significant changes were taking place in the period around the years 400 to 600 in political, economic, and intellectual terms. On the other hand we catch a glimpse of a significantly greater continuity in development than is immediately apparent if our attention is only fixed on conspicuous events, as for example the triumph of Christianity or the disintegration of the Roman empire. Clearly there is no place in this chapter for more than a schematic treatment of all these changes, the common context of which is far from being explained in an historically exhaustive way. So we must be content with noting some of the events that had immediate consequences for the intellectual and academic situation of posterity.[1]

The Roman empire was the playground of numerous tribes, each with its own religion, and therefore without religious unity. Beyond these native religions, however, a more universal series of movements

---

[1] On chapter 2 generally see A. H. M. Jones, *The Later Roman Empire 284–602*, vols. I–IV, Oxford, 1964; F. Lot, *La Fin du Monde Antique et le Début du Moyen Âge*, 2nd edn, Paris, 1948; B. Altaner, *Leben, Schriften und Lehre der Kirchenväter*, 2nd edn, Freiburg i.B., 1950.

in the first centuries of our era can be seen unfolding, which clearly proves that the traditional tribal religions were no longer felt to be satisfactory.

Among these new religions the cult of the Roman emperor took pride of place. Not least as a consequence of Syrian influence the emperor's position increased its religious status over the years, as is evident from the number of titles that were heaped up about the office of the emperor. As *consul* he was the supreme head of the Roman government with an increasingly insignificant senate as the instrument of his decisions. As *imperator* and *dominus* he was field marshal and lord of the empire. As *pontifex maximus* he was in addition high priest of the old native Roman religion, and finally, as *augustus* and *divus*, he was the object of a religious cult which was required of all citizens of the empire. At the same time other peoples were allowed to follow their own customary beliefs in peace. The emperor-ideology and the cult that followed from it thus had the purely political aim of using religion as a tool to strengthen the unity of the imperium.[2]

Of a quite different sort was the religious metaphysics that, under the name of Neo-Platonism, spread from Egypt all over the world in the course of the third century with Plotinus, a thinker resident in Rome (*c.* 205–270), as its foremost spokesman.[3] This philosophy was deeply engaged in the problem of the oneness of existence, regarding God as 'The One', from whom all existing things had emanated step by step, with matter as the lowest and least worthy form of existence. The soul's salvation therefore comes from turning one's back on this world and preparing the spirit for its return to its rightful, invisible homeland, once it is released from the tomb of the body and is no longer infected with matter. Clearly this was a religion for the refined intellectual elite who had been scandalised by the confusion of polytheistic tribal religions and disgusted by the crass materialism in the traditional mythologies.

Where the emperor cult lacked intensity and Neo-Platonism wanted popular appeal, an array of Middle Eastern mystery religions had greater power of attraction. Not least this was true of the cult of Mithras, a mythological hero in the old Persian religion who fought

---

[2] On the religions of the imperial age see F. Cumont, *Oriental Religions in Roman Paganism*, New York, 1956; L. Ross Taylor, *The Divinity of the Roman Emperor*, New Haven, 1931.

[3] W. R. Inge, *The Philosophy of Plotinus*, vols. I–II, London, 1929; see also the excellent monograph (in Danish) by Poul Johs. Jensen, *Plotin*, Copenhagen, 1948.

with the power of light against the forces of darkness, and who therefore came to be identified with a sun-god. His teaching was secret, and so not adequately documented even today; but it is known that Mithras was worshipped in temple grottos with a ritual – that is bull-sacrifices – to which only initiates had access, and in which women, to judge from the evidence, could not take part. Certainly this cult won an enormous following in the army, as archaeologists keep finding underground Mithras temples in all places where Roman legions were once stationed.[4]

Finally there was the Christian religion which slowly but surely in these centuries spread out in society through all walks of life, and which without question had more cards in its hand than the other universal religions. Belief in God as a creator of also the material universe stood in strong contrast to Neo-Platonism's pale contempt of the world, but by the same token appealed to the moral consciousness of the individual. It had mysteries (sacraments) and initiations, as did the cult of Mithras, but men and women were treated as equals. It finally secured an international structure as a universal church with an ever more developed leadership in the form of a hierarchy of priests and bishops, among whom the bishop of Rome enjoyed a certain supremacy even in the earliest days. Christianity also distinguished itself from the other religions of the Roman empire by its absolute unwillingness to grant the emperor any form of religious worship. This was the background for a series of persecutions, the last of which started in the year 303 AD under the Emperor Diocletian (284–305), with his fellow emperor Galerius as its true begetter.[5]

That this so-called Diocletian persecution was unusually bloody at times presumably means that the Christians were now so numerous that their protest against the emperor-cult was felt to be a serious threat to the unity of the empire. Only after the death of Diocletian in 313 did it blow over, when the new pair of emperors, Constantine (306–337) and Licinius, with the so-called Milan Edict introduced full religious freedom over the whole empire. This could be done within the general framework of Roman law, by having the churches made into corporations on the same footing as temples. Thereby the churches got the right to obtain and own property. In 315 the emperor went on to exempt church properties from taxation, and in

[4] On Mithras see Cumont, *Oriental Religions*, ch. VI, note 2.
[5] T. C. Christensen, *Galerius Valerius Maximinus*, Copenhagen, 1974.

321 the first day in the week was made an official holiday throughout the empire. This was not only a gesture for the Christians, who could now observe it as the Lord's Day: *dies dominica*, but also a kindness to the Mithras cults, which celebrated the day as the Sun's Day: *dies invicti solis*. With this stroke of genius the emperor ensured the good will of both church and army. That Mithras' official birthday on 25 December was later made into Christmas Day, on the other hand, must be seen as a move to counteract the Mithras cult, whose greatest feast day was thereby given a Christian context.[6]

In this way Constantine made Christians and non-Christians equal before the law, in an attempt to shape a religious peace on the home front in order to defend the empire all the more powerfully on the frontiers. Yet in spite of his openly growing sympathy for Christianity, Constantine was careful not to offend the old religion. So he refrained from being baptised until on his deathbed, just as to the last he continued to hold the imperial office as *pontifex maximus*. In his time it would still probably have meant political suicide to give up a title which in non-Christian eyes lent the emperor's position religious authority and ensured its connection with the Roman past.

Unfortunately this tolerance did not even last the century out. Already the young Emperor Gratian (375–383) did not see himself in any way able to function as *pontifex maximus* and abolished the office as such. This was the beginning of the end for the old religion's association with politics, and a few years later Gratian also deprived it of its economic base by scrapping the non-Christian priesthood's corporate status and bringing temple property into the government's coffers. His fellow emperor of the east, Theodosius I (379–395), went even further and abolished religious freedom itself in 380, when in a decree issued in Salonica he commanded all inhabitants of the empire to accept the Christian faith. In 392 he had the temples closed by the police, and a new edict three years later deprived heretics of their civil rights. This is the background for the famous letter in which one of the fathers of the church, Jerome (348–420), describes a visit to Rome in which he saw the Capitol lying waste and the temples covered in cobwebs, while in the city people gathered at the graves of the martyrs.[7]

---

[6] A. Alföldi, *The Conversion of Constantine*, Oxford, 1948; H. Kraft (ed.), *Konstantin der Grosse*, Darmstadt, 1974; N. H. Baynes, Constantine the Great and the Christian Church, *Proceedings of the British Academy* 15 (1929) (bibliography).

[7] Hieronymus, Epist. 107, *Migne PL* 22, 868.

Obviously the situation had reversed itself in less than a hundred years. Having won its hard-fought freedoms, the church could now order its internal affairs in the full glare of publicity and with the support of the government, as was the case in the great church assemblies which were organised in Nicaea (325), Constantinople (381), Ephesus (431), and Chalcedon (451), and which clarified the main tenets of Christian dogma. In compensation, to some extent, the church had allowed itself to be harnessed to the wagon of imperial politics as an instrument in the emperor's struggle to hold his domain together. By making Christianity into a state religion and forcing paganism underground, Theodosius the Great had in reality only revealed that he, just like Diocletian, was bound to the ingrown Roman conception of one emperor and one faith – notwithstanding that this was now a new faith. Firstly, this meant an end to Constantine's tolerance. Secondly, it became the starting point for one of the strongest ideological factors in the politics of the middle ages – the dream of establishing God's Kingdom on earth in the form of a Christian empire. At any rate, the church had been able to maintain its independence and integrity to such an extent that no later emperor dared to set himself up as *pontifex maximus* of the new state religion. On the contrary, before a hundred years was out and while the empire still existed, the strong Pope Leo the Great (440–461) was able unopposed to appropriate the old title for himself as a symbol of the Roman bishop's steadily stronger claim to be the supreme spiritual head of Christendom. This meant essentially a distinction between spiritual and secular power which was a new feature in the culture of antiquity. From now on there were two poles of loyalty for Christian citizens – and consequently many later conflicts on the right interpretation of the relationship between church and state.

While the shift in religion was taking place, there were also crucial changes in the political arena. Already under Constantine strong tensions appeared between the eastern and western parts of the empire, and even if he kept control over both of them he contributed to the polarisation by transforming the old Greek colony Byzantium into the new Constantinople, which as 'the New Rome' gave the eastern part of the empire a new centre of gravity of steadily increasing importance. After Constantine's death in 337 the empire was at times united and at other times divided. The final breach came after the death of Theodosius I in 395, when the empire was shared between his two incompetent sons, Honorius in the west and Arcadius in the east.[8]

This weakness meant new political opportunities for several tribes living immediately outside the frontiers of the empire. These had often supplied the emperors with mercenaries led by generals who knew Rome and Byzantium from personal experience and sometimes spoke both Latin and Greek. One such former general of the *foederati* was the Ostrogoth Alaric, who invaded Greece in 395/396 and was thereupon made regent in Illyricum by Arcadius, whose aim was to turn Alaric's aggression away from the Greek to the Latin zone of the older empire. After several campaigns in Italy and a series of fruitless dealings with Honorius in Ravenna, Alaric stormed Rome in 410, and only his death in the same year prevented the city from becoming the centre of a big Ostrogothic kingdom.

These wars weakened the defence of the western provinces. Thus the 20th legion was recalled home from Britain, though this did not stop the Vandals making themselves lords over Gaul and Spain in the years after 409. Between 429 and 439 the Vandals conquered the North African provinces which had been the breadbasket of Rome. They got into Rome in 455 under Genseric, but then lost the city again. In 476 came the final blow, when the German Odoacer deposed the last Roman shadow-emperor, Romulus Augustulus, and was recognised by Zeno, emperor of the east, as the lord of Italy. In 493 Odoacer was killed by the Ostrogoth Theoderic I, who thenceforth established himself in the whole of Italy.

Even before the fifth century was out, the earlier west Roman territories had turned into a group of independent individual states, with rulers of northern origin and usually with the original population significantly increased by immigrant races. The Vandals had established themselves in North Africa. Spain and the south of Gaul were ruled by the Visigoths, forced in their turn southwards by the Franks, who after Chlodoveg's assumption of power and the founding of the Merovingian dynasty in 481 counted as one of the most dynamic tribal groups in Europe. In Britain the void left by the Roman legions was already being filled up with Angles, Saxons, and Jutes, and in the Italian homeland the Ostrogoths ruled from

---

[8] On Byzantium see G. A. Ostrogorsky, *A History of the Byzantine State*, Oxford, 1956; H. W. Haussig, *Kulturgeschichte von Byzanz*, 2nd edn, Stuttgart, 1966; J. M. Hussey (ed.), *The Byzantine Empire*, vol. II: *Government, Church and Civilisation* (The Cambridge Medieval History 6, Part II), Cambridge, 1967.

Ravenna – the last imperial town – over a large area stretching as far as the Danube in the north and pushing to the edge of the Byzantine empire in the east. This last remnant of empire embraced Epirus and Greece, the whole of Asia Minor, Syria, Palestine, and Egypt.

Yet in economic terms there was far more continuity, owing to a number of different factors.[9] Firstly, the new 'barbarian' rulers, in spite of their name, were not wild savages cutting down everything before them. On the contrary, most of them were more or less influenced by the culture of Rome, just as the immigrant tribes with the exception of the Franks normally practised some form of Christianity. For a Germanic king in Spain, Gaul, or Italy the most important problem was how to get the new kingdom to work as a viable economic entity. This was best done by taking over as many of the old Roman institutions as possible, and as it were taking on the role of the former provincial governor, supported by the many officials with the administrative and economic expertise of former times who had nothing against going into the service of the new rulers, at least if the machinery was working. Roman agricultural production had essentially been based on large estates or *villae* both in Italy and in the provinces. They were large enough to clear any passing crisis on their own and so survived the shift in power without great changes in the way they were run, and perhaps also without very many of their farm-hands discovering that the profit of their labour no longer went to Rome. Finally, the most important provincial towns came to play a new role as episcopal sees and administrative centres of the church. It was the church that now remained the sole international organisation in the western world.

That the first stage of the transition took place successfully without catastrophic consequences is probably due to the fact that the new kingdoms, just as the former provinces, were grouped around the western end of the Mediterranean. Then as before this inland sea functioned as a link between them and made possible a wide-ranging sea-trade whereby surplus products from individual countries could be exchanged to mutual advantage, just as the Mediterranean at this period carried considerable trade with the empire of Byzantium in the east. That the Roman road network fell into decline in western Europe, because there was no longer any

---

[9] On the economic development of the period, see *The Cambridge Economic History of Europe*, vol. I, Cambridge, 1971, pp. 180–264; also H. Pirenne, *Economic and Social History of Medieval Europe*, London, 1936.

military need to maintain it, had less effect for this reason on the local economies.

This many-sided development did not pass without consequence for science and education. Here also things turned out very differently in east and west. The Hellenistic culture had had its centre of gravity in Alexandria, where already in the fourth century the schools had begun to become Christian, with the result that theological quarrels often forced teachers to emigrate. In this way knowledge of the Greek language and Greek science spread over a wider area. Thus the school in Antioch flourished at the same time as a Greek centre was established further east in Edessa. In Edessa, however, the school came under the influence of the Nestorian sect, for which reason the Emperor Zeno closed it in 489, causing its teachers to reestablish it in Nisibis, after which it was finally moved lock, stock, and barrel to Seleucia on the river Tigris.

Byzantium also in the fourth century opened its doors to a respectable influx of professors from unsettled Alexandria, with the result that its school began to grow; in 475 it had a library of 120,000 volumes. Events first really gathered pace when the Emperor Justinian (527–565) ascended the throne and soon afterwards started his master plan to strengthen the empire within and without. This led to costly expeditions on the frontiers, in which among other achievements the Vandal supremacy in North Africa was destroyed and for a time both Italy and parts of Spain were brought under Byzantine rule. Justinian's cultural policy was heavy-handed right from the start: in 529 he closed Plato's old Academy in Athens, which still existed as the only non-Christian school of importance within the borders of the empire. Its last seven teachers emigrated to Jundishapur in Persia, where a Greek school they founded became the last outpost of Hellenism in the east.

While Athens was thus deprived of its last institution of learning, something was achieved in Byzantium of the greatest relevance to later European history in east and west, when an imperial commission of four professors and eleven advocates undertook a thorough revision and codification of Roman law. The commission first read through 2,000 classical legal texts totalling 3 million lines, and made an abstract of 150,000 lines which they divided into 50 'books' or extracts and published under the title *Digesta* (or *Pandectae*). Half of the material came from Ulpian and Paulus. Shortly after there followed a collection of imperial laws and constitutions called the

Codex Justiniani together with a legal textbook in four 'books' with the traditional title *Institutiones*. Towards the end of Justinian's rule the *Codex* was supplemented with the so-called *Novellae*, made up from his own imperial laws and for the most part in Greek. Together these four works have gone down in history as the *Corpus Iuris Civilis*; when 'Roman law' is mentioned henceforth, it is this collection that will be referred to. During the supremacy of Justinian in Italy, Roman law came back to its homeland. In the coming centuries it became the basis for legal teaching in a number of small schools in different Italian towns, until it later reached its peak of importance in the history of political and academic ideology.[10]

In this way, paradoxically enough, the Latin Roman law received its finishing touches on Greek soil. That such a comprehensive work could be carried out in the course of only four years (since only the *Novellae* fall outside the period 530 to 534), shows first and foremost the strength of intellectual life in Justinian's Byzantium. Secondly, the very execution of the work is proof that the emperor wished to regard his eastern kingdom as the direct continuation of an undivided empire that was based on the same system of laws and the same fundamental state ideology. Last but not least, late Roman imperial ideology in Byzantium was quite unequivocally reinforced. In the constitution *Deo Auctore*, with which Justinian in 530 put his work on the *Digesta* in motion, he laid great stress on the old wives' tale that 'all legal authority and all power regarding the Roman people was committed to the imperial government' (by a special *lex regia* discussed by Ulpian, but certainly an invention). Justinian interpreted this in such a way that he, as emperor, was the true originator of the new compilation – regardless of what classical authorities it was based on: 'We are entitled to ascribe everything [i.e. in the law] to ourself in consideration of the fact that it is from us that their [i.e. the jurists'] authority is derived.' Roman law was therefore not valid because it came from the earlier emperors, but because it pleased Justinian to confirm it once more as 'Regent under authority of God over our empire, which is given over to us by His Heavenly Majesty'. Thus the imperial ideology was revived on Christian soil and with a pseudo-

---

[10] The legislative work of Justinian is described in H. F. Jolowicz, *Historical Introduction to the Study of Roman Law*, Cambridge, 1961, ch. 28; see also A. Honoré and A. Rodger, How the Digest Commissioners Worked, *Zeitschrift der Savigny-Stiftung, Romanische Abteilung* 87 (1970).

Christian foundation that was to be of fateful importance in the history of Europe.[11]

While Greek leaning for purely linguistic reasons was given the opportunity to survive in the Byzantine empire, the situation in the west was essentially different. There the linguistic confusion had always been greater, and this increased after the dissolution of the empire. The provinces had been administered in Latin, whereas Greek had been generally adopted by educated circles to the extent that the Romans had never felt the need to translate all the main works of Greek learning into their own language. Now after the dissolution of the western empire, Greek teachers soon disappeared. Thereby the tradition of learning also faded in the west, and only the compilations of the Latin encyclopedists were left as hollow monuments to the results of the scholarship of the ancient world with no chance of mediating its methods. In this sense we must recognise that the political sundering of the empire led to a cultural regression. That this was also the contemporary view is often witnessed in the literature. Towards the end of the sixth century Gregory of Tours (c. 538–594) wrote in the introduction to his *Historia Francorum*, that 'the towns of Gaul have allowed learned studies to decline or even perish ... It is no longer possible to find any person who, as a grammarian trained in dialectic, would be capable of reporting on events either in prose or in verse. Most mourned this and said: Woe for our age, for scholarship has died out among us – *Vae diebus nostris quia periit studium literarum a nobis!*'[12] And with this Gregory was not thinking of the knowledge of Greek that had disappeared, but of the even more basic knowledge of Latin and even of the art of reading and writing.

That there was still even now a modicum of strength left in Latin culture comes from the fact that clear-sighted personalities in the sixth century could recognise where everything was heading; while there was still time, they tried to counter the situation and ward off its worst effects. Foremost in this rescue attempt were Flavius Magnus Aurelius Cassiodorus (c. 490–c. 583) from Calabria and Anicius Manilius Severinus Boethius (c. 480–524), often described as 'the last Romans'. Both received high positions in the administration under the Ostrogothic king Theoderic the Great (455–526), who had

---

[11] O. Treitinger, *Die oströmische Rechts- und Kaiser-idee*, 2nd edn, Darmstadt, 1956.
[12] Gregory of Tours, *Historia Francorum*, Praefatio, *Migne PL* 71, 159f.

subjected most of Italy to his rule in 493. We can get an excellent idea of this aspect of Cassiodorus' work in the collection of 468 letters and other acts which he drafted in his time as minister, and then carefully classified in a collection known as the *Variarum Libri XII*. This work became the book of diplomatic letters and forms of the middle ages and is still an important source for the history of the period. After working for some time under Theoderic's incompetent successors, Cassiodorus gave up his office to devote himself to a cultural endeavour of greater calibre. He tells us about this in the introduction to the second part of the treatise *De Institutione Divinarum Scriptuarum*:

When I saw clearly that the study of profane literature flared up on account of a great lack, in such a way that many people thought themselves hereby capable of obtaining cleverness for themselves in this world, then I confess that it caused me deep pain that there was a want of public teachers in Holy Scripture. And since the profane authors would without doubt stand firm on the base of a great tradition, I committed myself together with the blessed Agapithus of Rome with shared economic means to find proper teachers for a Christian school in Rome (just as it is said that long ago such study was constituted in Alexandria which is now being developed with great industry for the Hebrews in Nisibis, the chief town of Syria), from which the soul might partake of eternal salvation and the tongues of believers be made beautiful with clean and sober speech. But since this my intention could not on the whole be performed on account of the raging wars and bewildering battles being fought in Italy, as much as the desire for peace finds no home in the time of strife, I appear to be forced by God's love to write these introductory works for you with His help in the role of teacher, by which, following my understanding, both the Holy Scriptures and a thorough knowledge of the profane literature, thanks be to God, can be extended. Perhaps they are less well written, since in them one finds no assumed eloquence, but only the necessary context. Yet they seem to be of great benefit if one learns from them whence both the salvation of the soul and profane wisdom appears to result.[13]

From this it appears that together with Pope Agapithus I (535–536) Cassiodorus strove for nothing less than to give Rome a high school that could become the spiritual and intellectual centre for the Latin world. The motives for this seem to have been many, but the decisive one was surely religious. It appears from the text that even now there were schools in Rome for orators still industriously studying the profane literature, while the now inaccessible school in

---

[13] Cassiodorus, *De Institutione*, Praefatio, *Migne PL* 70, 1105f.

Alexandria and its offshoot in Nisibis had long been Christian. Cassiodorus' plan clearly required him to summon Christian teachers, presumably from the east, to bring the schools in Rome into line with Alexandria as the workshop of a Christian culture.

He thereby suggested a programme to which the middle ages gradually devoted itself, and which it finally believed it had carried out. As late as 1384 the Paris Master Thomas of Ireland claimed that there were in Paris 'four faculties for theology, law, medicine and liberal arts, and they have been there just as long as the university in Paris, and that is the oldest in the world – for it is the one that was first in Athens and from Athens came to Rome and from Rome was moved to Paris'.[14] This theme of the migration of studies – *translatio studii* – recurs in many authors right through the middle ages, pathetic proof indeed that despite the breakdown of culture the ancient universities were still remembered, with a conscious desire to create a link back to the schools in Athens and Alexandria.

What Thomas of Ireland did not know, on the other hand, was that the Greek schools had never reemerged as a university in Rome. Cassiodorus' plan went wrong because of the political changes afoot in Italy. The result was that the Latin world had to dispense with such a centre in the following centuries. And yet to keep something of his idea alive, Cassiodorus tried another route and founded a monastery in Vivarium, his estate in Calabria, whose relatively comfortable design and beautiful surroundings are depicted in detail in his *De Institutione*.[15] To the extent that there were already monasteries in the west, this was no new idea. As early as 372 St Martin of Tours (*c.* 316–397) had founded the cloister of Marmoutiers near this town, and at the beginning of the fifth century St Victor was established outside Marseilles by Johannes Cassianus (*c.* 350–433), with whose ascetic writings Cassiodorus was familiar. An offshoot of St Victor was the monastery on the isles of Lerins (outside the French Riviera), that was founded by St Honoratus (d. 429). These institutions took the older Egyptian and Greek monasticism as their model, but differed in that they put more emphasis on the community life of monks. From the Roman provinces the movement

---

[14] The quotation is from a document of a law suit instigated in the 1380s by the Paris faculty of Canon law against the canons of Notre Dame, *Chartularium* III, 320 (no. 1486). The identification of the author with Thomas of Ireland is due to Gilson, pp. 193ff, where there is more on the topic of the *translatio studii*.

[15] The Vivarium is described by Cassiodorus in his *De Institutione*, ch. 29, *Migne PL* 70, 1143ff.

extended to Italy, where St Benedict of Nurcia (c. 480–c. 544) founded Monte Cassino in 529 – the same year as the school in Athens was closed and only a few years before Cassiodorus' Vivarium was built.

What was completely new about Cassiodorus as a father of monks, however, was his interpretation of the purpose of monasticism. The monastery was to be not only the context of the monks' religious community life in isolation from the world, but also the seat of other cultural endeavours. In *De Institutione* he enjoined the brothers to the special task of collecting books, making copies of them and thereby taking care to preserve the old literature.[16] As a former civil servant himself, he understood the importance of classifying relevant documents, to which his *Libri Variarum* bears witness. Possibly he simply imagined Vivarium as an archive where the old literature could be cared for and preserved until the day of more favourable political conditions when it could again be used in a larger school.

However this may be, the *De Institutione* was first of all a handbook for those who would attend to such a work. Cassiodorus' own experience as an orator and chancellor shines clearly through in his instructions on how texts should be copied, mistakes corrected, and defects improved. This cannot take place unless the writer is in possession of a certain general education. In a special extract of the work entitled *De Disciplinis* Cassiodorus therefore surveyed the seven liberal arts in association with Varro's text, mentioned on p. 23, leaving out medicine and architecture. Since this extract, too, was written as a guide for scribes in the scriptorium, the trivium assumed the predominant place, while the four mathematical disciplines in the quadrivium were dismissed with a few short paragraphs and literary references. Grammar was presented in a thorough way with constant reference to the grammarian Donatus (fourth century AD), but rhetoric took up even more space with a useful survey of the different stylistic models of which a speaker or writer can avail himself. Here Cicero was evidently the example. Yet the greatest emphasis was placed on dialectic, which was presented here as the

---

[16] On Cassiodorus and his influence see A. Momigliano, Cassiodorus and Italian Culture of his Time, *Proceedings of the British Academy* 41 (1955), pp. 207–46, and L. W. Jones, The Influence of Cassiodorus on Medieval Culture, *Speculum* 20 (1945), 433ff and 22 (1947), 254ff. On the copying programme see *De Institutione*, ch. 30, Migne PL 70, 1144–64.

art of philosophical argument, with among other things an extensive survey of the doctrine of the syllogism in Aristotelian logic.

That Cassiodorus paid so little attention to the quadrivium may be due to the fact that before him Boethius had made a serious attempt to save the mathematical subjects from oblivion.[17] In contrast to the practitioner Cassiodorus, Boethius was of a scholarly and philosophical temperament. He had possibly planned a complete translation of both Aristotle and Plato, a task which would surely have exceeded his powers even if he had not been executed in Pavia in 524 at a relatively early age after being accused of treason. Among his extant writings is the *De Institutione Arithmetica Libri II*, the *De Institutione Musica Libri V*, and an *Ars Geometrica*, which were all highly regarded handbooks right through the middle ages. He translated furthermore a commentary to Aristotle's *Categories* by Porphyry (c. 232–305) and thereby bestowed the chief work on logic to a posterity which for several centuries had no access to other Aristotelian works in Latin. Thanks to a letter from Cassiodorus, it seems that Boethius had also translated Ptolemy's *Almagest* and Archimedes' *Mechanics* (i.e. the treatise *On the Equilibrium of Plane Figures*). There is no trace of these works now, so they must have gone missing almost as soon as they were completed, as ill-luck would have it – a circumstance that paralysed medieval physics and astronomy before they even started.[18] In prison before his execution, Boethius finally wrote *De Consolatione Philosophiae*, a work that, as a deeply philosophical and religious meditation on the potential of philosophy and science to be a counterweight to the corruption of life, was loved and used throughout the middle ages and had the honour of being one of the few works of philosophy to be translated into vernacular languages – into West Saxon by King Alfred (849–900), into German by Notker Labeo (c. 950–1022), and into French by Jean de Meung (c. 1250–1305). Also a work on theology, *De Trinitate*, came to play an important role in the theory of science, thanks to commentaries by Thomas Aquinas and other scholars.

This development laid the foundations for monastic learning. In the following centuries this would be the only form of scholarship in

---

[17] On Boethius and Cassiodorus see also E. K. Rand, *Founders of the Middle Ages*, Cambridge, Mass., 1928. For the extensive literature on Boethius see the long article on Boethius by L. Minio-Paluello in *DSB*, vol. II, pp. 228–36, New York, 1970; cf. also B. Bonnaud, L'éducation scientifique de Boèce, *Speculum* 4 (1929), 198ff.

[18] Cassiodorus' letter to Boethius was included in his *Libri Variarum* I, 45, *Migne PL* 69, 539.

western Europe. Here the decisive impulse was undeniably the clear and conscious programme of culture underlying the efforts of Cassiodorus, Boethius, and St Benedict, which again presupposed their own Roman education. The scattered experiments with monastic life in the west obtained power and unity through the Rule of St Benedict, which gradually penetrated many of the already existing foundations and nearly all the later ones. Instigated by the *De Institutione* of Cassiodorus, scholastic study became a natural legitimate part of the monks' labours, even though it would be very wrong to overestimate the number of brothers in the cloister who were busied with this alone.[19] Finally, Boethius' writings achieved conclusive status as a mathematical-scientific supplement to the doctrinal matter of the Bible and the fathers. This made a natural basis for study in such a way that this or that interested monk could find inspiration for his own work on the quadrivium.

Often the period of monastic learning has been characterised as the dark ages. This term arose in a time when this period looked like an empty gap in the history of scholarship, simply because little was known about its intellectual life, with the result that many scholars hastily concluded that there was none. Today we know that this was not the case. Yet it is true that these ages are still dark to the extent that they make up the worst-researched and least-accessible era in the whole history of Latin learning. The sources are few and far between, and in the following remarks many seemingly secure statements will really be open to question. Nevertheless, we cannot ignore the problems of the expansion of monastic learning, its concrete scholarly content and ideological self-understanding in the light of the character and needs of early medieval society.

As regards the geographical expansion of monastic learning, a distinction can be made between an early period, in which monasteries grew up quite spontaneously in the former Roman provinces, and a late period in which social authorities in the form of pope and emperor exerted themselves to take control over this development.

In the first instance, from the fifth century the monasteries in Gaul were of direct relevance to the Celtic churches in Britain and Ireland. Here the tradition is extremely dark and uncertain, but it is

---

[19] On the activity of monastic scriptoria see e.g. L. W. Jones, The Scriptorium at Corbie, *Speculum* 22 (1947), 191–204 and 375–94, and also R. Branner, The Art of the Scriptorium at Luxeuil, *Speculum* 29 (1954), 678–90.

presumed to be true that the Irish student by the name of Patrick once living in Lerins returned to found the see of Armagh in about 450 and furnished it with a *Teach Screapha* or *Scriptorium* as a basis for the education of priests in the diocese. Surviving from this school is the famous *Book of Armagh* from 807. Other Irish schools were Clonard – 'from whence there came as many learned men as Greeks from the Trojan horse' – founded by St Finnian in about 520, Clonmacnoise from *c.* 544 and Bangor from *c.* 560. Working at the same time elsewhere in France was Gildas (*c.* 516–570), a monk from Britain, who in his *De Excidio Britanniae* described the ruin of Britain after the end of the Roman empire.

This expansion of the monastic life in Ireland is without doubt closely linked to the rather loose structure of Irish society, that never had any firm central organisation. This made it difficult to introduce the Roman church structure in which the visible exponent of religious unity was the bishop, mainly permanently resident in a town. Such an episcopal concept of the church based on the existence of towns hardly suited the tribal nature of Irish society, which felt religious life to be more at home in a monastic village. With the abbot as the central figure – and the bishop as a purely spiritual official under him – the cloister began to play a social role which reinvigorated its religious and intellectual activity. This took place so quickly that the effects were soon to be noticed outside the island, in such a way that Irish culture was able to pay the Merovingians back in the seventh century for what it had received from their Gallic forerunners a hundred years earlier.

Here the central figure is St Columban (*c.* 540–615) from Bangor in the north of Ireland, who criss-crossed the continent for many years and founded cloisters everywhere on the Irish model.[20] Thus in 589 he established Luxarium in the Vosges (the later Luxeuil), which for a time with its 600 monks was the most important monastic centre north of the Alps and an obvious counterpart to Monte Cassino. Later he founded Bregenz in present-day Switzerland before, at the end of his life, establishing Bobbio in Lombardy, whose library was famous throughout the whole middle ages. The movement was continued by his disciples and bore fruit in St Gallen

---

[20] See Jonas of Bobbio, Vitae Columbani et Sociorum, in *Monumenta Germaniae Historica, Scriptores rerum Merovingicarum* IV, 1–60, Hanover, 1902 (cf. *Migne PL* 87, 1011–46); also L. Gougard, *Les Saints Irlandais*, Louvain, 1936, and R. Aigrain, Columban, in *Catholicisme* II, Paris, 1950, pp. 1317ff.

(614) in Switzerland, among other places. In France Columban-style monasteries grew up in Faramoutier (617), Fontenelle (648, the later St Wandrille), and Jumièges (631). This success on the continent presumably came about because Merovingian society too was quite loosely organised with regard to ecclesiastical and social life; in one way or another this gave the monks of Columban an advantage over the Benedictines, in spite of the far stricter rule of their order.

The influence of Irish monastic learning on England came to be very important for the development of culture in Europe. Even before the Romans gave up their sovereignty over the British province once and for all in 410/411, parts of its Celtic population must have accepted Christianity, since we hear of British bishops taking part in the Synod of Arles in 314. After the non-Christian Angles, Saxons, and Jutes steadily overran most of the country in the years following 450, the original population was forced out to the boundaries in Cornwall, Wales, and Scotland, where the Celtic culture and church survived, supported by its links with Ireland and Gaul. But of course an Irish culture making its effects known as far as Italy could not ignore neighbouring England, and already in 563 on the small island of Hy (later called Iona) in the Hebrides a monastery was founded by the Irishman St Columba, who had been trained in Clonard and was famous as an excessively hard-working scribe. No fewer than 300 manuscripts are thought to have been copied by him, among which the psalter *Cathach* from before 600 survives as the oldest known example of the typical Irish miniscule hand. In the course of time a sizeable school of writers and authors was working on Iona, such as Adamnan (abbot 679–704), whose biography of Columba is an important historical source for this whole period. Another island cloister of less significance was Lindisfarne out on the east coast of Northumbria; it was founded by St Aidan of Iona in about 635. Among other products of this place is one of the best-executed gospel manuscripts of the period. There are certain indications that some knowledge of Greek was still alive in these schools, even if this is disputed. Thanks to these cultural outposts, the contact between the Celtic and English cultures became more and more lively, and with the conversion of King Edwin in 627 as the most marked event the church took firm root in Northumbria. Soon afterwards we find Irish foundations spread out as far as in Malmesbury in Wiltshire, Burgh Castle in Suffolk, and Bosham in Sussex.

A reaction was bound to take place against this powerful expansion of Irish culture. On one hand the princes in Gaul and Francia would fear that the large, well-manned, and highly educated settlements of Columban might turn into states within a state and threaten the very fragile existence of Merovingian society. On the other hand the Benedictine order was backed up from the south with no less power than that of the monks of Columban in the north, and in the end the Roman church and the papal throne had to look with unease at the expansion of an 'Irish' culture structure of a character much looser than the Roman and different to it.

In the political sphere the reaction affected Columban himself, who was driven out of Luxeuil after a quarrel with the Merovingian King Thierry. Soon afterwards royal power and the Benedictine order can be seen in unison taking consistent counter-measures against the monks of Columban in the building of a new network of Benedictine monasteries, or in the introduction of the far more lenient Benedictine Rule in existing foundations. Thus the monastery at St Pierre-et-Paul (later St Geneviève), founded in 511 in Paris under Chlodoveg, was now reformed, and under King Dagobert (622–638) the same happened to the older St Denis north of Paris. Corbie, established in 550, was turned into a Benedictine establishment in 622 for monks from Luxeuil who had become Benedictines. Stavelot (c. 650) and Malmédy (c. 650) were part of the same movement in Belgium.

The reaction in England, on the other hand, went on at the direct insistence of the papacy, which from the early seventh century onwards made persistent attempts to win back the lost British province for the church and convert the new Germanic element of the population. The beginning was made by Pope Gregory the Great (590–604), who in 596/597 sent a band of Benedictines led by St Augustine (of Canterbury) to Kent, where King Ethelbert (who was married to a Christian Merovingian princess) probably let himself be baptised on his deathbed in 617, after the foundation of the archbishopric and monastery of St Peter in Canterbury in 605.[21] Despite repeated setbacks, Christianity in the next two generations slowly pushed through East Anglia and approached Northumbria. There was a showdown between the Irish and Roman systems in a

---

[21] The principal source for the Roman mission in England is Bede's *Historia Ecclesiastica Gentis Anglorum* from AD 731, *Migne PL* 95, 23ff. Among the many English translations is the *History of the English Church and People*, transl. by L. Sherley-Price, London, 1955.

combined synod in Streoneshalch or Whitby Abbey (founded 657) in 663, at which King Oswin of the Northumbrians adjudicated the matter in favour of the Romans. A small flock of Irish extremists emigrated after this to Mayo in Ireland while the church in England was united under the constitution and rites of the Roman church. Soon afterwards even the church in Ireland went over to the Roman system, and Iona surrendered as the last Celtic bastion in 716. Thereby the Celtic phase in monastic learning was over, and soon the monasteries of Columban on the continent also adopted Benedictine observances. Yet for a long time afterwards Anglo-Saxon students continued to visit monasteries in Ireland to gain some of the education that could be had there until the Viking attacks provisionally ended it.

In England the new Benedictine learning was given decisive momentum in 664 when Pope Vitellian (657–672) sent Theodore the Greek and Hadrian from Africa in the footsteps of Augustine, through which the connection with Roman culture was strengthened once more. How eagerly the newly christianised English took advantage of this step can be seen most clearly from the activity of Benedict Biscop (c. 628–690).[22] This thegn at the court of King Oswin was consecrated as a priest at the age of twenty-five and thereafter travelled for the first time to Rome in 653. In the time of Pope Vitellian he revisited Rome once more, whereupon he supplemented his education for two years by staying at Lerins, before he took himself to Rome a third time so as to accompany Theodore and Hadrian to Canterbury. Here he ran the monastic school for two years, before visiting Rome for the fourth time, returning thence with a huge mass of theological works bought in Rome and Vienne, a town which he passed through on the return journey. In 674 he founded the monastery of St Peter's in Monkwearmouth and for that reason was obliged to take a tour to France to fetch stone masons and glaziers for the church that was to be raised there in the Romanesque style. When the monastery was finished, he was once more in Rome, his fifth visit, from whence he came home with a teacher of Gregorian chant together with 'a measureless quantity of books of all kinds'. In 681 he founded another monastery in Jarrow, St Paul's, in the immediate vicinity of St Peter's, and was able to

---

[22] On Benedict Biscop see D. Knowles, *The Monastic Order in England*, 2nd edn, Oxford, 1966, pp. 21ff; on Augustine, see M. Deanesley, *Augustine of Canterbury*, London, 1964.

proceed to Rome for the last time to bring home relics, vestments for the mass, and even more books. Thereby Benedict had created the most substantial library in England, and like many other incorrigible book collectors, stipulated in his will that all his books should remain together after his death as the basis for study in future generations.

Six trips to Rome in one short human lifetime was no mean feat in seventh-century Europe. It was also a sufficient proof of the vigour with which the monastic movement looked to Rome as the place from which both spiritual inspiration and literary aids to study could be brought even as far as the furthest corners of the earth. How fruitful the link would become is best seen from the progress made in Benedict Biscop's monasteries after his death. Here from the 680s onwards was the most learned man of the whole period, the Venerable Bede (c. 673–735), whose short autobiography gives a cursory sketch of the life of this industrious scholar:

> Bede, servant of Christ and priest in the cloisters of the holy apostles Peter and Paul situated in Monkwearmouth and Jarrow. Born in the neighbourhood of this first cloister, at the age of seven I was entrusted by my parents to the very reverend abbot Benedict and then to Ceolfrid [abbot in Jarrow] to be brought up by them. Since then I have spent all the days of my life in this monastery and used my industry in study of the scriptures. In that I have always observed the rule of the order and the daily singing of the hours in church, my desire has always been either to study or to instruct or to write.[23]

Among Bede's pupils was the later archbishop of York, Egbert, and Egbert's colleague and successor Aelbert, among whose pupils in the York cathedral school was Alcuin, later to become the chief proponent of the reform of education in Europe and the subject of closer discussion in the next chapter.

After this sketch of the expansion of monastic learning, we might consider its substance and the means by which it came about. If we look first at a contemporary source, there is Bede telling us that both the Benedictines Theodore and Hadrian mentioned above

> were so learned in both profane literature and Holy Scripture that they drew to them a great number of students into whose souls they poured day after day the waters of healthy knowledge. Apart from instructing their pupils in the Holy Scripture they also taught them poetry, astronomy, and

---

[23] Bede, *Hist. Eccl.* v, 24. On Bede, see A. Hamilton Thompson (ed.), *Bede, His Life, Times and Writings*, Oxford, 1935, and P. H. Blair, *The World of Bede*, New York, 1970; see also R. B. Palmer, Bede as a Textbook Writer, *Speculum* 24 (1959), 573–84.

From ancient science to monastic learning

the computation of the ecclesiastical calendar. Proof of this is that some of their disciples are alive today [i.e. 731; Bede refers in particular to Bishop Tobias of Rochester] being as skilled in Greek and Latin as in their mother tongue.[24]

The last claim should be treated with some reservation, but the statement shows, at any rate, that Bede was impressed. The same was the case with St Aldhelm of Malmesbury, who found from personal experience what the leap from Irish to Latin monastic learning implied.[25] In his youth he was trained in Malmesbury by the Irishman Maidulf, but moved thereafter to Canterbury with the result that 'I, who already believed myself to have become a teacher, must become a student once more.' In a letter to his friend Lentherius, Aldhelm gives a sketch of the Canterbury curriculum, which included Roman law: *Regum Romanorum Iura*, metrics, prosody, rhetorical figures, arithmetic (fractions included), and astronomy in accordance with what Bede reported above about Hadrian and Theodore. It is worth noting that Roman law was now taught in the monasteries notwithstanding the separate legal traditions of the Anglo-Saxon people. Finally, in lyrical turns of phrase in a Latin poem on the bishops and saints of York, *Poema de Pontificis et sanctis Ecclesiae Eboracensis*, Alcuin describes the education that he received in around 750 from Egbert of York, whom we mentioned earlier. A somewhat halting translation of an extract of this poem goes as follows:

> Here he watered thirsty hearts with streams of learning
> And with the sparkling dew of study in various ways.
> Grammar and its causes he industriously conferred on some,
> While others were embued with the floods of rhetorical
>   forms of speech.
> A few he took care to polish finely with jurisprudence.
> Some he taught to sing Aeolian songs together in unison,
> While others were taught to perform on Castalian flutes
> And wander on Parnassus with the feet of poets.
> Yet others the master allowed to gain the knowledge
> Of Heaven's harmony and the darkening of sun and moon,
> Of the world's five zones, the seven ever-wandering stars,
> Of the laws of fixed stars with their rising and setting,

---

[24] On Thomas of Rochester, see Bede, *Hist. Eccl.* v, 8.
[25] On Aldhelm, see Bede, *Hist Eccl.* v, 18, and G. F. Browne, *St. Aldhelm*, London, 1903. A. F. Leach, *The Schools of Medieval England*, London, 1915, ch. 3 (in particular pp. 38ff), considered Maidulf to be a fictitious person.

> Of the soughing of storms and quaking of earth and ocean,
> The essence of man, cattle and birds and animals,
> Different types of number and diverse figures, and
> Certainty he gave of the return of Easter festival.
> Yet mostly he interpreted Holy Scripture and its riddles
> And showed an abyss of cruelty of the Law of the Ancients.
> All talented young men that came before his eyes,
> He bound to himself...[26]

These slightly stereotyped descriptions function almost as standard depictions of the ideal teacher, but on the other hand reflect a certain conformity in the basic syllabus. The same subjects are named again and again: the Bible, grammar, rhetoric, mathematics, and astronomy. The rudiments of the old oratorial training of the Romans live on as a framework for new subject-matter. The monk, the priest, and the missionary are trained as Christian rhetors with the Bible as the first and most essential book – but still with the *artes liberales* as the intellectual basis of education. Even when Aldhelm of Malmesbury writes a dissertation *On Virginity* (*De Virginitate*) on a typical virtue of the cloister, he can sprinkle it for this reason with quotations from Virgil, Horace, Terence, and Juvenal.

However, we shall gain a much fuller picture of the substance of monastic learning if we consider not so much this evidence, briefly summarised, as its literary legacy, which is still extant by and large and makes up a Latin literature of no mean extent. In Migne's great *Patrologia Latina*, the writers of the period from Cassiodorus to Bede and Alcuin fill no less than thirty-five copious double-columned volumes. Even though this is less than the earlier Christian literature from late antiquity (sixty-four corresponding volumes), it is still equivalent to about 70,000 normal-sized pages or over 200 modern books of the format of the present book.

Quite a few of these authors were extraordinarily productive. This is not least true of Bede who gives a list in the epilogue of his *Ecclesiastical History* of the eighty-five treatises, or thereabouts, that he had managed to complete from the time he was ordained at the age of thirty, to the time he put the finishing touches to his masterpiece twenty-nine years later.[27] In this list all the most significant genres in the literature of the monasteries are represented. First of all:

---

[26] Alcuin's poem is printed in *Migne PL* 101, 814–46. The passage quoted here is on col. 841.
[27] Cf. Bede's list of his own works in *Hist. Eccl.* v, 24.

A. Bible commentaries, the most commonly found genre in the whole literature. Above all others, the Bible is now the book from which almost all the authors of the period find material for their own works. After this come

B. Theological dissertations, still quite few in number, in any case in the form of independent treatises on specific problems of theology or morality. Mention has already been made of St Aldhelm's *De Virginitate*, to which can be added, for example, a writing *On Poverty* (*De Paupertate*) of Martin of Braga from before 580, the *Moralia in Job* of Pope Gregory the Great, and his *Liber Pastoralis*.

C. Saints' lives are an extremely popular genre. From the modern point of view they are stereotyped and uncritical; the same miracles recur from one work to another and the individual features of the picture are often erased by a plethora of pious phrases. The genre is intended for reading aloud during meals in the monastic refectory, and moralising and the edifying parts are very much in the foreground. Yet today we would be essentially worse informed about the history of the dark ages, had we not for example the *Vita Martini* (St Martin of Tours) by Venantius Fortunatus (*c.* 530–600), or Adamnan's *Life of Columba*, already mentioned.

D. Historical works in the usual sense of the word are represented in a small series of indispensable texts that all seem to have been written out of a need, understandable in the midst of cultural decline, to preserve some ephemeral link with the past or to depict contemporary events for future generations. This motive comes out clearly in the prologue to the *Historia Francorum* (AD 591) of Gregory of Tours:

While booklearning fell into decay or more correctly perished completely in the towns of Gaul, and while a great many things, good as well as bad, were going on, while the popular wildness raged and the king's madness worsened ... there is no man among us who can commit the incidents of our time to a book. These and similar complaints have awakened in me the desire – though my language is unpolished – to portray the lives of generations gone before so that our descendants may yet know something of them.[28]

Other historical works of lasting value are, for example, the *History of the Ostrogoths* by Cassiodorus, a corresponding *History of the Visigoths* by

---

[28] Quoted from the prologue to Gregory of Tours, *Historia Francorum*, Migne PL 71.

archbishop Isidore of Seville (*c.* 565–636) and a more popular *History of the World* up to 642, ascribed to a certain Fredegarius but in reality composed by a group of three anonymous Burgundian historians.

Head and shoulders above these works is the towering *History of the English Church and People* of Bede, the *Historia Ecclesiastica Gentis Anglorum* of 731, which is notable for the exceptional care that Bede gives to the research that he carried out in order to write the work, and for his critical attitude to the authorities and sources he uses. It is impressive that a monk in one of Christendom's most remote monasteries was capable of procuring and publishing written material from the papal archives in Rome. To this he added written sources from Lindisfarne, other monasteries, and a group of English bishops, along with personal interviews with 'innumerable trustworthy witnesses who either know or remember events other than what I know myself'. The work contains only a few positive errors, and modern historical research has to a large extent been able to confirm it. Admirable is also Bede's ability to marshal his huge material in such a way that irrelevant details are cut out; what remains is worked into a beautiful composition that can still be read with pleasure today.[29]

E. *Artes Liberales* are represented by a great number of writings which, however, are usually short and without much value, even when compared to the second-hand works from antiquity on which they are normally based. On the trivium there is a number of small grammatical or rhetorical dissertations for the purpose of elementary instruction in Latin. As regards the quadrivium the situation is even more serious. The Greek sources for the mathematical subjects are no longer read, and the period's own productions never reach the standard, for example, of Boethius' handbooks, which are not yet circulated very widely. Yet there is one area in which monastic learning has made an original contribution, namely concerning time-reckoning (see next section).

F. The ecclesiastical calendar with its complicated calculation of Easter (about which the Romans and the Irish had long quarrelled) required no mean insight. Pioneer works were the *Liber de Paschale* and the *De Ratione Paschae* of Cassiodorus' friend Dionysius Exiguus,

---

[29] Bede was using the London priest Nothelm, who had examined the papal archives in Rome, according to the preface to the *Hist. Eccl.*

a monk in Rome who knew Greek and established the final calculation of Easter. These texts are the first of a long series of short treatises that make up the *computus* literature of the early middle ages and are the basis for monastic teaching in time-reckoning and chronology for centuries to come. In this area too Bede rendered a unique piece of work in his extensive *De Ratione Temporum*, a very clear and thorough treatise that was never superseded in the middle ages. This deals with all the problems of calendar and chronology along with a list of related questions; among other things, there is a chapter on the tide that shows Bede not only building on earlier authors, but also on his own observations of nature. It is Bede, last of all, who inaugurates the Christian era in his being the first to count the years from the presumed date of the birth of Christ.[30]

G. The encyclopedia as a scholarly genre has been mentioned above as characteristic of Roman culture, and so lives on in this age. The best example is Isidore of Seville's *Etymologiarum Libri XX* (*Twenty Books on the Origin of Words*), which can almost be regarded as a kind of lexicon of conversation and was so used for many centuries.[31] This gives a systematic view of knowledge in both the theoretical and the practical area, divided in the following way:

1 Grammar
2 Rhetoric and dialectic
3 Arithmetic, geometry, music, astronomy
4 Medicine
5 Law
6 The Bible, the church calendar
7 God, angels, saints, martyrs, bishops
8 The church, Christianity, the other religions
9 Tribes, their languages and descent
10 An alphabetical dictionary
11 Mankind
12 The animal kingdom
13 The four elements
14 Geography
15 Architecture and surveying

---

[30] A good introduction to the *compotus*-literature is found in C. W. Jones, *Bedae Opera de Temporibus*, Cambridge, Mass., 1943; see also O. Pedersen, The Ecclesiastical Calendar and the Life of the Church, in G. V. Coyne, M. A. Hoskin and O. Pedersen, *Gregorian Reform of the Calendar*, Vatican City, 1983, pp. 17–74.
[31] See J. Fontaine, *Isidore de Séville et la Culture Classique*, Bordeaux, 1959.

16 Mineralogy
17 Agriculture and horticulture
18 Warfare, military games, sport
19 Shipping, tools, textiles
20 Cooking, kitchen utensils, wagons and harness

The sciences take up about 40 per cent as against for example the 15 per cent of theology and church history. The material is clearly ordered, and it is easy to look things up. But above all, Isidore is a philologist and thinks he has said something crucial also in terms of science when he gives an (often crazy) etymology of a word. This can be seen for example in the excerpt on astronomy, where a chapter on the names of the stars fills six and a half pages, while the remaining chapters on astronomy only get a few lines each. The source material is naturally second-hand, and even in the scientific chapters Virgil is the authority most often cited. Yet this serves to show the positive significance of Isidore's encyclopedia in one area outside lexicography: thanks to the author's sharp distinction between astronomy and astrology and resolute contempt of the latter as superstition, astrology lacked any foothold in the spiritual life of the middle ages for the next 500 years.[32]

H. The scholarly compendium, appearing now as a new genre. Here, too, Isidore made a start with a treatise *On the Nature of Things* (*De Natura Rerum*), which is dedicated to King Sisebert (612–620) and in forty-eight chapters deals with time-reckoning, the structure of the universe, the movements of planets, meteorology, oceanography, earthquakes, and volcanoes in a more complete form than had been possible in his encyclopedia. Here it becomes clear to what a great extent the church fathers now emerge as scholarly authorities, not least Ambrosius of Milan (*c.* 340–397) and his *Hexaëmeron*, a comprehensive commentary on the creation narrative of the Bible. Bede also wrote a *De Natura Rerum* that was better than Isidore's, largely because Bede builds too on Pliny, whom Isidore seems not to have known. Thereafter the genre of compendia becomes common.

There is one literary genre that falls outside the literature of the monastery, but ought to be cited here nonetheless, partly because of its historical significance, partly because it could hardly have arisen

---

[32] For Isidore's dismissal of astrology, see his *Libri XX Etymologiarum* III, 27. The background to the critical attitude to astrology in the early middle ages was the sharp condemnation in St Augustine, *De Civitate Dei* v, 1–8 and *Confessiones* VII, 6.

without the intellectual assistance of monastic schools. This concerns the growing collections of laws that grew up in the 'barbarian' kingdoms which had been raised on the ashes of the Roman provinces.[33] Here the legal conditions were of a quite special character, in that the view of the ruling Germanic races towards the law and its origin stood nearly diametrically opposed to Roman law, which, as we have seen, finished up by regarding the emperor as the only lawgiver and source of justice. Among the Germans, on the other hand, the law was not something handed down from above. Law already existed in the tribe's unwritten tradition, from which it had to be ascertained whenever there was call for it in their assemblies. The king's job was therefore not to give new laws but to safeguard those already in place.

If the law applies to the tribe, it becomes something personal, to the extent that each person has the right to be judged according to the law of his own tribe regardless of where he is. Thus it was said in the *Lex Ribuaria*, one of the first collections of Germanic laws to be written down, that 'It is also our decree that any Frank, Burgundian, Aleman, or member of whatsoever nation who is accused before the law in the land of the Ribuarii, shall answer in accordance with the law of the land in which he was born. If convicted, he shall not suffer the penalty asked by the law of the Ribuarii, but that of his own law.'[34]

The important consequence of this principle of the personal nature of the law was that the new rulers were obliged to respect Roman law in the case of the original inhabitants of the former Roman provinces. This can be seen in the very first European collection of laws, the *Lex Romana Visigothorum*, which was made up of extracts and interpretations of Roman law applicable to Gauls under Visigothic sovereignty and put into force by King Alaric II in Toulouse in the year 506, after it was ratified by an assembly of laymen and bishops. At about the same time the *Lex Gundobada* appeared in written form, being not so much a collection of laws as a guide to Roman law for Germanic judges in Burgundy.

In this way the 'barbarians' got a certain acquaintance with

---

[33] On the codification of the 'barbarian' laws, see Ullmann, ch. 6, and the synoptic tables in E. Jenks, *Law and Politics in the Middle Ages*, London, 1919, pp. 327ff. On the development of Saxon law, see G. Theuerkauf, *Lex, Speculum, Compendium Juris*, Cologne, 1968.

[34] Quoted from Jenks, *Law and Politics*, p. 16.

Roman law. This helped those engaged in the reworking, codification, and transcription of their own laws, an activity which became ever more necessary in kingdoms of mixed population. The first result was the famous Salic law, *Lex Salica*, published by the Merovingian King Chlodoveg I in about 510. First of all it concerns itself with criminal law and has an interesting preface that informs us of the way the work was carried out: four chosen men – whose names and homesteads are stated – ascertained the law, such as it was, by questioning the chairmen of the legal assemblies all over the country. The *Lex Ribuaria* mentioned above appeared about a hundred years later and was put into force by King Dagobert I in about 623 to 625; it applied to a part of the Frankish area around Cologne.

Several other examples of such codified *Leges Barbarorum* could be mentioned. It is worth noting that all of them – with the exception of some Anglo-Saxon laws in England – consistently avoid the vernaculars in favour of Latin, even though they are full of Frankish expressions and turns of phrase in Latinised form. This clearly shows that in their final form they were edited by people of learning, which in this period is to say by bishops, abbots, or clerics in the king's service. The *Lex Ribuaria* also shows clear influences from Christianity and a few reminiscences of Roman law.

That the bishops came to play a part in this juristic work was due not only to their Latin education but also to their own activity as judges. Already from the first days of Christianity they had, on account of their office, looked after the daily life of their own communities, with the words of the Bible and the *canones* or decrees of the first synods as guidelines for the discipline of the church. After Christianity was made the state religion this role came more into the foreground. Besides, an older decree of 321 had established that two parties in a civil action at any time during the proceedings, with common consent, might plead their case under the bishop's jurisdiction, which was thereby incorporated into the civil (non-ecclesiastical) legal system. In the following centuries purely ecclesiastical lawgiving grew at quite a pace. The many councils and synods produced a multitude of *canones*, and the steadily more conspicuous Roman see dispatched ordinances or *decretales* on virtually anything between heaven and earth. All these decrees worked as judicial rules for the bishops and together made up the basis for Canon law (church law), that distinguished itself from the codified (and thereby fossilised) Roman law largely in being a living judicial system, *lex animata*, the extent of which grew steadily in pace with the needs of the moment.[35]

The outcome of this development in the legal area was that early medieval Europe was burdened with three completely different systems of law. Firstly, there were the remains here and there of Roman law that had survived in isolated pockets in Italy and in the former provinces. Secondly, Canon law, partly based on church decrees, partly, in want of these, on Roman law. Thirdly, there were the codified 'barbarian' laws, which by their very existence in Latin came to safeguard traditions that were for long able to prevent the penetration of Roman law into the purely Germanic areas of the north. As we shall see later, these three strands were woven each in its own way into the fabric of the later history of the university.

Formally, the most typical feature of monastic learning was its marked penchant for compilation. To be sure, Gregory of Tours and Bede in their historical works rely heavily on material gathered in their own day, but in the other disciplines such independent observations are few and far between. As mentioned earlier, this ties up closely with the fact that surviving Latin sources offered only summaries of the results of research done in antiquity, but neglected to give its methods, so that in the beginning scholars in the middle ages could simply not know how to do research at all. Books became the main source of knowledge in all areas, including those where only empirical methods can make new progress possible. It is therefore important to know the extent of the literature that the learned monks had at their command. This is not an easy task, for just as saints' lives and monastic chronicles tell of the industry with which bishops and abbots collected books, the same sources are often reluctant to disclose which books they were. For this reason we are restricted to minute and tiresome analyses of direct or concealed quotations in an author's works, if we wish to establish the extent of his working library. This has been done in a small number of cases; for instance, we have a tolerably fair knowledge of the books that were at Bede's disposal in the monastery library in Jarrow, where the

---

[35] On the development of ecclesiastical law, see P. Fournier and G. Le Bras, *Histoire des collections canoniques en Occident depuis les Fausses Décrétales jusqu'au Décret de Gratien*, vols. I–II, Paris, 1932; on the concept of *lex animata*, see Ullmann, note 33, pp. 117ff.

founding stock consisted of the texts that Benedict Biscop had brought home from his travels.[36]

With all the uncertainty that naturally attaches itself to such enumerations on the basis of more or less easily identifiable quotations, the outcome is that when Bede completed his own writings he made use of a collection of about 150 texts of in all about 80 different authors. All works are in Latin, with the exception of a couple of Greek Bibles, which surely raises the question of how much Greek Englishmen knew at this time. Most strongly represented are the four great Latin church fathers Ambrosius, Augustine, Gregory the Great, and Jerome, who make up together about a third of the collected contents of books. Augustine alone is the author of eighteen of these works. Bede knew a major part of his collected writing, of which the main works are *Confessiones*, *De Civitate Dei*, *De Doctrina Christiana*, *De Genesi ad Litteram*, *Enchiridion*, and *Tractatus in Ioannis Evangelium*. In addition, there is a long list of various texts of other Latin fathers such as Arnobius, Cassian, Cassiodorus, Cyprian, Hilary, Lactantius, Prosper of Aquitaine, and certain others. The Greek church fathers Athanasius, Basil, Chrysostom, Gregory of Nazianzus, Origenes, and Theophilus are represented in a series of translations. All this shows that the theological output of the fathers is the all-dominant nucleus of the library.

To this can be added a series of historical works used by Bede, including some biographical texts concerning saints Anthony, Germanus, Ambrose, and Augustine. Out of real historical literature Bede read Gildas, Gregory of Tours, Isidore of Seville's *Chronicon* and Prosper's corresponding work, and Latin translations of Josephus' *Antiquitates* and *De Bello Iudaico*, along with Eusebius' *Chronicon* and *Historia Ecclesiastica* in the translations respectively of Jerome and Rufinus.

If we finally inquire about literature pertaining to the *artes liberales*, the selection is more sparse. As regards the trivium, Bede had at his disposal a rather important collection of the old grammarians, whereas the quadrivium is almost totally unrepresented. Most important here are eight of the thirty-seven books of Pliny's *Historia Naturalis* that Bede knew, unlike Isidore. Of the latter author Bede had both the *De Natura Rerum* and the twenty books of *Etymologiae*.

---

[36] See M. L. W. Laistner, The Library of the Venerable Bede, in A. Hamilton Thompson (ed.), *Bede*, Oxford, 1935, pp. 237–66; cf. R. Davis, Bede's Early Reading, *Speculum* 8 (1933), 179–95.

Apart from that there is practically nothing. It is worth noting that Bede seems to have had no knowledge of Boethius. But sources for some of his scientific statements can certainly be found in Ambrose's *Hexaëmeron* and in a corresponding text of Basil, together with Macrobius' *Saturnalia*, and finally in Virgil, who seems to be the only classical author of any importance in the whole collection.[37]

In the light of the gigantic libraries of antiquity in Alexandria and elsewhere, the monastery library at Jarrow was undeniably small and impoverished. Of course it could have been larger than the catalogue above indicates, since Bede might perfectly well have had access to other books without quoting them. On the other hand, it cannot be ruled out that he obtained a great many of the works he used on loan from Canterbury, Lindisfarne, or other monasteries he was associated with. But, all things considered, we have to conclude that a library in the seventh century could have been a source of national pride without exceeding 200 works. The setback that scholarship suffered in the early middle ages is here illustrated in a striking way.[38]

Which was the ideology underlying monastic learning in the dark ages? No central or dominant form of power existed any longer in Europe, now fragmented into many lesser and relatively weak and unstable societies. The only international organisation of any significance was the church, with the Benedictine order as the most important instrument of cultural policy. In many ways the education system of the order was an offshoot of the old Roman orator's training – but the spirit had changed. Underneath the outward form is the suspicion of a content moulded not so much by Cicero, as by the thinker who more than any other shaped the whole spiritual life of the middle ages – the church father St Augustine of Hippo (354–430).[39] As a bishop in an insignificant North African town, Augustine played no part in education elsewhere, but through the Benedictine

---

[37] See Wise, and Brigitte Englisch (ed.), *Die Artes liberales im frühen Mittelalter (5.–9. Jh)*, Stuttgart, 1994 (Sudhoff's Archiv Beihefte 33).

[38] On English libraries in this period, see J. D. A. Ogilvy, *Books Known to the English 597–1066*, 2nd edn, Cambridge, Mass., 1967, and also J. S. Beddie, The Ancient Classics in the Medieval Libraries, *Speculum* 5 (1930), 3–20. On the spiritual basis of monastic learning, see J. Leclerq, *L'amour des lettres et le désir de Dieu. Initiation aux auteurs monastiques du moyen âge*, Paris, 1957.

[39] An outstanding biography of St Augustine is P. Brown, *Augustine of Hippo*, London, 1967; on Augustinian thought see E. Gilson, *Introduction à l'étude de Saint Augustin*, 3rd edn, Paris, 1949; see also H.-I. Marrou, *St. Augustin et la fin de la culture antique*, 4th edn, Paris, 1959. A very systematic and comprehensive exposition of Augustine's world of ideas is A. Portalié on

promulgation of his writings his thoughts on Christian training gradually spread to the furthest reaches of Christendom.

With Augustine, theology, philosophy, and scholarship are indivisible. Christ is at once God, Saviour, and Teacher: 'The true philosopher is the man who loves God',[40] as said in his main work *On the City of God* (*De Civitate Dei*). All scholarship must therefore look to God as the final objective and the supreme authority. If not, Augustine can be harshly critical, as when he writes thus about certain ancient astronomers, in his huge commentary on the first Book of Moses (and the creation narrative), *De Genesi ad Litteram*: 'Let them but write what they will on heaven – yet they know not Our Father who is in heaven. If we should give ourselves up to subtle speculations on the size of the heavenly bodies and their distance from us and apply in such a way the time that is required for better and more important subjects, then it would seem neither right nor proper to us.'[41] Sometimes this position even seems to force Augustine to sweep the whole of learning as such off the table: 'Even though a Christian were ignorant of the works of philosophers; though he did not know how to apply in discussion the phrases no-one had taught him; though he cannot describe that part of philosophy that examines nature, such as *scientia naturalis* in Latin or *physis* in Greek ... yet he is not for this reason ignorant of the learning by which we recognise God and ourselves, neither of the grace that makes us blessed in being united with Him', he says in *De Civitate Dei*.[42]

This stress on faith as a form of wisdom higher than learning is the most common of the fundamental ideas that Augustine passes on to the middle ages. But in addition to this, he expresses his thoughts in a philosophical world of ideas coloured by Neo-Platonism. Thus he shares the negative attitude of all Platonists to empirical knowledge, and warns against those philosophers who take the bodily senses as witness to the criterion of truth – *iudicium veritatis* – 'and who believed they could measure all our knowledge by the yardstick of these faithless and deceitful rules, and who claim that what is deduced comes from the senses and that the senses are the founda-

---

Augustin, *Dictionnaire de Théologie Catholique* I, Paris, 1902, English version: *A Guide to the Thought of St. Augustine*, New York, 1960.

[40] *De civitate Dei* VIII, 1.
[41] *De genesi ad literam* II, 16.
[42] *De civitate Dei* VIII, 10.

tions of what we learn and teach'.[43] The reason is of course that the senses can only show us the chance or changeable part of things, but not the constant, unalterable relations that exist between them. In another typical passage, Augustine says:

> If I were able to grasp numbers with my senses, I would still be unable to understand with these senses that which is essential about the compounding and distinction of numbers [i.e. the laws of mathematics]. Nor do I know how long anything I touch with the senses of my body will exist, for example this sky or that country or the things I can perceive in it. But seven plus three makes ten, and not only now, but always. Nor has seven plus three made anything else in the past, just as it will never make anything else in the future. Therefore I said that this intransitory truth is common to me and to anyone else who uses his reason.[44]

In this way, mathematics and the rest of learning in general is a doctrine for Augustine of eternal and unalterable truths that are not visible to the senses but are accessible to reason. Even the factual existence of mathematical truths forces him to acknowledge reason as the source of truth side by side with the authority of Christian revelation. Thus in *Contra Academicos* he says that our knowledge rests on a double foundation: 'It cannot be doubted that we are impelled to accept a doctrine on the double basis of authority and reason',[45] and in a letter he says: 'what we know consists of things that are either seen or believed. Concerning the things that we see or can see, we ourselves are witnesses. But regarding things that are believed, we are moved to believe them through the witness of others.'[46] However, this common recognition of faith and reason in Augustine does not lead to any doctrine of a double truth, since he establishes an inner harmony between the two sources of truth by means of an adaptation of the Platonic theory of ideas. What we see with the soul's inner eye are not so much the Platonic ideas as the 'eternal reasons' of things – *rationes eternae* – that are hidden in God and are only revealed to reason because 'The true light illuminates each person who comes into the world' (cf. John 1: 9). Henceforward this so-called 'theory of illumination' recurs throughout the whole middle ages, remaining almost unquestioned until about 1200, when the great scholastics begin to dispute it.

Even if reason regards the *rationes eternae* of things in an inner light given from God, this happens in many cases at the instigation of

---

[43] Ibid.   [44] *De libero arbitrio* II, 8.
[45] *Contra Academicos* III, 20.   [46] Epistola 147, III, 8; *Migne PL* 33, 600.

sense impressions. After all, Augustine still has a use for *artes liberales* in the system of learning that he sketches in a small treatise known as *De Ordine*. Here he shows how 'The liberal disciplines raise up the intellect to divine things; therefore these free arts must be learned partly because they are useful in life, partly because they lead to knowledge and to contemplation.'[47] The trivium in particular is useful, whereas the quadrivium is chiefly the starting point for contemplation. All in all the *artes liberales* teach us 'to seek truth with zeal, pursue it with endurance and maintain it in love'.[48]

In consequence it is no wonder that Augustine himself composed a treatise, *De Musica*, and started several unfinished works on the other *artes*, among which he seems to have replaced astronomy with philosophy. In summary, one can say that with the high position Augustine gives the liberal arts as tools for the development of the soul, he is not so far removed from Cicero's ideal of *humanitas*, even though the context is different. In this he differs from most of the early Patristic writers, some of whom would rather reject the profane subjects as an expression of superfluous and unjustifiable worldly learning.

As mentioned earlier, Augustine has no difficulties in uniting this vision of learning with his understanding of the authority of faith, which is and remains of primary importance: 'We believe so that we can know – we do not know so that we can believe.'[49] But on the other hand he knows the difficulties that can arise in the case of statements in the Bible that appear to contradict reason or experience. In such cases it is generally claimed that 'either the text is in error, or the commentator is on the wrong track, or you have not understood it'.[50] Furthermore he warns strongly against interpreting the Bible in direct contradiction of science, thus bringing God's word into disrepute in the eyes of men:

In many cases people have obtained without being Christian much knowledge about the earth, heaven, the other elements in the world, about the movements of heavenly bodies, their rotations, distances and sizes, about the nature of animals, plants, and minerals ... knowledge which in all certainty they gain through reason and experience. But there is one thing even more disreputable and dangerous, namely one of these unbelievers hearing a Christian talk about these things out of Holy

---

[47] *De Ordine* II, 16; *Migne PL* 32.   [48] *De Ordine* I, 8; *Migne PL* 32, 987.
[49] *In Joan. Evang.* XL, 9; *Migne PL* 35, 1668.
[50] Epistola 82; *Migne PL* 33, 277; cf. *Contra Faustum* XI, 5; *Migne PL* 42, 249.

Scripture and hearing him come out with so many follies that he ... can scarcely forbear laughing. The worst is not that this man is ready to grin at a person who has succumbed to delusions. The worst is that a person outside the church can attribute such opinions to [our] Biblical authors ... Such people want to be persuaded in advance that these texts are full of errors in questions that they have examined themselves through experience or ascertained by means of incontestable calculations.[51]

Thus Augustine keeps a balance between the precedence of authoritative faith on one hand and the positive value of human science on the other. His attempt to find a conceptual synthesis of these two elements would set the trend and decide the substance of monastic teaching for several centuries. Yet it soon became apparent that not all his disciples had the intellectual stature to maintain the same balance. Thus with different aspects of Augustine's world of ideas as starting points, we can observe in the following centuries two competing currents of thought in the age of monastic learning.

One of these currents can already be found in Cassiodorus, with whom the vision of *artes liberales* is significantly narrowed. To be sure, they are accepted as being useful for the different conditions of life, especially the trivium, which was a necessary prerequisite for the work of the writer-monks and is therefore rather in evidence in Cassiodorus' texts. But where Augustine had given the quadrivium a place of honour in the progress of man towards the contemplative life, in mathematics and science Cassiodorus can only see possible tools for Biblical exegesis of no great human value. Even more – even though Cassiodorus refers to the available classical literature on astronomy, it is really only the Bible he wishes to make use of as the base of his knowledge: 'But for us it is enough to know as much of that art as can be read from the Holy Scriptures' – *sed nobis sufficit, quantum in scriptoris sacris legitur tantum de hac arte sentire.*[52]

An even clearer disparagement of the profane teachings emerges in Gregory the Great (*c.* 540–604), who, having completed a traditional Roman education, became a Benedictine monk, nuncio in Byzantium, secretary to Pope Pelagius II and finally pope himself in 590. Gregory was one of the most powerful leaders of the church, instigator of the Anglo-Saxon mission and of important reforms in the liturgy, and finally a very productive writer. A humanist he was not. He knew no Greek, and judging by his writings he seems to have had no knowledge of the classical Latin authors either. He

[51] *De genesi ad litteram* I, 19–20; *Migne PL* 34, 260f.   [52] *Migne PL* 70, 1213–14.

relied on Augustine without having the same stature and without being able to maintain this father's calm equilibrium between renunciation of paganism and recognition of authentic values in the old writers. Accordingly, Gregory's work is dominated by the more culturally pessimistic of Augustine's thoughts. *Artes liberales* interest him only to the extent that they are directly applicable to Bible study, and even an ostensibly innocent subject such as grammar becomes dangerous in his eyes, as far as it uses non-Christian writers for examples. Archbishop Didier of Vienne in Gaul had done just that when, in despair at the general decline in this subject, he started to teach Latin, for which he was reported and got a sharp reprimand from the pope – could anyone believe it, a bishop teaching grammar?[53] Can Jesus and Jupiter be praised in the same breath! In his *Moralia in Iob* Gregory takes this scepticism so far that he consciously puts the more perfect language of the classical writers to one side, in favour of the Latin in Jerome's Vulgate Bible, even if this was full of Grecisms and Hebraicisms. These imperfections in Gregory's eyes were still legitimate forms of Latin, because Holy Scripture uses them. For the pope it would be 'unworthy to enslave the message of God's word under the rules of Donatus'.[54] Similar views can also be found in Cassiodorus. Thereby the ecclesiastical Latin of the middle ages in principle disowned its link with the classical past and could now go its own way.

Through his enormously famous *Liber Regulae Pastoralis*, Gregory's puritanical understanding of culture left its mark on the spiritual life of the early middle ages. The text was a handbook for preachers, and it bears witness to great practical psychological insight into different categories of audiences of whose individual requirements the speaker must take note; but regarding the substance of the sermon, precious little mention was made of more than a narrow-minded cramming of what alone was needful for redeeming the soul from the sin and misery of the world.

While Cassiodorus and Gregory unilaterally administered a certain part of the inheritance of Augustine, others put more emphasis on other aspects. This was already the case with Boethius, whose efforts to save as much of the quadrivium as possible from oblivion not only relied on these subjects for exegesis, but also on a

---

[53] On Didier, see Gregory the Great's Epistola XI, 54; *Migne PL* 77, 1171f.
[54] *Moralia in Job*, Epistola missoria cap. 5; *Migne PL* 75, 516,

clear understanding of their independent human value. In the beginning of *De Institutione Arithmetica* the exact sciences are described 'as a road to the peaks of learning, so that it is along this fourfold road [*quadrivium* – this is the first time the word is used] that they may go whose uplifted souls – engendered by us with the senses – shall be brought to surer knowledge'.[55] And in *De Institutione Musica* there is another echo of Cicero's *humanitas*, when Boethius says that 'nothing is more proper to humanity (*proprium humanitatis*) than to relax with delightful music',[56] and this not only during prescribed study or at a certain age, but one's whole life long, so that children, the young, and the old can rejoice in music and song as spontaneously as their natures incline them. Most of all, Boethius seems to have emphasised astronomy, to which he returns several times in *De Consolatione Philosophiae* as a starting point for reflections on the human lot. On one hand the smallness of man in relation to the universe fills him with humility, while on the other, the high heavens draw up his thoughts to the harmony lacking in life on earth. In other words astronomy leads us to that contemplation which Augustine took to be the real purpose of studying the quadrivium.[57]

The same attitude underlies Isidore's words in the *Libri Etymologiarum*, where he says that 'it is unworthy to use astronomy for superstitious purposes. Among the seven liberal arts astronomy comes last, in order that whenever earthly wisdom confuses us we shall lift ourselves with its help up to a contemplation of the highest things.'[58] With Isidore this contemplation often takes the form of a mystical reflection on nature in which natural phenomena appear as signs or symbols of more spiritual truths. The sun is thus an image of Christ, the moon of the church. The old analogy between *macrocosmos* (the universe as a whole) and *microcosmos* (man) also crops up in Isidore. And yet he never draws scientific conclusions from these allegories, though there is scarcely any doubt that in his eyes, at any rate, they make just as important a contribution to the understanding of nature as an objective scholarly analysis. This double view of nature would henceforth become a characteristic part of the spiritual life of the whole middle ages.

If we look back on monastic learning in its entirety, we must

---

[55] *De institutione arithmetica* I, 1.
[56] *De institutione musica* I, 1; cf. E. J. Dehnert, Music as Liberal in Augustine and Boethius, in *Arts Libéraux*, 987ff.
[57] *De Consolatione Philosophiae* II, Prose 7.   [58] *Libri XX Etymologiarum* III, 71.

frankly admit that compared to the knowledge of the Hellenistic age it was small and impoverished. For linguistic reasons it was cut off from the Greek roots of learning. Without the support of any central authority in society, only the cohesion of the Benedictine order linked it across frontiers from one country to another. No-one can deny that the future of European learning in this period hung by an extremely thin thread. Nevertheless, scholars managed to keep a meagre continuity with ancient culture. Rudiments of the Roman system of education were brought into the cloisters, and the copying of classical literature steadily kept the dream of antiquity alive. But the basis of this period's own cultural efforts had changed. Christianity was now the obvious context for any life of the mind, and the first cultural debate grew up in the attempt to find a place for Virgil, Horace, Terence, and Ovid in an environment where the Bible was the starting point for virtually every kind of intellectual activity. The streams of puritanism and *humanitas* still flowed in the same channel, but each was already beginning to claim its own followers. The Augustinian balance was in danger, and only the fact that the sole task of monastic learning was to train monks and missionaries kept the internal tensions under control. A new development would only come about if European learning could find its place in a new social order.

CHAPTER 3

The Carolingian Renaissance

In and around AD 800 the cultural situation in western Europe underwent a series of important transformations which are normally described as the Carolingian Renaissance. This was not a spontaneous expansion of the inherent cultural energy of the west, rather a reaction to political events which, in the last analysis, can be traced back to the appearance of Islam on the political stage.[1] Here we must go back to the year 622, when Mohammed transferred his activity from his birthplace Mecca to the nearby Medina, from which the Arab expansion took off soon after. Firstly, the Arab peninsula was united, and after the prophet's death in 632, one after the other the surrounding countries were subjected to the power of the Arabs. Damascus was conquered in 635, and Jerusalem fell two years later. In 638 the Arabs were overlords of parts of Mesopotamia, and from 640 to 641 Alexandria and most of Egypt yielded, while the whole of Persia was subdued in 643. Thereby the whole of the Near East was united under the caliphs of the Umajjad dynasty in Damascus, and Jews, Christians, and Mohammedans were forced into a kind of coexistence which would be of great cultural significance in the course of time. Then it was the turn of North Africa, and in 711 the 'Moors' crossed to Spain, where the last king of the Visigoths, Rodrigo, fell a couple of years later. Shortly afterwards the first Arab troops appeared north of the Pyrenees.

This violent expansion had enormous consequences for both east and west. In the east it meant a substantial diminution of the Byzantine empire's sphere of influence, and in the west, Spain and North Africa were both turned into Moorish caliphates. Thereby the

---

[1] On this chapter in general, see M. Manitius, *Geschichte der lateinischen Literatur des Mittelalters*, vol. I, Munich, 1911; C. Dawson, *The Making of Europe*, London, 1932; on church and state, see Jedin, vol. III, pp. 1, 3–196. On Islam see the *Cambridge Medieval History*, vol. II, 302–90, Cambridge, 1967, and N. Daniel, *The Arabs and Mediaeval Europe*, London, 1975.

western end of the Mediterranean became an Arab lake, 'where the Christians could not even throw a peg into the water',[2] as the Arab historian Ibn Khaldoun (1332–1406) later expressed it, in picturesque terms. This meant a complete breakdown in the earlier economic system based on overseas trade in the Mediterranean. What had once been a bridge now became a barrier that separated east and west in a way the Germanic invasions had never been able to achieve. At the same time as Gaul was threatened militarily, her lines of economic communication to south and east were cut through. Logically, therefore, the chances of escaping Arab domination in Europe would depend on a northern initiative, which the weak Merovingian kings in the lands between the Rhine and Loire were not capable of providing.

In this Frankish zone the real power shifted in about 717 to Charles Martel (?688–741), who step by step pushed the Merovingians out and in 732, together with the duke of Aquitaine, had the fortune to defeat the Moors in a big battle at Poitiers, with the result that Islam was driven back across the Pyrenees, and Charles' power stretched out over most of present-day France. In 751 his son Pippin the Short was able to depose the last king of the Merovingians unopposed and put him into a monastery. This new position of power for the Franks did not go unnoticed south of the Alps, and in 753 Pope Stephen II (752–757) became the first pope to take the unusual step of travelling to France to seek contact with the new ruling dynasty. The immediate outcome was the coronation of Pippin as the king of France in 754. This led to a permanent alliance between the papacy and the Carolingians. Pippin himself undertook at the pope's encouragement an expedition against the Longobards and thereby stopped their expansion towards Rome, where he was himself created a Roman patrician and the protector of the city. The contours of a new European system were already forming.

The development continued with increased momentum under Pippin's son Charlemagne (?742–814), or Charles the Great, who after the death of his brother Carloman in 771 became the sole ruler of France. Thereupon Charles quickly began an intensive effort to extend his power-base and secure its boundaries with yearly campaigns in all directions. The army was constantly on a war footing.

---

[2] Ibn Khaldoun's remark is quoted from Pirenne, *Economic and Social History*, p. 3.

In 772 began the first of Charles' many wars against the Saxons in the east. The next year brought a victorious expedition in Italy, where Charles assumed the title of king of the Longobards. In 777 Charles began a protracted struggle against the Moors, who had to move out of Barcelona in 801. In 783 Widukind, king of the Saxons, was defeated, following which Charles was able to consolidate his power beyond the Elbe. However, this was only achieved after mass executions and the replacing of parts of the Saxon population with the Slavic Obotrites, who thus became Denmark's closest neighbours to the south. The culmination of this in 800 was Charles' coronation as emperor in Rome by Pope Leo III (795–816), who already at his election had sworn an oath of fealty to Charles in his capacity as a patrician of Rome.

The formidable military and political success of the Carolingians after only three generations had brought them a kingdom whose extent far exceeded that of all previous Germanic states. The emperor's coronation in Rome was the symbolic expression of the view of Charles himself: that his kingdom was nothing less than a resurrection of the old Roman empire of the west following the chaos of the age of migrations, and that he himself was the legitimate heir of the western emperors. That is also how many summarised these events at the time. In reality the situation was rather more complicated. In the ideological sphere there was the difficulty that the imperial ideology of Roman law could no longer be applied without substantial modifications. Even if Charles (who knew hardly anything of Roman law) could adopt the Roman title *imperator*, the accompanying dignity of *pontifex maximus* had belonged to the pope since the time of Leo the Great. Now and again Charles intervened in quarrels of dogma, but thanks to the existence and growing international authority of the papacy it was no longer possible to combine spiritual with secular power under one title. The harmony between the two regimes was therefore conditioned by a more or less viable accommodation between pope and emperor – a state of affairs that is the key to a large part of the political history of the middle ages and one of the starting points for the political philosophy and theory of government of this time.

In the time of Charles' own rule this harmony was almost perfect. Pope Hadrian I (772–795) wrote to Charles with reference to the expansion of the Longobards into Italy that 'Thy salvation is our safety. Thy ennoblement is our joy, since, next to God, we put our body in the keeping of no stronger arm than thine.'³ Charles repaid him by handing over a few of his Italian conquests, which became the beginning of the papal state. Thereby the pope's fortunes changed in a fateful way, in that he not only deepened the growing rift between Rome and Byzantium, but also became an Italian prince with his own territory to defend, with all the possibilities which that entailed for confusing the mission of the church with the politics of the papacy.

However, the emperor's chief difficulty was this: while his kingdom in its extent could nearly measure itself by the old Roman empire of the west, in the beginning at least it completely lacked the administrative structure that had determined the existence of Rome. The Roman balance between centralised and decentralised control was gone, and the primary task of the new central power was to create an expedient administration. Even under the Merovingians a social system had developed towards the later feudalism with a division of the individual kingdoms into smaller units, each administered by a local count. Charles Martel, furthermore, had endeavoured to improve this system by parcelling out confiscated church property as knights' estates so as to create an economic base for the heavy cavalry which – after the introduction of the stirrup – became the mainstay of the Carolingian army.⁴ Clearly Charles had to take over this system, but he also modified it substantially. For one thing, he assumed the right to install and remove the counts, who thus became directly dependent on and responsible to the royal power. For another, he resumed an old principle of Roman administration by sending out special inspectors, *missi dominici*, who each had to control a number of counties and to see that the king's orders were carried out. These orders were called 'capitularies' and were laws in the same sense as the earlier Roman imperial edicts had been. It is clear that when Charles saw himself as a lawgiver, he was closer to Roman law – even if built on another foundation – than to Germanic legal tradition.

Another thing was that Charles' idea of a purely western, Germano-Latin empire was strange to the view of the emperor as *dominus mundi* – the ruler of the whole world – which permeated Roman law. Inevitably this idea aroused amazement in the east,

---

³ Hadrian I, Epistola ad Carolum Regem (AD 777), *Migne PL* 98, 312.
⁴ On the importance of the introduction of the stirrup, see White, pp. 1–38.

where there was already an emperor in Byzantium who could claim to be regarded as the true successor of the Roman emperors with more right than Charles. Here the image of a local western empire without a connection to Byzantium appeared as contradiction in terms. In the meantime the Byzantine empire had been greatly weakened because of the loss of the eastern provinces to Islam, against which Charles' power was growing. After some difficult negotiations the whole thing ended with a resurrection of the theory of the late ancient world of separate eastern and western empires, and in 812 Byzantium recognised Charles solely as emperor of the west.

The central administration itself – which presumably only functioned through the emperor's constant journeys around the kingdom – presupposed the existence of a special class of officials capable of drawing up in the royal chancellery the steady stream of decrees that went out to all corners of the empire. It was surely Charles' need for such civil servants as much as for local administrators which led to that concern for education which became one of the most interesting features of Charles' personality.

This concern, however, had a cause in the third of the difficulties Charles met in his newly created empire – its very disparate populations. In the Frankish provinces the after-effects of the Roman civilisation had never wholly disappeared, and already in the second and third centuries Christianity had taken firm root, with the result that paganism had totally disappeared in all but a few backwaters. But in the new provinces to the east the Germanic population was as good as untouched by Latin or Christian civilisation, despite a few scattered missionary attempts on the part of the Anglo-Saxon Benedictines. In this way, the Northumbrian Willibrord (*c*. 657– *c*. 739), having completed his education in Ireland, preached among the Frisians, assisted some of the time by the monk Wynfrith of Wessex (*c*. 672–754), who was known in later history as St Boniface, Apostle of Germany.[5] Boniface was ordained in Rome in 722 as the first bishop of the Germans, and thanks to him a diocese and an important monastery were founded at Fulda and also a diocese in Mainz. Both of these Englishmen ended their days as martyrs among the Frisians. After the suppression of the Saxons, Charles

---

[5] Th. Schieffer, *Winfried-Bonifatius und die christliche Grundlegung Europas*, Freiburg, 1954, cf. Jedin, vol. II/II, pp. 95ff and vol. II/I, pp. 9ff.

threw himself into a fervent attempt to achieve political unity with the aid of religion, first and foremost on the foundations laid by these English missionaries, by spinning a web of new bishoprics in the conquered areas – Paderborn, Minden, Münster, Osnabrück, Verden, Hildesheim, and Halberstadt, in addition to which Bremen was made the northern outpost of the church in 788. From these centres the population was Christianised by all available means, and after the assembly of Salz in 804 Saxony could be numbered as one of the Christian provinces of the empire in which religious tensions had thereby considerably decreased. This German church owed its existence to the emperor and in recompense submitted to him to the extent that the bishoprics were also placed under the firm control of Charles' *missi dominici*. With this development there grew an additional need for educated administrators, and it was at this time that Charles saw the possibility of using precisely these new bishoprics and monasteries as a basis for an organised system of education.

Charles' repeated initiatives in the area of schooling are interesting as the first attempt in Europe – and quite unwitting at that – to carry out Plato's old idea of the responsibility of the state towards education. Already in 788 Charles ordered Bishop Bangulf of Fulda in a *capitularium* to pursue studies in his diocese:

> It must be known to Your Beatific Piety that we together with our believers have found it profitable that those bishoprics and monasteries which through Christ's mercy are entrusted to our government, should also, besides placing importance on the conduct of life in keeping with the rule of the order and on monastic life according to religion, devote themselves to the appreciation of learning and to the education of those who, each according to his fortune, have received from God the ability to learn in such a way that speech is arranged and embellished through the zeal to teach and instruct, just as the decrees of the order arrange and embellish good morals so that they who strive to please God with right living by no means neglect to please Him by expressing themselves correctly ... Therefore we call upon you not only not to neglect learned studies, but also in efforts both humble and pleasing to God to compete in learning that which enables you better and more easily to penetrate the mysteries of Holy Scripture ... Thou must not omit to send copies of this letter to all thy assistant bishops and monasteries if thou wilt otherwise have my favour.[6]

This letter shows that Charles was concerned with introducing

---

[6] *Monumenta Germaniae Historica* II, Capitularia regum Francorum I, 79.

proper study as a substantial part of the activity of Benedictine monks, quite in the spirit of Cassiodorus, and it looks as if his letters in this respect are meant as a supplement to the Benedictine Rule.

After a while Charles' ideas on schooling took steadily greater proportions. While in 778 he had addressed himself to the bishop of Fulda, in 789 he issued an *admonitio generalis* to all the clergy of his kingdom. There it is decreed that regular instruction shall be organised in all monasteries and cathedrals, for both monks and canons should order their existence in such a way that 'many by their good conduct of life shall be drawn to God's service, so that not only children of unfree status but also the sons of freeborn men may meet and join in, so that schools of reading may be set up for children'.[7] In other words, this is an ordinance for the general enlightenment of the people through schools for children under ecclesiastical guidance. Of any compulsory education there is naturally no word, nor scarcely of any general right to education. Yet at any rate Charles wishes to see the possibility of general education put into effect. In the rest of his letter he goes into the question of subjects to be taught and the relevant methods. Subjects are the psalter, music, song, *compotus*, and grammar, and care shall be taken to use books that have been cleared of errors. For this reason too, children must not be allowed to spoil the books when reading and writing, and if it is necessary to copy a new gospel, psalter, or missal, this shall be left to capable scribes of a mature age. The subjects mentioned are mainly relevant for the liturgy of church and cloister, and this phase of Charles' plan of education should possibly be seen as an effort to normalise the liturgy in the different parts of the kingdom in further easing of the religious tensions between countries.

Such a comprehensive programme presupposed a staff of qualified teachers who had to be brought in from abroad, given the state of learning in Charles' realm. After Lombardy was conquered, we see Charles making consistent efforts to enable Italian scholars to move north of the Alps. The first one to do so seems to have been the otherwise completely unknown deacon Peter Pisanus, who mainly attended to the education of Charles himself from about 780 onwards. In his youth Charles had been to school, but had received hardly any special book-learning and had never learnt to write. His

[7] Ibid., I, 52f.

mother tongue was High Franconian, and his interest in Germanic culture is evident in the tradition that he had old Germanic lays collected and recorded in an anthology, now lost. At any rate, he learned from Peter how to speak Latin fluently, though the legend that he learned Greek too must surely be treated with caution. In 781 in Rome Charles made the acquaintance of the learned Longobard Paul the Deacon (*c.* 725–*c.* 797) who wrote to him to procure the release of his brother captured in 776. Paul the Deacon at this time was a monk in Monte Cassino, but had formerly been secretary to Desiderius, king of the Longobards, and teacher to his daughter; he was one of the few scholars of the 700s who mastered Greek. From 781 to 787 he stayed at Charles' court as teacher of the king, his family, and other students before once more returning to Monte Cassino to finish his great historical works on Rome and the Longobards, *Historia Romana* and *Historia Gentis Langobardorum*. Another Italian, the patriarch Paul of Aquileia (d. 802), was at work at Charles' court in the same period, where gradually there grew up an important school, the *Schola Palatina*, which followed the court on its journeys round the kingdom but which slowly began to be associated with Charles' preferred residence in Aachen.

The smaller courts of the Merovingians had already had schools for the training of scribes, but Charles' court school became markedly different, because right from the outset it attracted representatives of the best scholarly tradition in Europe. Here were not only the Italians already mentioned, but also the Englishman Alcuin of York (735–804), through whom English monastic learning from the time of Bede now took root on the continent. Alcuin was related to Willibrord, whose biography he later wrote, and he was educated in the school of St Peter's in York by Aelbert, who accompanied him to Rome to obtain books for the school's library. When Aelbert became archbishop of York in 766, it was Alcuin who became the master of the school. On the way back from another trip to Rome in 781 he met Charlemagne in Parma and was persuaded to work at his court school, with the revenues of the great abbeys of Ferrières and Troyes as his payment. From 781 to 790 Alcuin operated as Charles' minister of education, so to speak, and it was certainly he who was the main instigator of the *admonitio generalis* on general education cited above. At the same time he played an important role in the efforts to normalise the liturgy, by revising the missal and editing a Latin Bible, which he presented to Charles on the occasion of his coronation as emperor in 800. From 790 to 796 Alcuin stayed mostly in England, before returning to France as abbot of St Martin's in Tours, where he set up a library and a scriptorium and made this very prosperous monastery into the most significant centre of learning of the age. It was here that he died on 19 May in 804. After this the driving force in educational reform was the Visigoth Theodulf, whom Charles had engaged following one of his Spanish expeditions, and who, with the bishopric in Orléans as his base, ensured that the monks and priests in his own diocese observed the emperor's command in establishing elementary schools.

Alcuin himself has left us a comprehensive list of writings which, albeit without any original form, continue the English tradition with books on the *artes liberales*, consisting mainly of a grammar and some dialogues (between Alcuin and Charlemagne) on rhetoric and dialectics. To this can be added a theological treatise, *De Fide Trinitatis*, an important collection of letters, and a series of poems, among which is the poem mentioned before on the church and school of York. While his medieval reputation as a philosopher is undeserved, his significance as a cultural figure must be conceded without reservation, as one who consciously strove to encourage the state of learning in Europe with the tolerant and liberally scholastic tradition pertaining in England as his intellectual background. In a letter to Charles he says, for example:

Unhappily I now lack many of the books which I had at my disposal in my homeland, where they were procured by my teacher Aelbert, or by myself. I inform Your Majesty of this that your constant love of wisdom may be able to move you to send some of my letters to Britain, wherefrom they will be able to fetch all these British flowers back to France. Then will the Garden of Eden no longer bloom between the walls of York alone, but it will be seen shooting forth in French Touraine like a branch from the Tree of Paradise.[8]

In the last year of his life Alcuin summarised his life's work in another letter: 'In the morning of my life I sowed the seed of learning in Britain. Now, when the evening of my life has come and my blood is thickening, I continue to sow this seed in France, and with all my heart I beg that it may sprout in both kingdoms. As regards myself, I

---

[8] Alcuin, Epist. 43 ad Carolūm Magnūm AD 796, *Migne PL* 100, 207–10. On Alcuin see C. J. B. Gascoin, *Alcuin, His Life and Work*, London, 1903; F. S. Duckett, *Alcuin, Friend of Charlemagne*, New York, 1951; L. Wallach, *Alcuin and Charlemagne. Studies in Carolingian History and Literature*, New York, 1959.

comfort myself by thinking along with St Jerome that even though everything else perish, Wisdom will remain and will not falter in its increasing.'[9]

Thanks to Alcuin's Anglo-Saxon training the intellectual milieu at the court school remained open and tolerant. The culturally pessimistic bias from the time of Cassiodorus and Gregory the Great was held in check, and the *artes liberales* got a prominent place in the system. While the school decrees from Charles, mentioned above, were essentially directed at theological and liturgical education, the scope was gradually broadened. An *epistola generalis* from the emperor says that 'Since it is urgent to us that the state of our churches steadily improves, we are busied with the repair of our workshop (which through neglect was nearly wholly destroyed) for wakeful study of the highest sciences.'[10] This certainly refers to the institution of the court school to relieve the languishing scribal schools founded by the Merovingians. Charles continues the decree with a sentence showing which sciences he thought of as the highest: 'As far as we are able, we invite everybody through our own example to become familiar with the study of *artes liberales*.' Precisely the same idea emerges in the preface which Charles dictated for a treatise of Paul the Deacon: 'With all the zeal we can muster we assume ourselves the task of bringing back to life those studies which have been abandoned on grounds of the neglect of our forebears, and we call on all our subjects to cultivate according to their ability the *artes liberales*, and go before them with our own example.'[11] We have another impression of Alcuin's openness in a dialogue on the virtues, *De Virtutibus*, in which he explains that virtue, truth, and learning have an independent value that Christianity must respect. Charles then raises the question of the pagan philosophers of antiquity, to which Alcuin replies: 'They have known these things to belong to human nature and have cultivated them with extreme care.' Charles: 'What difference then between such philosophers and Christian ones?' Alcuin: 'Faith and baptism alone.'[12]

How strongly the idea of the value of classical education and the dignity of human thought marked the milieu of Charles' court is best seen in the so-called academy in which the emperor met for discussions with his professors and courtiers. The classical precedent

---

[9] Alcuin, Epist. 43 ad Car. Mag., *Migne PL* 100, 209.
[10] *Mon. Germ. Hist.* II, Cap. Reg. Franc. I, 79–81.
[11] *Migne PL* 95, 1159–60.   [12] *Migne PL* 101, 943f.

appears in the names adopted by members of the circle: Alcuin called himself *Flaccus* in memory of Horace; Theodulf was called *Pindar*, the courtier, architect, and later excellent biographer of Charles, Einhard (educated in Fulda, *c.* 770–840), was named *Calliopus*; and the Abbot Angilbert of St Riquier, *Homer*. That the academy was Christian, however, is stressed by the emperor's own appearance as *King David* and that of the abbot Abelard as *Augustine*. Today this children's comedy might cause a smile, but there is no doubt that the participants took the joke seriously. The analogy with Plato's academy but also the Christian character of the circle was emphasised by Alcuin, who wanted to 'found a new Athens' in France, and who could write in one delighted moment, that 'with no instruction other than Plato's disciplines that place [i.e. the school in Athens] gleamed with the science of the seven arts, while this place [i.e. Charles' academy] surpasses all the wisdom of this world in worthiness, for it is also enriched by the seven gifts of the Holy Ghost'.[13] Here the theme once more is the *translatio studii*, the transfer of scholarship from Athens and Rome to the new empire. Even more than a hundred years afterwards Notker Balbulus would claim without any hesitation that 'Alcuin's teaching bore such rich fruit that modern Gauls and Franks became the superiors of the old Athenians and Romans.'[14]

Even if this pronouncement presupposed a serious ignorance of ancient culture, it gives a correct impression of the dream of its rebirth in the Carolingian age. The flourishing of scholarship in Charles' empire has often been described as the Carolingian Renaissance, and it is certainly true that Alcuin's contribution bore fruit. Through his pupils in the court school, the Anglo-Saxon tradition of learning spread to monastic and cathedral schools in the empire, and after a generation we find his pupils teaching in many different places. Next to Alcuin the most significant figure was the German Hrabanus Maurus of Mainz (776–856), who received his first education in the monastery school of Fulda, from which he was sent by the abbot to St Martin to study under Alcuin. After the latter's death in 804 he returned to rule the school at Fulda, which thanks to his comprehensive learning and pedagogic ability became for a time the

---

[13] Epist. 86 ad Car. Magn. AD 798; *Migne PL* 100, 282.
[14] *Mon. Germ. Hist. Script.* II, 731, probably not by Notker, but by an anonymous editor of the *Chronicle* of St Gallen. On Charlemagne's academy, see K. Langosch, *Profil des lateinischen Mittelalters*, ch. 2, Darmstadt, 1965.

most important intellectual centre in the empire. From 822 Hrabanus was abbot of the monastery, until twenty years later he withdrew to devote himself to his studies, before he became archbishop of Mainz in 847. His activity and huge production of textbooks got him the name of the Teacher of Germany, *praeceptor Germaniae*.[15]

It was Charlemagne's wish to involve the monasteries in the enlightenment of his people, by linking public education to the already existing training of monks. How such an institution of learning could have been set up is evident from an extant map of St Gallen which was possibly drawn up by the emperor's architectural adviser Einhard. Just before the eastern end of the church, right up to the monks' private hospital, the map shows the *schola interiora*, formed as a miniature cloister with its own chapel, dormitory, refectory, and hospital, and designed for the future members of the order. Moreover, north of the church and near its public entrance and the monastery's common guesthouse, is a *schola exteriora* with an estimated 150 students. It is obvious that the lay school was meant to be kept sharply separate from the novices and that different teaching methods were to be used there.[16] How far this sketch was really followed in St Gallen, or how it resembled other places, is hard to say. At any rate, it is certain that the Carolingian monasteries provided the real framework for intense teaching throughout large parts of Europe.

Even if this development proceeded by and large along parallel lines in England – that is to say, outside the empire – it is the Carolingian school system in particular that impresses, in its conception and in the strength with which the emperor sought to establish it. On the other hand it cannot be denied that these schools never came to fulfil their original aims, that is, to shape a system of general popular education supplemented with higher training of such character that the new empire was provided with enough administrators to keep its coherence, and with teachers in sufficient numbers to create a somewhat uniform culture for the ironing out of tensions between individual elements in the population. There were several reasons for this.

---

[15] D. Turnau, *Rabanus Maurus Praeceptor Germaniae*, Munich, 1900. See also S. Fellner, *Compendium der Naturwissenschaften an der Schule zu Fulda*, Berlin, 1879.
[16] The groundplan of St Gallen is illustrated in *Encyclopedia Britannica*, 11th edn, Cambridge, 1910, vol. I, 13.

Firstly, the lack of teachers worked against the successful conclusion of the project. The schools were supposed to build up in unison the necessary number of teachers by their own instruction; according to the nature of the case this would have to take rather a long time. Added to this, the Benedictine monasteries did not seem to be as willing to cooperate on this task as has been claimed. They were principally institutions for the contemplative life, and even if they united work with prayer, preferably this would go on in isolation from the world on which the monk in the act of his *conversio* or *conversatio* (the words are used indiscriminately of entry into the cloister) had turned his back once and for all. To induct a large number of young people with no monastic vocation into the society of monks so as to prepare them for a 'secular' career, therefore, had to be a troublesome task of a more suspicious kind than, for example, quietly copying manuscripts in the unruffled peace of the scriptorium. In this connection it can be understood that in 817, only three years after the emperor's death, a synod in Aachen, his own capital, was able quite consciously to disregard his decisions with an unequivocal decree that 'no school may be kept in the monasteries unless for oblates' (i.e. for pupils belonging to the order).[17]

Yet this did not mean complete ruin for Charles' ideas on schooling; even if to some extent the monasteries failed in public education by withdrawing into themselves, there were still cathedral schools. Here as a rule the canons were secular priests with a communal life less strict than that of the monks, and with tasks oriented to the outside world a more acceptable occupation. Already in 826 Pope Eugenius II (824–827) points to this expedient:

From these places we receive complaints that no teachers can be found nor are the schools cared for. Therefore let care be taken, among bishops and their subordinates and at other places where this is necessary, with industry and devotion, that masters and teachers be engaged to teach permanently in *studia litterarum* and in the principles of *artes liberales*, since it is chiefly through their help that God's commandments are expounded and understood.[18]

In this way general education became more and more the responsibility of the bishops, while the abbots looked after their novices. How the system worked can be seen in a story of how King Alfred

---

[17] On the Aachen synod of 817, see Mansi, XIV, App. 397.
[18] Eugenius II quoted from a synodal decree of 826, included in the *Decreta* I, 37, 12.

(849–901) sent his youngest son Aethelwald to the cathedral school in Winchester where 'he prospered well under his teacher's attentive care, together with children from nearly all the noble families of the land and many who were not noble. Books in both languages, namely in Latin and English, were diligently read in the school. They also learned how to write and become industrious and capable in the liberal arts before they were old enough for such pastimes of manhood as hunting, and whatever else is suitable for a free man.'[19] Here if you like is an early example of the typical English public school for the education of 'gentlemen'.

That there were at least attempts to educate the people more widely as well can be seen in a circular of bishop Theodulf of Orléans, who had himself been educated at the court of Charlemagne. Theodulf says that 'in towns and villages priests shall keep schools. When one of the community entrusts his children to him, he shall receive them and not refuse to teach them ... For his teaching they shall demand no payment, nor shall they assume that the parents of their own free will shall tender them something to show their gratitude.'[20] Yet it is difficult to say to what degree such an institution of elementary schools was a consequence of the Carolingian movement.

The internal difficulties of building up a general system of schools were far from the only ones. A much greater hindrance to the execution of the programme was the external political and military events caused by Viking raids, of which the effects were first felt in England. One warning of what these could mean for cultural life had already been given in 793, when Norwegian Vikings destroyed Lindisfarne and plundered Jarrow a year later, after which they raided the Hebrides and Ireland. In 835 the Danish attacks on England began, and already in 842 assaults were made on London and Rochester. The following year Canterbury was stormed, while Winchester fell in 860 and York in 867. Three years later, King Edmund was killed, after which the Vikings 'overran the country from one end to the other and laid waste all the monasteries they came to. At the same time they came to the monastery in Medehamstede [the later Peterborough] and burnt and made it waste and killed the abbot and the monks, and all they found there, so they

---

[19] Asser, in his biography of Alfred, quoted from Leach, 73. On the schools in general see L. Maitre, *Les écoles épiscopales et monastiques en Occident avant les universités*, 2nd edn, Paris, 1924.
[20] Theodulf, Capitula ad presbyteros, cap. 20, *Migne PL* 105, 196.

annihilated what had been once a very rich foundation' – and that so thoroughly that when Bishop Aethelwald of Winchester nearly a century later came to rebuild the monastery (in 963), 'he found nothing but old walls and the forest growing wild'.[21] Alfred the Great's counter-offensive in about 870 led to the reconquering of London and to an unstable *modus vivendi* with the Danes. But the damage in both material and cultural terms was enormous, and the monastic schools, in particular, could be rebuilt only slowly in the Danish areas in East Anglia and Northumbria, where the conquerors had yet to be pacified and converted to Christianity. In Ireland, similar events led to a new wave of Irish scholars heading for the continent, where schools in this way received the last impulse of the old Irish tradition.

An interesting effect of the Viking depredations became clear at the end of the ninth century, when Alfred the Great had driven back the Danes and had to some extent consolidated his control. As a result of the wars the churches and monasteries had suffered burning and looting for half a century, and the knowledge of Latin was severely weakened, even among the clergy. This is the background to the conscious efforts Alfred now made to give the English language a place within education as well as outside it. He even found the time to have important works of translation carried out, so that texts such as the *Liber Pastoralis* of Gregory the Great, Paulus Orosius' *History of the World*, Bede's *History of the English Church and People* and Boethius' *De Consolatione Philosophiae* could now be read in the vernacular.[22] Added to this should probably be an anthology of the church fathers, a part of the Book of Psalms, and a now lost Anglo-Saxon martyrology. This activity went on in the court school which this king established, with teachers brought in (John the Saxon, Grimbold from the continent, and Asser, Alfred's biographer, from Wales); but as we have seen, this also led to some kind of teaching in English, in any case at the Winchester school. The idea of a scholarly application of the vernacular obviously came more naturally to the

---

[21] The main source for the extracts on the Vikings in England is *The Anglo-Saxon Chronicle* of which there are several translations, such as the Pelican version by G. N. Garmondsway, London, 1962; see also F. M. Stenton, *Anglo-Saxon England*, 2nd edn, Oxford, 1947, and Else Roesdahl, *The Vikings*, London, 1992.

[22] On King Alfred's literary programme see P. G. Thomas, in *The Cambridge History of English Literature*, vol. I, pp. 88–107, Cambridge, 1932, and also G. F. Browne, *King Alfred's Books*, London, 1920. Dorothy Whitelock, The Old English Bede, *Proceedings of the British Academy* 48 (1962), 57–90, argues that Alfred himself did not translate Bede's *Ecclesiastical History*.

English, who already had a literature in their own language dating from the days of Caedmon and Cynewulf. This was scarcely the case on the continent in the same period, where only a few attempts were made in this direction. Thus Hrabanus Maurus drew up the first German–Latin dictionary *Glossaria Latina-theodisca*, but for the time being without further consequence for a literature still dominated by Latin.

On the continent the Scandinavian expansion was also strongly felt, especially in Flanders and northern France, where in 885 the Vikings set up winter quarters outside Paris itself. This shows that Carolingian society at this time was severely weakened, in such a way that it would be wrong here to attribute its cultural regression to the Viking army alone. It had become clear much earlier that the tension between different population groups was too great, and that the school system had not had time enough to smooth them out by making a more uniform culture that could have held the empire together. Perhaps Charlemagne had realised this himself when before his death in 814 he shared out his kingdom among three of his sons, of whom only Louis the Pious (814–840) survived him. Louis had inherited his father's cultural awareness, but not his strength and political insight. When he therefore undertook a new division of the kingdom between his own three sons Pippin, Louis (the German), and Lothar (as emperor) – the days of the empire were as good as over. The quarrels between Louis and his brothers made a decentralised collective government impossible, powerful vassals set themselves up against their lords, and in the course of the ninth century political decay increased irresistibly. In France the Carolingians were forced out completely when Count Odo of Paris in 888 assumed royal power, ruling the French part of a Europe that was now just as fragmented as it had been when Charles Martel had begun to unite it one and a half centuries earlier. Only with the accession of Hugo Capet to the throne in 987 did affairs settle slowly down again in France, while the German owners of the imperial title worked on their side of the frontier between the French and German parts of Europe to consolidate 'the Holy Roman Empire of the German Nation'.

It is not easy to estimate what these events meant for the European system of education. On the continent things had never gone so catastrophically as in England, for even during times of war the monasteries were allowed to lead their own inner lives according to an unbroken tradition. For this reason the cloister schools continued too, and even in the darkest times in the tenth century there is proof of studying and literary output. Even if the lines of communication between monasteries were severely restricted, and even if schools were deprived of the dynamic that came from Charlemagne's attempt to involve them directly in the secular life of society, the life of the mind was not completely drawn into the collapse of the empire. Within their own walls the monasteries could gather themselves around the religious life that could be lived without regard to the confusion outside. No political suspension of this life was allowed for in the Rule of St Benedict, which once more assisted in keeping learning safe through the crises of society. That this was the actual state of affairs can clearly be seen in the progress of the scholarly literature of this time. In scope this literature was about the same size as that which was described in chapter 2 as the literary legacy of the monasteries, and by and large it contained the same genres. Yet here and there new forms cropped up, and new ideas were proposed for debate in texts which brought about polemical rejoinders.

If we turn first to the fundamental *artes liberales*, we will find in the Carolingian age a number of summary and introductory works, which in their quality, at any rate, do not excel those of the period before. Yet there is a certain development of the disciplines of the trivium, in which, for example, the grammarians in some cases broaden their areas with works on language history. One example of this is Hrabanus Maurus' *De Inventione Linguarum*, although it concerned itself less with the history of language than with that of the alphabet, and among other things, gave an account of runes. In St Gallen Notker Balbulus (c. 840–912) in his *Notitio de Viris Illustribus* gave us a kind of patristic literary history, and in Liège in about 848 the Irish Sedulius Scotus, who knew Greek, completed his *Collectaneum*, which contains numerous extracts from ancient pagan and Christian authors. The abbot Servatus Lupus of Ferrières (c. 805–862) understood the significance of literary textual criticism, and his pupil Heiric d'Auxerre (841–c. 880) made commentaries on ancient tracts on literature and logic.

More striking is the development of dialectic, which still involved cramming the student with Aristotelian logic, but which also, little by little, started to consider problems that essentially belonged to philosophy. Famous in this way is the battle about the epistemological status of the universals, or general concepts. This goes back to a text with the droll title *A Letter on Nothing and Darkness* (*Epistola de Nihilo et Tenebris*) by Alcuin's fellow Englishman and pupil Fredegise of Tours (d. 835). He claimed that words such as 'nothing' or 'darkness' may represent something real – 'darkness' in Fredegise's opinion must be a substance, since if it were not, no-one would be able to give it a name. This promptly brought forth a reply from another disciple of Alcuin, Agobard of Lyons (769–840), with the title *A Book Against Abbot Fredegise's Objections* (*Liber Contra Objectiones Fredegisi Abbatis*). Later Remigius of Auxerre (c. 841–908), a pupil of Heiric and a teacher in Paris and Rheims, maintained that a general concept such as 'man' represents a common human substance independent of all individuals, while his teacher Heiric in refutation regarded general concepts as pure and simple names.[23] This nominalist dispute is no doubt the first example of a philosophical feud about an abstract problem – the relation between language and reality – which would later become one of the great themes of medieval philosophy.

The greatest name in philosophy in this period, however, was an Irishman, Johannes Scotus Erigena (c. 810–877), who was working at the Schola Palatina from 847 onwards on the basis of a training now unknown.[24] In 867 he completed his main work *On the Division of Nature* (*De Divisione Naturae*), which contains the first detailed metaphysical system of European origin since antiquity. Erigena's premises were essentially Neo-Platonist, in connection with the Greek Fathers and mystics such as Gregory of Nyssa, Maximus the Confessor, and Dionysius Areopagites, of whom, with his distinguished knowledge of Greek, he had translated several treatises into Latin. Through his text – which was later condemned as heretical – a strongly Neo-Platonist tradition was implanted into the spiritual life of the middle ages independent of the Augustinism which otherwise prevailed.

When we look at the quadrivium, we see at once that the subjects of pure mathematics (arithmetic and geometry) are in an extremely weak position. Not one single text on these subjects survives from this period. The textbooks of Boethius mentioned above were obviously all that was needed to fulfil the modest needs of the time. Astronomy, too, was at a low ebb, even though there was much literature on the

---

[23] On Fredegise and Agobard, see Gilson, pp. 196ff.
[24] See M. Cappuyns, *Jean Scot Erigène, sa vie, son oeuvre, sa pensée*, Louvain–Paris, 1933; cf. G. Mathon, L'enseignement palatin de Jean Scot Erigène, in *Arts libéraux*, pp. 47–64.

subject, along with treatises on the calendrical system. How low the level was is seen in Paul the Deacon's *History of the Longobards*, in which the tides are described in a very detailed passage. The author has heard of the maelstrom in the Lofoten islands and believes the ebb and flood-tides to be caused by similar whirlpools in various places in the abysses of the ocean – without realising the connection between this phenomenon and the movements of the moon, which had already been recognised in ancient times and is even described in Bede's treatise on chronology.[25] Similarly, it is no wonder that Hrabanus Maurus' encyclopedia *On the Nature of Things or On the Universe* (*De Rerum Natura seu de Universo*) shows a predominant interest in the allegorical and mystical meaning of things and can scarcely be thought of as a contribution to the advance of astronomy, and the same is true of a corresponding text of Walafrid Strabo. A little more factual, however, is a commentary to Martianus Capella made by Remigius of Auxerre. Only with Johannes Scotus Erigena is astronomy touched on in a significant way; Erigena knows the so-called geo-heliocentric theory of the planets which is often, though probably unjustly, attributed to Heracleides of Pontus (*c*. 390–*c*. 310 BC), according to which Venus and Mercury circle around the sun, which circles around the stationary earth at the centre of the universe. Erigena develops this system further, when he assumes that Mars and Jupiter also circle around the sun. Had he added Saturn to this number, his theory would have been almost identical with that of Tycho Brahe 750 years later.[26] In connection with astronomy, we must mention geography, on which a particularly relevant text is *On the Size of the Earth's Sphere* (*De Mensura Orbis Terrae*) of 825. This is written by the otherwise unknown Irish monk Dicuil, presumably in Clonmacnoise, and is far from being a general compilation, in that the author builds not only on older works but also on reports from contemporary travellers. Thus he is able to give the first description of Iceland, which an Irish expedition had visited in 795, just as he knows of the ancient canal, closed in 767, linking the Nile and the Red Sea.[27]

In one area alone did the schools in this period contribute

---

[25] For Paulus Diaconus on tides and currents see his *De Gestis Langobardorum* I, 6, *Migne PL* 95, 444ff.
[26] See P. Duhem, *Le système du monde*, vol. III, pp. 44–62, Paris, 1915, and vol. V, pp. 38–75, Paris, 1917.
[27] On Dicuil, see Sarton, vol. I, p. 571, Baltimore, 1927.

independently to the development of the quadrivium, namely in music.[28] This subject had earlier attracted attention because of its importance for the liturgy (just as the discipline of *computus* was necessary for the ecclesiastical calendar), and Charlemagne had engaged Italian teachers in Gregorian chant at the cathedral schools of Metz and Soissons. By the seventh century, a special notation had developed with strokes over the words to indicate pitch, which turned into a more lucid musical notation in the form of the so-called neums. In the ninth century the first texts on the theory of music appear with a *Harmonica Institutio* of Hucbald of St Amand (*c.* 840–930) as one of the first known examples. This was followed by a *Musica Enchiriadis* of Abbot Hoger of Verden (d. 902), in which for the first time real bar-lines are used with keys, while his contemporary Regino of Prüm (d. 915) treated the doctrine of harmony in *De Harmonica Institutione* in connection with an antiphonary entitled *Tonarius*. Later this development reached a provisional high point in the Italian Guido of Arezzo, who in about 1030 wrote *A Short Account of the Art of Music* (*Micrologus de Disciplina Artis Musicae*) in which he introduced a system of four bar-lines. Akin to the quadrivium is medicine, which in this period gave rise to very few writings, though we must still mention the *Book of Horticulture* (*Liber de Cultura Hortorum*) of Walafrid Strabo (*c.* 808–849), which was really a botanical work describing twenty-three plants of interest to pharmacology.

Nor where jurisprudence was concerned is there much to tell, although a few texts remain which reveal an increasing tendency to systematise canonical law. Already in 774 Pope Hadrian I presented the emperor with a collection entitled *Dionysiana-Hadriana*, which gradually found several imitations, among others a *Codex Carolinus* gathered by Charles himself, from a time after 791. Later synodal manuals of Regino of Prüm in Germany (*c.* 906), Abbo of Fleury in France (*c.* 945–1004), along with an Italian collection dedicated to Anselm of Milan (*c.* 882), bear witness to the work of ecclesiastical jurists.[29]

On the other hand, this period gave rise to a wholly new genre in the form of the so-called Mirror of Princes. These were handbooks on the art of governing for the use of kings, sometimes also

---

[28] On Guido and the music of the Carolingian age, see A. Machabey, *Essai sur les formules usuelles de la musique occidentale des origines à la fin du XVe siècle*, Paris, 1928.

[29] On Canon law, see Fournier and Le Bras.

containing technical material on the *artes liberales*.[30] Charlemagne had already had such a *Via Regia* or *Royal Road* drawn up by Abbot Smaragdus of St Mihiel at about the same time as Paulinus of Aquileia wrote a *Liber Exhortationis* or *Book of Exhortation* for the use of Count Heiric of Friaul. Later Bishop Jonas of Orléans (*c.* 780–843) composed an *Institutio Regia* for King Pipin. These and many other texts of the same kind are interesting as showing how the people of the church were now systematically trying to create a theoretical basis for the new royal power.

As regards political philosophy Charlemagne was in a difficult position, at least to start with. The political integration of the empire meant that none of the many existing laws of tribe and country could be used as a basis for the universal legal system which had to supplement local laws if the unity of the kingdom were to be achieved and maintained. In any case it was difficult to find a theoretical justification that would enable the emperor to give laws for everything. Here Charles' Germanic background was of no help, for there the role of the king was more to respect the existing laws than to promulgate new ones. While Emperor Justinian in the east had based his authority without hesitation on the imperial ideology of Roman law, this was no longer possible in the west, nor did ecclesiastical law at this time know the concept of a Christian *imperator*. Charles thus had no other course than to rely on his personal advisers at court. As we have seen, nearly all of them were churchmen, nourished on a spiritual diet with the Old and New Testaments as the main ingredients. It is no wonder that the new imperial ideology was built more on the Bible than on Roman law. The point of departure became the Old Testament concept of the king as 'God's anointed', the perfection of whose power derives from God in so far as he himself obeys God's law. Thereby the idea of sacral kingship was implanted into European political philosophy.

This found clearest expression in a long series of works by Hincmar of Rheims (*c.* 806–882), among which the most important is a book *On the Person and Office of the King* (*De Regis Persona et Regio Ministerio*), dedicated in about 860 to Charles the Bald. The bishop here expresses himself with great freedom, for example when he says to the king that 'Thou hast not made me archbishop of Rheims,

---

[30] On the ideology of kingship, see W. Ullmann, *Medieval Political Thought*, London, 1975; cf. P. L. Ward, The Coronation Ceremony in Mediaeval England, *Speculum* 14 (1939), 160–78.

rather I together with my colleagues have chosen Thee to rule the kingdom on the condition that Thou respect the laws.'[31] It was also Hincmar who more than others was the instigator of the new coronation rites that carefully avoided any reference to the previous popular elections of kings. The king can be accepted or designated by his subjects in advance, but the decisive factor is his subsequent 'election' by the bishops signifying that he can only exercise his divine authority after being anointed by them. As sources for an ideology that endured in principle until the abolition of monarchic power in the different states of Europe, these texts are thus of wide-ranging importance.

One effect of this theocratic principle was that the anointed king or emperor could give laws for his subjects in God's name. Another was a new idea that it would be sinful to dispute the king's authority as long as he subjugated himself to God's law – even though the middle ages in practice had no more trouble than other epochs in accommodating a usurper, provided he had luck on his side. In the end this gave the bishops a new position in society, for who could explain to the anointed prince how to exercise his authority under God's law unless it was those officially appointed to invigilate over all spiritual affairs? With Charles' Frankish biographer Einhard, it is possible to read between the lines how hard it could be for a German to reconcile himself to such new-fangled ideas, which pulled the ground from under the feet of a time-honoured Germanic tradition, at the same time as it laid ecclesiastical constraints in principle on the king's exercise of power.

Despite the unmistakable interest in the period for *artes* and above all for trivium, it should not be forgotten that now as before theology was the most important object of monastic learning. In addition to what he otherwise wrote, practically every single author has left behind him commentaries on one or more of the biblical texts more or less in the manner of the fathers. But the flowering of the schools ensured that Bible study became more intense, and soon we see theologians beginning to use new genres and write treatises on specific problems in which new and personal points of view were championed. Bishop Theodulf of Orléans wrote *On the Holy Ghost* and *On the Rite of Baptism* (*De Spiritu Sancto* and *De Ordine Baptismi*),

---

[31] Hincmar as quoted in Ullmann, *Medieval Political Thought*, p. 88. See further J. Chydenius, *Medieval Institutions and the Old Testament*, Helsinki, 1965; P. A. Van der Baar, *Die kirchliche Lehre der Translatio Imperii*, Rome, 1956; G. Falco, *The Holy Roman Republic*, London, 1964.

while Paschasius Radbertus of Corbie wrote *On Faith, Hope and Charity* (*De Fide, Spe et Caritate*, c. 845). And just as the dialecticians pursued their feud around general concepts, the theologians had their own battle from 844 onwards on the doctrine of the eucharist, with Paschasius Radbertus and Hincmar of Rheims on one side and Hrabanus Maurus, Ratramnus of Corbie, and Johannes Scotus Erigena on the other, and with numerous texts of controversy *On the Lord's Body and Blood* (*De Corpore et Sanguine Domini*) as a result. Ratramnus and Radbertus also fought each other in a dispute on the question of the Virgin Birth, while Hrabanus Maurus' pupil, Gottschalk (c. 805–c. 866), started a very violent debate, in which most theologians of the time took part, on the doctrine of predestination. The outcome of the battle as far as Gottschalk was concerned was a twenty-year prison sentence for heresy. Also in the more pastoral sphere a new and copious literature appeared on the rules for living for both priests and monks, which space prevents us from considering here in any detail.

In none of the areas specified above is there any justification for saying that the schools of the Carolingian age pursued original research, if by this we mean conscious efforts to bring new knowledge into being. As in the age before, learning was built on inherited, strongly restricted source material that was studied in increasing depth, it is true, but always with respect for the old writer's authority. The only realistic possibility for really new research, therefore, had to lie within an area in which the older authors had nothing to contribute – that is to say, within the history of the age itself.[32] Thus it was in the historical area that the period came to yield its main harvest. Here many different genres were cultivated. The least valuable for posterity are the various expositions of universal history, from the creation, from the founding of Rome, or from the birth of Christ up to the author's own time. Here, among other works, we have the *Historia* of a disciple of Alcuin, Freculf of Lisieux (d. 852), the first one written on French soil, while the genre was introduced to Germany by Regino of Prüm with his *Chronica* from the birth of Christ to the year 906. These works are annalistic and note only important events in chronological order, and usually in an extremely uncritical fashion. Far more dependable are the numerous annals

---

[32] On medieval historiography, see B. Guenée, *Le métier d'historien au moyen-âge*, Paris, 1977, and B. Lacroix, *L'historien au moyen-âge*, Paris–Montreal, 1971.

describing the history of individual monasteries or dioceses. As a rule these are written year for year, roughly contemporary with the events depicted, often in the form of simple notes in the margin of the monastery calendar. Finally there are accounts of contemporary events over a shorter period of years in which the author himself lived or for which he knew witnesses. This is true, for example, of a chronicle for the years 804 to 843, written by Charlemagne's daughter's son Nithard (d. 844), an account of the period 893 to 995 by Richer de St Remi (c. 945–c. 1000), and Abbo of St Germain-des-Prés' versified *Bella Parisiacae Urbis*, which describes the siege of Paris by the Vikings from 885 to 886.

One particular historical genre is the biography, which was eagerly cultivated. As mentioned earlier, the biography of saints was the most frequent form, ranging from stereotyped accounts or imaginative novels of lesser-known persons to thorough and reliable life-stories of the saints whom the author himself had known. Insufficient expositions often gave rise to improved versions. Walafrid Strabo (c. 808–849) thus revised the old *Vita Sancti Galli*, just as he did the otherwise excellent *Vita Caroli Magni* of Einhard, and the *Gesta Hludovici* by Thegan concerning Louis the Pious, which was written even before Louis died. Finally it should be remembered that several authors of the time left behind them important collections of letters, whose value as source-material cannot be overestimated.

If, to conclude this chapter, we attempt to appraise the Carolingian Renaissance in general, the results will depend on the background against which we regard it, and on the point of view from which we judge the advance that it created in history. The darkest picture comes from comparing the learning and education of the Carolingian age with the developments made in corresponding areas of knowledge outside Europe, in particular the impressive flowering of science that took place at precisely the same time within Islam. We shall return to this briefly in the next chapter. Here we shall only remark that such a comparison is not wholly just, seeing that Arab scholars had the great advantage over their Latin contemporaries of having gained access to the scholarly literature of the ancient world, and thereby to the scientific methods that European schools missed most of all. On the other hand, if we see the contribution of these schools against the background of the preceding dark ages, the picture becomes more detailed. It is true that scholars were just continuing along the same trail as regards their use of source-material, just as the quadrivium had ground to a halt owing to a lack of interest in the exact sciences (leaving aside music) in the given social context. Yet in the trivium progress had been made – one important philosopher (Erigena) had emerged, and the first independent debates on fundamental problems of philosophy had taken place. And, apart from these particular advances, it has to be conceded without any doubt that this period made a general contribution of the greatest relevance: for the first time, society in Latin Europe had admitted some responsibility for education, and Charlemagne's dream of providing educational opportunities for the laity was of seminal value, despite the fact that the material conditions needed for carrying it out were not yet at hand.

CHAPTER 4

The schools of the middle ages

We have now reached that period in the history of Europe which immediately precedes the genesis of the university and which creates the concrete requirements for restructuring higher education. This space of time stretches from the tenth to the middle of the twelfth century and in many ways marks a turning point in the history of the middle ages. After the deep political and cultural drawback following the Carolingian period and the fearful expectation of the end of the world in the year 1000, a distinct age of prosperity set in. The middle ages now began to show their true colours in the development of a number of institutions and ideas, which in the political, economic, social, and spiritual spheres, built a new framework for human existence. As a background to the history of the medieval university, we must consider this framework a little more deeply; and even if this takes us rather far afield outside the history of learning in the narrow sense, the historical details in the following pages seem relevant for the understanding of the universities as the typical medieval institutions they were.[1]

In general terms the most important political change is certainly to be found in the fact that Europe had at long last reached the end of the long period of invasions that began with the first migrations in the last days of the Roman empire, and ended with the last Viking raids. To the east the Hungarians were now settling down in their domain. Among the Slavonic tribes the church was slowly moving forward, with civilising influences stemming from both Rome and Byzantium. To the south in Spain, Islam was halted, and a tolerant

---

[1] For ch. 4 in general, see M. Manitius, *Bildung, Wissenschaft und Litteratur im Abendlande von 800 bis 1100*, Crimitschau, 1925; R. W. Southern, *The Making of the Middle Ages*, New Haven, 1953; M. Deanesley, Medieval Schools to c. 1300, *The Cambridge Medieval History*, vol. v, Cambridge, pp. 765–79; N. Orme, *Education in the West of England 1066–1548*, Exeter, 1976; P. Riche, Recherches sur l'instruction des laïcs du IXe au XIIe siècle, *Cahiers de Civilisation Médiévale* 5 (1962), 175ff; P. Delhaye, L'organisation scolaire au XIIe siècle, *Traditio* 5 (1947), 211–68.

modus vivendi between Mohammedans, Jews, and Christians was able to survive the first Spanish attempts to reconquer parts of the territory. To the north and west the steam had gone out of the Viking attacks, and once Rollo had established a permanent dukedom in Normandy, the Normans there adopted both the French language and the Christian faith. The renewed Danish attacks on England in about 1000 led surely to the fleeting rule of Canute the Great over a union of England and Denmark, but gave no cause for the wild acts of destruction and pillage that had taken place 150 years earlier. Even the Danes were now becoming Christians, and in this process England was rich enough to give them powerful assistance from the west. Finally, the Norman conquest of England in 1066 and the years following was the last time the island kingdom was invaded, a point at which the independent existence of Anglo-Saxon culture came to an end and the conditions were right for the slow development of a mixed Franco-British culture in its place. All these transformations resulted in Europe now enjoying peace along its borders for the first time in centuries; soon the Crusades would show that aggression could be directed elsewhere.

These more peaceful conditions meant in no way any return to the political system that had begun to delineate itself under Charlemagne. On the contrary, the idea of empire was replaced by a conception of society that has often been characterised by the vague and unwieldy notion of feudalism. There is no place here to go into the many and often contradictory historical theories on the origin of feudalism. But as a background to understanding the society that created the universities, it is necessary to stress some of its most striking characteristics.

As we have seen, Charlemagne tried to administer his empire with the support of local dignitaries or chieftains whom he claimed the right to dismiss. These 'vassals' were thus only officials, servants of the central administration, each of them being responsible for a province of the kingdom under the emperor's sovereignty and control. After the long years of disruption there was nothing left of this system. The central power was gone, and the previous vassals had been able to establish themselves unopposed as landed gentry in their own domains, which were now passed down from father to son as in royal houses.

In a sense the idea of feudalism can be seen as an attempt to build a state out of this political chaos on the basis of a network of personal bonds that extended across all members of society with the aid of the terms 'lord' and 'vassal'. At the top was the king, whose lord was God, and whose vassals were the highest chieftains of the kingdom. Each of these was lord over other vassals of lower rank right down to the free farmer under the lord of the local manor. These bonds were seen as contractual relationships among free men with well-defined rights and duties guaranteed with the help of personal oaths of fealty. Each lord had the duty to protect his vassals and in return received various repayments in the form of military service, taxes, or work. Outside this system of contracts were in principle only serfs or the unfree, whose social status hardly differed from that of slaves in ancient times.[2]

This system had firstly a military rationale, in that each lord could claim armed support from his vassals and only from them – a state of affairs that also made it impossible for a feudal king to mobilise the peasantry directly. Secondly, there was an attempt to make this system into an economic structure with the idea that each vassal owns his land 'off' his lord, to whom in certain circumstances (breach of faith, lack of heirs, and so on) it could revert. In reality the feudal system was only a theory which reflected more or less correctly the way things were. It was never introduced everywhere in Europe or to its full possible extent. Obviously, in times of unrest, it was quite easy to get the common people to submit to the nearest chieftain whose warriors could protect life and property. This had been done already in the last days of the Roman empire and in the dark ages afterwards. It was far more difficult to do this in times of peace or further up the social hierarchy. The history of the middle ages is full of rebellious vassals who occasionally maintained their rights to rise up if the king failed to observe his contractual obligations. Precisely because of the reciprocity in the feudal contract, absolute monarchy ran counter to the system's basic principles.

While Charlemagne's empire was now a thing of the past, nonetheless in the ruins of the imperial idea a new concept arose that was to become a uniting force of some importance in political

---

[2] On feudalism, see the principal works of M. Bloch, *La société féodale*, vols. I and II, Paris, 1939–40, and F. L. Ganshof, *Qu'est-ce que la féodalité?*, Brussels, 1944; cf. R. Colbourn (ed.), *Feudalism in History*, Princeton, 1956, and the analysis in O. Brunner, 'Feudalismus' – ein Beitrag zur Begriffsgeschichte, *Neue Wege der Verfassungs- und Sozialgeschichte*, 2nd edn, Göttingen, 1968, 128ff. See also the two chapters of P. Vinogradoff in *The Cambridge Medieval History*, vol. II, Cambridge, 1968, pp. 631–55 and vol. III, pp. 458–84.

thought. Already Augustine had claimed that 'there is one society of all Christians', in which, characteristically enough for 'society', he applied the Roman term *res publica* without thinking of a political empire.[3] Now half a millennium after Augustine it was clear that the inhabitants of the more or less self-governing areas in fragmented Europe only really had one thing in common – Christianity. Already in the ninth century the notion of 'Christendom' emerges as a designation for spiritual, and to some extent cultural community existing across frontiers and independent of the shifting political scene. That this Christendom had its centre in Rome was underlined by Pope Nicholas I (858–867), who wrote to the Byzantine emperor describing himself as 'the supreme pontiff on the throne of Rome, whom You have denigrated, but whom the whole of Christendom with one soul looks up to'.[4] This fine theory did not last long, and it finally came to grief in the great schism between eastern and western churches in 1054. This breach was not caused alone by the steadily stronger claim of the popes to be the supreme spiritual authority in law over the whole of Christendom. It also had roots going further back to Charlemagne himself and his attempt to establish an empire solely in the western lands and wholly independently of the other emperor in Byzantium. The outcome was that 'Christendom' became more and more a western idea, while consequently and unbelievably the Latin conquest of Constantinople in 1204 became known in history as the fourth 'Crusade'.

On the ideological level this development had inevitable consequences for the relationship between the papacy and the princely houses of Europe. Earlier Charlemagne and Pope Leo III had united in sharing the responsibility for European progress in both spiritual and secular areas – with the emperor as a fully equal partner whose nomination of bishops and interference in synods went unquestioned by Rome. This state of affairs was now over, and while the princes lost more of their power, the pope appeared increasingly as the stronger party who not only claimed full sovereignty over ecclesiastical matters but also the right to call the princes to order in the political sphere. Nicholas I had already asserted that no secular power could sit in judgement over a spiritual authority, all Christians being in a way the subjects of the pope and deriving the power they

---

[3] Augustine, *De Opere Monachorum*, cap. 33, *Migne PL* 40, 575; cf. J. Rupp, *L'idée de chrétienté dans la pensée pontificale des origines à Innocent III*, Paris, 1939.
[4] Letter from Pope Nicholas I to the Emperor Michael III, *Migne PL* 119, 935.

had with all said and done from the Holy See. In the middle of the twelfth century this view was pregnantly expressed by John of Salisbury (d. 1180), who explained in his *Polycraticon* that the sword was carried by princes, but so to speak on behalf of the church and only because priests were forbidden to shed blood themselves. The quarrel over the investiture of bishops between the pope and the German emperor accentuated the claim of the church for absolute mastery over ecclesiastical posts, and the Lateran synod in 1059 explicitly forbade the clergy to receive offices from laymen, with the fight against simony as the justification. In 1077 the most powerful pope of the time, Gregory VII (1073–1085), forced Emperor Henry IV to accept this new course, which was confirmed for all practical purposes in the concordat of Worms in 1122, even if in the form of a compromise. Thereby the church had in principle freed itself from the political powers – at the same time as numerous bishops effectively carried on as secular rulers in their dioceses.

The ideological development within Christianity, as much as the changed relations between society and the ecclesiastical authorities, is the background to the Crusades, of which the first (1096–1099) and the second (1147–1149) fall inside the period we have to consider here. These wars must partly be understood as the result of efforts to stabilise peace inside Europe by channelling the aggressive tendencies of feudalism outside it into a gigantic action against 'the infidel'. This was clearly expressed in the *History of Jerusalem* (*Historia Hierosolymitana*), also known as the *Gesta Francorum Jerusalem Expugnantium*, of Fulcher of Chartres (1058–c. 1130), who says of the crusaders that 'they go forth in a just war against the infidel ... which teaches them to keep themselves from the fatiguing battles of earlier times against true believers'.[5] The idea of a Holy War is fairly obvious here, at the same time as it developed, thanks to the Crusades, among the 'infidel'.

How soon such ideas could transform the concept of Christendom into a self-caricature can perhaps be seen most clearly in a growing intolerance in Europe itself. Thus the first Crusade started with a bloody massacre of Jews in the Rhineland, and the risk was appreciably great also for Christians of divergent or heretical views. In 1022 thirty heretics died at the stake in Orléans, the first use in a spiritual quarrel of a penalty that earlier had only been employed

---

[5] Fulcher of Chartres, *Historia Hierosolymitana* I, 1; Migne *PL* 155, 828.

occasionally against criminal offenders.[6] The wars against the French Cathars in the twelfth and thirteenth centuries is also part of the picture of intolerance that ensured that the greater political stability in Europe did not go hand in hand with greater intellectual security for those who, for whatever reason, were unable to conform with the ever more intolerant principles of Christendom.'[7]

As regards the intellectual institutions, the monasteries are the most important centres in this period too, even if after a while the cathedral schools were to run a close second. Throughout the earlier unstable period, the Benedictine monasteries had proved their fitness to survive a very critical phase in the development of society everywhere, except where, as in England, they had been destroyed. From the start they were meant to be isolated enclaves, whose independence from 'the world' also caused them to be largely self-sufficient in all the produce they needed. One reason for this was that the Benedictine order was very loosely built without any central government, in such a way that individual monasteries also in spiritual ways were capable of bearing long periods of isolation. All things considered, the monasteries kept their role in this turbulent time as the centres of the learning and science of the age and as a refuge for men and women who were inclined to turn their backs on the world.

Yet it would soon become apparent that the popularity of the monasteries was influenced more by the desire to renounce the world than by conscious efforts to preserve its culture. As early as 910 in the most turbulent period of all and directly resulting from the Viking depredations in France – we can observe how Abbot Berno founded Cluny in the heartland between Paris and Lyon, in an attempt to make monastic life even more isolated from the world.[8] Where the life of monks in the dark ages had lost some of its original aims, and thereby its firmness and discipline, Berno wanted to reform it by taking it back to its source, that is, back to the Benedictine Rule. This happened with a hitherto unknown severity: the day was divided up minutely with a nearly unbroken liturgy as

---

[6] The burning of heretics was first decreed by King Robert I Capet in 1017, see Mansi, *Collectio XIX*, 373, and Ullmann, p. 147.

[7] For a brief summary of recent studies on the Cathars, see F. Niels, *Albigeois et Cathares*, Paris, 1962.

[8] On Cluny and the ecclesiastical reform, see H. E. J. Cowdreay, *The Cluniacs and the Gregorian Reform*, Oxford, 1970, and Jedin, vol. III/2, pp. 365ff. See further D. Knowles, *The Monastic Order in England*, Cambridge, 1966.

the most typical feature. To the prevalent monastic vows of poverty (i.e. common property), obedience, and celibacy, there was added a fourth: absolute silence, which only the abbot could break.

This was the beginning of the Cluniac monastery reform, which in the next centuries spread through Europe taking over one Benedictine abbey after the other, at the same time as new Cluniac foundations budded out from existing ones – all with the general abbot in Cluny as their head, a form of centralisation that had previously been alien to the Benedictines. The success of the new movement can be seen from the 1,450 Cluniac monasteries existing in about 1100 with an estimated number of 10,000 monks.

Parallel with the flowering of Cluny there was a widespread rebuilding of the destroyed monasteries in England, for example in Malmesbury (before 941), Glastonbury (943), and Peterborough (972), after which it was the turn of Whitby and Bede's old cloister, Monkwearmouth. The new Danish supremacy did not interrupt this process. On the contrary, Canute the Great is reported to have replaced the canons in Bury St Edmund's with monks. Nor did the coming of the Normans in 1066 halt this development, but on the contrary gave occasion for the building of several new foundations, for example Battle Abbey (1067) on the battlefield of Hastings itself. While about a hundred monasteries might have been counted in England in 800, the ensuing destruction ensured that the number in 1100 was no higher than eighty-eight, after which in the course of the twelfth century it rose to about four hundred. A corollary was that more and more land fell into church hands. In 1066 the monasteries in England had obtained for themselves through gifts and wills about 15 per cent of all landed property, a figure which was to double by 1216. In this way, the Benedictine abbots were effectively turned into administrators of large estates on a par with other feudal lords.

The impetus of the Cluniac movement was already dying out before 1100, and new orders sprang up, proof of the abiding strength of the monastic idea. In 1084 La Grande Chartreuse was founded, from which the Carthusian order grew; in 1119 the order of Premonstratensians was founded by regular canons, and at about the same time the explosive growth of the Cistercians began. Their order goes back to the little monastery of Cîteaux, founded in 1098 by Robert of Champagne and the Englishman Stephen Harding. St Bernard (1091–1153) entered here in 1113, before he founded the daughter monastery of Clairvaux two years later; this became the real point of departure for the new movement. With the usual motto: 'Back to the Rule!', the Cistercian monasteries spread like wildfire over the whole of Europe, and soon the expansion was so strong that the general chapter of the Cistercians in 1151 had to put a brake on the development by forbidding the founding of new monasteries.[9]

The monastic movement reached Denmark from 1000 onwards, with the Cluniac monastery of St Michael in Slesvig and All Saints in Lund, and then in a great surge in the following century: Odense (*c.* 1100), Essenbæk (*c.* 1140), Næstved (1135), Ringsted (*c.* 1135) and other places, while the Cistercians can be found in Esrom (1154), Øm (1165), Vitskøl (1158), Sorø (1150), Løgum (before 1171), and the Premonstratensians in Roskilde (*c.* 1177) and Børglum (before 1139). Various others could be named, quite apart from the numerous convents of nuns.[10]

The monastic reforms were of lasting importance for the whole of the later history of education. Indirectly this was because the reformers believed that the monk's life was the Christian life in pure essence and should be emulated as widely as possible by Christians in the outside world. The belief in the regular life as an especially deserving form of existence later became part of the pattern for many university colleges which – without being monasteries in the technical sense – bound up the student's life in a web of rules hardly less strict than those of an order. Celibacy was one of them, made obligatory for all clergy on the top three rungs of the church hierarchy (priest, deacon, and sub-deacon) by Pope Gregory VII in 1074 under the influence of Cluny. Since many students wanted a career in the church, this meant that in the middle ages married students were rare, even if far from unknown. Thus two important characteristics in the living conditions of the medieval student can be directly attributed to the attempts of Gregory and Bernard to press the spirituality of a religious order down on the heads of common lay people.

If we turn from these political and ecclesiastical matters to the more secular economy, we can observe in this period first of all an important increase in food production as a result of new agricultural methods. The wheeled plough should be mentioned here, as being a

---

[9] See A. Fliche, *Le Réforme Grégorienne*, vols. I III, Louvain, 1924–37.
[10] See H. N. Garner, *Atlas over danske klostre*, Copenhagen, 1968. On Odense and Evesham, see Knowles, *Monastic Order* note 8, pp. 163f.

development from as early as 800. It was expensive to produce and demanded a large team, for which reason it was often bought in common by the men of a village. Yet it had the advantage of being heavy and able to go deeper into the earth than earlier types of plough, so that it was able to break up hard soil, which meant that new lands could be put under the plough. This in itself meant an increase in yield.[11] Even more important was the change in methods of cultivation. As a consequence of deficient manuring it was necessary to give the land a rest at intervals. Previously the crop had been taken from one half of the field while the other lay fallow; the following year it was done the other way round. This was the classic two-year crop rotation. The new three-year system had been invented in the Carolingian period, being first described in 763 in the annals of St Gallen. Here only one-third of the field lay fallow whilst the two other thirds were sown with winter or spring seed according to the season. A simple calculation, already described in Walter of Henley's book of farming from about 1250, shows that with this system one could obtain the same profit with less ploughing work; or that with the same amount of ploughing one could put one's profits up by putting new land under the plough.[12] Together such technological advances ensured higher levels of production which would soon lead to an appreciable growth in population, besides an extension of trade.

In the Carolingian age and in the following years of strife, European trade had been of modest extent, by and large confined to local markets where the farmers of the district put their surplus up for sale. Travelling merchants from time to time sold a small selection of the more luxurious items that had been brought overland with great trouble from Byzantium or Italy after being carried there from the east. With rising standards of production and prosperity this international trade expanded, in spite of the many obstacles put in its path in the form of tolls to the local princes, bandits on the roads, and the general lack of legal protection for foreign travellers. This was the reason why merchants moved in armed 'companies' bound together by a common oath of loyalty. An example from the

---

[11] On the importance of the wheeled plough, see White, pp. 41–57. On the general development of agriculture, see *The Cambridge Economic History of Europe*, vol. 1: *The Agrarian Life of the Middle Ages*, Cambridge, 1971.

[12] D. Oschinsky, *Walter of Henley and other Treatises on Estate Management and Accounting*, Oxford, 1971.

eleventh century is the 'Union of Italian Merchants Visiting Markets in Champagne and the Kingdoms of the Franks' (Universitas Mercatorum Italiae Nundinas Campaniae ac Regni Franciae Frequentantium).[13] That this union is indicated by the word *universitas* shows that it is a corporation in the Roman sense of the word, and that it is hardly a coincidence that we first hear of merchant corporations in Italy, where Roman legal institutions had never been quite forgotten. In the course of time these institutions acquired a generally acknowledged status and were protected by an initially unwritten merchant code, the *lex mercatorum*, which in many ways made them immune from the local systems of justice.

With the livelier trade there came a new development of urban societies not least when the opening of the western Mediterranean for traffic enabled the quantity of imports to be significantly increased. Added to the cities which had survived from antiquity was now a number of purely medieval towns growing up around marketplaces, whose favourable positions had attracted an especially large trade. Here the merchant corporations often played an active part; thus it was the society of merchants of St Omer who in 1082, in agreement with the lord of the manor, took the initiative to pave the streets and to surround the town with earthworks.[14]

While the towns thus grew up as new centres for economic activity, they were in some way foreign elements in the society of their day – seen from an administrative point of view. As owners of land in the town and often also of farming estates in the surrounding country, the townsmen were in principle subject to the general conditions of land ownership, something that implied yields of one kind or another to the local lord, vassal, bishop, or abbot, along with the duty to have their mutual quarrels decided at his court. These were not the most favourable conditions for an urban society which did not base its economy on land ownership but on crafts and trade. This is the explanation for the general efforts of the towns to free themselves economically and legally from the local powers of authority, a process that as a rule was only accomplished in several moves involving sometimes violent, but most often peaceful means. To give an example, the men of Cambridge began the liberation of their town by obtaining, between 1120 and 1131, a royal privilege

[13] On *universitas* and the *lex mercatorum*, see Pirenne, *Economic and Social History*, pp. 53 and 96.
[14] Ibid., p. 166. Cf. J. Le Goff, *Marchands et banquiers du moyen âge*, Paris, 1956. See also P. Boissonnade, *Life and Work in Medieval Europe*, London, 1937.

that concentrated sea-trade for the whole county in the town of Cambridge itself and referred the lawsuits pertaining to this to a royal court, to be decided there *coram iustitia mea* and not by any local law. Later Henry II (1161–1189) freed them from the obligation to pay taxes to his vassal of the borough against the disbursement of a yearly tribute paid directly into his own coffers. In 1201 a new privilege followed from King John, who gave the townsmen the right to set up a merchants' guild, a *gilda mercatoria*, that was granted dispensation from certain tolls and taxes, along with the privilege of legal immunity from prosecution outside the town walls (unless they also owned land there). At the same time duels were forbidden as a means of deciding legal cases. Confirmation of an old privilege to hold a large market each year ensured the incomes of corporations by charging duty to stallholders. Finally a new privilege in 1207 granted citizens the right freely to elect their own *praepositus*.[15]

In this way, economic and judicial freedoms went hand in hand. From now on citizens could govern their own affairs and keep their own order. The merchants seem to have been the driving force in this development, which has parallels everywhere. But it is worth noting that the formal instrument of this liberation from constraint was nothing other than the traditional Roman doctrine of corporations. The term *praepositus* for the mayor or alderman is literal proof of this fact, which is all the more remarkable in that hitherto England had hardly been influenced by Roman law at all.

Urban society became increasingly important for the birth and development of the universities. Its material growth meant an increased quantity of dwellings in which students could find a place in unoccupied rooms or apartments. The transition to a cash economy, furthermore, meant that students could be accepted in great numbers without their taking part in farming or trade, by paying for their board and lodging. Just as important, however, was without doubt the citizens' practical demonstration that a population group could guard common interests by 'incorporating' itself, that is to say, by forming a corporation (society or guild) with well-defined rights and duties. It was not until this corporative idea began to spread right through the twelfth century that one of the most serious obstacles to the creation of universities was removed.

---

[15] See F. W. Maitland, *The Charters of the Borough of Cambridge*, Cambridge, 1901, and also his *Township and Borough*, Cambridge, 1898, repr. 1964. Cf. C. Stephenson, *Borough and Town, A Study of Urban Origins in England*, Cambridge, Mass., 1933.

Closely linked to the flowering of urban society was the technological development which also gained momentum in the period with which we are concerned. It is in the towns that we find the many categories of craftsmen and merchants whose activity was essential if the transition from village to town and from mere subsistence to cash economy was to be realised. Here there were masons of different kinds: stonemasons, house and ship's carpenters, farriers, toolmakers, and master casters. The stained glass and leaden roofs of cathedrals are witness to the existence of glass-makers and roofers, and the growth of coinage made mint-masters indispensable in many towns. Of all these occupations it can be said that they were still largely utilising tools and methods that had been known in principle since antiquity and that had not been forgotten since then. But more than anything else it was the concentration of such crafts that turned medieval towns into functional economic units, and made the basis for the trade by which many of them grew rich and powerful.

The whole of this progress in social, technological, and economic activity had the obvious consequence of increasing the need for training in both practical and theoretical areas. In this respect the monasteries might have been expected to lead the way, since they were not only the traditional home of theoretical learning but were also leaders in certain technical fields. This is illustrated in their attempt to industrialise their own food production with watermills, that spread over Europe in this period and – together with windmills, introduced a little later – made the first essential change in energy supply.[16] But it did not work quite this way. The monasteries were determined more than ever before to live in isolation from the world, and this tendency was strengthened with each new reform. If we thus compare the layout of great abbeys such as Cluny and Clairvaux with the plan of St Gallen discussed earlier, we find hardly any *schola exterior* in these cloisters. Time after time St Bernard and other great monastic fathers of his day stress that the monastery is a *schola caritatis*, 'a school of divine wisdom and charity', or a *paradisus*

---

[16] On power machines of the middle ages, see R. J. Forbes, Power, in *History of Technology*, vol. II, ed. C. Singer, E. J. Holmyard, A. R. Hall, and T. I. Williams, pp. 589–622, Oxford, 1957, and B. Gille, Machines, ibid., pp. 629–658. A very readable account is found in J. Gimpel, *La révolution industrielle du moyen âge*, Paris, 1975. On watermills in particular, see White, note 11, pp. 100ff, and M. Carus-Wilson, An Industrial Revolution in the 13th Century, *Economic History Review* 11 (1941), 39–60.

claustralis, 'a cloistered paradise', in which the wisdom of this world has nothing to say to those who only seek the one thing that is necessary.[17] While it is true that the Cluniac monks still took part in the scholarly progress of the age, the Cistercians kept themselves at a distance from it. This is not the whole story: for example, to a great extent medieval medicine was cultivated in connection with monastery hospitals and nursing homes. But by and large the triumphal expansion of the monastic movement in this period meant that public education had to find another basis in society. From another perspective, this segregation meant no less significantly that education had the chance of becoming something more than a mere training for monks. Perhaps European culture was rescued thereby from a theocratic system of learning that would scarcely have been able to supply the needs of either society or the laity as such.

In this context cathedral chapters came to play an ever greater role. In England, Herman of Bury says of Canute the Great that 'whenever he came to a cathedral or a fortified town, he handed over to the monks or canons not only the occasional boy of good family, but also the more distinguished boys among the poor, to be instructed at his expense'.[18] And Abbot Samson of Bury reports that Canute 'instituted *publicas scolas* in the greater and lesser towns, appointed teachers at state expense and sent them boys with the ability to learn grammar – even the freed sons of slaves'. This was clearly an attempt to exploit the reserves of intelligence in society regardless of social status. It is also worth noting that the term 'public school', *Publica Schola*, is used here for the first time.

The structure and function of the cathedral chapter, above all, was determined by its main task, that of running and maintaining the church and performing the daily liturgy along with assisting the bishop with the administrative work of the foundation. In the *Institutiones* issued by St Osmund, presumably in connection with the organising of the cathedral chapter in Salisbury in 1091, four different assignments or offices are listed: 'the cantor shall lead the choir, whatever hymn is sung. The treasurer shall look after the endowments of the church. The chancellor shall run the school and carry the books, and an *archischola* shall hear the lessons, determine,

---

[17] The source for the monastic industry at Clervaux is the *Vita Sancti Bernardi*, in Migne PL 185, 570–2. On the monastery as an enclosed paradise, see E. Gilson, *La théologie mystique de Saint Bernard*, Paris, 1947.

[18] On Herman of Bury, see A. F. Leach, *The Schools of Medieval England*, London, 1915, pp. 91f.

carry the church seal, compose letters and documents and notify the lectors [of services] on the board, just as the cantor does with regard to the hymns.'[19] In this way the chancellor of the cathedral was responsible for teaching, which was reasonable enough, since normally he was also in charge of the cathedral library and scriptorium. However, it is clear that he already had another canon to assist him with the teaching itself.

After a while it became customary for the two offices to be separate in such a way that the chancellor functioned as the school governor, while the teaching was delegated to a schoolmaster, *magister scholarum*, to whom the bishop gave the monopoly of public education in the town, presumably after testing his qualifications in some way. Thus when Bishop Henry of Blois was vicar in London in 1138, he bestowed this privilege upon a certain Henry who was *magister scholarum* at St Paul's, and ordered the deacon to excommunicate all 'those who without the permission of master Henry presume to teach in London, apart from those who represent the schools at St Mary le Bow and St Martin le Grand'. The last two leading churches were excused on the grounds that they contained independent chapters each with its own school.[20] The main thing, therefore, was that a *magister scholarum* required episcopal authorisation, but in return had a monopoly in teaching and thereby the income this could bring, from pupils who could afford to pay.

Standards in education and teaching could vary a great deal between individual schools. This was above all a consequence of the lack of teachers, which in the nature of things, at least in the beginning, goes with any effective extension of education. As was already the case in the Carolingian age, teachers appeared to be a restless lot, frequently on the road from one school to the other. An outstanding teacher could therefore make a previously unimportant cathedral school into a leading intellectual centre, thereafter letting it sink once more into obscurity by moving to another school, which would then flower in turn. With respect to this period, it is thus easier to shed light on the history of famous teachers than on that of the schools themselves.

A good example of this uncertainty can be found in Denmark,

---

[19] The *Institutiones* are quoted from Leach, *Schools*, pp. 73–5. Other functions of a cathedral chapter are described in F. Harrison, *Life in a Medieval College*, London, 1952 (on the chapter of York).
[20] On Henry of Blois, see Leach, *Schools*, p. 111.

where the story of the first Danish schools is extremely obscure. Here we have to assume that from the first moment some kind of teaching went on, in association with the cathedral chapters which after the independence of the Danish church at the start of the twelfth century, could be found in Lund, Roskilde, Odense, Børglum, Viborg, Aarhus, Ribe, and Slesvig; but as to a 'teacher for boys', *magister puerorum*, only a single name appears, that of St Keld (Ketil) of Viborg (*c*. 1100–1150). Even he is named not so much for his work as teacher and book copyist as for his glory as a saint, confirmed after his death by his canonisation in 1188. Yet we also hear of Archbishop Eskil of Lund (*c*. 1100–1181) bestowing rich gifts on the cathedral chapter's *scholasticus*, just as the Bishops Peder Vognsen of Aarhus (d. 1204) and Homer of Ribe (d. 1204) gave collections of books to their churches.[21] However, it was only at the end of the period that Danish schools made more contact with European centres of learning, thanks to the former Paris students Archbishop Anders Sunesøn of Lund (*c*. 1167–1228) and Bishop Gunner of Viborg (1152–1251).

If we turn from the organisation of the schools to the teaching itself, the shift of scholastic activity away from the monasteries to the cathedral schools may be observed as early as Gerbert of Aurillac (*c*. 945–1003), who was without question the most learned man of the tenth century. He received his first education in the monastery of Aurillac, which Odo of Cluny had reformed. Thus he can be seen as a child of the Cluniac movement, untypical as he was of it. In his youth he stayed for a time in northern Spain, where he was influenced in a decisive way by Arab science. After a stay in Rome he came at some time between 970 and 972 to the court of the German emperor, as tutor for the later Otto II (955–983). Later he was known as a teacher in the school at the cathedral of Rheims. Here he first shone in teaching logic, concerning which his pupil, the historian Richer, says:

Gerbert first examined Porphyry's *Isagoge* [i.e. Introduction] in the rhetor Victorinus' translation, and thereupon the same text in Boethius' version. He also explained the *Categories* and *Predicaments*, which are books of Aristotle's, and as regards *Perihermenias* or *De Interpretatione*, he showed its whole difficulty clearly. Thereafter he went on to inform his audience of the

---

[21] On the gift of books of the bishops of Aarhus and Ribe, see H. Koch, *Danmarks Kirke i den begyndende Højmiddelalder*, II, Copenhagen, 1936.

Topica, a book translated from Greek to Latin by Cicero and glossed in a commentary of six books by the consul Boethius.[22]

This is enough to show that Gerbert could command the main elements of Aristotelian logic. Of what he wrote himself in this area, only a small text on dialectic has survived; unfortunately it does not show him to be of any merit as a philosopher.

What particularly distinguished Gerbert from other teachers of his time was his interest in the quadrivium, which is also said to have been why he became the tutor of Otto II since 'music and astronomy were nearly completely unheard of in Italy'. In this area he has left a series of smaller writings that heralds a new age in the curriculum of schools, namely some letters to his pupil Constantine of Fleury on calculation with the *abacus* (bead-frame), on spherical astronomy, and small commentaries on Boethius' *Musica et Arithmetica*. Added to this is a larger independent work, *Isagoge Geometriae*, and finally a *Book on the Astrolabe* (*Liber de Astrolabio*), the first treatise in Latin on this important instrument for measuring and computing in astronomy. Gerbert certainly got to know the astrolabe in Spain, from where it slowly began to penetrate Europe as an aid to the teaching of astronomy. For the same purpose he himself constructed an armillary sphere to demonstrate the circles of the celestial sphere, together with a globe of the heavens – perhaps the one he sent to Remigius of Trier in exchange for a manuscript of Statius' *Achilleis*. Gerbert was namely one of the most industrious collectors of books in the middle ages, always on the lookout for a good manuscript, and several of Cicero's dialogues are extant only thanks to him. When he returned to monastic life in 982 as abbot of Bobbio, it was perhaps so that he could use the large library this monastery possessed. Meanwhile France drew him once more, and in 991 he was elected archbishop of Rheims. Seven years later he became archbishop of Ravenna, and finally in 999, just before the expected day of judgement at the change of the millennium, he was elected pope with the name Sylvester II, no doubt the only mathematician ever to fill the Chair of Peter. Legend soon endowed him with the fantastic abilities of a magician, and with no apparent foundation in reality rumours of a terrible death soon began to spread. Gerbert's

---

[22] Richer, *Historiarum libri IV*, cap. 46, *Migne PL* 138, 102 (chapters 43 to 65 are the main source of Gerbert's history). See further H. Pratt Lattin, *The Letters of Gerbert*, New York, 1961, and J. R. Williams, The Cathedral School of Reims in the Eleventh Century, *Speculum* 29 (1954), 661ff.

activity soon left its mark in numerous disciples and disciples of disciples. In his all-round learning he was unique among contemporaries, but as the typical wandering professor he was imitated by hundreds of others, of whom only a few made notable contributions to the schools.

The period after Gerbert was unable to utilise the whole of his legacy, since by and large the schools ignored the quadrivium in favour of the trivium.[23] This was understandable, for the quadrivium had only very poor literary material to build on, while the trivium, despite all deficiencies, could use large parts of a classical Latin literature that was still read, analysed, and compared. As a result, new points of view and methods gradually appeared that made themselves known in various ways in all subjects of the trivium.

The discipline of grammar already had a firm tradition in the schools, part of whose responsibility was to instruct future priests and others in Latin, usually with a classical grammar of Donatus as a textbook and one of the collections of exempla from the church fathers or the classical authors as a textual base. Yet, through purely pedagogical needs, after a while there emerged a technique of close reading, or 'declination', through which the pupil not only learnt to translate the text but also to pay attention to the inflections and derivations of individual words, in such a way that the inner structure of the language came alive. Lingusitic arguments were conducted in a logical style in such a way that a real science of language was now under way. However, this tendency first really blossomed in the numerous dissertations on the philosophy of language that appeared in the thirteenth century.

Rhetoric also changed its character. Formerly this discipline aimed at the technique of beautiful and correct presentation, especially when preaching was concerned, classical Latin authors being often used as models. This was done with fear and trembling, and many passages had to be passed over, if they gave too clear evidence of the paganism or frivolous morals of antiquity. Typical of this attitude was Hrabanus Maurus, who says, concerning the pagan literature, that 'if we find anything of profit therein, let us turn it to the good of our own teaching (*ad nostrum dogma convertimus*). But if we find superficial things pertaining to idols or erotic love or absorption

---

[23] On the liberal arts in the period after Gerbert, see M. T. Gilson, The *Artes* in the Eleventh Century, in *Arts libéraux*, pp. 121–6, and J. R. O. Donnel, The Liberal Arts in the Twelfth Century, ibid., pp. 127–35.

in worldly affairs, let us weed them out.'[24] Yet unfortunately the more the classical authors were studied, the harder it was to refrain from reading them in context or to avoid making sense of them in their own terms. It was particularly in the twelfth century that this study of literature flowered, with sincere admiration for Virgil, Horace, Ovid, Cicero, and Seneca. The knowledge of such authors once again became an important part of the ideal education. They were now read without suspicion, no doubt because Christian culture was sufficiently well established to allow such a daring glimpse into the non-Christian world, even to the extent of learning something from it. Thus the study of literature was converted from being an appendix to grammar to being a subject in its own right with obvious human value. Not without reason has the twelfth century been described as a period of humanism, with the wise and tolerant bishop of Chartres, John of Salisbury, as a typical figure. A real history of literature was still lacking at this time, but an attempt can be found in the *Dialogus super Auctores* of Konrad of Hirsau from about 1150.[25]

Most striking of all, however, was the progress in dialectic, which prior to Gerbert seems to have been a heavy-handed memorisation of the basic principles of Aristotelian logic in association with the *Categoriae* and *De Interpretatione* (*Logica Vetus*). That Gerbert incorporated Aristotle's other texts on logic into his teaching syllabus gave logic a new impetus, witnessing to the new philosophical interest; the old battle on general concepts flared up again in the itinerant Roscellinus (*c.* 1050–*c.* 1120), who advocated an extreme nominalism. With this development, dialectic was well on the way to separating epistemology and metaphysics from logic as distinguished and independent disciplines.

Of great importance for the whole development of the intellectual life in the middle ages was the confrontation between dialectic and theology which began in the eleventh century. The dialectician's

---

[24] Hrabanus Maurus, *De clericorum institutione PL*, 18, *Migne* III 107, 396.
[25] On rhetoric, see R. McKeon, Rhetoric in the Middle Ages, *Speculum* 17 (1942), 1–32, and H. Caplan, *On Eloquence: Studies in Ancient and Medieval Rhetoric*, Ithaca–London, 1970. On the literary renaissance of the twelfth century, see C. H. Haskins, *The Renaissance of the Twelfth Century*, Cambridge, Mass., 1927 and G. Paré, A. Brunet, and P. Tremblay, *La Renaissance du XIIe siècle, les Ecoles et l'Enseignement*, Ottawa–Paris, 1933 and also the polemic between W. A. Nitze, U. T. Holmes, and E. M. Sanford in *Speculum* 23 (1948), 464ff and 26 (1951) 635ff. See also B. Munk Olsen, *La réception de la littérature classique au moyen age (IXe–XIIe siècle)*, Copenhagen, 1995. On Roscellinus, see F. Picavet, *Roscelin*, Paris, 1911.

urge to illuminate problems with the help of reason did not stop for theology, and Roscellinus caused havoc in just this area when he applied his nominalism to the doctrine of the Trinity. The Italian Anselm of Canterbury (1033–1109) made an attempt of a hitherto unknown kind to enlist philosophy in his aid in the debate on the general question of belief. 'As I see it', says Anselm, 'it is a sign of slackness, when once we have found the faith, to make no effort to understand what we believe.' To Anselm philosophy was an aid to the self-understanding of faith, but not an invitation to rationalism: 'Before we can profit from discussing the depths of faith, the heart must be purified and the eye illumined by the observance of God's commandments ... where we discard the love of the flesh and live according to the spirit.' Anselm himself gives examples of such considerations on dialectic and theology in a text *Cur Deus Homo?*, on the Incarnation, in the manifesto *Monologium* with the central motto 'I believe so I can understand' (*credo ut intelligam*), and finally in the *Proslogium*, in which he puts forward his famous logico-metaphysical proof of God's existence.[26]

This systematic approach to theological problems gave rise to important innovations in methodology. In the very nature of the case, theology had to build constantly on inherited material – the Bible and the church fathers. For a long time various collections of the fathers' sayings had been used as teaching material. As soon as these collections were arranged on more systematic lines, however, the discrepancies between the fathers' observations on specific questions became clearer. Whenever two or more church fathers expressed themselves differently on a problem, a single pronouncement from one of them could no longer be used as an authority, and it became difficult for systematic theologians to resolve such discrepancies. This gave rise to new genres in theological literature which soon became the precedents for scholarly works within other subjects. The pioneer here was Roscellinus' pupil Abelard (1079–1142), another wandering professor, whose unusual autobiography *The Story of My Sufferings* (*Historia Calamitatum*) describes his fate and his stormy relationship with Heloïse.[27] His main work of theology *Yes and No* (*Sic et Non*) contains 158 theological questions, each of

---

[26] See Eadmer, *The Life of St. Anselm*, ed. and transl. by R. W. Southern, Cambridge, 1963; E. Rosas, *Saint Anselme de Cantorbery*, Paris, 1929. The first quotation is from *Cur Deus Homo?* 1, 2, *Migne PL* 158, 362, the second from the *Proslogium* cap. 1, ibid., 227.

[27] See D. Luscombe, *Peter Abelard*, Cambridge, 1979, and *The School of Peter Abelard*, Cambridge,

which is illuminated by opposing quotations from church fathers and other authorities, without any attempt to mediate between them. With this work, which was otherwise not absolutely new in its form, theology was liberated from the purely edifying character it had previously had, and likewise from a meditative form that had still been the hallmark of Anselm's writings. After a while it became normal to present problems in the form of such *quaestiones*, which could be arranged in great systematic compilations. The best-known example of the period in the latter genre were the four *Four Books of Sentences* (*Libri Quattuor Sententiarum*) of Peter the Lombard (d. 1160), which were read and commented upon by all theologians right up to the Reformation.[28]

Yet dialectical theology would hardly have been so prominent had it not evolved hand in hand with dialectical jurisprudence, which under pressure of outside events was now increasingly affecting canonical law. The various efforts to give the many rules of ecclesiastical law a more transparent and systematic form have already been mentioned. Up to 1100 this work was vigorously stimulated by the rivalry between emperor and pope. Their struggle revealed not only strong social tensions that demanded a solution; it also showed that the juridical legacy of the church was full of contradictory clauses that could not exist side by side if ecclesiastical law should remain a practically applicable guide for the daily life of Christians. This was underlined by Bishop Ivo of Chartres (*c.* 1040–1116), the arbitrator in the French part of the quarrel over investiture, in his collection of decrees arguing for a fundamental *consonantia canonum* (concordance between rules of church law) which could only be effectively demonstrated by applying the methods of dialectic. This development will be treated in closer detail later.

Both the *sic et non* method in theology and the dialectical canon law were based on a fundamental faith in there being only one true answer to each individual question, and in the ability of reason being able to find this answer through a process that begins by pointing out obviously contradictory observations. This was the beginning of

---

1971. Cf. also L. Grane, *Peter Abelard*, Copenhagen, 1974, and for his relations with Heloïse, E. Gilson, *Héloïse et Abélard*, Paris, 2nd edn, 1948.
[28] See A. M. Landgraf, *Einführung in die Geschichte der theologischen Literatur der Frühscholastik*, Regensburg, 1948; L. Höd, Die dialektische Theologie des 12. Jahrhunderts, *Arts libéraux*, pp. 137ff. J. de Ghellinck, *Le mouvement théologique du XIIe siècle*, 2nd edn, Gembloux, 1948. J. N. Espenberger, *Die Philosophie des Petrus Lombardus*, Münster, 1901.

the famous scholastic method, which, as we shall see later, became the preferred intellectual instrument of the early universities. It has not always been noted that intellectual needs besides those of ecclesiastical politics were behind this form of dialectic.

This penetration of dialectical methods into theology did not come about without resistance from conservative theologians, who felt that the new approach was a threat to the Christian faith and its time-honoured tradition. The strongest exponent of this anti-dialectical position was the very ascetic Peter Damian (1007–1072), who as a young man had taught in Ravenna, before he first became a hermit, and then archbishop of Ostia and cardinal at the time when Gregory VII was busy with his ecclesiastical reforms. He was of the pure of heart who want only one thing – salvation of the soul, sweeping everything else aside as useless and harmful. God's omnipotence was incomprehensible to the mortal mind and a thing that puts all scholarship to shame. The first grammarian taught Adam to decline 'God' in the plural and was the devil himself. In his treatise *On the Omnipotence of God* (*De Omnipotentia Divina*) scholarship is made the slave of faith: 'If knowledge of these *artes* is occasionally applied to Holy Scripture, it must not push itself forward with arrogance, but must itself remain in the position of servant – as a maidservant to her lady. If philosophy comes before Scripture, it is mistaken, and by drawing conclusions from outward words it loses sight of the inward truth.'[29] In his book *On Sacred Simplicity* (*De Sancta Simplicitate*) Peter correspondingly notes that 'when God wished to save the world He did not send philosophers or orators but rather simple people and fishermen'.[30] After this it was no wonder that in *On the Ordered Life of Hermits* (*De Ordine Heremitorum*) Peter could publish a sort of approved list for a monastery library, which comprised only the Bible, the martyrology and biblical commentaries of Ambrose, Gregory the Great, Augustine, Jerome, Prosper of Aquitaine, Bede, Remigius of Auxerre, Amalarius, James of Auxerre, and Paschasius Radbertus.

In the following century, this anti-intellectualist approach was followed chiefly by St Bernard of Clairvaux (1091–1153) and his spiritual kinsman Peter the Venerable (*c.* 1092–1155), who was abbot of Cluny. Both fought Abelard's theological methods violently, and

---

[29] Petrus Damiani, *De Omnipotentia Dei*, Migne *PL* 145, 603.
[30] Petrus Damiani, *De Sancta Simplicitate*, Migne *PL* 145, 697. Cf. J. A. Endres, *Petrus Damiani und die weltliche Wissenschaft*, Münster, 1910.

The schools of the middle ages 113

yet with no more personal hostility than in Peter allowing the ageing and hard-pressed Abelard to take his final refuge in Cluny. All these attempts to hold back the innovations within theology were not of much avail, as the abbot of St Geneviève, Etienne de Tournai, had to admit at the end of the twelfth century in his letter to the pope, complaining that 'the students are no longer interested in anything but the new and fashionable things. Teachers – who before all things seek their own fame – are each day composing new summaries of theological works diverting and deceptive to those who listen, as if the writings of the fathers were not enough – they who expounded Holy Scripture.'[31] The torrent could not be stopped, and the new scholastic method was well on the way to penetrating all branches of learning when study was given a new structure by the universities.

After considering this theoretical teaching, we must move on to the more down-to-earth problems that arose in connection with the growing need for technical training, a need which followed in the wake of urban economic growth. Here we have a completely different picture. No schools catered for technology, a range of sciences that were already very much a part of the social structure in this period; this frustrated any fruitful contact with the theoretical sciences. This was a direct result of the emergence of professional unions of craftsmen, which, to a steadily increasing extent, following the example of the merchants' guilds, became the social framework of medieval crafts and technology. Normally a union contained all the workers in a particular craft, masters and apprentices alike. These were led by elected aldermen, and even if the declared aim in the beginning was often a religious one, the social function of the guilds was to see above all that the standards and competitiveness of the craft were kept high. This was done by limiting the intake of members so as to prevent their status from lowering to a proletarian level. Everywhere the guilds strove to ensure that their crafts had the monopoly, through privileges from the town council or royal power, that guaranteed their articles of association. In the end, the freedom to trade freely was only found in a few professions among, for example, itinerant coppersmiths and tinkers.[32]

Of special relevance to the state of education was the fact that the guilds themselves paid attention to training in their crafts. Young

[31] Etienne de Tournai, Epistola 251, *Migne PL* 211, 577.
[32] C. Nyrop, *Danmarks Gilde- og Laugsskraaer fra Middelalderen*, vols. I–II, Copenhagen, 1899–1904, repr. 1977.

people were put into apprenticeship with a master in a period of normally seven years, ending with a test which decided if the applicant should be taken into the guild. By this system access to the guild could be regulated, the standard of work could be kept high, the methods of technology on which the monopoly was based could be kept secret, and finally – thanks to the privileges – unorganised labour could be stamped out.

The guild-society meant that in the whole period, until long after the end of the middle ages, all technical education took place in closed circles and on a purely practical basis. Methods were acquired on the job, and there was no use or wish for textbooks, which would have revealed the secrets of the profession and enabled outsiders to use the same skills. This is why only extremely few texts on technology are known from the whole middle ages; one of the most interesting examples is a sketchbook of the French architect and engineer Villard de Honnecourt (*c.* 1200–1260).[33] If we are looking for information on medieval tools, for example, or the ways in which they were used, we must go to other sources: for example, the numerous scenes of working craftsmen depicted in illuminated prayerbooks and Bible-commentaries, often showing ship's carpenters at work on Noah's ark, or the walls of the Tower of Babel under construction. These pictures are drawn with just the naive anachronism that makes them valuable for the history of medieval craftsmanship.[34]

Above this closed training in practical technologies came theoretical teaching in the schools. This was open and accessible in principle to anyone who had the opportunity to follow it, but it was based on textbooks and other literature prohibiting any form of shop-guild secrecy. The separation of these two kinds of training in the middle ages excluded any fruitful collaboration. The 'cultural divide' often cited in our own day is therefore no recent thing; contrary to the present day, in the middle ages, however, this does not seem to have been regarded as a great tragedy. Certainly people did not know all the special techniques used in craftsmanship, but on the other hand they were not alarmed by them, probably because all could see how immediately vital to society their products were. As long as the

---

[33] *Album de Villard de Honnecourt*, facsimile edn, 1906.
[34] On paintings as sources for the craftsmanship of the middle ages, see G. Binding and N. Nussbaum, *Mittelalterliche Baubetrieb nördlich der Alpen in zeitgenössischen Darstellungen*, Darmstadt, 1978.

masons, smiths, or weavers produced goods that everyone needed, there would be no trouble in allowing skilled workers to keep their secrets undisturbed. In principle a 'cultural divide' can only be alarming when within a closed-off area – as in some branches of modern industry – there is a secret activity whose relevance to society is unknown or directly harmful.

However, the middle ages permitted itself some thoughts as to the basic position of the technical sciences. As a rule this happened in connection with the introductions to scholarship which emerged in schools in the twelfth century and later became a very extensive literary genre. One of the first examples of this is a text *On the Division of Philosophy and Science* (*De Divisione Philosophiae*) by the translator Dominicus Gundissalinus, in which he gives a general view of all human activities in scientific and practical work, and classifies them according to whether they are harmful, vain, or profitable. The practical arts are seen everywhere as related to the theoretical sciences. In the same way, in his grand summary *Didascalion*, Hugo of St Victor (1096–1141) links each theoretical discipline with its practical applications.[35] This can be seen as the result of the schoolmen's understanding that practical subjects have in fact theoretical premises, and it ought to have led to an integrated system of education. Yet no medieval school ever taught a technological subject, something which would also have been strongly opposed by the guilds. Even the gradually petrified system of *artes liberales* would have been broken up in such an attempt. In this way, the divide between technology and science or scholarship was made so secure by the social order that no-one dreamed of bridging it.

Yet one cannot ignore certain reservations. Indeed, Hugo of St Victor reflects a strange duplicity in his work. On one hand he recognises a fundamental coherence between theory and practice, in that the theoretical sciences are seen as coming into being as a consequence of the practical needs of humanity, becoming systematised only later; but on the other hand he seems to have cherished a certain contempt for purely technical matters. By means of an erroneous etymology he describes the mechanical sciences as 'fornicating arts', as if the spirit was infected by intercourse with the material world – a train of thought that clearly continued the

---

[35] On Hugo of St Victor's view of science and technology, see his *Didascalion* II, 2, *Migne PL* 176, 706.

attitude of many ancient philosophers. In opposition to this, Hugo glorifies the *artes liberale* because they free the spirit, just as he refers to the ancient times when they were the privilege of free men as opposed to the despised manual labour of slaves. With this attitude he runs counter to the general medieval view of the situation. For in the twelfth and thirteenth centuries the Neo-Platonist scepticism of the material universe was largely being overcome, thanks to the Christian doctrine of the universe as created and essentially good. This was how, for example, Francis of Assisi expressed it in his so-called hymn to the sun. Added to this was an acknowledgement of physical labour as befitting human dignity, something that the Benedictine life and rule, for example, had vouchsafed for centuries. That Hugo saw it another way can be put down to his tendency to flirt with Greek thought, though he had scant knowledge of the Greek language, and to his admiration of many aspects of the ancient lifestyle. Now and again, however, loose references can be found throughout the middle ages that without destroying the general picture show a certain academic arrogance – as when a rector of the University of Paris in 1494 was still lamenting his students' disorderly life and describing them as 'bad lots, carrying weapons, consorting with "gens mécaniques" [manual workers] with their loose ways'.[36]

In fairness it must be said that even if the technical subjects, in spite of their incapsulation in the guilds, should have wished to have their basis in theoretical science, they would have been hard-pressed to find it. The schools had unilaterally cultivated the humanist disciplines within the trivium, but the exact sciences within the quadrivium were at a standstill through a lack of sources. To recreate Greek mathematics and science from the basic works was obviously out of the question, since even the knowledge of how to do research had passed into oblivion. The sketchy contact with the Byzantine world – with Greek monks, for example, who had sought refuge in Italian monasteries from iconoclasm and intolerance at home – was hardly an adequate remedy. That the study of the exact sciences did not end in a blind alley, was due to a completely different stream of culture now spilling out of Arab civilisation into the Latin world.

In the first century after the Arabs began to expand their territories, Islam was focussed in the caliphate of the Umajjads in

---

[36] The rector's complaint of 1494 is quoted after M.-D. Chenu, Arts 'mécaniques' et oeuvres serviles, *Revue des sciences philosophiques et théologiques* 29 (1940), 314.

Damascus. We do not hear much of independent Arab science in this period, the efforts being spent on the military and political consolidation of the lands they had conquered. Only when the Abbassid caliphs of Persia (750–1258) took over and founded Baghdad as their new capital in 762, did the great age of Islamic culture begin.[37] Under the seventh caliph, Al-Mahmun (809–833), a 'House of Wisdom' was built in Baghdad that became the foremost academy of the Arab world until the Mongols destroyed it in 1258. It was equipped with a large library which among other treasures contained numerous Greek manuscripts found locally or obtained by purchase in Byzantium, to which town a legation was sent for this purpose.

Similar institutions with libraries, schools, and observatories were later built in Cairo, in 1005, and in the Spanish Cordoba. Islam now had three centres of learning of a size and quality the world had seen nothing to match since the heyday of the school in Alexandria. Many schools were founded in smaller towns, such as Seville, Marrakesh, Jerusalem, and many other places, and Greek, Syrian, Egyptian, and Mesopotamian scholars could be found in Baghdad, Merv, and Basra alongside scholars from Persia, India, and Afghanistan. Many scholars of widely differing race and religion worked together here to create an 'Arab' culture, which would have made the modest learning of the Romans seem pale and impoverished if a direct comparison had been possible.

However, the term 'Arab culture' should be taken with some modification, since the contribution the Arabs made was modest. This was confined by and large to the Mohammedan religion and to the Arabic language, normalised by the Koran, which now, almost as Latin previously in Europe, came to function as a link between different elements in the population. The big names in Arab philosophy and science are proof that what unity there was in the Mohammedan world was chiefly a linguistic one. The first Islamic philosopher was Al-Kindi (*c.* 800–*c.* 873), who came from Basra, but worked in Baghdad. Here Al-Farabi (*c.* 870–950) also worked, a

---

[37] On Islamic learning, see D. L. O'Leary, *How Greek Science Passed to the Arabs*, London, 1947; A. Mieli, *La science arabe et son rôle dans l'évolution scientifique mondiale*, Leiden, 1939 (repr. 1966), B. Carra de Vaux, *Les penseurs d'Islam* i–v, Paris, 1921–5 (in particular vol. ii); F. Sezgin, *Geschichte des arabischen Schrifttums*, in particular vols. v and vi, Leiden, 1975, 1978. On faith and philosophy in Islam, see L. Gardet and M. M. Anawati, *Introduction à la philosophie musulmane*, Paris, 1948.

native of Turkestan, while the most universal thinker and man of science in Islam, Ibn Sina or 'Avicenna' (980–1037), came from Bukhara. On the other hand, the best-known Arab philosopher in Europe and commentator on Aristotle, Ibn Roshd (1126–1198), worked in Cordoba and was soon known in the west as Averroës.

The scholarly basis for Arab culture was the Greek learning of antiquity, which still lived on, though not creatively, in the schools of the conquered territories. Even before Islam, a number of Greek texts had been translated into Syrian, which is a Semitic language like Arabic; but after the Baghdad academy was founded, the amount of translating increased until in the course of a few centuries practically all main extant works of Greek scholarship had their Arabic versions. A good many of the ancient texts are only known today because of these translations. This is true, for example, of works as important as Ptolemy's *Optics* and parts of Apollonius' *Doctrine of Conic Sections*. Yet it would be wrong to think that the Arabs confined themselves to a slavish appropriation of Greek results. In practical and in theoretical matters Islam faced problems that gave rise to the development of an independent philosophy and science.

One occasion for philosophical and theological disputes lay in the fact that Islam, just as the Old Testament, put its faith in one everlasting and almighty God, Who made all things. So, too, Mohammedan thinkers were faced with the problem of how this faith could be united with the Greek view of the universe. In this dispute both Neo-Platonist and Aristotelian tendencies can be discerned side by side with more narrow attitudes for which dogma and the Koran needed no philosophical support. The problem of faith versus philosophy thus became an important incentive for Mohammedan thought, just as was the case later within Christianity.

An example of how purely practical tasks promoted scientific knowledge is given in the new problems in astronomy that Islam faced. One of these was the question of how to determine the *qibla*, or the direction to Mecca from any given place in a far-flung region.[38] Another problem was the need to navigate safely in the Indian Ocean, something that demanded astronomical methods that had not been necessary in the voyages of former times in the Mediterranean or along the coasts of Europe. Both questions

---

[38] The quibla-problem can be studied in Al-Biruni, *The Determination of the Coordinates of Cities*, transl. J. Ali, Beirut, 1966.

necessitated further advances in spherical astronomy and spherical trigonometry; and in all essentials, the development of trigonometry is the work of Arab mathematicians.

The whole of this cultural flowering took place inside Islam with scarcely any contact with Europeans, who by and large were ignorant of what was happening there. The exchange of embassies between Charlemagne and Harun Al-Rashid was a solitary event with no lasting consequences. It is also wrong to think that the first contacts were made in the Crusades, as the view used to be. Firstly, it can hardly be imagined that European warriors in the east possessed the necessary inclination to learn philosophy or mathematics from the Arab scholars they might have come across in Antioch or Jerusalem. In addition, the first evidence of translations from Arabic to Latin circulating in Europe comes long before the Crusades. There is no doubt that this movement started in Spain, where Muslims and Christians had learnt to live together in peace, and where even in the tenth century a lively cultural exchange was going on within the monastery of St Maria de Ripoll in northern Spain and other places. Gerbert stayed down there for purposes of study, as we have seen, one of the things that he brought back to France being the knowledge of the astrolabe. A little later Herman the Lame (Hermannus Contractus) from Reichenau (1013–1054), translated two small treatises on this fascinating instrument from Arabic to Latin and retained many Arabic names for stars and technical expressions which he had not been able to explain. Arabic numerals too (which originally came from India) slowly began to emerge, though they only became common in the thirteenth century.[39]

Around Europe there were now schools that operated as assimilation centres for Arab science mediated by Latin teachers, who in increasingly large numbers undertook long or brief journeys to study south of the Pyrenees. This was a small-scale movement in the eleventh century, but numbers increased drastically in the period following. Famous in this respect was Adelard of Bath (d. 1145), who translated into Latin in about 1126 the *Liber Alchorismi* of the Arab

---

[39] On the translation of scientific works, see G. Sarton, *Introduction to the History of Science*, vol. II, Baltimore, 1931, p. 167. See also A. van de Vyver, Les plus anciennes traductions latines médiévales de traités d'astronomie et d'astrologie, *Osiris* 1 (1936), 658–91. A. C. Crombie, *Augustine to Galileo*, London, 1962, contains on pp. 23–40 a useful handlist of the more important translations of works on the quadrivium and medicine. See also J. T. Muckle, Greek Works Translated Directly into Latin before 1350, *Medieval Studies* 4 (1942), 33–42 and 102–14.

mathematician Al-Khwarizmi (d. c. 850) and his astronomical tables, while giving a summary of his new knowledge in his own *Quaestiones Naturales*. Other smaller texts, too, on the abacus and the astrolabe are owed to him; and yet all these things are obscured by the fact that Adelard translated all fifteen books of Euclid's *Elements* from Arabic to Latin and thereby eventually made the main works of Greek mathematics available in Europe.

A central figure in this work was the Italian Gerard of Cremona (1114–1187), who settled in Toledo as a professional translator.[40] Toledo was taken back from the Moors in 1085 by King Alfonso VI of Castille, becoming in the next couple of centuries the most considerable meeting place for Arab, Jewish, and Christian scholars. There was a lively group of translators working in Sicily, too, where there were many Arabs in the population, just as the island had good trading links with the east and many Greek-speaking inhabitants. The latter circumstance was why Greek learning was being increasingly drawn straight from the original sources. This was important not least because the translations from Arabic were often checkered with interpolations or inaccuracies, which for a large part had their origin in opinions peculiar to Arab thought, for example, about astrology. Scholars became more critical after a while, in the way that for instance in about 1269 Thomas Aquinas encouraged a Dutch Dominican, William of Moerbeke (c. 1215–c. 1286), to make exceptionally good translations directly from Greek of authors as important as Aristotle and Archimedes.

Without belittling the importance of the philosophical texts that, thanks to these translations, were now accessible again – and this is true first and foremost of all Aristotle's works – it has to be said that the great twelfth-century wave of translations was beneficial most of all to the undernourished quadrivium. If, for example, we consider the three most productive translators, Adelard of Bath, Gerard of Cremona, and Dominicus Gundissalinus, it appears that together they accounted for about 116 translations, of which no less than 84 were texts pertaining to the quadrivium or medicine and natural history. How strong this interest was in mathematical and scientific fields appears also in the fact that various texts were translated several times, usually in steadily improved versions. This was the

---

[40] See K. Sudhoff, Die kurze Vita und das Verzeichnis der Arbeiten Gerards von Cremona, *Archiv für Geschichte der Medizin* 8 (1914), 73–82.

case with Ptolemy's *Almagest*, first translated straight from Greek in about 1160 in Sicily. Thereafter it was translated by Gerard of Cremona from Arabic in about 1175, and fragments are even known of two more translations from before 1300.[41]

All this meant that, even before 1200, the schools had at their disposal the most essential works of Greek science along with a number of translations from textbooks of the Arabs themselves, which were often easier to get hold of. Considering that this new material was acquired by teachers and students whose background was still Boethius and the *De Rerum Natura* literature, it is easier to understand that part of the reason why the universities originated was the great intellectual difficulties that twelfth-century scholars met with in their attempts to assimilate the huge amount of newly available knowledge.

However brief and incomplete this sketch of events, it should still give a motley picture of a society in which strong powers were causing big changes in many different areas. A certain political stability had arrived. The influence of the church had grown, and with the Crusades and the partial reconquest of Spain and the Mediterranean, aggressive tendencies had been somewhat diverted from Europe. New methods of farming had increased food production and had formed the basis for economic progress and population growth, strengthening the position of the towns as increasingly independent enclaves in the existing system of property. The idea of corporations had once more shown its practical use for population groups with a common interest. The need for education had grown sharply, and after the monasteries failed in this respect, the cathedral schools sought to meet the demand, with some success in the sphere of humanist theology. The spread of monastic ideology had led to a new religious intensity in many circles, its own norms at the same time being established as ideals for all Christians. Last but not least, by an odd roundabout way, peaceful cultural exchange between Christendom and Islam had reopened the road to ancient learning. In the next chapter we shall see how nearly all these factors played a role in creating the conditions in teaching that led to the lasting contribution of the middle ages to education in Europe.

---

[41] On translations of the *Almagest*, see C. H. Haskins, *Studies in the History of Mediaeval Science*, Cambridge, Mass., 1924, pp. 157ff.

CHAPTER 5

From school to studium generale

The strong economic and political changes in medieval society following the first millennium were accompanied by a rapid transformation within higher education.[1] To a great extent this development can be attributed to the steadily increasing contact with 'Arab' culture, mediated by the hard industry of translators. Through these efforts Latin Europe came into possession of a scholarly literature of great extent for the first time since antiquity. Some of this literature was of high quality and comprised crucial parts of the best literary legacy of Greek scholarship, along with the works of many great thinkers and men of learning who had worked within Islam. In reality this was a true explosion of information that would clearly mean an enormous intellectual challenge for twelfth-century teaching and science. Later ages have often cherished an image of medieval polymaths, people capable of cultivating all subjects with equal competence. But this view is exaggerated. There is no doubt that after these translations appeared, the collected literature became too copious for any single teacher to cope with. An Alcuin or a Gerbert was no longer thinkable, and in no previous time had the situation seemed so hard to grasp for a teacher who wished to be universally oriented. In this context it can be understood that the schools of the twelfth century reacted to this challenge in the most logical way, namely by specialising. Everywhere we can spot a tendency to divide the work up by subject. This had the most far-reaching consequences for the whole system of education.

Let us begin with the developments in Salerno in southern Italy, where an important centre for medical training and the healing arts grew up.[2] In Italy, during the whole medieval period, the situation in

---

[1] The main sources for this chapter are Denifle; *Chartularium*; Rashdall. See also D'Irsay; Cobban; and H. de Ridder-Symoens (ed.), *Universities in the Middle Ages*, Cambridge, 1992.
[2] On the Salerno school, see the introduction to B. Lawn, *The Salernitan Questions*, Oxford,

teaching was somewhat different to that north of the Alps. The cultural collapse had been a trifle less complete, the dark ages a little lighter, than elsewhere. In a good number of Italian cities there were schools that were able to trace their existence back to antiquity; as noted above, Charlemagne was able to fetch his first teachers from Italy. As regards Salerno, in particular, a doctor from this city is mentioned as early as 848, and a hundred years later there is one more at the court of Louis IV in France. Of the latter it is said that 'even if he was not in possession of any book-learning, yet he had great practical experience through his natural ingenuity'.[3] Everything points to these doctors from Salerno being pure practicians, and as such widely sought as personal physicians for people of standing all over Europe.

The origin of the Salerno medical school is lost in obscurity. Perhaps it was directly linked to the tradition of antiquity, but neither can a connection with Monte Cassino be ruled out. This monastery had been destroyed by the Arabs in 884, but was rebuilt in 949, after which it showed an unusually high level of activity in the copying of medical manuscripts in the monastery scriptorium. Yet even if Salerno was dependent for its literature on Monte Cassino, it was no monastery itself but an independent school numbering clergy and laity among its students. We know otherwise very little about the way it was organised in this first period. The real flowering of the school first began with the Benedictine Alfanus, who was archbishop of Salerno from 1058 to 1085 and left a number of medical writings behind, of which *De Quatuor Humoribus* and *De Pulsibus* survive. These are directly based on the Hippocratic tradition of medicine and presume a knowledge of Greek, which had not completely died out in this region at the time when, in about 1100, Adelard of Bath visited Salerno. At this time the town was already known far and wide as *Civitas Hippocratica*.

The further development of the Salerno school was due mostly to Constantine Africanus (*c.* 1027–1087), the convert and pupil of Alfanus.[4] Constantine carried out a long series of translations from Greek of the works of the greatest physician of antiquity, Galen of Pergamum, along with many medical works of Byzantine and Arab

---

1963, and T. Meyer-Steineg and K. Sudhoff, *Illustrierte Geschichte der Medizin*, 5th edn, Stuttgart, 1965, pp. 121–39.
[3] The quotation is taken from Rashdall, vol. I, p. 76, note 1.
[4] On Constantinus Africanus, see P. O. Kristeller, The School of Salerno, *Bulletin of the History of Medicine* 17 (1954), 138–94.

authors. Thus the medicine of the middle ages began to receive the effects of the translations, and soon also a good number of original textbooks and teaching manuals saw the light of day. The so-called *Antidotarium Nicolai* was widely circulated, as was a pharmacopoeia or collection of recipes written by Nicholas of Salerno before 1100, a surgery textbook by Roger Fugardi (*c.* 1170), and the somewhat later, versified *Regimen Sanitatis* on diet and pharmacology.

In the twelfth century the need for doctors grew, owing to the upsurge of the towns which made local hospitals necessary as bodies independent of the infirmaries of the Benedictine monasteries in the countryside. Many famous town hospitals existing today can be traced back to this period. This is true of St Bartholomew's in London, built in 1133 by Canon Rahere at St Paul's,[5] and also of Hôtel-Dieu in Paris, founded in 1157. These foundations were inspired by new religious orders based in the towns, whose speciality was nursing the sick. Most notable among them were the Order of St John of Jerusalem, and the Brothers of the Holy Ghost who even before 1200 had no less than eighty-four hospitals spread all over Europe. The shift of hospitals from country to town was encouraged by the church, which even in 1139 forbade the monks to leave their monasteries to study secular medicine and law – *ad physicam legesve mondanas legendas*[6] – and which looked with growing scepticism through the century on the blurring of the priest's profession with the doctor's. The result was that – like that of the lawyers – the class of physicians gradually grew secular with an education of a level high enough to support a layman and his family.

This new need for doctors could obviously not be met from Salerno alone, and already at the beginning of the twelfth century this town had a serious rival in Montpellier. The origin of this school, too, is lost in obscurity, but it is no coincidence that it grew up in an area of typically mixed culture. In the nearby towns of Arles and Narbonne there were Jewish schools of medicine; there was still a Greek population to be found in Marseilles in the eleventh century; and finally Islam was not far away. There is evidence for this school in 1137. At about the same time St Bernard of Clairvaux

---

[5] On Rahere, see N. Moore, *The History of St. Bartholomew's Hospital*, vol. 1, London, 1918.
[6] On the secularisation of medicine, see P. Delauny, *La médecine et l'église*, Paris, 1948. The prohibition *Ad physicam legesve* was contained in Canon 9 of the second Lateran Council (1139) and confirmed by Pope Alexander III at the Council of Tours (1163) after which it became Canon law, see the *Decretales* III, 50, 3.

describes Montpellier as the place to which the archbishop of Lyon betook himself to seek a cure, and 'where he spent all that he owned and even more on the doctors'.[7] That the school may only have had a quite loose structure, or perhaps none at all, can be seen in the count of Montpellier in 1180 allowing anyone to teach medicine in the town who so wished. What helped Montpellier to grow at the expense of Salerno was possibly a better medical curriculum.[8] Thus it made use of Gerard of Cremona's translation of the great *Canon Medicinae* of the Arab physician and philosopher Ibn Sina (the Avicenna of the Latins), who lived from 980 to 1037.[9] In the four centuries that followed, this treatise was to be the main work of reference in medieval medicine. In his five books Avicenna gave a clear picture of general medicine, pharmacology, pathology, nutrition, and hygiene, all based on a synthesis of Hippocratic and Galenic observations and on Aristotle's ideas on biology. With its clear clinical descriptions and precise therapeutic notes, the *Canon* gave the art of healing in the middle ages a solid foundation – more solid perhaps than the theories on which it was based. Its importance in the story of medieval teaching can hardly be overrated, and to this day it is read with respect as the most superior work in this area that the past has ever produced.

What Salerno was for medicine, Bologna became for law. There had already been schools further north in Lombardy, where the Carolingian Renaissance had also left its mark. Thus the Emperor Lothar in 825 founded schools in eight of the most important towns in the province,[10] and a year later Pope Eugenius II (824–827) followed the emperor's initiative with a decree that teachers in *artes liberales* should be appointed in all the larger churches. In the tenth century Archbishop Atto of Vercelli, influenced by the Cluniac reforms, sought to make the parish clergy hold schools also in the villages. In the next century there is a report of the young Lanfranc, later archbishop of Canterbury, studying in Pavia where he was born, in the schools of *artes liberales* and secular jurisprudence, in accordance with the custom of his country.[11] From this it can

---

[7] Bernard of Clervaux, Epist. 307, *Migne PL* 132, 512.
[8] On Montpellier, see Rashdall, vol. II, pp. 16ff, and on the privilege of 1180, see ibid. p. 122.
[9] See O. C. Gruner, *A Treatise on the Canon of Medicine of Avicenna*, London, 1930.
[10] On the schools founded by Emperor Lothar, see Rashdall, vol. I, p. 90, note 3.
[11] See *Vita Lanfranci*, *Migne PL* 150, 39ff; cf. A. F. Macdonald, *Lanfranc. A study of his life, work and writing*, 2nd edn, 1944.

certainly be inferred that Lombard law was taught in Pavia. This legal tradition clashed in Bologna with Roman law, that had been honoured by the rhetors and advocates since ancient times. This meeting of two differing legal systems is part of the reason for Bologna's central place in law; but it is also due to the disputes between emperor and pope in this period for supremacy in Europe; the ideological part of this struggle was provided with a superstructure of legal arguments, and therefore made demands on the work and interest of legal scholars.

In Bologna a distinction should be made between two schools with different teaching matter and organisation.[12] One was the juridical school of civil Roman law, based on the *Corpus Juris Civilis*. Its teachers were simply the advocates of the town who took young people into their homes and for a payment instructed them in law and the special juristic form of rhetoric. In accordance with old Roman usage, law was viewed as a part of rhetoric, and could be formally incorporated into *artes liberales*, contrary to medicine. There is much to show that these jurists already had a loosely developed organisation in the early twelfth century, perhaps without detailed statutes. No sources concerning this teaching have been preserved, but it is unthinkable that such teachers in unison would have failed to protect the interests of their class and keep strangers out of a lucrative profession by means of one kind or another of guild or corporation. In any case they would have fulfilled the most important condition of Roman law to be able to form such a corporation, in having citizenship in the town and knowing a profession.

In the first half of the eleventh century the school in Bologna flowered, due to the scholarly work the jurists carried out in order to become more confident in the classical sources of Roman law.[13] The rediscovered Justinian *Corpus Juris Civilis* – in a manuscript of the seventh century that came to Bologna in about 1080 – was analysed systematically and minutely with the result that classical Roman law came to play a much greater role in both legal teaching as such and in the progress of medieval law and politics. The pioneering work

---

[12] On the study in Bologna, see Rashdall, vol. 1, pp. 87–268; and Sorbelli.
[13] The principal work on Roman law is still F. K. Savigny, *Geschichte des römischen Rechts im Mittelalter*, I–VI, Heidelberg, 1815–31; see also the various articles on law in *Dictionary of the Middle Ages*, vol. VII, New York, 1986, pp. 394–528. Denifle, p. 204, contested the existence of an original teachers' corporation in Bologna, but Rashdall gave weighty reasons for accepting at least some form of union of colleagues.

was carried out by the jurist Irnerius (*c.* 1075–1130), who was presumably of Germanic descent and closely linked to the Emperor Henry V. His literary legacy was a collection of commentaries or *glossae*, continued by his pupils, the famous 'four doctors of law' Bulgarus (d. 1166), Martinus (d. 1157), Jacob da Porta Ravennate (d. 1178), and Hugo de Alberico (d. 1168), who together became known as the glossators.[14] Among the many later compilations of this kind, the *Glossa Ordinaria sive Magistralis* of Accursius (*c.* 1185–1263) was widely used. An important consequence of this activity was that theoretical law was eventually separated from rhetoric as a science in its own right – and as an arsenal from which princes and kings could draw weapons for their political ventures, using civil law to legitimate any privileges that had been due to the Roman emperor of the past.

Just as significant were the changes in ecclesiastical law taking place at the same time in Bologna. Whereas the sources of Roman law lay collected in the completed *Corpus* of Justinian's time, synods and popes added ever more material to canonical law with council decrees (*canones*) and papal letters (*decretales*) on questions of the day pertaining to moral life or ecclesiastical discipline. It has always been so; but as time went on, this material became increasingly unwieldy, a new codification ever more pressing. As mentioned earlier, shortly after 1100 Ivo of Chartres, Algers of Liège, and other canonists in France had finished their own compilations. However, these lost their importance when, in about 1140, a Camuldulensian monk in Bologna by the name of Gratian produced a collection of ecclesiastical law that later became known as the *Decreta*.[15] The real title was *Concordia Discordantium Canonum*, or *Harmony between Discordant Rules of Law*. Problems were systematically presented and illuminated by the often contradictory pronouncements of the sources, so as to be solved in a way that was at once critical and sought to give every authority its due. Thus the *Decreta* also became an important contribution to the development of the scholastic method.

Gratian's work was a conscious attempt to give ecclesiastical or canonical law the same systematic construction as Roman law had had for a long time in the *Corpus Juris Civilis*, which was the direct

---

[14] On Irnerius and the four doctors, see Savigny, *Geschichte*, vol. IV, pp. 9–101, and Rashdall, vol. I, pp. 89–125.
[15] Gratian's *Decreta* are printed in *Migne PL*, 187ff; on the codification of ecclesiastical law, see Rashdall, vol. I, pp. 126–41, and D. D. Hazeltine, Roman and Canon Law in the Middle Ages, in the *Cambridge Medieval History*, vol. V, pp. 697–764.

model of the *Decreta*. Thereby many of the methods and principles of Roman law came into Canon law, which thus emphasised its universality and general validity throughout Christendom in the same way as Roman law had been valid in the empire. This state of affairs, in connection with the existence of the papal state and the political activity of the popes, was one of the main reasons why the church increasingly came to resemble a kingdom of this world, with the pope in the role of emperor as universal lawgiver.

Gratian's codification of Canon law was just the beginning. Ecclesiastical law was a 'living law' in constant change, not least in the hundred years following the publication of the *Decreta*, in which there were no less than four ecumenical councils and a long list of very active popes. One of these was Gratian's pupil and successor as teacher in Bologna, Roland Bandinelli, who later became Pope Alexander III (1159–1181) and started a new wave of ecclesiastical legislation, partly as a result of his lifelong battle with Emperor Frederic Barbarossa and the attempts to split the German church away from Rome.[16] As Justinian had supplemented his *Codex* with his own *Novellae*, the lawyers of the church therefore had to compile supplements to the *Decreta*. In about 1190 these were collated by Bernard of Pavia in the so-called *Breviarum Extravagantium* or *Extravagantes*, which were in turn succeeded by several *Compilationes Antiquae*. The result was a new unwieldiness that was to make work for canonists in the century to come. The school of Canon law in Bologna came directly under the bishop's authority and had no structural link with the school of civil law, with which it often had a tense relationship. Its teachers were all clergy and the students were in any case tonsured clerks, even if not necessarily members of the higher degrees of the hierarchy.

North of the Alps the tendency to specialise was strongly marked in the cathedral school in Chartres, which had been founded at the turn of the millennium by Gerbert's Roman pupil Fulbert, later bishop of Chartres from 1007 to 1028. The school can thus be seen as the direct product of Gerbert's teachings.[17] This school flowered in the twelfth century and was known over the whole of Europe as a centre for the study of *artes liberales*. The interest in the trivium has

---

[16] See G. Le Bras, *Le droit romain au service de la domination pontificale*, Paris, 1949; cf. M. W. Baldwin, *Alexander III and the Twelfth Century*, 1968.

[17] See A. Clerval, *Les écoles de Chartres au moyen âge*, Paris, 1895; J. M. Parent, *La doctrine de la création dans l'école de Chartres*, Paris–Ottawa, 1938.

already been mentioned. It led to the upsurge of the new humanism of this period and had a characteristic spokesman in John of Salisbury, bishop of Chartres.[18] The base of the school was in any case broad enough to take in the quadrivium also, so that twelfth-century Chartres became the home to a series of thinkers more interested in problems of natural philosophy than was the case in cathedral schools elsewhere.

Of this group the first *magister scholarum* was Bernard of Chartres (*c*. 1080–1124/30), who worked as the school's chancellor from 1119. He was succeeded in this office by Gilbertus Porretanus or Gilbert de la Porrée (1076–1154), who moved to Paris in 1141 or 1142 and ended his days as bishop of Poitiers. He was followed by his pupil, Bernard's younger brother Thierry (*c*. 1090–*c*. 1154), and finally the philosophers Guillaume de Conches (1080–1145) and Bernard Silvestris of Tours (*c*. 1100–1160) also belonged to this circle, along with other lesser-known authors of surviving works on natural philosophy. Common to them all was an attempt to put the quadrivium into a larger human context, as sciences that would liberate the soul from the darkness of ignorance and thereby wipe out one of the consequences of the Fall. The liberal arts here were not only the handmaidens of theology, but had an independent role to play in the work of salvation. This gave the philosophers of Chartres the frankness to study the natural sciences and the subjects connected with them without ulterior theological motives. Even if their assumptions were still influenced by the *Timaeus* and Platonism in general – the great wave of translations had not yet really hit Chartres – we can still see in their works a good number of ideas that were alien to their time. Gilbert de la Porrée, with his *Book on the Six Principles* (*Liber Sex Principiorum*) became the most important logician of his century, and he was more Aristotelian than his colleagues. By accepting the atomic theory, Guillaume de Conches went against the current idea of matter as built up out of the four elements (fire, air, water, and earth) and otherwise showed a striking independence from the church fathers; he did not escape being accused of heresy by Guillaume de St Thierry (*c*. 1085–1148) in a letter to Bernard of Clervaux. In Thierry de Chartres we can observe the effects of the

---

[18] John of Salisbury's works are in *Migne PL* 209. There are interesting autobiographical passages in his *Policraticus*, transl. J. Dickinson, New York, 1927, as well as in his *Metalogicon*, trans. D. D. McGarry, Berkeley–Los Angeles, 1955. See also B. P. Hendley, John of Salisbury's defense of the trivium, in *Arts libéraux*, pp. 753–62.

first translations from Arabic works on mathematics, astronomy and medicine.

One final example of specialisation was in Paris, where there were no less than four schools going back to earlier times. Firstly, and certainly since the Carolingian age, there existed a *schola interior* in connection with the Benedictine monastery of St Germain des Prés. As a purely monastic institution this school was not a public one, and it had no teachers of note in the period with which we are concerned. Its influence abroad was thus minimal.[19]

Secondly, there was a cathedral school linked to the church of Notre Dame which advanced to the first rank of the public schools of Europe in the twelfth century, mostly because of Guillaume de Champeaux, its first important master. Abelard was one of his pupils and later a teacher at the school himself from 1113 to 1119. Here, furthermore, worked Peter the Lombard, 'Master of Sentences', in the middle of the century; and after him, a long line of his pupils such as Odo of Paris (chancellor 1164–1168), Peter Comestor (d. 1178), Peter of Poitiers (c. 1130–1206), Peter Cantor (d. 1197), and later the Cardinal Stephen Langton (d. 1228). Together these men inaugurated the long line of medieval commentators on the *sententiae*. In this way it can be said that the new systematic dialectic theology of the twelfth century had its best resort in the cathedral school whose chancellors were in charge of the teaching.

Thirdly, there was a public school linked (unusually so) with the monastery of St Geneviève. This school started with secular teachers and (just as the cathedral schools) occasionally admitted lay students. It flourished in the first half of the century, large because Abelard taught there for a short time. In 1147 St Geneviève shared the fate of many other schools, when the secular teachers were driven out in favour of regular Augustinian canons. After this it increasingly appeared as a bastion of conservative theology in a relationship of extreme tension with the cathedral school, not least under Abbot Etienne de Tournai, who held office from 1176 to 1192.

Last but not least there was the school at St Victor, a community of regular canons, which had been established in 1108 by Guillaume de Champeaux at about the time he abandoned the 'world', that is to say the cathedral school. St Victor received external students and

---

[19] On the schools of Paris, see Denifle, pp. 655–82, and the material in A. Tuilier, *La vie universitaire parisienne au XIII' siècle*, Paris, 1974, pp. 25–34.

was originally intended to counterbalance the often mentioned 'disorderly conduct' of students in the 'secular' schools and the new scholastic theology. However, it was St Victor which eventually reduced the tensions between the progressive and conservative theologies to some degree, mainly through Hugo of St Victor (1096–1141) from Blankenberg in Germany, a very important thinker, who wrote not only the *Didascalion* (as mentioned earlier) but also the first systematic textbook of dogmatics, *De Sacramentis Fidei Christianae*. His successor was the Scottish mystic Richard of St Victor (d. 1173), who applied dialectic methods in a text *On the Trinity* to mysticism itself, and thereby contributed ultimately to the easing of the tension.

All this meant that twelfth-century Paris became the most important theological centre of its time, with a permanent milieu of teachers of high quality. Specialisation had thereby become acceptable also in theology. Yet despite the dominant position theology had in Paris, it should not be forgotten that there was also a thriving instruction in *artes liberales* taught by secular teachers living in the quarter around Petit-Pont. At the beginning of the century Adam Parvipontius worked here; he was the teacher of John of Salisbury and at the end of his life bishop of Wales. Towards the end of the century these small schools spread south of the Seine into the Rue Garlande and Rue de Fouarre, which lay on the land of St Geneviève and therefore outside the jurisdiction of the chancellors. Canon law and medicine were also taught in twelfth-century Paris, but without filling any prominent place in the scholastic life of the city.

In spite of having different specialisations, the big schools of Salerno, Bologna, Montpellier, Chartres, and Paris had one feature in common – they were all built in towns. The explosion of knowledge cited earlier seems to have removed the rural monastic schools from the field. The general unwillingness, especially of the Cistercians, to become involved in worldly affairs was the reason why no medieval university ever grew up in the country. It is also illuminating to see how the success of the schools was determined by the general development of twelfth-century urban societies. Only in towns were there the right conditions for a large student population, with rooms to let out, places to eat, and the like, and only towns could give conditions for a richer scholarly milieu than the previous schools had been able to achieve. The mere existence of no less than four theological schools in Paris, each with its own staff of teachers, meant in itself that more theologians were gathered within these town walls than anywhere else. This was why conflicts could develop between different views – in Paris between the new and old theologies – and the debate could proceed in a far more lively way. It goes without saying that the Paris schools would act as a magnet to the solitary theologian of a provincial school who was normally excluded from the possibility of fruitful exchanges with colleagues in the same subject.

In this context, the Paris schools grew steadily throughout the twelfth century. Before long teachers and students were streaming there from all corners of Europe, drawn by the prospect of sitting at the feet of a famous teacher. The Canon Fulques de Deuil illustrates this movement in graphic terms in a letter to Abelard:

> Rome sent thee her sons for educating: even if Rome herself was formerly accustomed to give her students insight into all sciences, now she has sent all her pupils to thee and has thereby admitted in the light of day that thy wisdom was greater than hers. No wild landscapes, no steep crags nor valley gorges, no road filled with dangers or harassed by bandits was enough to keep them from hastening to thee. Throngs of young Englishmen would not be frightened by the ocean blocking them with its storms and waves. With contempt for all these dangers they have streamed to thee as soon as hearing thy name spoken. Far Brittany has sent thee her coarse-grained young fellows to be polished. The people of Anjou have conquered their wildness and have served thee through their sons. The inhabitants of Poitou, the Basques and Iberians, Normans and Flemings, Germans and Swabians have constantly desired to extol the fiery power of thy spirit – not to speak of the townsfolk of Paris and of the Gallic lands lying near or far, who have thirsted so strongly for your teaching as though every form of wisdom were to be found with thee.[20]

Never mind that such a letter was written to flatter or console – it still gives contemporary proof of Abelard's unique position as well as the general tendency of students throughout Europe.

In this period it is otherwise worth noting that Denmark and Norway were also drawn into the general current down to the great centres of learning in the south. Previously Archbishop Eskil had maintained links mainly with Clairvaux, whereas Absalon (1128–1201) had studied in Paris, possibly the very first Dane ever to do so. When he replaced Eskil as archbishop of Lund in 1178, there was a change of policy, and promising young clerks were directed to Paris for their education. Thus we see the brothers Peder Sunesøn (c. 1161–1214)

---

[20] Fulques de Deuil, Epistola ad Abaelardum, *Migne PL* 178, 371f.

and Anders Sunesøn (c. 1167–1228 moving to St Geneviève, where, also, a Danish prince named Valdemar was a canon till his death in about 1184. Anders Sunesøn supplemented his stay in Paris with a study of law in Bologna, later went to Oxford and finally back to Paris, but now as a teacher, before returning to Denmark to replace Absalon as archbishop of Lund in 1201. By virtue of this training Anders Sunesøon emerges as the first Dane to undergo European teaching, as clearly reflected in his own – though not especially epoch-making – didactic poem, the *Hexaëmeron*.[21] It is also at this time that we meet Saxo Grammaticus (c. 1150–c. 1216), the most important Danish historian of the middle ages. We do not know where he studied, but his *Gesta Danorum* (ending in 1185) is evidence of the author's deep familiarity with the whole tradition of European scholarship.[22]

What has been said above of Paris is by and large true also of Bologna and Montpellier, and to some extent, of Chartres. At these places the teaching staff become more and more international, and students flocked there from every country in Europe. Thus these schools acquired an international status and prestige that the others could not rival; soon they also got their special designation as *studium generale*, a term which was beginning to get a foothold. It was already in use in the twelfth century and became commonplace in the thirteenth. Its precise meaning cannot be wholly determined, as it was only gradually that it won right of place in academic usage. The main word is *generale*, which indicates chiefly that such a school took students from all over Europe. It also seems to have presupposed that the school taught not only the introductory *artes liberales* but also one of the three advanced subjects, medicine, law, or theology. Finally, it was part of the nature of such study that the teaching was taken care of by a staff of several teachers.

It should be noted that the twelfth-century schools of Paris, Bologna, and Salerno won their renown as *studia generalia* by the merit of their own teaching efforts, not as any result of prompting or support from the social authorities or the church. It was the learned world itself that by its own efforts lifted the schools above the earlier

---

[21] *Andreae Sunonis Filii Hexaëmeron*, ed. S. Ebbesen and L. B. Mortensen, in *Corpus Philosophorum Danicorum Medii Aevi*, vol. XI, pp. 1–2, Copenhagen, 1985–8.
[22] The intellectual background of Saxo is described in I. Boserup (ed.), *Saxostudier*, Copenhagen, 1975. On the concept of the *studium generale*, see Denifle, pp. 1–29, and Rashdall, vol. I, pp. 6ff.

level of excellence. On the other hand, it cannot be emphasised enough that these specialised schools, far more of course than the lesser cathedral schools, addressed the growing needs of society in just those categories of higher education that were most needed, by producing teachers, physicians, jurists, and theologians. It was the use society made of the teaching of specialised schools that determined their success. A *studium generale* which for example had Greek as its special subject would have been received with enthusiasm by the scholars of the middle ages, but would not have thrived in the twelfth century, simply because it was irrelevant to the needs of society.

Another result of the specialisation, from a medieval point of view, was rather more alarming. Though it is true that a more solid education could be had within a *studium generale* than elsewhere, this was at the expense of completeness. Anders Sunesøn experienced this when consciously or otherwise he prepared himself to become archbishop of Denmark. While he could better obtain the necessary theological grounding in Paris than elsewhere, there was no way that he could also find there the qualifications in law that were so necessary for a prelate. As a result, he was obliged to supplement his education in Paris with a course of study in Bologna. Numerous other students had the same experience, and consequently the itinerant student became a typical figure of the twelfth century.

How changeable such an existence could be appears in a very vivid way in Abelard's autobiographical *Historia Calamitatum*: Abelard arrived in Paris about 1098 from his birth-place of Le Pallet near Nantes to study under Guillaume de Champeaux at the cathedral school in Paris. After a dispute with his teacher he left the town and in about 1101 founded his own school in Melun, but soon afterwards moved it to Corbeil. In 1103 he was in Paris again studying theology, and soon after that teaching at St Geneviève. After a rest in Brittany, he went to Laon to be a pupil of the famous Anselm of Laon (*c.* 1050–1117), who was in charge of the local cathedral school. From 1113 to 1119 he worked once more in Paris as a teacher in the cathedral school, in which he celebrated his greatest academic triumphs. It was also at this time that he met Heloïse, married her and so aroused the wrath of her family to such an extent that one night he was maltreated in the cruellest way. Wounded and sick, he was forced to take refuge in the monastery of St Denis outside the city, while Heloïse went into a convent in Argenteuil. In

1121 Abelard was in Soissons for a short time, then again in St Denis, until he finally found peace for a while as a hermit in Le Paraclet near Nogent-sur-Seine. But by 1126 his rest was over; Abelard had been ordained as a priest and received the post of abbot over the Benedictine monastery of St Gildas in Brittany. He retired as abbot in 1136 to try his luck again as a professor in Paris. This only lasted a year; from 1137 to 1141 it is not known where he stayed, only that he was revising his work during this time. In 1141 he was received as a guest in Cluny by Peter the Venerable, and a year later he died while on leave at Chalon-sur-Saône.[23]

In medieval eyes, a life of this unsettled kind was in many ways an abomination. The church felt particularly ill at ease about it, owing to the fact that most students were clerks, that is to say, they had taken orders of a lower degree and wore the tonsure to show it. The church had thus taken responsibility for them in legal matters; since the time of Gregory VII, tonsured clerks were under a bishop's jurisdiction and could not be prosecuted at law in a civil court. How, then, could the church take responsibility for a social group as unstable as itinerant students?

In addition, there were other objections. From ancient times the monastic fathers had emphasised the importance of a monk staying in the same place to weaken his understanding of the spiritual life, not to be distracted by any vagabond existence. This attitude rubbed off on other clergy, and as early as the first ecumenical council of Nicaea in 325, bishops, priests, and deacons were enjoined to stay in one place and not to move from one town to another. Augustine in his *De Ordine Monachorum* ridiculed the many hypocrites knocking about in a monk's cowl – some as dealers in relics, others making a show of inquiring after pretended relatives who did not exist. Similarly the Benedictine Rule contained a sharp section on the itinerant monk – *gyrovagum* – who can never stay in one place for longer than three or four days, while it upheld *stabilitas* as a fundamental rule of the order.[24] Throughout the middle ages one synod after the other sought to put an end to this nuisance, but the very fact that these injunctions for priests only to travel with their

---

[23] Abelard's roving life is depicted in his autobiographical *Historia calamitatum*, Migne PL 178. See also J. G. Sikes, *Peter Abailard*, Cambridge, 1932, and D. E. Luscombe, *The School of Peter Abelard*, Cambridge, 1971. On his relations with Heloïse, see E. Gilson, *Héloïse et Abélard*, Paris, 1948.

[24] See *Regula Sancti Benedicti*, chs. 1 and 61.

superior's permission were repeated so often shows that the church was not successful. The *vagantes* were there and would not be made to disappear, even if the system also had great drawbacks from their own point of view. They never ceased to complain of the hard life with journeys on foot over hill and dale, and of uncertain rest in strange beds. And even if the tonsure gave the poor clerk the right to alms, the itinerant student would have regarded poverty as his most serious problem, to judge by the many surviving petitions for support.[25]

Yet there were many sides to this question. Firstly, it is clear that the existence of a wandering student could easily obstruct his studies. The numerous critics of the *vagantes* stress the worldly temptations that these young people could fall into in taverns and country inns, and several times synods forbade clerks to visit such dangerous places. That it was a serious matter to break off a course of study was related to the fact that many students wore the tonsure as clerks, and therefore to a certain degree they were liable to the punishment as well as the protection of the church. The problem was what the church should do with a clerk who had not completed his education and consequently could not become a member of the proper hierarchy. One solution was to reduce the clerk to layman's status, but the church looked on this with reluctance; it was seen as degrading the church authorities besides the clerks concerned, who in any case lost their ecclesiastical privileges. On the other hand, it was intolerable that clerks should choose civil occupations, as was the case in Languedoc in the thirteenth century, where bakers, butchers, hucksters, and innkeepers took the tonsure – thus exempting themselves and their trades from the control of any civil authority or from guild agreements designed to limit competition, given that the bishops had no wish to give up jurisdiction over them. Situations such as this caused a great deal of trouble throughout the middle ages.[26]

Only one position was acceptable to all sides where a clerk not in orders was concerned: he could become a teacher. But it is easy to see how itinerant teachers could be a thorn in the flesh of those

---

[25] The principal work is Waddell; appendix E contains a summary of the many condemnations of the *vagantes* in ecclesiastical law; cf. *Decreta* II, 16, 17–18. An interesting map of the travels of Thomas Aquinas and Bonaventura is found in A. Tuilier, *La vie universitaire parisienne*, pp. 133 and 144.

[26] On tonsured craftsmen in Languedoc, see Waddell, p. 187.

anchored to one place. One example of how badly things could work out is again the story of Abelard, who finished his study with Guillaume de Champeaux by holding lectures himself on dialectic, thus emptying Guillaume's auditorium and much of his purse as well, since teachers at cathedral schools normally supplemented their prebends with payments from their students. A similar story is told of the St Denis community, where the legitimately appointed master complained of unfair competition from an itinerant teacher, who was drawing all the children away from the school to his own establishment simply by entertaining them with his violin.[27]

Finally, it should be remembered that there was also a minority of students who were not clerks. These were not the many young people frequenting the cathedral schools to prepare themselves for a career in civil occupations, but students who came to a *studium generale* to receive a higher education without regard to ecclesiastical appointments. This was particularly the case in the medical schools of Salerno and other places and in the law schools in Bologna. Here it was not so much economic problems that mattered, for many of the students at the school of civil law were rich enough to invest their own means in an education that was a prerequisite for a promising and lucrative career as an advocate or government official. It was because of this social status that the students of Bologna were addressed as *Domini*. Yet complications came in the social and legal sphere, due to the confusing number of different legal systems which existed in medieval Europe. Not least in Italy were matters very complicated as a result of the lively mixing of populations in the age of migrations. In the towns the original populations continued to follow the traditions of Roman law, while the incoming tribes that had just arrived brought their own laws with them, as we have already seen with regard to the Lombardic law. Roman law also acknowledged the right of newcomers to keep their own laws, with the result that the citizens of one and the same town could have different legal status within the same community.

This system meant that a layman newly arrived as a student in Bologna kept the legal status he had at home. This could seem helpful, but was effectively a hindrance, given that the home in question was rarely able to offer him assistance. The free traffic of the middle ages across the frontiers without passport or visa was a

---

[27] On the violin-playing teacher of St Denis, see Waddell, p. 192.

good thing in itself, and indispensable to the existence of wandering scholars or teachers – but there was undeniably another side to the coin. Free travel was possible – but at private risk, without protection, and therefore with the chance of possible prosecution anywhere according to unknown foreign laws. No consulate existed to take charge of the interests of the traveller, and if the layman took himself abroad, he also took his life into his own hands. For clerks it was another matter, in that everywhere they were under the jurisdiction and protection of the church, and had the right to be judged by Canon law, which they would already know from home.

Added to the legal difficulties faced by a Bologna student was his economic security. Even provided that he had the means to pay his teacher and complete his study, when it was over he found himself quite literally out on the street. The Bologna council of this period consistently refused to give foreign students citizenship in the town, probably under pressure from the corps of teachers. On one hand, the town was to a great extent economically dependent on the students and was therefore interested in keeping them; on the other hand, regular citizenship would have meant that any student, having finished his studies in Bologna, could have settled there as a lawyer or teacher. This would have ended the lucrative monopoly on teaching enjoyed by the lawyers of the city.

Yet there was always one thing such a student could do: he could move to another school, become a canonist, and supplement his training in civil law with a course in ecclesiastical law. In many cases this would also be of use to him later, in that ecclesiastical law came to dominate more and more aspects of medieval society. However, such a step brought with it certain consequences. Since canonists were clerks, it was practically impossible for a layman to study ecclesiastical law if he was married. Even if he was not married, by changing his course of study and receiving the tonsure he would come under the jurisdiction of the bishop of Bologna. Thereby his legal status with regard to his homeland would also change. This might be unfortunate for a promising career in civil law at home.

In this way, the strides forward in education in the great schools of the twelfth century were linked with conditions that became increasingly intolerable both for staff and students. Growing student numbers intensified the problem. The attempt to put an end to all such disadvantages was the direct cause of the formation of the universities. After what has been said so far, it is no wonder that the beginning of all this was a kind of legal game in Bologna, illustrating in a very interesting way one of the most fruitful interactions in history between the conceptions of Roman and Germanic law.

Unfortunately the sources for the development of the Bologna schools into the first proper university in Europe are extremely sparse. An often-quoted tradition shows that when Emperor Frederic Barbarossa pitched camp outside Bologna during his Italian campaign at Whitsuntide in 1155, he received emissaries from the town with teachers and students among them.[28] To the emperor's questions on why the students preferred Bologna to other places, and how they were treated by the city government, they answered that they were satisfied with their conditions of study, but that their legal protection was inadequate; for example, students were sometimes ordered by the courts to pay back debts that their fellow students had incurred. After taking advice from his vassals the emperor is said to have issued a decree which placed the students under his personal protection.

It is hard to decide the truth of this report, but it is certain that the emperor did in fact issue such a decree in November 1158. This happened at the famous assembly on the plain of Roncaglia near Piacenza, in which four scholars of law from Bologna took part.[29] These four professors were joined by two judges from each of fourteen different towns, and together they made up a sworn commission entrusted with the elucidation of the legal practice on certain matters already pertaining in northern Italy. Even if the four experts from Bologna were thoroughly experienced in Roman law, here they put their technical competence at the service of a typically Germanic procedure – the investigation of the law already in force. The results of their labours were settled in the so-called 'Authentic' *Habita* – the peculiar title is simply the *incipit* or first word of the writ – which is the sole surviving document of any importance for the history of the University of Bologna at this time.[30] It is expressly

---

[28] See P. Muntz, *Frederick Barbarossa*, London, 1969. The tradition of the first contact between Barbarossa and the jurists of Bologna in 1155 comes from a later, anonymous poem, see Rashdall, vol. I, p. 144, note 1.

[29] On the Roncaglia parliament, see Rahevin's *Gesta Frederici* IV, chs. 2–4, in *Monum. Germ. Scriptores* XX, Hanover, 1868, pp. 445–6; on the procedure at the parliament see Otto Morena, *Historia Frederici* I, ibid., new series VII, Berlin, 1930, pp. 58–61. On the interpretation of this event, see Denifle, pp. 48ff; Rashdall, vol. I, pp. 142ff; and H. Koeppler, Fredrick Barbarossa and the Schools of Bologna, *English Historical Review* 54 (1939), 577–607.

[30] *The Authentica Habia* is printed in *Mon. Germ Hist. Constitutiones* I, Hanover, 1893, 249.

declared that all travelling '*scholares* ... shall be legally protected in the places to which they come, and where they live and study'. This is followed by the provision that students accused in law should be able to decide for themselves whether they were to be judged by the bishop's court or by their own teachers; the latter provision refers to an old decree of Justinian, according to which professors of law had authority of judgement on a par with bishops. All those attempting to put students in front of other judges should themselves be punished.

With this ordinance a big step forward was taken towards improving the legal situation of the academic world. The only problems lay in which region the law was valid and at whom it was aimed. As regards the former question, the *Habita* makes no direct reference to Bologna, for which reason it should be taken as a general decree for all Italian possessions of the emperor. Furthermore, what was happening in Bologna would make it particularly relevant there, where the need for such reforms was more pressing than in other places. There is hardly any doubt that it was intended directly for those who were studying Roman law. It is true that the decree refers also to some *divinarum atque sacrarum legum professoribus*, from which it has been concluded that teachers of ecclesiastical law were also included in the provisions of the decree. These would have been superfluous anyway, since they were already covered by the jurisdiction and protection of the church. For this reason there is hardly any doubt that this particular passus was intended for civil lawyers for whom, now as in antiquity, Roman law was a *lex sacra*.

Seen from this perspective many things fall into place. It is possible that Frederic's contact with the civil lawyers of Bologna in 1155 opened his eyes to certain possibilities. After all, Roman law would have presented a hitherto quite insignificant German prince, occupied with the building of an empire and looking for an ideological base that Germanic law could not provide,[31] with a doctrine of the emperor as the *dominus mundi*. That he indeed adopted this doctrine can be seen from his frequent habit of referring to his predecessors as *divi reges et imperatores*, 'divine kings and emperors', which could only be meaningful in the context of Roman law. Even if the contents of the *Habita* were brought out in a

---

[31] On the shortcomings of Germanic law as a basis for imperial policy, see Ullmann, pp. 89 and 93, and Kibre, p. 11.

From school to studium generale 141

Germanic procedure, it was promulgated nonetheless as an imperial edict and as such embodied in the *Corpus Juris Civilis*. If the *Habita* is justly regarded as the forerunner of all later university privileges, it is inevitable that the birth of the universities must be seen as closely linked with German imperial policy, even though it still took some time before Bologna appeared as a university in the proper sense of the word.

However, not all problems regarding the student's legal relationship to Bologna and its citizens were solved by the issuing of a privilege, which after all only guaranteed a student's legal position, but not his social status. In the following decades there were numerous attempts on the part of students to improve their living conditions in the town, using the only weapon they had – the threat to leave. No-one could prevent them moving away and thereby dealing the town a serious blow, since a mass exodus would have meant a catastrophic fall in local incomes. Also for teachers it would have been synonymous with economic ruin, unless they were willing to follow the students elsewhere.

There is an indication that the pupils of the civil school had already played this card by the end of the twelfth century. In 1189 the town council suddenly required teachers in civil law to swear on oath that they would not teach Roman law anywhere else than in Bologna.[32] This can only mean that something like this had been discussed. It means again that the students must have threatened to leave, that their teachers must have seen themselves compelled to go with them simply to go on providing for their families. At this time the town had no power to force the students to stay; but by preventing the teachers from leaving, they could make departure meaningless for their pupils, who would not be able to get the equivalent teaching elsewhere. This shows that the teachers' economic dependence on their students was really the cause of their own weak position in case of a conflict; the only card they could play was their high scholarly competence. Thus we can assume that the teachers would have had no objection to swearing the oath.

The sources are silent on this matter, and it is not possible to decide with any certainty what the controversies were that lay behind this affair. It looks, however, as if it was the accommodation

---

[32] On the demands of the town council in 1189, see Denifle, p. 194 and Rashdall, vol. 1, p. 169, note 1.

problem that got the students to act. One of the few documents preserved from this time is a bull issued in 1189 by Pope Clement III (1187–1191) to confirm an existing agreement that neither teachers nor students might offer a landlord higher rent for a room that was already occupied by a student.[33] This attempt to keep room prices down is the only thing we know of what students were doing at this time, and so it is not unreasonable to assume that the battle was fought over this question, even if there is no documentary evidence for it. The outcome was a victory for the students. It was laid on the bishop or his successors each year to have the bull read aloud before a plenum of students and teachers – *in communi audientia magistrorum atque scholarum* – and an agreement was struck with the town by which room prices should be pegged by a rent tribunal of four people, two to be chosen by the town and two by the students.

The students could only exert their strength by threatening to move out all at once, if they were all agreed on it. This means that they must have had an organisation of some kind. That this was the case in the thirteenth century is confirmed by a number of documents. That it was so early as the late twelfth century also is an inevitable conclusion. The later well-documented student combinations are known by the name of 'nations', in that they took the form of unions of students from the same or closely related nations. Consequently these unions must have been formed early on, and they must have had the character of unions of mutual aid and support for students who came from the same area.[34]

The problem is simply what status such combinations had. Sometimes they have been seen as student guilds or corporations in the usual medieval sense, from the natural idea that the students could have formed their own guilds just as merchants and craftsmen did. But in the beginning this was hardly the case. A guild was a privileged union of colleagues in the same trade, recognised by the authorities as an artificial person and allowed to keep justice among its own members. However, the students did not formally meet the aforesaid conditions to form a corporation because they were still in training themselves and so in no position to practise a trade. At the end of the twelfth century the jurist John Bassianus expressly takes issue with the students' right 'to elect aldermen', *consules eligere*, in

[33] On the bull of Pope Clement III in 1189, see Rashdall, vol. I, p. 148.
[34] On the nations in Bologna, see Sorbelli, pp. 150–8, Denifle, pp. 135ff, Rashdall, vol. I, 154ff; cf. P. Kibre, *The Nations in the Mediaeval Universities*, Cambridge, Mass., 1948.

consideration of the fact that an equivalent right was not exercised by towers and the apprentices of other craftsmen, who merely left it to their masters.[35] Other jurists claimed, with *Corpus Juris Civilis* in hand, that autonomous corporations could only be founded by those who 'were known to carry out a profession' (*professionem exercere noscuntur*), and by no others.

Thus in the beginning the student unions cannot be seen as guilds in the proper sense, but should rather be compared with organisations such as those established by merchants to help each other abroad. They were free unions which were not properly incorporated, and which in the beginning did not have the equivalent negotiating rights with the town council. But in the long run this inevitably led to corporative status, and with customary cleverness the lawyers knew how to find grounds for justifying the town's change of policy. Thus Peter Ancharano explained that there should be a distinction between students and craftsmen's apprentices: the former are subject to scholars and learning, while the latter are engaged in lower tasks and should therefore have lesser rights. Once more the ancient distinction between *artes liberales* and *artes serviles* served as a basis for academic privilege.[36]

The number of these nations became very great. A catalogue from 1265 names no less than thirteen just for students from countries north of the Alps.[37] However, this does not mean that every people in Europe was represented by a student nation in Bologna; so few students could come from a certain country that they could not form an independent group but had to join one of the others. When, for instance, the Danish mathematician and astronomer Peter Philomena de Dacia stayed in the town in 1291, we find him on the list of the German nation.[38]

Later in the thirteenth century the nations were clustered in two big groups, a transalpine one embracing all non-Italians, and a cisalpine one for Italians who did not belong to Bologna; the children of the city in any case had full rights of citizenship and needed no organisation of their own. At the head of these groups

---

[35] On John Bassianus, see Denifle, pp. 140 and 172ff.
[36] On Petrus Ancharono, see Denifle, p. 174.
[37] The list of nations of 1265 is in Denifle, p. 156.
[38] On Peter de Dacia, see O. Pedersen, The Life and Works of Peter Nightingale, *Vistas in Astronomy* 9 (1968), 3–10. Peter's works are now available in an excellent edition by F. Saaby Petersen in *Corpus Philosophorum Danicorum Medii Aevi*, vol. x, 1–2, Copenhagen 1983–4.

was a foreman elected by the students; he seems originally to have been called *consul*, but his name soon became *rector* – a designation in keeping with the fact that the same title had been used for aldermen of the guilds in Bologna since 1194. To be wholly precise, it should be emphasised that the full title of the alderman was *rector scholarium*, which may be translated 'leader of the students' and should not be confused with *rector scholarum*, used of the head of the schools.[39]

The situation is thus that in Bologna before 1200 we have two large academic groups: the combination of teachers in civil Roman law on one hand, and the students' nations on the other. It was the second group that had an economic trumpcard good enough to win any controversy. In the course of the thirteenth century the students also succeeded in subduing the teachers' organisation, which preserved only one single privilege – to decide if the student was qualified to join the proper legal profession on a par with his teachers. That the students could not wrest this privilege from the teachers was logical if the teachers formed a real corporation, so that it fell only to members to decide on new intakes. The same thing must have happened as in the craftsmen's guilds, with the normal qualifying tests for apprentices similar to the examination for students. The academic examination in Bologna can thus be seen as the test of entry for the teacher's guild. It consisted of an *examinatio* of the candidate's qualifications, a declaration that he had been accepted as qualified (*admissus*), and finally a ceremony at which he was taken into the guild (*conventus, principium, inceptio*) and was allowed to call himself *doctor, master,* or *professor* – titles that were originally used indiscriminately.

There is evidence that the two main academic organisations met from time to time in common cause. Thus it is said that when the jurist Buoncompagni's new work *Rhetorica antiqua* came out it was read aloud ceremonially 'before a gathering of professors of civil and canonical law and a large group of student scholars' (*coram universitate professorum juris canonici et civilis et aliorum doctorum scholarium multitudine numerosa*). This took place in April 1215, and it is the first time that the word *universitas* is attested as a description for the collected academic world in Bologna.[40] Perhaps this date can be regarded as the birthday of the universities, though this is a slightly misleading

---

[39] On the terms *rector scholarum* and *rector scholarium*, see Denifle, pp. 145f and Rashdall, vol. 1, p. 162. On the titles master, doctor, professor, see Denifle, pp. 203f.

[40] On the reading of 1215, see Rashdall, vol. 1, p. 115 and 146; cf. L. Thorndike, Public

interpretation, as there was nothing special in the word *universitas*. This was a purely technical term taken from the doctrine of corporations in Roman law. It means no more than that such corporations of teachers and students now existed. It has no special ideological content and is used quite neutrally of the total mass of teachers and students at the Bologna law schools. It was only much later that the word acquired a specially philosophical meaning: in the middle ages *studium generale* was and remained the official term for the university.[41]

If we now turn to the schools in Paris, we see a situation that differed in a decisive way from that of Bologna. In nearly all respects this can be derived from the fact that in the process of specialising Paris had developed itself first and foremost into a *studium generale* in theology.[42] The theological nature of the big Paris schools meant firstly that all teachers were clergy, either canons or monks, whereas civilian or eventually married teachers were an unknown concept. Not for nothing did Abelard crate a furore by entering into marriage with Heloïse, and even this was an absolute exception that only served to confirm the rule of teachers' celibacy. Secondly, the precedence given to theological study meant that the large majority of students arriving in Paris were already tonsured clerks intending to continue an ecclesiastical career. However, increasingly, secularised medical students were also coming to Paris.

From the legal point of view this state of affairs made the situation more simple in Paris than in Bologna, where as we have seen the students' confused legal affiliations were one of the main causes of the emergence of the university. The matter was straightforward in Paris – both teachers and pupils were clerks and thus subject to the jurisdiction of the church, which was held by the bishop or his superior, the archbishop of Sens. On the other hand, it also meant that students and teachers together would necessarily make a state within a state; long before university organisations had begun to develop, these clerks formed *de facto* a common-interest group that

---

Readings of New Works in Medieval Universities, *Speculum* 1 (1926), 101–3, and the same author's Public Recitals in Universities of the Fifteenth Century, *Speculum* 3 (1928), 104ff.

[41] On the term *universitas* and the concept of corporations, see P. Michaud-Quantin, *Universitas: Expressions du mouvement communautaire dans le Moyen-Age latin*, Paris, 1970.

[42] On the university of Paris, see Rashdall, vol. I, pp. 269–584, and Kibre, pp. 85–267. The old work by Bulaeus, *Historia Universitatis Parisiensis*, vols. I–VI, Paris, 1665–73, is the most comprehensive history of this university and still useful for the many documents published here, but otherwise unreliable.

could go united before the town council with demands for special treatment in courts of law. This state of affairs constantly gave rise to difficulties: on one hand the town was to a high degree economically dependent on students, the greatest part of whom lodged with the townsfolk and brought them a not insubstantial income. At the same time, this form of life implied in itself many possibilities of conflict, with civil and criminal lawsuits to follow. On the other hand, however, the citizenry were excluded from prosecuting students in the general courts; the student in question could plead for judgement in an ecclesiastical court, which the citizens thought was a plot of the ecclesiastics as a whole against the interests of the common people. No-one ever found a proper solution to this problem; but as we shall see, it was just such a dispute that brought about the founding of the university.

The marked theological nature of the courses of study in Paris also had economic consequences. The average student in Paris was a young clerk who had come to town to augment his theological training in the hope of an eventually promising career in the church hierarchy. His economic basis was in many cases one form or other of support from his homeland, often in the form of a church prebend that could not always cover living costs abroad. But in a number of cases the students had no secure incomes and were therefore reduced to living off the alms which, as clerks, they were privileged to take from anyone ready to give. It is obvious that this would easily lead to a reduction of the student population to the level of the proletariat, as the growing fame of the schools attracted greater numbers of disciples. The poverty of the students of Paris is partly the reason why the quarrel between clerk and citizen became unusually bitter here: no-one in Paris thought of addressing a student as *Domine*, just as wretched living conditions nourished the criminality that the townsfolk found it so hard to punish.[43]

Other difficulties were added to these economic problems, caused by the relationship between students and teachers. This was abundantly clear in Bologna – here the teachers received payment for teaching and were thus made dependent on the students and their organisations. In Paris, on the contrary, most students were too poor

---

[43] This summary of the circumstances of Parisian students conflicts with John of Salisbury's letter to Thomas Becket in 1164, in which he describes the good conditions of English scholars in the city, see *Chartularium* 1, 16–19; however, much later material points to the contrary, as shown by Waddell.

to pay their teachers for instructing them. As far as it went this was in keeping with the fact that the teachers in Paris were not family providers but members of a cathedral chapter or monastic society that took care of their maintenance itself. The only thing that could threaten the teachers' privileged status and their opportunity to make extra money was thus the possibility of education outside the existing schools. On the other hand, it must still have been extremely tempting for a graduate student simply to settle down in or near the town and start up on his own. We have already seen Abelard avail himself of such an option; others often did the same, until the church put a stop to this business.

This was done using the chancellor's office as the instrument. We have already seen that cathedral schools were responsible to the chancellor of the chapter, who appointed a *magister scholarum* to take care of the teaching itself. This explains how the chancellor's office in Notre Dame in Paris grew in influence and importance at the same pace as the pressure of the mass of students on the school, and consequently the pressure of graduate candidates without occupation. In the course of the twelfth century the chancellor contrived to get all public teaching under his control. Not only was he now leader of the cathedral school itself, but no other master was allowed to set up other schools in the diocese without his permission. This was given in the form of a special teacher's licence or *licentia docendi* that was the prerequisite for any future career in teaching and therefore worth some money. It goes almost without saying that the chancellor in these conditions would not have resisted the temptation to issue the licence for any consideration the recipient was willing to provide in expectation of future plenty.[44]

The evidence suggests that the first attempts to ease some of the problems for teachers and students in Paris was made by Pope Alexander III (1159–1181), who had previously been professor in canonical law in Bologna and author of one of the first big commentaries to Gratian's *Decretum*, with the title *Summa Magistri Rolandi*. During most of his time as pope he was involved in a life-or-death struggle with the empire and the anti-popes who were under the protection of Frederic Barbarossa from 1159 to 1177. One of these, Pascal III, gained notoriety in 1165 by canonising Charlemagne, in an attempt to put the church into the harness of imperial ideology.

---

[44] On the *licentia docendi*, see Rashdall, vol. 1, pp. 278ff.

Alexander III was only able to uphold his legitimacy and independence by working closely with the royal power in France, where he stayed in exile in the years 1162 to 1165. Without doubt it was the pope's constant and finally victorious battle with the emperor that opened his eyes to the possibility of making the theological schools in Paris into the allies of the papacy and a useful counterweight to the juristic centre in Bologna, which had got its first privileges from the emperor and was therefore under suspicion of being the empire's tool against the church. In any case, it is hardly a coincidence that some of the oldest extant documents concerning the University of Paris are a series of papal letters from Alexander III. Already on 26 July 1164 we see him recommending a student to study in Paris; later he interfered repeatedly in doctrinal disputes between Paris masters, just as the term *licentia docendi* first occurs in a letter from about 1170, in which he prohibits the prevailing trade in selling this authorisation for money.[45]

It was Alexander III again who was the driving force behind the Third Lateran Council in 1179, at which about 300 bishops sought to normalise education throughout Christendom by improving both teachers' conditions and student possibilities. In Canon 18 of the Council, it says that

Seeing that the Church of God like a good mother undertakes to care for the needy, regarding the maintaining of the body and the wants of the soul, a sufficient benefice shall be given in each cathedral for a master to teach both clerks of the same cathedral and poor students free of charge, whereby the teacher's need can be eased and the path to knowledge made open to his pupils, so that the poor who cannot be helped by their parents' means shall not be deprived of the opportunity to read and make progress. In other churches and monasteries this [benefice], as far as it existed in former times, shall be reestablished.[46]

For teachers this was an extremely important step forward, for here the church explicitly offered to take upon itself the economic responsibility for teaching in cathedral schools: prebends would be established for masters, who would then be in a position to teach their students free of charge. Presumably this would have roused

---

[45] See M. Pacaut, *Alexandre III*, Paris, 1956, and Baldwin, *Alexandre III*; cf. also the genial portrait in the last chapter of F. Heer, *Aufgang Europas*, Vienna–Zurich, 1949. On Pope Alexander III's recommendation of a student in 1164, see *Chartularium* I, 3f; his prohibition on payment for the *licentia docendi*, ibid. 4f. Cf. G. Post, Alexander III, the Licentia Docendi and the Rise of the universities, in *Haskins Anniversary Essays*, ed. Ch. Taylor, Boston, 1929.

[46] Canon 18 is quoted from *Chartularium* I, 10; cf. *Decretales* V, 5, 1–5 (*De magistris*).

teachers to applause rather more than what follows: 'no-one [i.e. no chancellor] may claim remuneration for a *licentia docendi* in any way, nor by teachers' pleading of use and custom ask for anything, nor by any means refuse petitions for a *licentia docendi* from any qualified person'. The last provision meant that even for students the prospect was brighter than before: if a student after finishing his study showed himself qualified, the chancellor could not refuse to give him the *licentia docendi* free of charge. Of course it could not be inferred from this that there would be an office waiting for the student when he finished. But his qualifications were established, and his chances of setting up a school himself and thereby making ends meet were greatly increased.

With this important step, Alexander III and the Third Lateran Council created the possibility of diverting the stream of students away from Bologna to Paris. Thereby the church strengthened the position of theology against law. The distinction is clearly illustrated by the fact that Roman law never found a place in Paris, while Bologna only got a faculty of theology as late as 1364. Thus the church's backing of the Paris schools should be seen as one more blow in the fight between emperor and pope, and as the beginning of the favour that the papacy bestowed in perpetuity on the teachers of Paris in their battle for autonomous status. This did not mean that the church was casting Bologna aside; but it is worth remembering that Alexander III's affirmation of the *Habita* only came late, when the emperor's power had weakened and the outcome of their struggle had been sealed by the treaty of Venice in 1177.

The Third Lateran Council was an ecumenical assembly whose decrees were valid for the church as a whole. It is not easy to say to what extent the decrees on free teaching in all dioceses were straightaway carried out in real life; but it is easy to see that this council decree was the condition for further developments in Paris in the next decades. Most importantly, the decree gave teachers in schools economic independence from their pupils. This prevented a Bologna-type development in which teachers would lose the struggle for power through their economic dependence. On the other hand the council made new difficulties for teachers by making it easier for their pupils to get their own authorisation for teaching as soon as their education was finished. This would imply an unhindered rise in the number of masters, something that again meant the danger of the whole class losing status in society. It goes without saying that a reaction to this change could be expected on the teachers' part.

Originally it had been an obvious and unspoken assumption that no-one could start teaching without first undergoing an education, or without the consent of his own teacher. The unwritten right of teachers to bestow the *licentia docendi* on their own pupils had been undermined by the chancellor's position of power, which in turn had now been repeated by the council. Gradually the tradition developed whereby the student upon finishing his education was given his *licentia docendi* by all the teachers together in a formal induction into the society of teachers; the term for this was *inceptio*. It comprised various ceremonies to be discussed in more detail in a later chapter. Added to this was a special fee which the master-to-be had to pay the guild; this was not seen to contradict the council's decrees, since the fee was never used to benefit individual teachers, but was applied to the common interest.

The whole ceremony of inception can only be interpreted in one way: the teachers of Paris had formed a corporation which admitted new members after a normal qualifying examination by a solemn act. Just when this guild was founded cannot be established with any certainty, but it must have happened quite a long time before 1200. The English Benedictine Matthew Paris (d. 1259) has left evidence of this in his life of the abbot of St Albans, John de Cella, who died at a ripe old age in 1214. Of him it is said that he frequented the Paris schools in his youth assiduously and 'earned the right to be admitted to the society of elected masters' (*ad electorum consortium magistrorum meruit attingere*).[47] It would be tempting to date this 'consortium' to the year 1179, though this is a hypothesis that cannot be documented. It is quite conceivable that the guild goes back even further, in which case the council's intervention in favour of the teachers in 1179 may have inspired them to strengthen their professional organisation.

The problem is now whether the teachers' corporation in Paris was ever balanced by a student organisation corresponding to the Bologna nations mentioned earlier. On this matter, however, the oldest sources are completely silent. There is no doubt that student fellowships are mentioned frequently at the beginning of the thirteenth century. Bishop Odo of Paris thus mentions a *communitas scholarium* in 1207, and Pope Innocent III (1198–1216) writes of an

---

[47] On John de Cella, see Rashdall, vol. 1, p. 292.

universitas scholarium in 1208–9.[48] But such terms are too general for any conclusions to be drawn from them; they refer only to students in general and do not presume any special organisation. It is only in a document dated October 1249 that the nations in Paris are unambiguously named.[49]

However, this fact does not prevent us from seeing the students as a group or a *communitas scholarium* that in many cases, when seen from outside, would appear as a unity. Together with their teachers they made up the academic world of the town. Just as in Bologna, it is this academic world, taken as a whole, that gave rise to the origin of the term 'university'. On this matter the sources are quite clear. A papal letter from Innocent III in 1205 is addressed to *universis magistris et scholaribus Parisiensis*, 'to all masters and students in Paris', and later in the same letter these are indicated by the general description *universitatem vestram*.[50] In the following years, *magistri et scholares* was the preferred name for the group of teachers and pupils as a whole, as used by the Cardinal Legate Guala Bichierus in 1208 and the Synod of Paris in 1213.[51] Two years later the term *universitas* came into circulation in the decrees issued by Robert de Courçon, in which there is talk of making some people responsible towards teachers and students together or 'towards certain persons designated by the university' (*coram universitate magistrorum et scholarium, vel coram aliquibus ab Universitate constitutis*).[52] In Paris therefore, just as in Bologna, the concept of *universitas* rose out of the general imprecision of language. Here too all it indicates is the whole community of students and masters without the slightest ideological meaning. Finally, the word emerges with the same neutral meaning in Montpellier in 1220, in a reference to *universitas medicorum tam doctorum quam discipulorum*, 'the assembly of physicians, teachers as well as disciples'.[53]

One centre of study other than Bologna and Paris was to start on the path of future university status before the twelfth century was out. This was Oxford, the initial history of which is unfortunately veiled in even greater obscurity, thanks to the state of the sources.

---

[48] For the term *communitas scholarium*, see *Chartularium* I, 65, and for *Universitas scholarium*, ibid. 67f.
[49] The document of 1249 is in *Chartularium* I, 215; cf. also G. Post, Parisian Masters as a Corporation, *Speculum* 9 (1934), 421–45.
[50] Pope Innocent III's letter to *Universis magistris* is printed in *Chartularium* I, 62.
[51] On Guala Bichierus, see *Chartularium* I, 66, and on the synod of 1213 ibid. I, 77f.
[52] *Chartularium* I, 78f.   [53] Rashdall, vol. II, p. 123.

But that there must have been particular problems associated with the history of Oxford University is already evident from the circumstances of the town. First mentioned by name in 912, Oxford was no autonomous bishopric in the middle ages, but belonged until 1541 to the bishop of faraway Lincoln. The town, therefore, had neither a cathedral nor accordingly a cathedral school that could serve as a stimulus to future development. Nevertheless Oxford was early on already an important centre for the church, and was controlled by an archdeacon working under the bishop. There were many churches within its walls, and several monasteries of importance in the immediate vicinity such as Abingdon, Osney, and others.[54]

The first evidence of proper teaching in Oxford outside the monasteries comes from the time around 1100, when a certain Theobaldus Stampensis, Doctor Cadumensis (Theobald of Etampes, doctor from Caen), was teaching theology in the town.[55] This must have gone on for a long time, for in about 1119 Theobald described himself as *Master Oxinefordie* in a still extant autograph manuscript containing a little treatise against the monks and the celibacy of priests. As an enemy of the monks he was possibly associated with the secular canons at the important church of St Frideswide. Otherwise an anonymous counterblast from the monks contains the valuable information that Theobald had sixty or a hundred clerks studying in Oxford under him. In about 1133 we see another theologian, Robert Pullen, holding lectures in Oxford for a period of five years. He was an important representative of the new dialectical theology, and his *Sententiae* was the immediate prototype of Peter the Lombard's work of the same name. Another Oxford scholar was Robert of Cricklade, who became prior of St Frideswide's in 1141 and whose works include an abbreviated version of Pliny's *Historia Naturalis* for the use of King Henry II (1154–1189).[56]

All this shows that some teaching was going on in Oxford before 1150, even if it was hardly as wide-ranging as that of Winchester, Hereford, or London at the same time. Everything indicates also that English students normally went abroad to supplement their education at home. This was true of John of Salisbury, often

---

[54] On the ecclesiastical status of Oxford, see E. Marshall, *The Diocesan History of Oxford*, London, 1882.
[55] See C. E. Mallet, *A History of the University of Oxford*, vol. I, Oxford, 1924, p. 20 and the more recent chapter by R. W. Southern in Catto, pp. 1–36.
[56] On these Oxford teachers, see Mallet, vol. I, p. 23, Rashdall, vol. III, 16.

mentioned previously, as well as of many others. The problem, therefore, is what caused the Oxford schools to grow in scope and importance so vigorously that by the early thirteenth century they could almost equal the stature of Bologna and Paris as a *studium generale*.

It has been argued that the impulse may have come from outside, as a side-effect of the struggle between Henry II and the archbishop of Canterbury, Thomas Becket (1117–1170). After opposing one of the king's demands, this time that clergy should be brought to civil law-courts, in 1164 the archbishop fled to France with a group of followers. To counteract the prelate's influence on the English clergy, the king issued a series of ordinances from 1164 to 1169, that decided, among other things, that no churchman could leave the country without permission of the crown, and that no English student abroad would keep his prebend if he did not come home within three months. Naturally this increased numbers of students concentrated in England itself. Added to this, 'France', so John of Salisbury tells us in a letter, 'this the mildest and most civilised of all nations, has expelled her foreign students.[57] This happened in 1167 and further helped to increase the numbers of students as well as finished masters at home. The most reasonable assumption is that most of these settled in Oxford, where there is evidence of academic activity in the years immediately following.

Thus in 1172 Robert of Cricklade is said to have preached in St Frideswide's on feastdays before clerks from different parts of England. A legal document from shortly after 1180 is witnessed by a scribe, a bookbinder, two parchment-makers and three illuminators, all living in 'Cattestrete', where, by the same token, there was now a substantial basis for significant book-production. In 1184 or 1185 the town was visited by the historian Giraldus Cambrensis (1147–1223), who spent three days reading aloud from his new *Topographia Hibernica* before 'a numerous gathering of doctors from different faculties and their best students'.[58] In about 1190 there is mention of a Dutch student embarking on the general *studium*, who was in Oxford, and finally Richard of Devizes claimed in 1192 that Oxford was so full of clerks that the town could barely feed them. Even if

---

[57] *Chartularium* I, 20f.
[58] On the reading by Giraldus Cambrensis, see Mallet, vol. I, p. 23 and Rashdall, vol. III, pp. 25–31. Cf. C. H. Haskins, A Further Note on a Note, *Speculum* 1 (1926), 221, and Thorndike's reply, ibid. 445ff.

these references are relatively few and far between, they speak in clear language of Oxford having become a *studium generale* and a destination for students not only from England but also from the continent.

How teaching was organised in Oxford in this period is still an open question. There was no bishop in the place, and no chancellor either to issue a *licentia docendi*. Possibly the teachers of theology went to the archdeacon for some kind of authorisation, or else they worked without formal ecclesiastical approbation as a free company of masters. In such a case they would have been able to decide whom they would accept as colleagues, just as they did in Bologna, which almost certainly presupposes their having the status of a corporation. Yet the existence of a guild of teachers before 1200 cannot be found documented in the sources. It is only in 1209 that the documents begin to speak seriously of study in Oxford; in 1210 a papal bull speaks of a rector for the schools of Oxford, and in 1214 we can begin to see the emergence of a proper university structure. But there is no reason to doubt that as early as the years 1167 to 1200 the new *studium generale* had got an organisation of teachers that determined how it would function.[59]

In this way, the decisive period of the early history of the university fell within the latter half of the twelfth century. Now the schools in Europe could break clear from their earlier isolation, provincialism, and individualism. Where the general cathedral schools had been only local centres of learning sustained by an individual teacher, one *studium generale* now followed another, each with a corps of several teachers and an international student clientele. The strength of these new schools is borne out by both the emperor and the pope trying, each in his own way; to keep a firm hand on a development based on the doctrine of corporations in Roman law, something with which neither of these authorities initially had any connection. Hereby the scene was now set for the battle of sovereignty over the universities, which was to become one of the most striking events in the cultural life of the thirteenth century.

[59] On the organisation of teachers in Oxford, see Rashdall,, vol. III, pp. 39f.

CHAPTER 6

The battle for the universities

In the last chapter the concrete causes of the origin of the university corporations were established – the huge increase in scholarly literature, the specialisation of the big schools, the growth in student numbers, the continuing internationalisation of students and teachers in each school. Behind all this was the economic recovery and society's increased need of people with a high degree of training. But even if the universities thus met the needs of society, they were not as a matter of course totally suited to the society they had to serve. Already at their beginning they ran into a number of problems that had to do with their social role and status. A little paradoxically, it can be said that many of these difficulties arose because in a manner of speaking the universities came into the world without knowing it.

A teacher or student in Bologna, Paris, or Oxford at the end of the twelfth century would not have felt himself a member of any 'university'. Perhaps he would use the word *universitas* now and again, but only as a neutral term for all people associated with his school either as teachers or students. The organisations which he could see right in front of him were not universities in the later sense of the word. They were only fairly loosely structured associations by means of which teachers and students each tried to defend their separate interests. If he thought more carefully about this matter, the student would accordingly have to admit that the position was weak in many ways. The corporation of teachers was certainly in keeping with the general social structure of the time and might be legally recognised, but on the other hand they still did not have the kind of privileges or guarantees that were needed to safeguard an ordinary guild. Even more uncertain was the situation regarding students, since their corporations could not be recognised as legal corporations – because their members had not yet 'served their apprenticeship'. But while the new organisations grew in this way without proper safeguards, it would soon be clear that a high level of protection was what they needed. It was because their numbers were so great and were made up, for the large part, of very youthful and lively elements, that many sectors of society kept a watchful eye on them and sought to control them.

This was true above all of urban societies, which for historical reasons had become the context of university activity everywhere. In reality the town faced an uncomfortable dilemma. On one hand the presence of a large, unruly, and international population constantly gave rise to incidents with the people of the town. Riots and feuds between students and citizens were perhaps the most distinguishing feature of student life in the middle ages, and the antagonisms between 'town and gown' required ceaseless intervention on the part of the town council. On the other hand, one could not be too hard on the university, for if this found circumstances too tangled and moved away, the town would lose an important source of income. In this respect some clarification was urgently needed.

The state government also had cause to be interested in the affairs of the universities. We have already seen how developments in Bologna were helped substantially by the imperial privilege of 1158 for students in Italy. Outside the frontiers of the empire, in England, France, and Spain, it was royal power which, by and large and in an equally positive way, supported the institutions from which the necessary officials could be recruited. In return, the king could also be seen seeking support from the university on questions of ideology, for example in the ongoing dispute on the relationship between church and state. Where this broke out into open conflict – in tandem with the incipient emergence of national states – the royal power had need of jurists who were a match for the canonists of the church and could give the state ideological backing, when attempting to keep the papacy at arm's length.

Finally, it was the church itself that had the possibility of interfering in many different ways in university affairs. Firstly, the local bishop by the power of his office was expected to see that the new schools did not teach false doctrine. Various conflicts between the church and the universities were caused by such interference in teaching on the bishop's part. Under him in Paris and certain other places was the chancellor of the cathedral chapter, who had previously been responsible for teaching in the cathedral school, but who now saw his power threatened by the academic corporations, and who had reason to regard the founding of the teachers' guild as a conspiracy of subordinate staff against the traditional leadership. Above the local level, it was the papacy that, as the only real international authority, might have a strong position over institutions of teaching with an international public. Last but not least was the influence of the new religious orders that grew up in the thirteenth century. While the older Benedictine, Cluniac, and Cistercian orders increasingly lost interest in public schooling, the Dominicans engaged themselves in it right from the start, and the Franciscans followed soon after. For both orders it soon became a major problem how to get a foothold in the universities and influence the teaching there.

In this way there were enough groups in society which had reason to regard the new seats of learning with attention; in a way, the social impact of the universities can be directly read from the number of parties who tried to take them over. But it should not be forgotten that it was not only groups or powers outside the universities who helped to bring conflicts about. There were also internal problems of no less serious a character. Even in the beginning it is possible to distinguish two different types of university. Bologna was a thoroughgoing students' university;[1] here the student organisations had absolute mastery over the teachers, in that the real initiative was in all cases with the student nations. Paris, on the other hand, was a typical professors' university, with the initiative coming from a teachers' guild that the church supported economically; here it was only later that the students got far weaker organisations of their own. Elsewhere were structures placed at various points between these two extremes. But whichever side had the initiative or greater influence, it cannot be concealed that of necessity there had to be two different interest groups in every university, between whom conflicts were unavoidable unless outer pressures forced them into solidarity for a time. I shall discuss these aspects further in chapter 7.

The rest of this chapter will be devoted to examining how the universities sought to safeguard their autonomy and independent status. This they did in a long series of battles that, in the beginning at least, nearly put a stop to the whole enterprise. The result was that the universities survived, but in a new ideological context, with a concept of the university that was no longer neutral. This phase in

---

[1] The term 'student university' was coined by Rashdall, vol. 1, p. 149.

the university's life had consequences for centuries to come, and it is no exaggeration that many of the topical problems of the universities in the twentieth century go straight back to events in the thirteenth, as described in the following paragraphs.

Firstly, the relationship between the universities and the civil authorities seems to have come to a head in Paris. Here a dramatic incident took place in the summer of 1200, when five clerks and laymen (probably students with non-studying companions) were attacked and brutally treated by a few malefactors led by a certain Thomas, described as *praepositus* and certainly a kind of policeman. The circumstances have not come to light. Presumably it was an ordinary disturbance on the street or in the tavern, but at any rate the police quelled it in such a violent way that the clerks of Paris were compelled to appeal to King Philippe Auguste (1180–1223) for help. That they were more than successful in getting that, appears from a royal decree of the same year, which is in any case our only source for the whole affair.[2] The very first statute decrees lifelong imprisonment for the officer leading the police – to be carried out even if he declared himself innocent! He could also elect to undergo the water-test, but, even in the event that he survived, he should be exiled. Thomas anyway elected imprisonment, but broke his neck in an escape attempt shortly afterwards. The other culprits had fled the town, but they were to be hunted down everywhere, apprehended, and imprisoned in Paris.

The suppression of these guilty men was only one side of the affair. The rest of the decree contained a list of ordinances designed to normalise relations and safeguard the position of the students in the life of the town. Thus each citizen of Paris was asked to swear an oath that he would give information to the authorities and appear as a witness if he ever saw a student attacked by a layman. If the layman was not acting in self-defence, he was to be seized at once and put up before the royal court. If on the other hand it was a student causing the disturbance, no hand was to be laid on him unless he was caught in the act; in this case he could be arrested, but he was to be promptly handed over to the ecclesiastical court; any civilian accomplices would be judged by the royal court. Finally, no-one could be appointed to the police force in Paris until he had made his oath before the *scholares* gathered in a church that he would

[2] *Chartularium* 1, 59–61.

abide by these decrees. Ten years later the king issued a sequel to these first university privileges with a new ordinance, stipulating that no *clericus* might be arrested unless he was caught redhanded in 'homicide, adultery, rape or similar grave offences, or at a scene of bloodshed with a club, rock, or weapon', in which case he was to be handed over to the judgement of the ecclesiastical authorities.[3]

Presumably these decrees only came about after direct application to the king, no doubt after complaints to the town council had proved to be fruitless. We do not know if these applications came from the professors or from the students, but it is clear that in this case the university as a whole succeeded in allying itself with royal power so as to establish an accommodation with the people of the town. This episode is important for being the first well-documented case of the king of France consciously recognising the university and seeking to protect its existence with privileges. That these may have been a thorn in the flesh of the city council is clear; but with regard to the scholars' clerical status the result could hardly have been other than what it was.

The documented history of Oxford University begins with a similar episode, even if it had quite a different outcome, thanks to conditions in England at that time. At the start of the thirteenth century, the situation was influenced by the persistent attempts of King John (1199–1216) to increase his power over the barons at home as much as over the church, whose pope at this time was the forceful Innocent III (1198–1216). This dispute led to a general interdict on England in 1208 and to the king's excommunication in 1209. Now in the winter of 1208–1209, it happened that a student inadvertently killed a girl in a place inside the town boundary called Maiden Hall, after which he fled. The town rose in uproar, and when the culprit could not be found, his lodgings were broken into and two or three of his fellow students were seized and later hanged outside the town with the king's blessing.[4]

In the first instance this judicial murder led to the depopulation of the university. Obviously, neither town nor king was interested in upholding the law. According to contemporary but no doubt exaggerated accounts no less than 3,000 students and teachers left the town and settled elsewhere. Some went to London, others to

[3] Ibid. 72f.
[4] See Rashdall, vol. III, pp. 33f, Mallet, vol. I, pp. 31ff, and R. W. Southern in Catto, pp. 26ff.

Canterbury, and yet more continued their studies in Paris. In the meantime another group settled down in Cambridge, possibly because they originally came from there. While the others later returned to Oxford, these stayed in Cambridge, and in 1229 King Henry III (1216–1272), could be seen offering asylum in England and the possibility of studying in Cambridge, among other places, to students in exile from Paris. A year later a chancellor is mentioned in Cambridge. Thus events in Oxford caused the foundation of the University of Cambridge, in the same way as Oxford had grown enormously from the exodus from Paris in 1167.[5]

In Oxford subsequent events ran their course in close harmony with political developments. In 1212 Pope Innocent III had formally deposed the king and had sent the bishop of Tusculum, Cardinal Pandolfo, to England to announce this measure and free the English from their obligations to their former ruler. John capitulated to the church a year later and received his kingdom back as a fief from the pope. Nor could Oxford stand its ground, and in the same year the town sent a deputation to the papal legate in London to get the peace reinstated. The cardinal absolved the town on condition that those guilty of the hangings should walk barefoot round all the churches of Oxford and ask for absolution from the parish priests. To regulate affairs in the future, the cardinal issued an ordinance in 1214 that may be seen as the first legal privilege of Oxford University, analogous to the decree of Philippe Auguste in Paris in 1200. One of the penances of the town was that rents in student hospices should be halved for ten years, and in the ten years after that, should not be increased above the rate already agreed earlier by the masters and the town council. Furthermore, there would be price-controls on food, and twice a year the town would pay a sum to the university for distribution among students in need. In this respect the university had won a victory over the town, but with the help of the church – and with no support from the king.[6]

The great tensions between town and university in Bologna have already been mentioned. To all appearances nothing went on here as dramatically as in Oxford or Paris, but there was constant cause

---

[5] The contemporary sources are chiefly Walter Map, see Rashdall, vol. III, p. 34. On the migration to Cambridge in 1209, see Rashdall, vol. III, pp. 274ff; cf. Cooper, vol. I, p. 34 (after Matthew Paris).
[6] On the 1214 Oxford pronouncement, see Mallet, vol. I, p. 32. The legal document in question is in H. E. Salter, vol. I, pp. 2f.

for friction in financial matters. As already noted, this students' university had essentially only one card to play – the threat to leave town and thereby to rob it of an important source of income. The policy of the town council was therefore concerned with preventing such an emigration. The oath required of teachers to prevent them from leaving has already been mentioned. But disaster struck in 1204, when a substantial group of teachers and students left Bologna and founded the University of Vicenza. This was set up with many masters and four nations of students each with its own rector, but in spite of much lively activity, it only lasted a short while until 1209.[7]

This emigration lay behind the next move of the town, which was meant to end all possibility of the students acting in a united group. In the town statutes of 1211 and 1215 there are prohibitions against any one student swearing an oath to another to leave the town at the latter's insistence (here, of course, they were thinking of the rectors of nations);[8] contravention of this would be punished by the confiscation of the student's property and following that, by his exile. It is almost certain that in this case the town's legal advisers were none other than law professors of the university. In the face of such a crude attempt to break the power of the nations, the university reacted by appealing to Pope Honorius III (1216–1227), who had once been archdeacon of Bologna and thus knew its affairs from the inside. In a bull of 1217, the pope placed himself on the students' side completely, and advised them to leave the town rather than let themselves be compelled to recognise statutes that infringed their freedom of action.[9]

In the first instance, this support from the pope seems not to have made any impression on the town, and in 1220 a new bull sought a compromise by requiring the town to halt its persecution of students while rectors were required to swear to refrain from new plans to emigrate. However, this did not work either, and by 1222 dissatisfaction had reached such a peak that a part of the university left Bologna once more, moved to Padua, and there established a university which later became at least as important as Bologna and the main seat of higher learning in the Republic of

---

[7] On the exodus to Vicenza; see Rashdall, vol. II, p. 6. Rashdall, vol. I, p. 598 gives a summary of contemporary migrations from Bologna.
[8] Rashdall, vol. I, p. 170; Sorbelli, pp. 161f.
[9] The bull of 1217 of Honorius III is printed in Rashdall, vol. I, app. I, p. 585, followed on pp. 586–8 by the bull of 1220.

Venice.[10] Not long after there seems to have been a renewed application to the pope, who in 1224 for the third time urged the town of Bologna to give up its hard policy.[11]

That the pope's appeal had a better outcome for the university this time, is probably connected with developments in southern Italy, where the Emperor Frederic II (1208–1250) ruled both Sicilies, neither of which had till then had an independent university of its own. The king of Spain, Alfonso VIII of Castile (1158–1214), had already founded the University of Palencia in 1208–1209 on the basis of a cathedral school that existed there previously.[12] With this example in mind, Frederic II issued a decree in 1224 for the foundation of a new university in Naples.[13] Its charter is clearly influenced by the imperial *Habita* of 1158 and the later developments in Bologna; thus a ceiling was put on rents, that were to be fixed by a commission of two students and two people of the town, just as in Bologna. Even if the emperor's love of scholarship was incontestable, the University of Naples should be seen before anything else as one more move in Frederic II's constant battle against the papacy. Thus an ordinance forbade any of the emperor's subjects to study anywhere other than in Naples – a decree designed to rob the University of Bologna, which the pope supported, of a large part of its Italian students, and which is also the first example of the academic ordinance which later became a common measure to ensure the survival of a new foundation.

In this threatening situation the Bologna town council must have realised the sense of going softly, and conditions now gradually improved. It is true that the notorious request of the rectors was formally upheld in the town's own bylaws up to 1288; but already in 1245 new statutes were formed which gave the different nations full freedom to elect rectors, at the same time as the students got full civil (but not political) rights in the town.[14] A set of statutes from 1289 went even further and confirmed the right of rectors to adjudicate in civil disputes between students. In 1321 indeed there was yet another emigration to the University of Siena, which had already been

---

[10] Rashdall, vol. II, pp. 9ff, and Denifle, p. 277.
[11] On the papal intervention of 1224, see Rashdall, vol. I, p. 171.
[12] Rashdall, vol. II, p. 65.
[13] Denifle, pp. 452f; Rashdall, vol. II, pp. 21ff.
[14] On the Bologna statute of 1245 and the migration to Siena in 1321, see Rashdall, vol. I, p. 172.

recognised in 1252; but it was clear that the students of Bologna were gaining the field. At a certain time (before 1432), they were even able to demand of the town that its *podestà* should swear an oath to the university that it would observe its statutes. Thereby the situation was turned around, and the full freedom of the university in the town was established.

In these battles between the universities and civil authorities it was the royal powers that had a changeable attitude in England and France, whereas the church intervened everywhere on behalf of the universities, often by means of direct intervention from the pope. However, the relationship between church and university became gradually more complicated. Firstly, the church had a great number of practical opportunities to influence change in the universities through its many local or international courts; it could also interfere in the curriculum through its own doctrinal authority. Secondly, with respect to forms of organisation, Roman law and ecclesiastical law were fundamentally different. This led to tensions that were only slowly reduced. The trouble was that the university system was developing on the basis of a modern adaptation of the doctrine of corporations of Roman law; but this doctrine had no counterpart in canon law. In the structure of the church it is true that there were some organisations with certain corporative features, chiefly cathedral chapters and religious orders. The canons of a cathedral (or the priests of another collegiate church), as well as the monks in a monastery, could own property in common; they could even regulate the intake of new members into the community, and elect their own leader, in the form of a bishop or an abbot. This built on a tradition hundreds of years old, which really went back to the great privilege issued by Constantine the Great, who gave the priests at Christian churches the same rights of corporation that the priests of non-Christian temples already possessed. Yet there were real differences between these ecclesiastical communities and corporations in the Roman sense; while members could elect their own head, they would find it very hard to vote him out, given that bishops and abbots were elected for life. In addition, the bishop by virtue of his consecration automatically moved up higher in the hierarchy, just as the abbot through the rule and tradition of the order had titles far in excess of those that fell to the lot of an ordinary *praepositus* of a secular congregation.

All these matters were settled in Canon law, with the result that the church and its men were initially sceptical of attempts to organise corporations of teachers, quite apart from students. A synod in Rouen in 1189 thus refers to 'certain clerks as well as lay people who enter into a league so as to grant help to each other in all lawsuits and negotiations'.[15] The same synod passed a prohibition against such non-canonical unions. This had no practical consequences, since the new corporations continued to consolidate the rights they had obtained over the years, even though it needed a sometimes hard battle to stop the ecclesiastical authorities from making cathedral chapters or religious orders models for universities. If things had gone the other way, the university organisations would presumably have had leaders elected for life and would have come under direct control of the church. Europe would then have had scholarly orders besides religious ones, and the whole later development of our culture would have been different.

In the following pages we shall see in more detail the machinations that were carried on in the early thirteenth century between chancellors, bishops, and pope on one hand, and the universities on the other. Before anything else we must consider the changes in Paris, which are better known than elsewhere. Here the fight between the university and the church authorities went into several rounds, the first of which ended in 1215. This fight took place on home ground, with the bishop, cathedral chapter, and chancellor as the university's main opponents and the pope as its distant protector; everything about this can be understood if it is clear what the different parties had to fear as a result of the birth of the university.

The pope had nothing to fear, but, on the contrary, could regard the theologically oriented University of Paris as a valuable instrument for spreading the faith. Pope Alexander IV (1254–1261) later expressed this in the usual florid curia style, in a letter to the university normally known as *Quasi lignum vitae* and dated 14 April 1255: 'The learning of the Paris schools is to Holy Church as the Tree of Life in the earthly paradise ... Misshapen in the congenital blindness of its ignorance, humanity regains its vision and beauty in Paris through the acknowledging of the true light that radiates outwards from the theology here.'[16] A similar point of view certainly moved Innocent III (1198–1216) to support the University of Paris

---

[15] On the Rouen synod of 1189, see Denifle, p. 142, note 25.
[16] *Quasi lignum vitae* is printed in *Chartularium* I, 279–85.

The battle for the universities 165

throughout his eventful period of office, with all his power and great diplomatic ability. It was also from Paris that he had a master's degree in theology himself, just as he had a law degree from Bologna. In 1205 he did his best to enable the masters of Paris to go to Constantinople to help in the Latinising of the city and to promote scholarship in the east.[17] Similarly two years later, on 14 November 1207, he tried to prevent the teaching staff of the university from becoming lower-class citizens, by commanding the bishop as far as possible to keep the number of masters of theology down to eight – though this ordinance was soon undermined, even by the popes themselves.[18] Even in 1218 Pope Honorius III (1216–1227) lamented that the chancellor was denying the *licentia docendi* to a certain master of theology by the name of Matthaeus de Scotia, by referring to the decree of 1207, notwithstanding that according to the pope himself it was no longer respected.[19]

It was another matter with Bishop Odo of Paris (accountable to the archbishop of Sens, the former Paris Canon Pierre de Corbeil). From the bishop's point of view the forming of a masters' corporation would look like a threat. The quick flowering of this body and its marked tendency towards autonomy spelt danger for the bishop: soon he would lose that control over theological teaching which his office obliged him to exercise. As bishop he could have no authority over a free, professional corporation – this in any case was the teacher's point of view – even if the royal privileges of 1200 had established the bishop's jurisdiction over all members of the university. There were only two possibilities left: either to undermine the university from within by excommunicating its students and masters, or to contest the very legitimacy of the teachers' guild. As we shall see, both options were tried.

We know little of the first clash between bishop and university; we only know of the after-effects from a letter of 1208, in which the pope's cardinal legate in France, Guala Bichierius, limited the bishop's immediate right to excommunicate *magistri* and *scholares*.[20] In future this would only be allowed to happen after two prior warnings, the first one delivered in general terms by the other masters, the second by the naming of the person in the school itself. From the form of the letter it appears that hereby the legate was

---

[17] Ibid. 62f; it was a consequence of the conquest of the city in 1204 and the establishment of a Latin kingdom under Baldwin I.
[18] *Chartularium* I, 65.   [19] Ibid. 85.   [20] Ibid. 66.

softening his own previous decrees. Consequently, the bishop's authority was being limited.

In this matter the Paris masters cannot have failed to notice that in the pope they had a powerful ally. That they did not hesitate to take advantage of this, appears from a papal letter of 1208–9 addressed to *Universis doctoribus sacre pagine, decretorum et liberalium artium Parisiis commorantibus*, 'To all doctors of theology, law and *artes liberales* living in Paris'.[21] First referred to here are certain doctors in *artes liberales* standing accused of unseemly dress, of not respecting order or the peace during lectures and disputations, of having neglected the requiem masses it was incumbent on them to celebrate; the last accusation strengthens the suspicion that it was the bishop who submitted the charge. These irregularities had led to the dismissal of a certain Master G. (the pope is content with the initial, leniently enough), whose reinstatement Innocent meanwhile demanded on condition that he observed the teachers' statutes.

This letter is of the greatest interest, because it shows the university now going directly to the pope over the head of the bishop, whose authority over the university is not even mentioned by the pope. It also shows that at this time there were already statutes for corporations of teachers in the subjects of theology, law, and *artes liberales*; that medicine is not numbered among them is only an oversight. However, these statutes have not survived.

We do not know what impression this reversal made on Bishop Odo, whom in any case Pierre de Nemours replaced soon afterwards. That the bishops constantly had a hostile attitude to the university was already apparent in a synod chaired by Pierre de Corbeil in 1210, in which the bishops availed themselves of their doctrinal authority to stamp out a heresy among the supporters of Amaury de Bene, who had been professor of logic and then theology up to his death in 1206–7.[22] A later list of his heretical doctrines shows him as a successor to Johannes Scotus Erigena, with certain pantheistic tendencies.[23] The synod decreed that Amaury's body should be disinterred and buried in unconsecrated earth, that four of his disciples should be imprisoned for the rest of their lives, and that ten more – most of them priests in or around Paris – should be handed over to the secular authorities, which burned them at the

---

[21] Ibid. 67f.   [22] Ibid. 70f.
[23] The list of Amaury's heresies is printed in *Chartularium* I, 71f; on his philosophy, see Gilson, pp. 383f.

stake in the same year. This extremely cruel measure revealed the desire of the bishop to make an example and to put fear into the university. Yet the decisions of the synod were also interesting for another reason: they contained an ordinance that 'Aristotle's books on natural philosophy must not be read in Paris either publicly or privately.' This is the first indication of the battle over Aristotelianism, that became so strongly characteristic of the first age of the universities as an ideological smokescreen covering the more fundamental fight for sovereignty over the institution itself.

One can easily imagine what an impression an interference of such force and cruelty must have made on the university. Even if hardly anyone wished to impugn the doctrinal office of the bishops and their right to take action where heresies were concerned, it was not a case of theology alone. The ban on reading those works of Aristotle that had just been translated and that now appeared as the very pillars of modern thinking – here the target was presumably the *Metaphysics* and the *Physics* – deprived masters of *artes liberales* of their most interesting object of study, and at the same time made it impossible for theologians to continue their work on formulating the doctrine of faith in that philosophical language that was now increasingly found to be the only one suitable.

In this situation the step the pope next took was highly remarkable. Innocent III formally overruled neither the 1210 synod nor the archbishop of Sens – this would have made problems for the church of an incalculable extent in France, at a time when the pope had his hands full in England. Instead, at the beginning of 1212, he appointed Robert de Courçon both as cardinal and as papal legate in France.[24] The point is that Robert was one of Paris University's own masters in theology, who suddenly thus got a higher status than the local prelates. With this move, papal diplomacy once more enabled itself to exert influence irrespective of the interests of the normal hierarchy.

Perhaps it was this handshake from the pope that made the university come out so firmly against the next move of the local church that came from the chancellor of the cathedral chapter, Johannes Cancellarius (Jean de Chandelle), who had entered office in 1209. From his point of view the university was no less menacing than it seemed to the bishop. As shown earlier, the chancellor had

[24] *Chartularium* I, 78f.

been the *ex-officio* director of teaching in the cathedral school. As such he had had the privilege of conferring the *licentia docendi* upon new masters, something that earned him a comfortable perquisite. After the teachers' guild was set up, the position of the chancellor became more questionable. There is nothing to show that he was necessarily a member of the corporation, even though this was not out of the question either. But in all cases the chancellor's claim to be the only one who could bestow the *licentia docendi* had been a thorn in the flesh of the guild, which, according to the general principles of the corporation, should have had the power itself to decide who should be inducted as a new member. Nor do we know the real cause of the struggle in detail, but on 20 January 1212 Innocent III wrote to Bishop Hervaeus of Troyes that it had come to his attention that in Paris Johannes Cancellarius was locked in battle with the students and was pressing them to pay dues which he turned to his own use.[25] This shows that the Lateran Council's decree concerning the free *licentia docendi* had been violated by Johannes, while nothing of this kind is known from the time of his predecessor Prepositinus. It is also worth noting that the pope here referred to the bishop of Troyes and not to Bishop Pierre of Paris, who would have been the nearest choice for taking on the case.

In the meantime the Paris bishop felt compelled to take over the affair himself, considering such a crude violation of a decree from an ecumenical council. Thus we have a memorandum from the bishop of August 1213 in which he arbitrates an agreement between the chancellor and the *magistros et scholares Parisiensis*.[26] This arrangement came into being thanks to six arbitrators, three appointed by the chancellor and three masters of the university. In general terms it was established that the chancellor should not take dues of any kind *pro licentia legendi*, that he should not imprison clerks without cause, and that he should immediately turn over imprisoned clerks to the bishop, who could let them out on bail. In those cases where the chancellor was himself the judge, he was not allowed to take payment from any of the parties. In addition, there was a series of special decrees that would only apply in Johannes' remaining period of office. Thus he was not allowed to refuse to give the *licentia docendi* to any student of theology if the majority of the teachers of theology found him of the appropriate standard; yet he could go on

[25] Ibid. 73f.   [26] Ibid. 75f.

distributing the *licentia* without the teachers' consent to whomsoever he himself found to be of the standard. Similar decrees are found for teachers of law and medicine, and yet here the bishop himself could give the *licentia* if the chancellor refused. With respect to students of *artes* a jury elected for six months and composed of three members appointed by the masters and three by the chancellor should decide the candidate's fitness with a simple majority, in case the chancellor refused to give the *licentia*; yet here too he could let candidates pass without the jury being consulted. The agreement was certified by Johannes Cancellarius in August 1213 in a short written statement, after which Bishop Hervaeus of Troyes proclaimed it publicly in November of the same year.[27]

A contributory cause of the Paris chancellor's defeat in this case was the fact that he was no longer alone in being able to bestow the *licentia docendi*, since the abbot of the monastery of St Geneviève had gradually arrogated the same authority to himself. This was confirmed in 1227 by Pope Gregory IX (1227–1241), and was made possible by the normal decree of ecclesiastical law that freed abbeys from the jurisdiction of the local bishop.[28] Students of the *artes*, in particular, availed themselves of this opportunity to get a *licentia* 'on the hill' (i.e. on Mont Sainte Geneviève), and in ever growing numbers they moved west to Vicus Stramineus (Rue de Fouarre), that lay in the abbot's territory. The street-name in due time became synonymous with the whole faculty.

In many ways, the battle with the chancellor was a very interesting proof of the university's collusion with the pope so as to ensure a freedom that was otherwise threatened by the chancellor's violation of the decrees of the Lateran Council. It shows teachers and students in the face of encroachments from outside uniting as one group to appeal directly to the pope over the head of the bishop. What is more, it appears that the pope consented to this procedure, and that in this case he made use of the help of a foreign bishop; since presumably he regarded the bishop of Paris as party to the case and therefore disqualified in it. In this respect it was expressly confirmed on the pope's part that the university in Paris was responsible to him and not to the local bishop. In other words the Paris institution became the university of the whole church, free of the interests of the

---

[27] The 1213 declaration of John Cancellarius is in *Chartularium* I, 76; on its publication, ibid. I, 77.
[28] Ibid. 511.

local clergy. Beyond this, this document is important for being the first evidence of the four categories of scholars in Paris: theologians, jurists, medieval scholars, and students of *artes*. At the same time it provides an outline of the first examination system (with jury) in the school of the *artes*.

After these two skirmishes, the bishops thus emerged masters of the sphere of education and dogma, while on the administrative side the university had won a victory against the chancellor. The tension was in no way diminished by this, however, and new action from the papacy was required. This came in the person of the new cardinal legate Robert de Courçon, who summoned a new Paris synod in 1213 at which he presided himself above the archbishop.[29] By and large, the decrees of this synod left the university in peace but regulated its relationship to the parish clergy and religious orders: the parish clergy could not continue their studies without the permission of their superiors, monks were recalled to their monasteries regardless of any earlier permission, and their further education was to take place within the cloister walls. These decrees may seem strange, but they would surely have been able to lessen the risk of clashes between the university and the bishop, by keeping the clergy immediately subordinate to him away from the scholars' world. Finally and with the direct mandate of the pope – *cum domini pape speciale habuissemus mandatum* – Robert de Courçon issued a set of laws in August 1215 concerning the ordering of university affairs. These rules were also given without the bishop's collaboration and may be considered the first known statutes of the University of Paris, by which it was formally established as a papal university.[30] The individual decrees talk in plain language of the problems that were the most real at this time.

Firstly, there was a series of detailed rules for study and examination at the faculty of *artes*. This will be discussed later in another context. After this, however, came a number of paragraphs most relevant to the existence of the university itself: first, a repetition of the decree that no payment was to be made for the *licentia docendi*; second, freedom of union was established expressly for teachers and students alike. The latter was something new; but both parties had unrestricted permission to associate to defend themselves against violence and assault, to evaluate rents and so on, just so long as

[29] Ibid. 77f.   [30] Ibid. 78–80.

nothing was undertaken that might destroy or dissolve the university. In general it is stated that no-one could be a student in Paris without a specific master, who would also provide teaching premises for his own students.

About other studies there is just the proviso that masters of theology should be no less than thirty-five years of age or should have studied theology for at least eight years. Scholars of law and medicine are not mentioned. Nevertheless, we can here distinguish the basic features of a system of study whereby a boy started with the study of *artes liberales* for six years and finished with an examination that gave him the title of *magister artium*. After this he could undertake an eight-year course in theology and become *magister theologiae*; or he could go further as a scholar of law or medicine – though this is not directly mentioned in the document itself.

Clearly these decrees would have served as the basis for an accommodation between the university as a teaching institution and the bishop as the controlling doctrinal authority. This meant that the prohibitions against dangerous writings made by the 1210 synod were upheld, even while masters were permitted to incorporate certain new features from Aristotle in their teaching. Yet from the university's point of view, the statutes of 1215 must have seemed as yet another victory over both bishop and chancellor. Now it could breathe more easily and could seriously set about extending the range of teaching without fear of constant interference on the part of the local authorities.

But this was not how it turned out. Scarcely was this battle's first round over when the second one started. In the following years it was obvious that bishop and chancellor regarded themselves as in no way defeated, but on the contrary were constantly trying to regain their power in all kinds of ways. Thus they unearthed an old ordinance against conspiracies and excommunicated the university *en bloc* for not adhering to it;[31] on inquiry they revealed that 'conspiracies' simply meant the corporations that the statutes had made legitimate. Not until Honorius III had issued a whole series of papal bulls did the bishop of Paris stop opposing the duly recognised freedom of union.[32] Something indicates that the university in these years kept a sort of permanent lobby at the papal court, so as to

---

[31] On the pronouncement against conspiracies, see *Chartularium* I, 87f, and Rashdall, vol. I, pp. 310f.
[32] *Chartularium* I, 87–90.

make its point of view constantly felt; the expenditure involved led to a heavy debt which was financed by money borrowed from merchants in Florence.

The extent to which the church authorities in Paris could make life difficult for the university appeared once more in the years between 1228 and 1230, when an otherwise trivial incident suddenly developed to catastrophic proportions and nearly caused the complete collapse of the university. It started with carnival antics in the winter of 1228–9, when some students quarrelled with an innkeeper about the bill. Riots inevitably followed, and with the help of some citizens, the students were chased out of the town.[33] The next day they came back with armed reinforcements, rased the inn to the ground, and let the wine run dry in the gutters. The police were called, and the bishop appealed to the reigning queen, Blanca of Castilla, who gave orders to clamp down hard. Then the police killed a number of innocent students who had taken no part in the riots. The role of the bishop in this affair is therefore much less flattering, as all the scholars were under his jurisdiction and protection; at any rate the police quietly turned a blind eye on the real perpetrators. Only a deep hostility between university and bishopric in Paris can explain this judicial murder.

The university's reply came swiftly and with a strength that showed how active and well organised both corporations of teachers and students now were. Notice was given that if this misdeed was not put right within one month, the university would disband for a period of six years.[34] After words came deeds; most teachers and scholars left town. Some went to Oxford and Cambridge, invited by King Henry III,[35] while others settled in various French schools, chiefly in Toulouse and Angers. To compensate for this reverse, King Louis IX in August 1229 confirmed Philippe Auguste's privileges granted in 1200, while there was lively activity from the lobby in Rome.[36] Only in 1231 did the university resume its work in Paris, at the same time as Pope Gregory IX again established and broadened its privileges with his bull *Parens Scientiarum*.[37] The right of the university to form its own corporative statutes was emphasised, and a new right was introduced to suspend teaching and go on strike in the event of any injustices not being expiated within fifteen days. At the same time, the wings of the

---

[33] On the riots of 1229, see Rashdall, vol. 1, pp. 334ff (after Matthew Paris).
[34] *Chartularium* I, 118; Rashdall, vol. 1, pp. 336f.
[35] Ibid. 119.   [36] Ibid. 120–2.   [37] Ibid. 136–9 (*Parens scientiarum*).

bishop and chancellor were clipped even further. There is a very telling paragraph confirming that no bishop could arrest innocent students in place of guilty ones, nor put a student in jail for debt, nor impose fines on them. The chancellor could not keep a jail of his own (this had already been decided by Honorius III in 1222,[38] but obviously had not been carried out), but was to move arrested persons straightaway to the bishop's jail, from which, as before, they could be released on bail. Finally the chancellor was to deposit on oath to be impartial in examinations and not to disclose which way individual examination jurors had voted! In a later letter of 10 May 1231, the pope further proclaimed that within a seven-year period no member of the university could be excommunicated without special permission from the Holy See.[39] This robbed the bishop of his most powerful weapon. The privilege was renewed in 1237 and later on after each period of seven years. On the other hand this bull gave the chancellor a little more authority than he had with the statutes of 1215, for now he was allowed to issue the *licentia docendi* if he had only taken advice from the teachers. The bull did not in any case invalidate the 1215 statutes, just as little as it corroborated them directly. All the same, it resulted in more peace and quiet in the university, and though to the end of the century there was still a marked chill in relations between the university and the cathedral chapter, it never came to such violent collisions as before – even if there had to be a constant stream of reminders from the pope to maintain the peace. Thus with the papal bull of 1231 the second round in the battle was effectively won.

With the bull *Parens Scientarum* the university had acquired the right to organise and to strike. This was owing to constant support from the papacy during the first two rounds of the battle for power. It is therefore a little ironic that the first time these rights were seriously used was in a dispute that came within a hairsbreadth of bringing the university into a position of permanent antagonism with the Roman See. This happened with the new attempts of the mendicant orders to get a foothold in the faculty of theology. The development of the relationship between the University of Paris and the orders of Franciscans and Dominicans therefore deserves a little closer attention.

These new orders can be viewed as the medieval attempt to adapt

---

[38] Ibid. 102–4.   [39] Ibid. 147.

the religious life to the steadily more complicated urban societies on which the older orders, in their cloistered isolation in the countryside, could not have any influence. Francis of Assisi (1182–1226) had conceived of a movement of laymen that was to offer renewed testimony of the gospel with a life spent in apostolic poverty. Through the cardinal Hugolin Conti, the church had transformed the movement into a real order with a special rule established in 1223 by Pope Honorius III, just as Hugolin, or Pope Gregory IX (1227–1241) as he became, later made scholarly studies part of the everyday life of the order.[40] On the other hand the Dominican order had always been conceived as an order of priests, founded by the Spanish Premonstratensian Dominicus (c. 1170–1221), and established already in 1216 by Honorius III.[41] One characteristic common to both orders was the ban on property and paid labour. The brothers were to live on alms – hence their name 'mendicants' or begging monks. At the same time the Dominicans had the avowed aim of working as preachers in any place where evangelising was urgently needed, such as areas with extensive heretical movements and in the towns.

The real need for these new orders is demonstrated by the speed with which they spread out over Europe. Already in 1217 there were Dominicans in Paris, in 1221 they were in England, and in 1222 Brother Solomon, the first Dominican to go to Denmark, settled in Aarhus.[42] Two other orders of mendicants came to characterise the life of the towns of the later middle ages, apart from many lesser ones which need not be discussed further here. They were the so-called Augustinian 'hermits' and the Carmelites, both of which had arisen out of previously loosely based societies that now organised themselves on much the same lines as the Franciscans and Dominicans.

As an *ordo praedicatorum*, an 'order of preachers', the Dominicans would naturally have had a special connection with study, and it is

---

[40] Ibid. 160. A major work on St Francis is P. Sabatier, *Vie de S. François d'Assise*, Paris, 1893 (numerous later edns) with its critical review of the source material. See also P. Gratien, *Histoire de la fondation et de l'évolution de l'Ordre des Frères Mineurs au XIIIe siècle*, Paris, 1928, and the excellent biography by Johannes Jørgensen, *Saint François d'Assise*, Paris, 1916.

[41] See P. Mandonnet, *Saint Dominique*, vols. I–II, Paris, 1937, and M.-H. Vicaire, *Histoire de Saint Dominique*, vols. I–II, Paris, 1957. An excellent survey of the new orders can be found in D. Knowles, *The Religious Orders in England*, vol. I, Cambridge, 1948, pp. 114–204.

[42] On the Dominicans in Denmark, see E. Wedel-Jarlsberg, *La Province de Dacie*, Rome–Tournai, 1889, and J. Gallen, *La province de Dacie*, vol. I, Helsinki, 1946.

no coincidence that their houses could soon be found in all university towns. In Paris they were warmly received by the university, which conveyed to them a site at St Jacques, which was to remain their most important religious house in France right up to the Revolution in 1789.⁴³ Dominican training required theology to be taught in each house of its order. The general chapter in Paris directly stated in 1228 that no house was to be founded without a lector in theology with four years of theological study behind him.⁴⁴ On the other hand no teaching in secular sciences nor in *artes liberales* was to be undertaken in any houses of the order. Clearly this syllabus had been drawn up in order to train preachers quickly, since it omitted the introductory study of *artes* that was the inevitable basis of university education and the precondition for any further study.

The success of the Dominicans in Paris immediately became apparent. At regular intervals the general master Jordanus of Saxony was able to write reports on the growing numbers entering the order, not least students and masters. In 1224 over forty novices alone entered between Advent and Easter, and in four weeks in 1226 a total of twenty-one arrived, six of them masters of the *artes*.⁴⁵ With this the contact between the order and the university was made a fact; at the same time something similar was happening with the Franciscans. The benevolent attitude of the university – brought about by many papal commands to receive the new orders well – is apparent in the fact that, even at an early stage, Dominican lectors in theology were taken in as members of the university, where one of the chairs in theology was now occupied by a Dominican, Master Roland. It cannot be inferred from this that a theologian of the order changed his position by becoming a member of the university. He continued to teach in his own religious house, but as a member of the teachers' assembly he had influence over the administration of the university and could submit his students for the examination and *licentia* on a par with the others. In 1231 the Franciscans also got a professor of their own, even if by another route, when a master of theology at the university, the Englishman Alexander of Hales (d. 1245), abandoned his secular status and entered the order.⁴⁶

In the meantime this harmony came under heavy strain in the university strike of 1229 to 1231. For the mendicants this meant a

⁴³ *Chartularium* I, 99f.   ⁴⁴ Ibid. 112f.   ⁴⁵ Ibid. 106 and 108f.
⁴⁶ On Alexander of Hales, see *Chartularium* I, 135n. (after Roger Bacon); on his philosophy, see Gilson, pp. 436ff.

loyalty crisis: should they be loyal to the order and remain in their religious houses in town, or to the university and follow the same diversion as the teachers? Here loyalty to the order took absolute precedence, and neither Dominicans nor Franciscans took part in the strike. It also seems that during the strike St Jacques fished in troubled waters by recruiting masters who had not left the town. One of these was the best-known teacher of logic of his day, Walter Teutonicus, who entered the order in 1229.[47]

This position would of course cause the university some unease, but did not lead immediately to any breach. From 1235 to 1238 we find both Masters Hugo de St Cher of the Dominicans (d. 1263) and Johannes de Rupella of the Franciscans (d. 1245) in the company of other theologians from the university as delegates on a commission to negotiate with Bishop Guillaume d'Auvergne.[48] Both men at this time kept their normal status in the teachers' corporation, just as the Dominicans got themselves suitable noticed by their scholarly efforts. Thus in 1236 under the guidance of the same Hugo de St Cher they completed the revision of the Vulgate which came to be the basis of the Latin text of the Bible that was later used everywhere.

Meanwhile a smouldering dissatisfaction grew, fanned by the many other orders that came into existence outside, and also by the older orders of Cluny and Cîteaux gradually abandoning their declared policy and setting up centres of study in the town, with a resulting demand on teaching facilities. In February 1252 the university reacted officially for the first time, prompted by the theologians, who were now starting to make use of their right to issue statutes on the admission of teachers in theology.[49] These stated that members of orders could not be taken into the *societas* of masters unless they had a *collegium* of their own; that only one member could be taken in from each religious house; and that all those concerned should have given lessons under a university teacher (i.e. should be university trained). The aim was obviously to limit the number of mendicants among professors, and the background was the loyalty dilemma mentioned above: in a crisis the teachers' corporation would lose its power to negotiate, unless a

---

[47] *Chartularium* I, 131f.
[48] Ibid. 157f, where the revision of the Vulgate is also mentioned; cf. *The Cambridge History of the Bible*, vol. II, Cambridge, 1969, pp. 148f.
[49] *Chartularium* I, 226f.

The battle for the universities

majority of its members sided with the university. This was something that the mendicants could never have done, either now or in the future.

While the religious orders seemed to have resigned themselves to this, events of the following year 1253 soon proved the university's scepticism to be fully justified. It all started in the usual way: a student was killed by the police during street disturbances, and in violation of the privileges of 1231 many others were jailed.[50] The university took up its old but now fully legitimate weapon and decreed a *cessatio*, or strike. The two Dominicans and one Franciscan among the theologians refused to cooperate, and appealed to the pope. Because of this the strike soon lost its impetus, whereupon the university demanded an oath of all its teachers to stand by each other in their claim for justice. This course the mendicants also refused, after which the teachers' corporation expelled them and forbade scholars to go to any of their lectures.

This was the beginning of the crisis which in the years to come shook the university more violently than anything ever before. In reality the situation was desperate: the university built its existence on papal privileges and could not ensure this existence as a body independent of the religious orders without offending the pope, the same source of their privileges, who had also taken the orders under his special protection. This meant that the university stood alone in this matter and had to weather the storm on its own. First it passed a resolution in April 1253, according to which no-one could 'be admitted to the company of masters or to the consortium of our university' unless he swore on oath to respect the statutes, and in particular, to take part in agreed strike action.[51] The resolution was dismissed by Pope Innocent IV, who repeatedly commanded the university to reinstate the expelled teachers and stop their spitefulness against the religious orders.[52] But the university stood fast, and on 4 February 1254 replied in an open letter, in which the problems were stated in detail, from the *corpus collegii sive Universitatis* and addressed to all prelates and university people in the world.[53] It appeared that there were now fifteen professors of theology in all (whereas Innocent III, as shown previously, had established a maximum of eight), of whom three were canons and nine mendi-

---

[50] On the riots of 1253, see Rashdall, vol. I, pp. 377f.
[51] *Chartularium* I, 242–4.   [52] Ibid. 247–51.   [53] Ibid. 252–8.

cants. This meant that only three positions were occupied by ordinary secular masters. In consequence, secular students had never had much prospect of gaining a chair. Furthermore it was maintained that there were far too many professors as against students, and that this had come about through the need of religious orders to further their own members' careers in the university.

Literary weapons were also brought into play in this feud. A Franciscan by the name of Gerardo de Borgo San Donnino, a lector in the Franciscan house in Paris, had published a fantastical, apocalyptic treatise entitled *Introductorium in Evangelium Aeternum*. This the faculty of theology cut to pieces in 1254, as containing thirty-one examples of heterodoxy – no doubt in the quiet hope of their condemnation discrediting the Franciscan order as a whole.[54] At the same time the theologian Guillaume de St Amour (d. 1272) issued a pamphlet called *De Periculis Novissimorum Temporum* (*On the Dangers of Most Recent Times*) with a violent attack on the friars in general, whom he presented as forerunners of Antichrist and harbingers of the last days. This was also condemned, of course, and by the pope himself in 1256.[55]

In the meantime Pope Alexander IV tried to calm the waters by issuing on 14 April 1255 the bull already quoted earlier, *Quasi Lignum Vitae*.[56] From the university's point of view this text offered a very unsatisfactory compromise. The chancellor was allowed to give the *licentia docendi* to as many candidates as he found appropriate – after having examined them personally himself. This would only mean a stream of new masters from the religious orders swamping the university without obeying its authority. In compensation there was a decree that all members of religious orders had to respect a strike; but this command was made illusory anyway by a new rule, according to which a strike could only be ratified by a majority of at least two-thirds; this effectively enabled the orders, who inevitably occupied more than a third of the chairs, to prevent any strike at all. On the same day the pope proceeded to command the university to reinstate the expelled teachers within a fortnight.

The university also tried to stand firm against these demands. In a joint communication on 2 October 1255 from masters and students in all faculties – not only theology, where the dispute lay – the pope was informed that the bull *Quasi Lignum Vitae* was damaging to the

[54] Ibid. 272–5. [55] Ibid. 319–23. [56] Ibid. 279–85.

university.[57] Their case was explained in great detail, and furthermore it was pointed out that the expelled mendicant professors could not be admitted at the pope's command, as the teachers' *consortium* was a free association whose members had come together through friendship, not compulsion. Rather than comply with the papal commands, therefore, they would renounce all privileges and leave the town, to set up another university elsewhere, or, should the pope oppose this, each one of them would go home to his people and there enjoy the freedom that in Paris was crushed by a compulsion which forced more and more people to leave the university, a body that would soon perish for ever as a result. Below the letter were the seals of the four nations.

Yet Pope Alexander IV was still unyielding. His reply came soon, on 7 December 1255, in the form of an order to the bishops to excommunicate all masters who would not respect *Quasi Lignum Vitae*[58]. Though with various manoeuvrings the university managed to stop it getting that far for the time being, the situation was more acute than ever before. In reality it had reached stalemate, for just as the university, on the basis of its earlier experiences, could not dream of existing without the support of the pope, so neither could Alexander IV make a final breach with them without ruining the whole education policy that his predecessors had carefully built up.

The secular professors of theology had felt without doubt that their position in this struggle was very strong – and with justice. For one thing they had a united university behind them, with both students and teachers rallying in rebellion against the pope, naturally not including the mendicants that the whole dispute was about. For another, they had done nothing to oppose the ordinances and statutes that earlier popes had recognised and confirmed. The pope had no legal case for forcing unwanted colleagues on them, and his attempts to get his way with threats of excommunication were a brazen fiat that had no effect on the united stand taken by the university. Finally, because of these statutes, he could not prevent the secular teachers from forbidding their own students to go to the mendicants' lectures. That such a boycott really took place, is known from a report by the Dominican general master, Humbert, on the

---

[57] Ibid. 292–7. Cf. M. M. Dufeil, *Guillaume de Saint-Amour et la polémique universitaire parisienne 1250–1259*, Paris, 1972.
[58] *Chartularium* I, 299f.

obstruction his order met with in Paris in 1256.[59] So all things considered, there was little chance of stopping the university from committing suicide if it really wished to do so.

It was in this situation that Alexander IV took a step allowing him to manoeuvre his way round a catastrophe while saving face and legality at the same time. In the beginning of 1256 he approached the chancellor in Paris and asked him to give one Thomas Aquinas (1225–1274), a young Dominican in St Jacques, the *licentia docendi* in theology.[60] Formally there was nothing wrong in this, since the chancellor, as already shown, had the right on the basis of a paragraph in the *Parens Scientarum* of 1231 to give the *licentia* to anyone he himself found qualified. But this hated paragraph had already ensured that the faculty was filled up with an abundant supply of unwanted friars, and in this affair the pope's decision to invoke it once more undeniably looked like a provocation to the university.

That the foundations were laid here for a fruitful development, at any rate, were probably due to Thomas Aquinas and to the fact that he was no commonplace lector of a religious order. As his name shows, he came from the south of Italy, and already as quite a young man he had shown his independence by leaving the Benedictine monastery on Monte Cassino for a life as a mendicant among the Dominicans. This had led him first to various religious houses in Italy, and then in the period 1245–8 to Paris, from which he followed his teacher Albert the Great (1193–1280) to the new *studium generale* of the Dominicans in Cologne. From here in 1252 he went back to Paris, where with his baccalaureate he started to teach theology. His great commentary to the *Sententiae* of Peter the Lombard was written from 1254 onwards.[61]

Thomas' teaching in Paris was an enormous success. His biographer Peter Calo says that 'when Thomas had taken on his duties as teacher and begun his lectures and disputations, the students flocked

---

[59] Ibid. 309–13.
[60] Ibid. 307, on Thomas Aquinas' *licentia*, which was given after the pope's consultation with Humbert and must have seemed provocative since Thomas was four years short of the required age of thirty-five.
[61] Of the very comprehensive literature on Thomas Aquinas, only the latest biography can be mentioned here: J. A. Weisheipl, *Friar Thomas d'Aquino, His Life, Thought and Works*, Oxford, 1975; but see also the popular, very lively, and accurate little work by G. K. Chesterton, *St. Thomas Aquinas*, London, 1933. Among studies of Thomas as a thinker are E. Gilson, *Le Thomisme*, Paris, 5th edn, 1947, and F. Copleston, *Aquinas*, London, 1955.

around him in such numbers that the auditorium could scarcely hold all those who were drawn there by the teaching of this outstanding master and spurred on to greater progress in learning. Many masters blossomed out in the light of his teaching. The reason for his success was the clever, clear, and plain style of his lectures.'[62] This last statement is quite correct, but is hardly the whole story; another biographer, Bernardus Guidonis, reveals a little more of the reason, when he says 'he brought new talents to his lectures, introduced new methods as proofs in his argumentation. Anyone, therefore, who heard him teach new theories and solve matters of dispute and other difficulties with new arguments, could not but believe that God Himself had illumined this thinker with the rays of a new light.'[63]

In another context we shall return to Thomas Aquinas, to see what his innovations were. For the time being it is enough to say that his activity brought the Dominicans remarkable academic success, and that this happened just in the period after 1256 which was the most critical for the university, when through its opposition to the Dominicans everything threatened to go to pieces. The Franciscans also enjoyed a part of the students' good will, thanks to their own outstanding theologian Iohannes de Firdanza, called Bonaventura (1221–1274), who got his *licentia* at about the time Thomas Aquinas did.

Perhaps it had been the concealed but shrewd intention of Pope Alexander IV to allow secular professors to rage as much as they liked against the mendicants, while the latter gently ousted them from their place in the regard of the students, through sheer scholarly and pedagogic brilliance. There is much to show the correctness of this assessment. In any case the university made no serious attempt to close itself down. Its opposition to the mendicant professors slowly smouldered the more the auditoria of these men filled and their own rooms emptied. After a while the striking secular professors quietly came back, were removed one by one from their excommunication and took up their work once more in free competition with their former enemies – regularly warned through papal letters to behave themselves properly. The death of Alexander IV in 1261 and the election as pope of a Paris master by the name of Urban IV (1261–1264) brought this turbulent period to an end. In

---

[62] Petrus Calo, *Vita S. Thomae*, ch. 11, in D. Prümmer (ed.), *Fontes Vitae Sancti Thomae*, vol. I, Toulouse, 1912.

[63] Bernard Guidonis, *Legenda S. Thomae*, ch. 11, ibid. vol. III, Toulouse, 1925.

due course the former conflicts were forgotten. The mendicants appeared to be more amenable than expected and contented themselves with getting one or two from their order made professors, and with being excluded from teaching in the faculty of *artes*. In 1318 they even accepted the oath on the statutes that they had refused to swear in 1253 – the cause of the whole dispute.[64]

How great was the role that the religious orders came to play in theological teaching in Paris can be seen from the list of theologians who got the *licentia docendi* in the period 1373–98. The total number was 192, implying an annual average of about eight. But out of these 102 were mendicants, 17 were Benedictine monks and only 47 were secular clergy.[65] This means that the great part of theology was based on the religious orders and their teaching. Yet the secular theologians in the second half of the thirteenth century acquired a strong power-base in the Collège de Sorbonne, which was very well provided for and gave them all the advantages of a religious house without subjecting them to any authority outside the university.

In this way, in the first hundred years of its existence the university of Paris was forced to test its strength in all spheres with both secular and ecclesiastical authorities. It is obvious that other universities in the same situation followed this battle with interest; however, in most cases they were spared the necessity of fighting the battle to the same extent. The result was that Paris came to act as the vanguard of the universities in general. For this reason there will be no further discussion here of the other universities' fight for freedom in Europe. Instead we must consider conditions in Oxford and Cambridge, which in many ways came to diverge from the pattern known on the continent.

The unique position of the English universities in these developments was chiefly due to the fact that neither Oxford nor Cambridge were episcopal sees. Oxford belonged to the huge diocese of Lincoln, and the bishop of Lincoln was a remote figure in the daily life of the town. Cambridge lay within the bishopric of Ely, being governed by an archdeacon resident in the town who had no association either with the Ely cathedral school or with any of the schools in Cambridge. This meant in practice that the chancellors at

---

[64] *Chartularium* II, 227f, and Rashdall, vol. I, p. 393; the oath also included the Cistercians and the Hermits of St Augustine.

[65] The number of theological candidates in 1373–98 is derived from the annual lists in *Chartularium* III.

the cathedral chapters in Lincoln and Ely from the outset had no real responsibility for teaching in Oxford and Cambridge respectively. Nor is there any evidence that the two chancellors ever tried to assume such a responsibility. On the contrary, it is clear that these two universities knew right from the start how to claim their independence from the local church authorities.

In Cambridge we hear of a chancellor for the first time in some decrees issued by King Henry III in 1231.[66] Here it appears that the chancellor and the masters could refer to the bishop of Ely, who in turn could ask assistance from the sheriff in keeping order in the university. That this chancellor was not the man of the church, but of the university, can be seen in the recently rediscovered Cambridge statutes from about 1250, whose first paragraph says: 'Since it is difficult for a university to reach unity by common consent or unanimous wish, we stipulate that all teachers (*regentes*) or a majority of them must nominate a chancellor according to their own choice.' The following paragraphs define the chancellor's authority in detail: he was to adjudicate in all cases involving students, unless the offence was so grave that teachers also were to appear in court. He was also to carry out the decisions of the teachers, as soon as he was familiar with them; but he could not alter the statutes without their consent.[67]

With this step the university got itself a leadership with only nominal obeisance to the ecclesiastical chancellor. In all the vicissitudes that followed, both Oxford and Cambridge managed to keep hold of this system. Essentially it ensured harmony with the local church authorities, as soon as the university chancellor's relations to them were made clear. In Cambridge this happened by means of an agreement with the bishop of Ely, Hugh de Balsham, who was persuaded in 1275 to allow the chancellor full jurisdiction over the university, as long as the archdeacon of Cambridge was confirmed in his rights as the supreme church authority over all other burghers in the town.[68] As a consequence of this clear arrangement the universities of England stayed out of any serious conflict with the church until the close of the fourteenth century, when John Wyclif was active in Oxford.

---

[66] See Cooper, 41f. Cf. D. R. Leader, *A History of the University of Cambridge*, vol. 1, Cambridge, 1988, p. 21.
[67] See M. B. Hackett, *The Original Statutes of Cambridge University*, Cambridge, 1970, p. 197.
[68] Cooper, p. 55.

All the more serious were the conflicts with the local town councils. In Bologna and Paris such clashes had ended with a compromise that safeguarded both the existence of the university and the right of the town to govern its own affairs. In England this development went much further. Here the universities ended up really making themselves masters of their surrounding towns. How this came about in Cambridge can be seen in a series of documents from the thirteenth century, the first of which is the royal decree of 1231 mentioned earlier, supplemented by a similar pronouncement from 1242.[69] Here it was not only decided that the chancellor had power of judgement over members of the university, but also that none of them could be arrested by the communal police force. A new royal privilege followed in 1268, stating that 'a layman who molests a clerk shall be promptly arrested and in serious cases held in prison, until reasonable indemnity for the clerk has been paid'.[70] But on the other hand if a clerk did harm to a layman, the townsfolk could only hold him in prison until the chancellor asked him to be handed over to the prosecution of the internal university court. A year later another decree followed, saying that 'since the burghers and night watchmen have not carried out their duty or shown themselves able to suppress the acts of violence that so often disturb the scholars in their studies', the sheriff was to place himself ready with a company of men sufficient to force all those who disturbed the peace of the university to desist from their evil deeds, and sufficient also to suppress anything that could harm the scholars.[71]

Behind all these decrees was the implication that it was the burghers of the town and their own police force that were accountable for law and order in the town, while the king's representative – the sheriff of the castle – was mainly at the university's disposal. This angered the men of Cambridge so greatly that during the king's visit in 1270 they presented him with a formal complaint. His reply was to appoint a permanent commission to stabilise the situation.[72] This came to consist of thirteen representatives for the university (five Englishmen, three Scots, two Welshmen, and three Irishmen) as against only ten for the town (seven townsmen and three from the suburbs). Members were to sit for one year at a time and swear joint oaths to provide for a peaceful coexistence between town and university. In particular, the thirteen university representatives got

[69] Ibid. pp. 41 and 44. [70] Ibid. p. 63. [71] Ibid. p. 52. [72] Ibid. p. 52.

the task of 'being of assistance to the townsfolk, as far as is compatible with their clerical status, in arresting all evil or rebellious students, as well as laymen'. Furthermore, the commission was to see that students were registered in the town's hostels, and also guarantee that no innkeepers took disturbers of the peace into their houses, but reported those who were already there.

The imbalance in favour of university members in the commission shows that the university constantly had the last word in cases concerning its own members. There were many examples of the chancellor knowing well how to make use of this fact. When in 1288–9 some Cambridge students were imprisoned in the Tower of London, he managed without more ado to get them transferred to the jurisdiction of his own court.[73] In 1290 he succeeded with the help of the bishop of Ely in getting not only a clerk released who stood accused of manslaughter before the king's court, but also his confiscated property. In 1293 the university took legal action against the mayor of Cambridge and his bailiffs, because in violation of the statutes they had freed a certain Adam Elyot, whom the chancellor had ordered to be jailed. The outcome of this case is not known.[74]

Examples of this kind are legion; but after some riots in 1304 the university went even further and requested a royal privilege also in purely civil cases involving all contracts between clerks and laymen. Hereby the whole issue of rents and any form of buying and selling would be transferred to the authority of the university. The king replied that the university could have an arrangement similar to the one in Oxford. As a result, the chancellor got the right to summon to his own court any town citizens and other laymen that members of the university might accuse. This was followed in 1316–17 by a decree that gave the chancellor the right to inspect the communal jail, to see if any of his people were being held in custody without just cause. On the same occasion it was decided that unless the chancellor or his representative were present at the deposition of a newly elected town mayor's oath to respect the university's privileges, this oath would not be valid.[75]

In the face of this slow but sure tendency to establish the university as the real authority over the town, the king's willingness to give the townspeople a bit of support now and then was not much help. Thus for example King Edward reacted to a complaint from the town in

[73] Ibid. pp. 62–3   [74] Ibid. pp. 67 and 70.   [75] Ibid. p. 82.

1327 by forbidding clerks in the university to buy up other men's debts and mortgage deeds – telling proof, if there ever was any, that the university was not only after jurisdiction over the citizens of Cambridge, but also sought to control the property market of the town.[76] All in all this development shows how cleverly the university could play off royal power against the local authorities, not to mention how the chancellor's importance within the university structure was steadily growing.

An even more dramatic change was afoot in Oxford, where friction still arose in spite of the regulations of 1214. Famous is the great battle on the eve of St John in 1306, when the tailors of the town celebrated midsummer with a big bonfire. After midnight they came out of their shops – *de shoppis suis* (*sic*) – full of high spirits, and began to sing and dance in the streets. This irritated a student so much that he set on the tailors with his sword drawn, after which the town went into general uproar.[77] It was even worse in the big three-day battle that started on St Scholastica's day on 10 February 1355 and led to the town's eventual loss of autonomy. This started with a few students in a pub near Carfax complaining about the quality of the wine and throwing bottles and glasses at the landlord's head. His friends rang the storm bells of St Martin's. An armed mob rushed up and attacked the scholars, and even the chancellor was driven back by arrows when he tried to restore peace. Towards evening the fight died down, but the next day the town stationed a corps of eighty armed men in St Giles' church, from where they made sorties against the students. One was killed and many others wounded, after which the colleges and lodgings were attacked and plundered. The murder and looting went on the following day, and some members of the university were even scalped.[78]

It was no wonder that the scholars of Oxford fled out of town, excepting a few who ensconced themselves behind the thick walls of Merton College. The chancellor went on the university's behalf to the king, who took action in consultation with the church authorities. The town was placed under an interdict for one year while a royal commission sat down to examine the affair from one end to the other. The

---

[76] Ibid. pp. 82.
[77] On the battle of 1306, see Rait, p. 127.
[78] On the fray of St Scholastica's day, see the many documents in J. E. Thorold Rogers, *Oxford City Documents*, Oxford, 1891, pp. 245–68, and in Salter, vol. I, pp. 148–71. Cf. Rashdall, vol. III, pp. 96ff. An earlier dispute in 1298 is documented in Salter, vol. I, pp. 43–81.

final result was that the chancellor obtained control of the major part of the town's trade and also the authority to punish clerks and laymen alike for illegally bearing arms. The town furthermore was ordered to pay an immediate penalty for this battle amounting to £250, together with an annual fine that was paid out by the town council to the university right up to 1825. Thus a complete victory for the university had been won, in the sense that in the following centuries Oxford was to all intents and purposes administrated by its university.

The general results of this long struggle for sovereignty were both positive and negative. As regards the basic issues of this contest, it has to be admitted from an external point of view that the universities were victorious in so far as no external power any longer threatened their existence. Internally the contest ensured that solidarity was strengthened, as the various corporations constantly adjusted their statutes and, taught by the harsh realities around them, gradually established a university structure able to look after the common interests of teachers and students. These problems of organisation will be discussed in closer detail in the next chapter.

Here it is enough to note that even if the universities came out of this battle with an extensive autonomy of their own, their victory had its limits and its price. The limits were defined by the same papal power that had removed the initial obstacles in relation to the secular authorities; but in turn, in the dispute with the professors of religious orders, the pope had gained a position of supremacy over the universities. In the time to come, these submitted one by one to the authority of the Holy See by accepting the statutes that the pope had issued or at least approved. The price of victory was discernible in two completely different areas. Firstly, it became more and more common for the statutes not only to define the university structure and form of government, but also the curriculum and textbooks. In the beginning this was beneficial: the 'modern' Aristotelian philosophy of the thirteenth century, for example, could hardly have gained a footing in the syllabus without strong statutory support from the highest powers. But in the long run this arrangement became a hindrance to advances in scholarship, given that the curriculum itself could not effectively be altered without corresponding alteration in the statutes. Even if this took place only much later, the procedure was potentially troublesome, because it gave one master the opportunity to interfere in another master's teaching, and led to bitter quarrels among colleagues.

Secondly, there was a price to be paid, in the real sense of the word, in that this dispute had cost money. In the battle with the chancellor and later with the mendicants, the corporations of the university of Paris had had to engage professional lawyers to plead their case to the authorities. As mentioned earlier, there actually seems to have been a permanent delegation in the curia. The university had no means for such undertakings, and the only solution to meet this expense was to get members to pay fees or subscriptions. These subscriptions were normally charged in *bursae*, a *bursa* being a fixed sum covering a student's weekly cost of living. Each master, *baccalaureus*, or student at the end of the thirteenth century, could be dunned for one or more *bursae* as a contribution to the payment of common expenses, a practise often confirmed by papal decree.[79] In this connection it should be also mentioned that the principle of teachers receiving their wages from the church became more fictional as their numbers grew, especially in the faculty of *artes*. This meant that teachers got the right to ask a return for their labours in the form of *collecta* from the scholars; the *Hörgeld* of the German universities up to our own days was the last remnant of this system. Part of these incomes went to the maintenance of the teachers, part to the pay of the permanently employed university functionaries or *bidelli*, of whom more will be said in the next chapter. In the course of the fourteenth century, this form of finance became so inadequate that many universities introduced permanent *salaria* to a number of teachers. In this way, one of the most perceptible results of the fight for the university was the end of the good old days when a student could stay at the university free, without paying more than his living expenses.

---

[79] *Bursae* and students' fees are first mentioned as a general fee for all members of the Parisian faculty of arts in 1254, see *Chartularium* I, 258f, with direct reference to the cost of taking legal action against the Dominicans. The fee was imposed on the whole university in 1284, cf. *Chartularium* I, 600f, and in 1339 also on bookdealers, parchment-makers, and copyists, ibid. II, 487. Cf. Kibre, pp. 105, 126, and 146.

CHAPTER 7

Structure and form of government

In the first century of their life the universities had to fight on many different fronts in order to ensure their existence and as much independence as they could achieve. Bishop and chancellor, town government and king, and emperor and pope – all wished to have their fingers in the pie. The fact that so many different authorities were involved, however, began to matter a great deal where the outcome of the struggle was concerned. One power could be played off cleverly against the other with the dexterous use of some diplomacy on the part of the university. The king's authority could be mobilised whenever a contentious town council had to be brought into line. In the face of a power-hungry bishop or chancellor who did not understand the difference between a traditional cathedral school and a new university, one could always appeal to the papacy, which more and more in this period was taking the part of the guardian of the universities. Only the pope had sufficient power to make local prelates toe the line, at the same time as the papacy in most cases was distant enough not to disrupt their day-to-day work. For this reason the alliance with the pope suited the universities very well. After a while it became a tradition to turn to Rome to get privileges confirmed, statutes certified, and thereby to obtain the valuable right to grant the *ius ubique docendi*, which assigned to each graduate of the university the whole of 'Christendom' (i.e. the territory of the western church) as a field of operation. It is obvious that in the eyes of the curia this was a welcome change that would strengthen the spiritual authority and international position of the pope, even throughout the fourteenth century, when the new nation states were consistently trying to reduce his political power.

These high political results of the battle for the universities were to become quite important for at least certain areas of life in Europe of the high and late middle ages. But from the university's own point of view this battle brought no less significant consequences, which internally took the form of an increasingly more permanent structuring of the framework of university organisation and administration. It was only armed with their good sense and starting with the Roman legal concept of corporations, that the university people ever succeeded in making a suitable structure for their system of teaching and a form of government for their institutions. Considering that the same structure was accepted everywhere (with lesser, local modifications), and also lived long after the end of the middle ages, this was an expedient measure. In this chapter our attention will be focussed on this process of structural reform, as much as it can be when we consider the deficient state of much of the source material. In the first instance we only need deal with the old universities, that grew up organically and had to win their unity of structure in a series of single moves. Each step forward of this kind most often started with a concrete battle of which the final outcome was settled in a document that would thereafter become a link in the university's growing chain of regulations. For brevity's sake we shall here consider only the development in Paris. This is because the fullest sources come from there, and also because in many ways Paris became the model for other universities. Even in an 'old' university such as Oxford, the bishop of Lincoln Robert Grosseteste required masters of theology in about 1240 to follow the Paris syllabus, and the pope made this compulsory on 20 May 1246.[1]

The constituting phase of this development in Paris spanned a hundred years. We must picture a situation at the end of the twelfth century where the town was full of teachers and students of many different subjects. Even at this time there was talk of four main tendencies. The Englishman Alexander Neckham mentions – in his poem *De Laudibus Divinae Sapientiae* of before 1200 – that study was flourishing in *artes liberales*, theology, Roman law, Canon law and medicine, even if Paris was above all a centre for theology.[2] Each teacher had a group of pupils in his own 'school' and was himself a member of a very loosely organised union or guild. A hundred years later this rather uncomplicated state of affairs was replaced by a highly developed and well-ordered university structure with a number of different organs and officials. Now there were nations,

---

[1] *Chartularium* I, 169f (Grosseteste) and ibid. 189 (the pope's answer).
[2] The reference to Alexander Neckham is taken from Rashdall, vol. I, p. 322.

faculties, colleges, rectors, deans, proctors, and chancellors, each with a distinct role to play in the system.

The development of this structure can be traced in the growing collection of documents that were used in the last chapter to illustrate the battle for the university's existence. First there were the (now lost) statutes that the teachers' guild may even have had before 1200. After that, there was King Philippe Auguste's privilege from the same year. There were also decrees from the synods of 1210 and 1213 and the statutes of Robert de Courçon from 1215. In the following years there was a long list of papal letters prescribing and regulating many various questions of detail. The bull *Parens Scientiarum*, which gave the university the right to strike and to make its own statutes, derives from 1231. From 1245 we have a number of new decrees relating to teachers' conditions which were passed by a general assembly of masters, and from the same year a resolution on teaching arrangements at the faculty of *artes*. A year later Pope Innocent IV allowed the university its own seal as a symbol of its corporate independence, and from 1249 an agreement came into being between students of the four nations on the election of rectors. In 1252 the masters of the English nation passed regulations for the baccalaureate examination. The year after, there was the unanimous declaration, mentioned earlier, that no teacher could be admitted unless he swore an oath to keep the university's statutes. In 1255 the faculty of *artes* approved a new syllabus which allowed the use of the previously banned writings of Aristotle, and in the same year Pope Alexander IV issued the bull *Quasi Lignum Vitae*.

This list could go on, but even as it stands here, it shows sufficiently clearly that what could be called the 'constitution' of the University of Paris only existed as a long series of internal decrees for the individual university organs, or as resolutions passed by the university as a whole, or as ordinances or privileges from king or pope. Something similar pertained to Oxford or Bologna, whereas the situation differed in universities that did not grow organically but were set up from scratch by one or other authority in society. As we shall see, this latter group was normally equipped from the outset with well-defined statutes.

As regards Paris, it is natural to start with the teachers' organisation, since Paris was a 'university of professors'. The first problem concerns the emergence of the faculties. Everything points to the conclusion that the teachers' corporation kept together for a fairly long time without troubling about subject boundaries. Even when the university conveyed the Dominicans in 1221 to St Jacques, this was done on behalf of all masters together, just as masses were required for the soul of each deceased master, 'whichever one of our faculties he belonged to'.[3] Yet 'faculties' are mentioned here, and in the long run, of course, it was inevitable that teachers would have to make up groups formed by subject, even if these groups acquired the name 'faculties' only slowly and casually. When, for example, a commission was set up in 1248 to investigate the Jewish Talmud, this was a task for theologians and jurists and not professors in medicine or *artes liberales*, who were excluded as not competent in the subject.[4] The bull *Parens Scientiarum* of 1231 expressly names the faculty of jurists and theologians, while bestowing in some matters a *facultas* upon masters of *artes* and medicine. The word seems at this point to have had a relatively non-technical meaning which was still close to the etymological root; thus the *facultas* of physicians could best be defined as the collected capacity of the professors of medicine within the university as a whole. There is a similar example in a letter from Pope Honorius III of 16 November 1218, which instructed the Paris chancellor to confer the *licentia docendi in facultate predicta* on three masters of theology – but no faculty is mentioned before, so the concept *facultas* in this case as well just means the teachers of theology taken together, but scarcely any real organisation.[5]

The first time all faculties were named together was in an oath deposited by the university in 1251 to the queen 'for the common good of the whole *studium* of Paris ... for masters just as for those scholars of theology, canonical law, medicine, *artes* and grammar ... who study at the faculties just mentioned'.[6] Thus the faculty structure must have been consolidating itself right at this time. Only it is peculiar that grammar is named here along with the other subjects. Right from the start it had normally belonged to the *artes liberales* as one part of the trivium; and neither before nor since is there any other record of a special faculty of grammar. The explanation is possibly that seeing that the university was promising in the same document to keep the peace in the town of Paris, it was expedient to let the grammar professors appear as a special group – for it was they who were responsible for the altogether younger scholars who were there in large numbers and perhaps gave rise to most difficulties.

[3] *Chartularium* I, 99f.   [4] Ibid. 209–11.   [5] Ibid. 85.   [6] Ibid. 222–4.

Structure and form of government

Among the four faculties the faculty of *artes* seems to have been the first to order its own internal affairs. Thus a syllabus of 19 March 1255 was approved by 'the *magistri artium* ... of our faculty', and was provided with four seals – one for each of the four nations described more closely below.[7] Furthermore, there is an examination decree from April 1260 which the masters of the faculty approved in concert and which was published subject to the approval of the faculty: *reservata tamen potestate facultati*.[8] The composition of the faculty was finally formulated exactly in 1275, where it was stated that members should be *magistri actu regentes*, or teachers actually occupied with practical instruction; a master would thus have to withdraw from the faculty if he went over to other work or left the town.[9]

The faculty of ecclesiastical law is already named in the *Parens Scientarium* of 1231, even if in a vague way. It should be noted that only Canon law was taught in Paris, since Pope Honorius III had forbidden the study of Roman law in 1219.[10] The intention was not to contest civil law as such, but to strengthen the position of the university as a theological high school of the church. This step encouraged specialisation and strengthened Roman law elsewhere, most of all in Bologna and also in Angers closer by, besides in the many universities of the later middle ages, where law was often the most important subject of all. In the Paris Talmud Commission of 1248 fourteen *magistri decretorum* are named, but no faculty as such. Presumably this was only finally constituted in 1271/2, when agreement was reached between the Chancellor John Cancellarius and the *decretorum facultas* on a special seal for this faculty, which was thereby able to certify its own documents.[11] This was one of the most telling indications that a new corporation – in the technical sense – had come into the world.

In Paris medicine had no great place of its own, even though medical teachers and schools are attested before 1200. Pope Innocent III completely omitted the physicians from his letter of 1208/9, whereas they were busy reaching a compromise with the chancellor in 1213. The physicians seem to have emerged as a proper faculty at about the same time as the jurists. In 1270 they gathered in a church on Île de la Cité and passed a motion that any bachelor of medicine who had got the *licentia docendi* without the consent of faculty or masters, 'shall be excluded from the *societas* of masters for ever', and

---

[7] Ibid. 277ff. [8] Ibid. 412. [9] Ibid. 530. [10] Ibid. 90–3. [11] Ibid. 503.

also from all academic activities in the faculty of medicine.[12] The following year the faculty passed a resolution directed against anyone who practised in Paris without an education recognised by the faculty, be he physician, surgeon, or apothecary.[13] While this last statute was aimed at Jewish doctors, among others, it was also without doubt a move against the chancellor's penchant for conferring the *licentia docendi* on his own initiative. Finally there is an *ordinatio* from 1274 from the same faculty, consisting of nine masters plus the dean, on the introduction of a particular seal with which the incorporation was formally made complete.[14]

The fourth and last faculty was theology, which, as is natural, had the pope's special favour and is mentioned time after time in the extant documents from 1218 onwards. It was also this faculty that took part more than any other in the fight with the mendicant friars. One of its first known documents is a statute of February 1252; in this it is laid down that access to a chair in theology should be made conditional on a normal university education, and one of the tasks of those concerned was to lecture on Peter the Lombard's '*Sententiae* in schools with an actively teaching master present'.[15] This of course would serve to exclude the mendicants, who had had no normal course of study. The statute was approved by the *doctores in theologia regentes* of Paris, but the whole university entered into it and provided it with its own seal. As a result the other faculties in this affair stood shoulder to shoulder with the theologians.

If we now return to the faculty of *artes*, long the largest through its special place in the course of study; we note that this is where every scholar began his career, right from arriving at the university often at only fourteen or fifteen years of age. The administration of such a numerous and youthful mass of students was without doubt a difficult problem for the masters of *artes*. This is the context of the faculty's gradual division into a structure of four departments, which came to be called nations, just as the student organisations of Bologna were. In Paris, however, there were different antecedents. As we saw earlier, the existence of these nations is only documented with certainty in the 1240s, but it looks as if the division into nations in Paris went back at least to the fight with the cathedral chapter, bishop, and chancellor in the years 1219 to 1222. Thus there is a letter from Pope Honorius III from 1219, from which it appears that the

[12] Ibid. 488.   [13] Ibid. 488–90.   [14] Ibid. 515.   [15] Ibid. 226.

bishop had complained in Rome about certain *conspirationes* of teachers and scholars who were prosecuting their case with the help of some *procuratores*.[16] A new papal missive in the same affair from 1222 speaks of the students *secundum nationes suas*, 'in accordance with their nations'.[17] In the following decades we hear occasionally of these nations with their rector and proctors. Only in October 1249, however, is the system mentioned in its final form in a document relating to a quarrel between the Gallican and the three other nations.[18] The other nations are not named, but they seem to have emerged as a special group, in that they had elected their own rector and thus clashed with the Gallican nation, which had elected a different person. In the document it is stated that in future one rector should be elected for all nations, and he should be chosen by their four proctors. Below the text is a seal for each nation, all of which must now be recognised corporations. From a document of 1267, to be discussed later, it is known that the nations concerned were Gaul, Picardy, Normandy, and England.[19] The Gallican nation was by far the largest and was divided into subsections called 'provinces'.

It was not long before the nations began to play an active part in internal administration, even though cooperation and unity were often lacking and higher authorities had to intervene. As early as 1252 the English nation took it upon itself to pass a statute for the so-called baccalaureate examination which will come up later. On the other hand the syllabus of 1255, which has already been mentioned, was the work of all four nations. As regards the quarrel over rectors, the Cardinal Legate Simon de Brie (later pope from 1281 to 1285 with the name of Martin IV) made a compromise in 1266, and gave the Gallican nation on one hand and the three others on the other the right in certain conditions to elect a rector for each party.[20] After a while relations became more harmonious, and normally only one rector was elected. With this the basic structure of the *artes* faculty was established. Masters were divided into four nations, each of which handled its own affairs and elected its own proctor; together the four proctors elected a rector. Beyond this, each nation had a *bedellus*, mentioned for the first time in about 1218.[21] The beadle seems to have operated as a kind of secretary to the proctor, with no authority of his own.

[16] Ibid. 87f.   [17] Ibid. 102f.   [18] Ibid. 215f.   [19] Ibid. 467–9.
[20] Ibid. 449–57.   [21] Ibid. 86.

Once the four faculties were established, the basic elements were in place for the future structure of the university. While it had previously identified itself with the mass of teachers as a whole, now it more and more came to be seen as a federation of four faculties, at the same time as these were strongly underscoring their independence. All this comes clearly out in a statute of 12 July 1281, which was passed by all the Paris masters teaching in all the faculties.[22] They solemnly declared that any acts, *facta*, performed by any of the four faculties, were to be counted as acts of the university, in so far as they respected its privileges or resolutions. After this it is clear that the term *universitas* now covered the four relatively independent faculties, each of which could make its own resolutions and have its own seal and could therefore act autonomously.

In the thirteenth century the faculties had no buildings of their own. Nor did the remaining administrative organs of the university, and faculty meetings normally took place in some church lent for the occasion. Yet a tendency could already be seen for geographically segregating the faculties. Of old the theologians had stayed near Notre Dame, and after a while the physicians and jurists also came to teach on the same island in the Seine. On the other hand, the big faculty of *artes* with its many schools was quartered on the left bank of the Seine around Rue du Fouarre and on the slope of Mont Sainte Geneviève, where the Latin Quarter is today. This was partly a result of the desire to come outside the jurisdiction of the cathedral chancellor, as we have already seen, and within that of the chancellor of St Geneviève.

The size of the individual faculties cannot be made out with much certainty, since neither registers of scholars nor other statistical information of even a barely systematic kind have survived from the first hundred years of this university's history. We have already seen that there were fifteen masters of theology in 1254, while there were ten masters of medicine in 1274, and at least fourteen in law in 1248. As regards the *artes* faculty, its size in about 1283/4 is known from a very long and thorough letter from the faculty to the pope answering a series of allegations that the Chancellor Philippe de Thori had made against the masters of *artes* with respect to their teaching and the discharge of their office.[23] From this letter it seems that at this time there were no less than about 120 masters who taught *artes*

[22] Ibid. 590. [23] Ibid. 605–22.

liberales. In numbers this faculty was thus far superior to the others, something that never changed throughout the middle ages. The statistics are better for the next century; the figures in table 1 are part of them.[24] The enormous preponderance of masters of *artes* is partly explained by the fact that according to the normal arrangement of study all scholars were obliged to undergo the whole course this faculty provided, before they could go on to another faculty or even leave the university to work outside in society on the basis of a master of arts degree alone. The inevitable drop-out of unqualified students also went on essentially at the faculty of *artes*, with the result that it could stay larger than the other three faculties combined. Since however we do not know the average number of scholars per teacher with any certainty, the drop-out percentage cannot be fixed; but everything indicates that it was big. That the figures show a considerable decline in numbers from 1348 to 1362 is for a large part due to the effects of the plague in 1347/9.

Table 1

Year	Theology	Law	Medicine	Artes liberales
1348	32	18	46	514
1362	25	11	25	441

Having considered the faculty structure of the university, we must turn to the question of how it was governed. The government of the university is not described, but it has to be extrapolated from a series of different statutes, each of which lets the administrative state of affairs shine through in some way. An otherwise unimportant document from 7 July 1267, on a defamation case between two masters, is interesting here, because it contains the names of all members of the university leadership of that time.[25] These were the following:

Oddo de Carnoto – dean of the Paris masters of Canon law
Petrus Lemovicensis – dean of physicians
Robertus de Winchelis – rector of the University of Paris
Oddo de Polengeio – proctor of the Gallican nation
Petrus Cornubiensis – proctor of the English nation
Matheus de Arginis – proctor of the Picardic nation
Guillermus de Insulis – proctor of the Norman nation

[24] See Denifle, pp. 123f.   [25] *Chartularium* 1, 467–9.

A peculiar thing about this list is the absence of the theologians. However, this omission only concerns the *faculty* of theology, for the document is otherwise issued by the apostolic public notary in conjunction with in all eight named masters of theology. This shows that the faculty of theology at this time had no formal leader of its own. The document can be supplemented with a papal missive from the following year, 23 March 1268, in which Clement IV (1265–1271) mentions all the leadership of the university, by referring to the deans of the faculties of medicine and law, the proctors of the four nations, the chancellor of Paris, and the masters teaching theology.[26]

It is now clear that at least two of the faculties were represented by deans in the university leadership. This was the case for the jurists and physicians, as confirmed in the ordinance of 19 October 1279, of the Cardinal Legate Simon de Brie on the manner of these deans' election.[27] In both faculties the dean was just one of the masters, elected by his colleagues to represent the faculty outside. Electors were all teachers of the faculty with a master's degree; only the young baccalaureate teachers seem to have been excluded, all in keeping with their status as under instruction and not yet having received the *licentia docendi*. Thus the system was fully democratic, to the extent that all graduated teachers took part in the election on an equal footing, and they were all eligible themselves.

That no dean of the faculty of theology was included on the list is no doubt connected to the fact that in earlier times it was precisely the theologians who had a particular association with the cathedral school, whose chapter and chancellor were originally in charge of their teaching. As we saw in the last chapter, the chancellor, in unison with the bishop and cathedral chapter, sought in the period considered here to assert his authority over the university as a whole. This had forced the pope to make repeated reprimands and conditions limiting the chancellor's power, as shown earlier. However, it seems that while the chancellor's title over the university as a whole became increasingly restricted to the formal right to confer the *licentia docendi*, he was still trying to keep a special position in relation to theological teaching. At about the same time at which there is mention of deans among jurists and physicians, there are two letters from Pope Urban IV (1261–1265), both dated 26 June 1264 and both

[26] Ibid. 475.   [27] Ibid. 577–9.

dealing with encroachments from Stephen Cancellarius. In the first one the pope requests a canon in Abbeville to organise an investigation into the case of the chancellor *propria temeritate*, 'in his own rashness', calling himself dean of the theological faculty; from the second letter it seems that the chancellor issued a *licentia docendi* without consulting with the masters of theology.[28]

This is another proof of infringements on the part of the chancellor that had infuriated the university so much before, and it explains why in the letter of 1267 the public notary, to make sure of the support of theologians, had to make do with individual teachers who quite openly had no desire to be represented by the chancellor. In the pope's letter of 1268 the situation was still unresolved, and Clement IV mentions the chancellor and masters of theology in the same breath. The quarrel blew up violently in the 1280s, when the above-named Chancellor Philippe de Thori demanded to be respected as the *caput* or 'head' of the university.[29] Arbitrarily conferring the *licentia* was another way in which he unfortunately got himself noticed; he was also offended at being summoned to a meeting instead of being respectfully invited to go there. The university reacted by suspending the chancellor from his office as professor of theology and by forbidding scholars to hear his sermons. Furthermore, there was a vain attempt to employ an independent university chancellor without association to the cathedral chapter; this would imply an ordinance such as the one in Oxford and Cambridge, by which the university itself came to run both examinations and the allocation of the *licentia*.

However, in this affair the university conflicted with the pope, in spite of having humbly declared, in the long letter mentioned earlier, that it had no other head than the pope himself. Even though the relevant documents here are missing, it looks as if the pope had refused point blank to lop away the connection with the cathedral chapter, whose chancellor still continued to be the main figure distributing the *licentia*. But after a while the university managed to clip his wings further, gaining full control over the examinations itself. Thus the chancellor's role became just that of presenting degrees to candidates whom the university's own examination committee allowed through their tests.[30]

---

[28] Ibid. 440–2.   [29] Ibid. 618f.
[30] See Rashdall, vol. 1, 400f. on the decline of the chancellor's office.

While the chancellor's star was now falling, the rector's was slowly but surely rising. After what was said earlier about the development of the nations, it is clear that in the beginning the rector could not be regarded as any real superior as such over the faculty of *artes*. His office was rather to coordinate the activities that each of the four nations had the statutory right to carry out through its proctor. Yet already in the thirteenth century, the influence and authority of the rector's office came to stretch much further. In the first place this was undoubtedly connected with the numerical superiority of this faculty, and with its special need for the pope's protection of its youthful student corps against the local church authorities. As we have seen, the proctors were originally just representatives who pleaded the faculty's case to the pope while the struggle with bishop and chancellor was in progress in about 1200.

Through papal missives and other documents we can observe how over fifty years the rectorate managed to win an increasingly stronger position of power. A statute of 1245 says that the infringement of certain decrees should be punished with exclusion, until 'the rector of the university and the proctors' had been satisfied.[31] Since this is a statute for the faculty of *artes* alone, the 'university' in this connection must denote all masters of *artes* together, who were thus delegating their authority to a collective organ with the rector as *primus inter pares*. But in 1259 the meaning of the word seems to have widened. Now the Pope Alexander IV (1254–1261), in a letter of 5 March, speaks of a debt to some Florentine merchants which had been incurred long ago by the rector of the university, together with the masters and students of Paris, *inter ... rectorem Universitatis et ipsam universitatem magistrorum et scholarium Parisiensium*.[32] The bond was witnessed by the university seal, and there is no doubt that all four faculties were involved in the case. It is therefore plausible that the office of rector was assumed here to be instrumental for the whole university. The same seems to be the case in a peculiar letter of 2 May 1274, from the 'rector of the University of Paris, the proctors and the remaining masters' of the faculty of *artes* addressed to the general chapter of the Dominican order, gathering at this time in Lyons. It contained a request to have the corpse of Thomas Aquinas, who had died the same year on 7 March, transferred to Paris, where

---

[31] *Chartularium* I, 178f.   [32] Ibid. 378–81.

they wished to bury him.[33] Now, as a teacher Thomas had been exclusively associated with the theology faculty, and in no way could the faculty of *artes* be particularly interested in his earthly remains, especially when we remember that the faculty was hostile to professors belonging to religious orders and normally did not admit them as members. The conclusion, therefore, must be that here the rector of the *artes* faculty, in union with its proctors, represented the whole university in its external affairs.

That a rector from the faculty of *artes* could reach such a strong position, is not only connected with the size of his faculty, but also with the requirement that each student of *artes* should have to make an oath of loyalty to the rector, if he were to be allowed to pass the first examination. This oath originally only applied as long as the student in question was a scholar or *baccalaureus* at the faculty, but in about 1280 its application was broadened 'to any situation he could come into in the future'.[34] Now the situation of many masters of *artes* in the future was to be members of one of the higher faculties. As a result of the oath they had put themselves therefore under the rector's orders. For example, he could summon them to general university meetings, and also – within the guidelines of the applicable statutes – make decrees which affected them. The method was simple and effective: to go further in his studies, a young student would have to swear an oath, which from that time onwards bound him to respect a university structure that he could hardly have understood very well at the moment he swore the oath. The only remarkable thing is that none of the masters of the three higher faculties protested at the ordinance, or asked the pope to free them from an oath that reduced their influence on university government.

Something indicates that certain groups in the university tried for a while to extend the rectorate's authority further, namely by asking the superior faculties of medicine and law to have their deans selected by the rector. Thereby they would come directly under the power of the faculty of *artes*. This would have led to a very awkward situation, since teachers at the higher faculties could not be members of the *artes* faculty, whose masters had to be practising teachers in the *artes* subjects. The Cardinal Legate Simon de Brie put the brakes on this manoeuvre when on 5 August 1279 he stated that deans should be elected by their respective faculties.[35]

[33] Ibid. 504f. [34] Ibid. 586f. [35] Ibid. 575.

Finally, a bull from Pope Martin IV (Simon de Brie), dated 7 March 1284, gave regulations for the financing of the university's common expenditure.[36] All masters and *scholares* would contribute two Paris *solidi* per head each week to a common chest. The money would be gathered by the abbot and chancellor of St Geneviève, which as an independent entity came to operate as inspectors of a kind, while the 'rector of the university, the deans of the faculties and the proctors of the four nations' were made jointly responsible for the way the money was spent. This is the same combination that we saw earlier in 1267 as the supreme university authority – but here the rector is the first one named. His special position was thereby confirmed, and in the course of the following century it became more and more prominent, until in the end he appeared at official occasions with the same rank and dignity as the bishop of Paris himself.[37]

The election of the rector, according to a statute of 1249, proceeded in such a way that the four proctors (or a representative of each of them) swore on oath that they would find the best man suitable for the job; thereafter the candidate was elected by a simple majority of the same four people.[38] In the event of a tie the outgoing rector was invited to make the casting vote. In the beginning the period of office was only six weeks, but was increased to three months in 1266; later the general term was one year. Any practising teacher in the faculty of *artes* seems to have been eligible. When a student is sometimes mentioned as the rector of Paris, this should not be understood to be a matter of a student at the faculty of *artes* itself. This would have been quite unthinkable in a professors' university such as Paris. The explanation is rather that in many cases a *magister artium* had become a scholar at one of the three higher faculties. His university status was therefore, from this point of view, that of a student and not a teacher.

From the developments sketched below the final structure of the university can be ascertained, as it would have been at the end of the thirteenth century; this is illustrated in diagram 3. The individual groups here represent the basic institutions of the

---

[36] Ibid. 600f.
[37] See Rashdall, vol. I, p. 403 on the growing status of the rector.
[38] *Chartularium* I, 215f.

Faculty of theology	Faculty of law	Faculty of medicine
DEAN	DEAN	DEAN

RECTOR

Faculty of *artes*			
Gallican nation	English nation	Picardian nation	Norman nation
PROCTOR	PROCTOR	PROCTOR	PROCTOR

Diagram 3

university – the four nations at the *artes* faculty and the three higher faculties. Each of these seven corporations bore its own seal, and all were thereby recognised as autonomous organs that could govern their own affairs and above all the arrangements of courses. This happened in a thoroughly democratic way, in that masters in the individual corporations got together from time to time jointly to make the necessary decrees. These decrees could then be reported to the university's central leadership, which consisted of

a *rector universitatis*
three deans of the higher faculties
four proctors of the nations of *artes*.

This official entity would meet together and make its decisions as colleagues working together. Here the powers of the rector were formally small. He was the *primus inter pares*, but he had no real authority over his colleagues. His most important internal work was to summon the university leadership to meetings, either in writing or with the help of the beadles. Externally he represented the university before other institutions. It is true that there is some evidence of a special court under the rectorate, but very little is known about how effective this office was. In all criminal cases the university, as shown earlier, was subject to the bishop's jurisdiction, so that a rector only had power of judgement in civil questions such as the endless disputes over rents.[39]

Finally, two more officials should be numbered among the university authorities, though the university regarded them as outsiders. One was the chancellor in Notre Dame, who still conferred degrees after each examination. The other was the chancellor at St Geneviève, who, as we have seen, could only distribute the *licentia* to masters of *artes*, and also looked after the university's economic means.

This is as far as we can go with the structural development of Paris University, where in many ways conditions were normative and typical of the time. This does not prevent frequent deviations from the norm that make the picture of the first universities of the middle ages considerably more varied.

In the beginning the faculties emerged on the basis of pre-existing specialised schools which now had a new life within the compass of the university as a whole. This explains their numbers. The four faculties in Paris were simply the remains of the teaching in theology, law, medicine, and *artes* that had originally taken place there. In this respect the University of Paris became the model for the complete university, comprising the four named faculties which were still able even now to cover the needs of society in the various categories of higher education.

Of the other universities, only a few were just as complete as Paris. In Bologna there were the original legal, and to some extent medical, schools, whereas Bologna only got its faculty of theology in 1364.[40] Nor in the beginning did the other Italian universities have theology faculties, so that students of theology here normally got some kind of preliminary training – usually in one of the study houses of the monastic orders – before they moved off to Paris to be examined by the chancellor and to receive the *licentia docendi* from him. This practice was connected with the energetic tendency of the popes in these times to strengthen and maintain Paris as the theological citadel of the church, and one which was protected from competition from other centres by a clear reluctance to set up new theological faculties. In this respect Toulouse was a noteworthy exception: from its inception, this university had a complete structure with all four

---

[39] See Rashdall, vol. 1, p. 405 on the rector's power of attorney.
[40] Ibid. pp. 252f.

faculties, though this was also because Toulouse was founded at the critical moment in 1229 as a partial substitute for Paris, which had had a doubtful future because of the big strike of 1229 t9 1231.[41] On the other hand, the pope's industrious founding of new theological faculties in the late middle ages probably shows that the University of Paris was no longer seen as the pope's traditional ally.

Where the supreme leadership of the universities is concerned, we also come across a number of systems more or less deviating from that of Paris. Yet in the main it was true that a colleague-based principle of leadership could be found at all the spontaneously emerging universities governed by the teachers, as a result of the desire to have as much wide-ranging autonomy as possible. In certain cases this tendency went even further than in Paris, where the chancellor of the cathedral chapter was rarely recognised as belonging to the university leadership, even if he kept his right to issue the *licentia docendi*.

In the beginning, Oxford University seems to have solved its problems of organisation by imitating the course taken in Paris. This was only to be expected, in view of the close relationship that had existed between the two centres of learning even before 1200. Where later developments diverged, however, it was probably because the two places had begun in different conditions. Here it is worth remembering that even if Oxford was a *studium generale*, it was never to be as international as Paris, being mainly visited by scholars from England, Scotland, and Ireland, and in consequence national divisions never made themselves so strongly felt as they did in the big universities of the continent. To start with there was a northern nation and a southern one, each of which had its own proctor on the Paris model, but in 1274 distinct nations were abolished; on the other hand the proctors went on as before as officials of law and order – which is their role in Oxford today.[42]

The most pronounced divergence between forms of government in Paris on the one hand and the English universities on the other, however, can be found in the differing styles of university chancellor. In the last chapter it was seen how as early as 1231 the chancellor of

---

[41] See Rashdall, vol. II, pp. 160ff on the founding of Toulouse.
[42] See Mallet, vol. I, pp. 40f and Rashdall, vol. III, p. 57 on the nations of Oxford. Cf. A. B. Emden, Northerners and Southerners in the Organisation of the University to 1509, in R. W. Southern, *Oxford Studies Presented to Daniel Callus*, Oxford, 1964, pp. 1–30. On proctors in Oxford, see M. B. Hackett, in Catto, pp. 83ff.

Cambridge was one of that university's own masters, elected by his equals and with no special association with the chapter of Ely Cathedral. This arrangement was already made law in the recently rediscovered statutes of Cambridge from about 1250.[43] In Oxford a similar development took place, in that here also was neither bishop nor cathedral chapter. The scanty documents from the early days of Oxford indicate that the chancellor's office grew in importance in the first half of the thirteenth century. The first real statutes of 1252 – produced after a fight between scholars from England and Ireland – thus establish a special means of keeping the peace in the university: a special commission of thirty or forty well-to-do men, either teachers or others, was to swear an oath to the proctors to supervise discipline and to report any breach of the rules to the chancellor.[44] This was happening at a time when in Paris the chancellor's jurisdiction over students had already been whittled away; but the crucial difference is that the Oxford chancellor was a master of theology, chosen by and from his colleagues with the double role of conferring the *licentia* and representing the university before the bishop in faraway Lincoln. In this way, right from the outset the chancellor of Oxford was one of the university's own, integrated into the system in such a way that any dispute with the cathedral chapter over the *licentia docendi* was impossible. Autonomy was thereby formally established, whereas its recognition in Paris had only been *de facto*. The chancellor's authority after a while would inevitably grow; it was he who took the chair in the general teachers' assemblies (the later Convocations), and who appeared before the inner and outer world as the supreme authority of the university. In this context it is obvious that there was no use for a rectorate in Oxford, where the job of the Paris rectors was included in the office of chancellor.

Elsewhere the deviation was even greater. This was true not least in the imperial university of Naples, which had not grown organically from already existing schools, but was founded by the decree of Frederic II in 1224.[45] Here was the absolute minimum of self-government, for in practically all areas the university was subject to the king who ruled it through his own chancellor. Examinations

---

[43] On the office of chancellor in Cambridge, see M. B. Hackett, *The Original Statutes of Cambridge University*, Cambridge, 1970, ch. 1, p. 197.
[44] On the Oxford statutes of 1252, see Mallet, vol. I, pp. 35ff.
[45] On the university of Naples, see Rashdall, vol. II, pp. 21–6, and Haskins, ch. 12.

were conducted in the presence of the court, and the chancellor conferred degrees in the name of the king. There were also cases of the king ordering the reexamination of the entire teaching staff, with subsequent dismissal of those who failed to pass. The University of Naples is the first example of an institution of higher learning whose status from beginning to end was that of a department under state control, with no real academic freedom or independence for either scholars or teachers. Yet for a short time (1272–4) Naples numbered among its pupils a man of learning no less outstanding than Thomas Aquinas.

The problem that remains is to assess the influence that student scholars had on the government of the medieval universities. From what we have seen already, it can be inferred that there was no great call for anything of this kind in Paris. Paris was a university of professors, constituted through teachers' corporations, with the scholars' nations as a relatively late development in the hierarchy. To this it can be objected that teachers and scholars are mentioned in the same breath very frequently in the documents cited above. Through the whole thirteenth century *magistri et scholares* was virtually a standard expression in both university letters and papal missives. Nor is there any doubt that the university as a whole regarded itself as a collected mass of teachers and scholars under one banner, or that it acted in most cases with support mustered from both groups. This was the case, for example, with the issue of the circular of 4 February 1254, which, as we saw earlier, can only be interpreted as the attempt of the university as a whole to stamp out the mendicant friars; but even this letter was drafted solely by masters at a meeting in the church of St Julien-le-Pauvre.[46]

In theory there was an opportunity for certain scholars, at any rate, to take part in the governing body – namely those who went on as scholars at one of the specialised faculties, after finishing their education at the faculty of *artes*. Such a student already had the status of *magister artium*, and as such could be summoned by the rector to general meetings of university teachers. And yet in practice, it seems that these students did not have any greater influence; in the higher faculties they were only scholars, and in the faculty of *artes* there were constant attempts to exclude from the decision-making process any members who were not *actu regentes*, that is to say,

---

[46] *Chartularium* I, 257.

members who were not teachers at the faculty themselves. We must therefore conclude that the influence of students in Paris was limited to masters of *artes* who studied at other faculties and yet taught at their own at one and the same time. It was only these older persons sharing the responsibility for teaching who could take part in the election of proctors, thereby gaining influence also on the election of the rector. It was roughly the same in the other professorial universities that made up the large majority of all institutions of learning.

Only in Bologna was the situation different, lasting from the time that this university entered the world as a group of corporate student institutions up to a time long after the end of the middle ages. The many nations of Bologna have been mentioned earlier. They organised themselves in the thirteenth century into two big groups, the Ultramontan and Cismontan, each with its own rector. This structure, however, was too simple to be able to cope with the problems of administering a mass of students whose numbers, even in the thirteenth century, were said to have been of the order of 10,000 – though this was no doubt exaggerated.[47] Formally the plenary assembly of all students was the highest authority of the university, but in practice the student nations continued to exist as sub-groups, each of which would elect one or two advisers – *conciliarii* – to act on its behalf.[48] The day-to-day governing of the university was managed by the two rectors in association with all the advisers. In any case there was nothing exceptional about a system with two simultaneous rectors. They had the same status, and if one was absent the other could act on his behalf. In the supreme council the rectors had no special powers, and matters were settled by a straightforward majority vote. The rectors were elected for two years at a time by the special electors' assembly consisting of all *conciliarii*, just as many special delegates plus the two outgoing rectors. Conditions of eligibility for the rectorate were that the candidate should be a secular clerk, unmarried, at least twenty-four years old and with at least five years' study in law behind him.[49]

The rectors of Bologna were of a very high rank. They took precedence over bishops, archbishops, and cardinals, except the

---

[47] On the student numbers in Bologna, see Rashdall, vol. 1, p. 180, quoting the jurist Odofredus, who died in 1265.
[48] *Conciliarii* are first mentioned in 1224 according to Rashdall, vol. 1, p. 163.
[49] See Rashdall, vol. 1, pp. 176f on the development of the rectorate.

bishop of Bologna. In time the two offices were made into one, and after a while they lost their relevance. An ordinance was introduced in 1609 after which proceedings were conducted by a *prior* elected by the scholars for a month at a time. This ordinance lasted until 1742, when the rectorate was reintroduced as a permanent institution, though henceforth it was to be placed in the hands of the cardinal legate of Bologna. Only when this happened did students' rights of self-government come to an end; unique throughout the world in this way, Bologna will remain an everlasting proof in history that, with the right economic conditions at any rate, a medieval university did not have to be a professors' university.

In this way, the universities of the middle ages managed after a while to bring about a structure allowing corporations of scholars and teachers to govern their own affairs, with the help of a number of academic officials who were elected by and from the university's own members. But beyond this there is some early evidence that a special group of non-academic functionaries was also growing that could take care of a number of practical tasks. The most important of these were the beadles mentioned earlier, *bedelli*, who seem to have acquired a well-defined status long before the first written records are found that regulated their activity. The oldest statutes of Cambridge of about 1250 fix the number of beadles at two, one of whom stood at the disposal of teachers of theology and canon law, the other attending to teachers of the other subjects. They were directly subject to the chancellor, whose orders and tasks they were to carry out, for example by announcing court sittings and by serving writs. In addition, they were also responsible for teaching premises in the schools; they were to ring the hours for the beginning and ending of lessons, and not too early or too late either (to do teachers a special service); they were also to be present at all official functions of the university, including vespers and funerals, always bearing the staffs that were a symbol of their dignity.[50] In Paris they were first mentioned in the dispute with the mendicants in 1254, as 'our public servants, whom we call beadles'.[51] Here they seem to have been mainly functionaries of the four nations, since each proctor had his own beadle. It was the beadle who announced the courses by presenting himself personally in all classes, as prescribed

---

[50] On beadles in Cambridge, see Hackett, *Original Statutes*, ch. 7, p. 207, note 43.
[51] *Chartularium* I, 256.

in a special regulation that dates from about this time.[52] Every morning the beadle would present himself also in the classes of the rector and the other proctors, presumably to receive his orders for the day, and it would be his responsibility to have a calendar that enabled him to report on which days teaching was cancelled for religious feasts or other reasons. In 1328, furthermore, the Gallican or French nation made beadles register all the teachers and their lectures, and then deliver the result to a five-man committee that had the role of what today we would call the study commission of this nation.[53] In certain cases the beadles operated as mediators between the university and the outside world. It was they, in this way, who visited the markets of Paris in 1291 to see that the parchment trade was conducted in the prescribed manner; just as they operated the gradually stricter controls on the price and quality of victuals, as we shall see later.[54]

All things considered, it is clear that the day-to-day running of the university largely depended on the performance of the beadles. For this reason, it is also clear that it became necessary to give them a special status within the university structure, notwithstanding their position as laymen and possibly fathers of families, as men who worked for payment, contrary to the academic officials of the university. This came out quite clearly in a statute of Padua from 1261, where it says that 'messengers or beadles of the university ... are to enjoy the same freedoms as doctors and scholars, which means that they are to be circumscribed by the newly reached agreements between the council and the University of Padua'.[55] Many later documents take special pains to show the beadles as expressly belonging to the circle of people covered by the privileges of the university. On the other hand this right seems to have been abused, where a layman in a university town, for instance, could obtain certain benefits in the form of tax exemption, ecclesiastical jurisdiction, and so on, simply by entering university service. It was in this context that a trial took place in Paris in 1416, which showed that these privileges were reserved for the genuine beadles of the university alone (*principales bedelli*), and not for the privately appointed servants of teachers or scholars.[56]

If a stranger had asked the way to the university in thirteenth-

---

[52] Ibid. 418, dated only between 1251 and 1260.   [53] *Chartularium* II, 307f.
[54] Ibid. 49–51.   [55] See Kibre, p. 58, n. 18.   [56] *Chartularium* IV, 311f.

century Paris or Bologna, he would not have been understood. There were as yet at this time no special university buildings, either for teaching or administration. Where teaching premises were concerned, it had long been the business of individual teachers to find suitable classrooms and auditoria. The wealthier teachers taught in the rooms of their own houses. The great majority of teachers, however, were left to rent classroom premises from private landlords. In practice this often led to quarrels with the landlords as well as to friction between teachers. It was to bring order into the situation that all teachers in Paris at a plenary session in 1245 passed a statute on the leasing of classroom premises, that established, among other things, that a teacher was only entitled to rent premises if he was a real instructor (that is to say, a *regens*); that he could only rent one place for his own use or for the use of a prospective *baccalaureus* who was likely to 'graduate' under him; that he could offer no landlord any more than the stipulated rent (a decree that shows that a system of assessment already operated at this time); and last but not least, it was decided that if a landlord refused to lease a classroom to a teacher who could pay the stipulated rent and offer surety for it, then his house was to be blacklisted for five years, during which time no other university teacher might rent it.[57]

Material accessories seem to have been spartan in the classrooms. There was a chair (*cathedra*) for the teacher and a desk for his books. In any case in the higher faculties there also seem to have been benches for scholars and sometimes even tables or writing desks. But this was no matter of course in the faculty of *artes*; in Paris, in any case, hulking boys in their first year at university would have had to put up with a place on the floor or on the straw bundles that the teacher's private beadle laid out for them. These could be bought at the end of the street where most teaching in the faculty of *artes* came to be based, which was called the Vicus Straminis or 'Straw alley' (now Rue du Fourarre). The resulting squalor can easily be imagined, nor did it do much to increase respect for the classrooms. That this street became notorious for disorder can be seen in a petition of 1358 that the masters of *artes* sent to Charles V, who was ruling the land at that time as the crown prince while his father was a prisoner in England.[58] The petition shows that people not only

[57] *Chartularium* I, 177f.   [58] *Chartularium* III, 53f.

poured their rubbish into the street at night but also broke into classroom premises, where teachers would find their 'cathedrae' covered in filth in the morning. The teachers therefore saw no option but to stop their lessons until something was done. Consequently they got permission to close off each end of the street with a gateway which could be locked at night.

The need for places of administration does not seem to have been great in the beginning. A *statio universitatis* is mentioned in Bologna, where the rectors and notaries kept an office, but there is no proof that this property belonged to the university.[59] The rector held court in the *statio bidellorum generalium*, which was probably the same place. Larger meetings where the whole university was assembled took place in a church borrowed for the purpose, or later in the Dominican monastery of the town, where the university seal and document chest were kept in the vestry. In Paris the only property of the university, at least to begin with, was the contested Pré-aux-clercs, a meadow that was used as a kind of recreational area. The seals were originally kept out of town in the abbey of St Geneviève, the archives in the Mathurine monastery, the chapel of which was often used for plenary sessions on the lines of the church of St Julien-le-Pauvre, which however was later used exclusively for the weekly teachers' meetings of the faculty of *artes*. Each nation borrowed a church for its national mass, while the general religious service of the university was held at the Dominicans' or Franciscans' place, or later in the chapel of the Collège de Navarre, founded in 1305, where the seal and archives were later transferred. This college now became one of the university's centres of administration, while finances were still run from St Geneviève. The English universities developed in a similar way. In Oxford the faculty of *artes* met in St Mildred's Church, the university sermons were held in St Peter in the East, while St Mary's was used for the 'congregation' (plenary sessions). The administrative life of Cambridge University was run from the great church of St Mary's in Market Hill, where the documents and seal were also kept.

[59] See Rashdall, vol. 1, p. 188, note 1.

CHAPTER 8

The material situation

In the picture of the birth and development of the universities so far, it might seem that we have lost sight of the students themselves. Thus in this chapter we shall look at the material conditions under which a student of the middle ages lived, to see what his chances were of commencing and completing a course of study, and how he might obtain its prerequisites: some preliminary education, money to live on, a place to live and something to eat and drink, social security and legal protection and, last but not least, enough peace and quiet to study in. There is much reason to take these practical problems into account, as it was the medieval universities that by and large dealt with them, helping individual students to find a tolerable existence while they studied, by trying to keep necessary outlays down to a minimum. It is already clear that student universities such as Bologna worked for this purpose; it was as corporations of scholars to safeguard such common interests that these universities had been formed. And history shows that even professors' universities such as Oxford or Paris were not long in following this example, in providing extensive support in most of the above areas. Finally, this side of the story is also important simply because the efforts the universities made to solve these material problems often led to conflicts with the burghers of university towns; and this had repercussions on the university's relationship with medieval society in general.

In principle the universities of the middle ages were open to all who wished to study there and could derive benefit from them. At any rate, the early sources never mention entrance exams or other criteria of admission. On the contrary, free entry was sometimes directly enforced. So the charter of Naples University says in 1224 that this institution was founded 'for the general good of all who may wish to study'.[1] The large number of students at the more famous schools also indicates that in reality the door was held wide open. The only restriction lay in the clerical status of students, which implied that they had to be Christians. In such an age this was a matter of course, and it was only in areas with many non-Christians that this measure was occasionally enforced. These were mainly Jewish minorities, as a statute from Perpignan indicates in about 1389.[2]

This free entry was a consequence of the state of affairs in education. We have seen how the chancellor of Paris was not allowed to refuse the *licentia docendi* to any qualified candidate. Inevitably this would lead to a surplus of teachers with the *magister artium* degree. Since any master could rent premises and start to teach *artes liberales*, a spirit of competition probably marked the faculty when it came to procuring students.

On the other hand, a course of study at a university naturally required certain qualifications. These were scarcely anything to do with the subject, since the teaching of the various *artes* began at a very elementary stage. On the other hand, the fact that teaching everywhere took place in Latin was a real restriction. The use of a universal language was itself a reason why, in the first place, an international system of education of this kind could work, but on the other side of the coin, any potential student had to be accomplished in Latin before there was any point in applying to the university.

University education therefore required a basic schooling with Latin as the main subject. It has already been noted how the cathedral schools flourished in the eleventh and twelfth centuries, and how in part they turned into the specialised schools from which the universities grew. These schools still continued, and in many towns they were supplemented by secular Latin grammar schools which had no necessary association with the cathedrals or monasteries.

The duration of this preparatory schooling in Latin cannot be known for sure, but a daily familiarity with the language for several years would surely have been necessary before pupils could read and write it well enough to be able to go further. In 1309 the Frenchman Pierre Dubois drew up a quite fantastical project for the education

---

[1] From an imperial letter quoted by Rashdall, vol. II, p. 23, note 1.
[2] See the English translation in Thorndike, p. 257.

and dispatch of young men to the Middle East to safeguard the Holy Land against Islam. In his *On the Recovery of the Holy Land* (*De Recuperatione Terrae Sanctae*), he estimates that with four hours' daily instruction, and using Donatus' Grammar, the Psalter and 'the Bible told in the manner of a child' as textbooks, even gifted pupils would need about six years to obtain the necessary skill in Latin to proceed to the more advanced texts of Cato and other classical authors.[3] In all it must be estimated that no pupil can have had anything like a sufficient knowledge of Latin before he was thirteen or fourteen years old; this matches what we know of many scholars starting at university at the age of fourteen or fifteen. It is also worth remembering that it was not only a matter of being able to read and write the Latin language itself; a student also had to acquaint himself with the often complicated system of abbreviations that were increasingly used to save time and parchment in the books and documents of the middle ages. In certain cases it was the Latin grammar schools that also took care of this training.

Provided he had the necessary ability, the most serious problem any potential student had was the funding of his preparatory education. Lessons were usually free in the cathedral schools, where living expenses were thus the only issue. But at many of the other schools teaching was no less than the daily bread of the master, who might well be a layman or even the provider of a family. For example, we know that a grammar-school boy in Oxford at the beginning of the fourteenth century would have had to pay four or five pence each term in school-fees.[4] This was no great amount in itself, compared with other expenses such as board and lodging, which was reckoned at eight pence per week, while the necessary grammar book, which contained about 6,000 words, cost three pence. In the first instance, the payment of these expenses was a matter for the parents, and a number of contracts between parents and teachers concerning this are still known.[5] In some cases the town council seems to have taken care that the charges were not set too high; there is a statute from 1253 in which the town of Ypres in Flanders fixes school-fees at a maximum of ten *solidi* or sous per year, just as extra charges for tables, benches, ink, and blood-letting (*sic!*)

---

[3] Ibid. pp. 138–49.
[4] Ibid. p. 403.
[5] On contracts between parents and teachers, see R. L. Reynolds, Two Documents Concerning Elementary Education in the Middle Ages, *Speculum* 12 (1937), 225–56.

were prohibited. In return the teachers were allowed a monopoly over school-teaching.⁶

Where the parents' means were not sufficient, there was often a chance that the church might help. As we saw earlier, the decrees of the third Lateran Council were not only aimed at higher education, but also at the founding of free elementary grammar schools for children. There is evidence that to some extent these decrees were observed; for example, there is a letter from Pope Benedict IX (1303–1305) from 2 November 1303 addressed to the rector and disciples at the school that Bishop Christian founded at Pugetoft near Ribe in Denmark, 'for the use of poor urchins wishing to dedicate themselves to the pearls of learning'.⁷ In the letter this school is allocated the incomes from the church at Henne, after a chaplain's expenses are deducted, in such a way that 'twenty poor pupils cultivating school subjects will be maintained in a suitable manner'. A year later Peder, the newly appointed bishop of Odense, tried to further teaching in his diocese by transferring the incomes of the church at Særslev 'to the advantage of the pupils in Odense'.⁸ This system of free school places in the middle ages effectively meant that higher education was not a privilege reserved for the higher classes, and by the same token, it helped to bring about a certain social mobility in medieval society.

After his schooldays were over, the next problem facing a potential student was the funding of his studies at the university. Here we can ignore the young men who by going into a monastery were able to have their studies paid for by the appropriate order. The most attractive option for others, without doubt, was to get a prebend, that is to say, to receive income from an ecclesiastical office, and at the same time to have this office discharged by a more poorly paid chaplain. The difference would be at the private disposal of the holder of the prebend. According to the Third Lateran Council teachers were normally to be remunerated in this way, but at about the same time the popes began to demand prebends for scholars under their personal protection. Thus in 1180 Pope Alexander III (1159–1181) wrote to the cathedral chapter of Paris, requesting that 'our dear son master Theobald' might have bestowed on him an office in the cathedral, to enable him to

---

⁶ On the Ypres statute of 1253, see L. Thorndike, Elementary and Secondary Education in the Middle Ages, *Speculum* 15 (1940), 400–8.
⁷ *Danmarks Riges Breve*, vol. II, pp. 5, 221f.   ⁸ Ibid. 248.

continue his studies.⁹ Since it was the right of the local bishops or cathedral chapters to fill offices in their bishoprics, this kind of request was not always received gracefully. When, for example, a canon's office fell vacant in Tournai, Innocent III (1198–1216) in the first years of his pontificate wished to have the place filled by a certain Bernard de Insulis, and this met with violent opposition from the bishop, Etienne de Tournai.¹⁰ The affair ended with the pope requesting the bishop of Paris to inform his colleague that if his original request was not followed up, he would be excommunicated.

This practice lasted indeed right through the thirteenth century, and after a while the bishops had to drop their opposition. The method was officially affirmed on 16 November 1219, when Honorius explained that 'as long as they teach in the schools, teachers as well as scholars at the faculty of theology are to receive the proceeds of their prebends or benefices for a period of five whole years'.¹¹ This was the famous *quinquennium*, that allowed the holders of church offices to be absent from them for five years in order to study theology. A similar *septennium*, good for seven years, was introduced by Pope Clement VI (1342–1352) in 1346.¹² In Denmark these decrees proved useful for Henry, the rural dean of Gamtofte in Funen, when he started a five-year course of canon law at the Curia University in 1303; according to two letters from Benedict IX to the church authorities in Denmark, he was able to enjoy the incomes of his deanery during this time by paying a vicar to fill the post in his absence.¹³

It was only possible to get a prebend if a suitable office was vacant. If it were not, a potential student would have to wait. This was the case with a certain master Hugo de Seghuin, whom Innocent IV (1243–1254) supported when he wrote to the bishop of Tournai in 1253, asking that Hugo should have an office at the cathedral or at another church as soon as one fell vacant.¹⁴ It could be hard for an applicant to judge where in the world such an empty post would be, and the large number of scholars also raised the competition. This is why faculties in the fourteenth century began to evaluate applicants by submitting to the church a list or *rotulus nominandorum* once a year, concerning students who by virtue of

⁹ *Chartularium* I, 10f.   ¹⁰ Ibid. 12–14.   ¹¹ Ibid. 90–3.
¹² *Chartularium* II, 574.
¹³ *Diplomatarium Danicum*, Copenhagen, 1943, vol. II, pp. 5, 247f, and 260.
¹⁴ *Chartularium* I, 241.

hardship, conduct, and suitability for study, could be recommended for prebends. Candidates were put down according to their seniority, in such a way that masters took precedence over students, and teachers over non-teaching masters. The earliest extant *rotuli* were sent from Paris to Pope Clement VI in 1349, but the custom probably goes back much further.[15]

In the middle ages the prebend system worked in a mixed way. In the beginning it seems that prebends were allotted to actual members of the priesthood who wished to add to their knowledge of theology or canon law. Later the system was seriously abused, when prebends were sometimes given to boys who were under the canonical age for orders, or to laymen without ecclesiastical status. Kings often knew how to save on salaries for higher officials of state simply by assigning them dioceses. These would consequently be run by cheap vicars, while the (frequently noble) incumbent would keep himself at court, just as was the case with most Danish bishops during the Reformation. With pluralism the system resulted in even worse abuse. This allowed an individual to receive incomes from more than one office. All in all this traffic in prebends was the main reason why the lower clerical orders steadily lost their position as the later middle ages went on; it was a perpetual source of criticism of the whole machinery of the church, and even a source for schismatic and heretical movements.[16]

However, only a small number of scholars had any hope of securing a prebend, at least at the beginning of their studies. The great majority of the very young students of *artes* therefore had to look around for other sources of income. Without doubt most of them resorted to the time-honoured custom of bringing money with them from home. The family would have had to operate as a financial safety-net, and should the money ever run out, there was nothing for it but to write home for more. This is what Nicolas Copernicus (1473–1543) had to do when he was studying in Bologna in 1499. In a letter to his uncle, Bishop Lucas Watzelrode, Nicolas painted his economic circumstances in somewhat dark colours – in spite of the prebend that he had already had since 1497 in Frauenburg – whilst his brother

---

[15] *Chartularium* II, 624–47. Cf. D. E. R. Watt, University Clerks and Rolls of Petitions for Benefices, *Speculum* 34 (1959), 213–29, and F. Pegues, Royal Support of Students in the Thirteenth Century, *Speculum* 31 (1956), 454–62.

[16] Pope John XXII condemned pluralism in 1318 in the famous bull *Execrabilis*, *Cod. Jur. Canonici* III, 1, but without spectacular results.

Andreas Copernicus simply threatened 'to offer himself as a slave in Rome so as to alleviate his need'. In this case the money was forthcoming.[17] In other similar situations the nearest thing to a solution in the short term was probably to raise a loan with one of the pawnbrokers in the university towns, if getting some part-time work during a course of study – for example, as a servant in a college or for a well-to-do comrade – was out of the question.

Another solution was to try one's luck by throwing oneself on the generosity and mercy of others. Here it is worth remembering that the clerks of the middle ages had the right to take alms, and begging in public was no great disgrace for a student who had perhaps observed even famous masters within the mendicant orders go from door to door with their begging bowls. In some of the student collectives, which will be discussed later, inmates were regularly sent out to beg for the common maintenance. Staying with philanthropic townspeople was also well known. There is even a story of a certain Thomas de Chanteloup of Paris, who not only supported a chaplain in his house, who celebrated mass in the morning before he went to the university, but also a great number of poor students.[18]

That a large number of (frequently Jewish) pawnbrokers flourished everywhere in the university towns shows that short-term loans, against a surety, were a last resort often taken by scholars in acute financial distress. From the earliest days the authorities were trying to counteract the unhappy consequences of this. An interesting example of this is the loan fund set up by the town council of Padua in 1260. This had a capital of 4,000 lire and was governed by four members of the university. The annual rate of interest was not allowed to exceed 4 to 6%; the municipality also tried to ensure that this ceiling was honoured by private moneylenders.[19] Elsewhere the university took the initiative and founded similar inexpensive loan funds for scholars. As early as 1240 Robert Grosseteste set up such a fund for the scholars of Oxford, who could then borrow small sums by pawning a book, a cup or a piece of clothing; if the article was not redeemed within a year, it was sold at auction.[20] Before the middle ages ended the number of such university-controlled funds in Oxford grew to about twenty. A similar development took place in Cambridge in 1290, when Queen Eleanor left the university 100

[17] Copernicus' letter is translated into English in Rashdall, vol. III, p. 409, note 3.
[18] Rashdall, vol. III, p. 405 note 1.   [19] Kibre, p. 58.
[20] Rashdall, vol. III, pp. 35f. See also T. H. Aston and R. Faith in Catto, pp. 266ff.

marks in her will, to be deposited in the Queen's Chest.[21] In 1348 Bishop William Bateman of Norwich set up a similar fund with capital of £100. This was soon reserved for the use of scholars at the college of Trinity Hall, which the bishop had founded. Here a master could borrow as much as £4, a bachelor 30 shillings, and a student 20 shillings, though in all cases against a surety.[22] Here many other funds sprang up, too, from which it seems that loans were made without interest.

There were also simple grants in great number which there was no need to pay back. After a while the universities managed to secure themselves incomes in various ways. Thus in 1278 when the monks of Saint Germain de Prés quarrelled once more with the scholars about the contested Pré-aux-clercs, King Philippe III condemned them to build two chapels for the use of the university and also to pay £20 a year for the salaries of the same number of chaplains.[23] In 1296 the university obtained three chapels in Châtelet as compensation for the killing of a master of *artes* by the name of Simon de Messemy.[24] In this way the university gradually had the title to a number of livings in and around Paris through which it was able to derive incomes independently of the local church authorities.

There were still other means of income. After the affair of 1278 the cardinal legate also intervened, sentencing the monastery to a colossal fine, in cash, of which £200 was placed at the disposal of poor scholars, to be divided among them. The records show that such fines after a while became no mean a source of income for the university, which also derived sums from donations in wills. An interesting example of this was the will of the Danish Master Peder Arnfast, who, as he had his own house in Paris, must have been quite wealthy. In an open proclamation from the public notary of Paris, dated 18 September 1284, it was announced that

Since Master Peder Arnfast, doctor in Holy Scripture and canon in Roskilde in the Kingdom of Denmark (on whose soul may God have mercy) has given and conferred in his will a house in Paris, situated in the eastern quarter on the Rue des Anglais, for the use and profit of poor students from Denmark, for the time that they study with industry in Paris, concerning the which house annually elected leaders and representatives of the scholars of Denmark shall preside and superintend in accordance with the wishes of the aforesaid doctor's last will and testament.[25]

[21] Cooper, vol. I, p. 62.   [22] Ibid. p. 100.   [23] *Chartularium* I, 567f.
[24] *Chartularium* II, 71f.   [25] *Danmarks Riges Breve* II, 3, 97f.

The material situation

It was not the intention that these scholars should live in the house. The house was to be let out, and after maintenance costs were deducted, the income so derived was to be divided among the Danish students upon application. God's wrath and disfavour 'betide them who, receiving something of the aforesaid income, straightway take it away with them without the intention soon to return and attend to their course of study'. In reality, thus, some kind of private scholars' fund existed that was based on revenue from fixed property. Unfortunately, we do not know how many Danish scholars might have had a chance to enjoy an education in this way. That in spite of everything there were only about 450 grants in the middle of the fourteenth century for a student population of about 10,000 shows that this support was only a form of almsgiving, beneficial on a small scale but of little use to the great majority, who were obliged to make their own living.[26]

Compared to the 'freshers' of our day, students starting out in medieval universities were very young. This fact is based on evidence from syllabuses and examination decrees in the faculty of *artes*. In Paris the statutes of Robert de Courçon laid down in 1215 that no-one under the age of twenty-one could teach in the liberal arts and a teacher also had to have attended lectures himself for no less than six years.[27] In 1252 the English nation in Paris managed to change these decrees a little; in order to 'determine' (i.e. take their exams), students would now have to be twenty years old, or at least in their nineteenth year, with proof that they had studied for five, or at a pinch, four years.[28] The interference was the same in either case, namely that scholars in the faculty of *artes* came to start their course as early as fifteen years old. This is well in keeping with what we have already seen concerning the age at which boys normally graduated from grammar schools.

This is not to say that the 'freshers' of the middle ages were children when compared to those of the present. The average life expectancy was lower, and in the thirteenth century a boy of fifteen would probably have been just as prepared to stand on his own two feet as an eighteen-year-old today. Nevertheless, there were surely many parents who, with some disquiet and feelings of dread, watched their young sons set out on the long journey to the university. The students of thirteenth-century Scandinavia, Germany, or Poland, for

---

[26] See Agrain, p. 37. [27] *Chartularium* I, 78f. [28] Ibid. 227ff.

example, had no university to go to closer than Paris or Bologna. This meant a journey of many weeks, often on foot and by roads that were only as safe as the knowledge of highway robbers that young men soon to be students would necessarily carry money abroad with them allowed them to be. In this context, it is easy to understand that the common ban on carrying arms was lifted for people going to and from university. In England there is even evidence that some parents entrusted their sons to a professional 'fetcher' who travelled round a district gathering students into a large band, in order to take them to Oxford or Cambridge.[29]

Highway robbery was not the only misfortune that could stop an itinerant student from reaching his goal. Medieval roads were full of gates and turnpikes where state or council officials had legal power to ask tolls and other duties on all goods – even, as in some cases, taxes on personal belongings or the food that was taken along for the journey. In 1246 Pope Innocent IV therefore ordered all bishops and archbishops to excommunicate any tax-gatherers so officious as to raise the cost of scholars' journeys to and from Paris.[30] This does not seem to have worked, for in 1251 we find the pope complaining to the French dowager Queen Blanca (who was regent during the absence of Louis IX on the Seventh Crusade), and also to Countess Margaret of Flanders, that students from Dacia on the lower Danube were still being asked for tolls from vital though slender means.[31] It was only with the decree of Philip IV in 1295 that the immunity of scholars from paying tolls was finally established.[32] A second decree two years later placed scholars directly under the king's protection on the roads to and from the universities of Paris and Orléans, regardless of their country of origin. But even in 1313 the king was obliged to go to court against Count Robert of Boulogne, who was continuing to take tolls from English students when they arrived from across the Channel.[33] The king reminds us of the 'hardship, the sleepless nights, the exhaustion, want, tribulation and danger that these students must bear in their search for the precious pearls of knowledge', and he commanded the count 'to consider how they have abandoned their friends, kinsmen and fathers' estates, their worldly goods and family income, so as to come here from distant lands to drink the waters of the fountain of life'.

[29] On the 'fetcher', see Mullinger, vol. I, pp. 345f. [30] *Chartularium* I, 194.
[31] Ibid. 221f.   [32] *Chartularium* II, 65; Kibre, p. 129.
[33] *Chartularium* II, 159f; cf. Kibre, p. 137.

History does not relate if this stylistic masterpiece from the king's chancellery ever had the desired effect.

Once the question of funding was solved, and the student had safely arrived in the university, the next problem was to find somewhere to live. Members of an order in many cases could stay in their own institutions and would naturally prefer to do so, so as to interrupt the regular pace of their studies as little as possible. For this reason many orders founded their own lodgings in university towns. This was most true of the mendicant orders, who normally based their existence on town society, whereas the Benedictines in their country abbeys lagged a little behind. In 1337 Pope Benedict XII (1334–1342) therefore ordered them to send one out of every twenty monks to university with a stipend from their order.[34] In Cambridge in 1428 this gave rise to the building of a separate hostel for the Benedictines of Croyland Abbey, so that they would not have to stay with the laity when they were studying. This house became known as Buckingham College, and reemerged after the Reformation as Magdalene College.[35]

The reason for Buckingham College's foundation reveals that private lodging arrangements were the order of the day. So there is no doubt that the renting out of rooms – with or without board – was an important source of income for the people of university towns, with all the opportunity for economically exploiting students that this offered. We have already seen how the first demands of the students of Bologna for the right to form corporations revolved around control of room prices by a special rent commission with representatives from the town and the university alike. A similar arrangement in Cambridge is known even from 1231, when King Henry III ordered the town mayor to see that the value of all houses where students were staying should be assessed, and the rent then established by a board of two masters and two men good and true from the town.[36] In the oldest Cambridge statutes of about 1250, this body is established in law with the added proviso that fixed rents should be entered in a publicly accessible protocol, and that the representatives of the university on the board should be the two rectors.[37]

---

[34] Cooper, vol. 1, p. 91; cf. B. F. Harvey, The Monks of Westminster and the University of Oxford, in F. R. H. Du Boulay (ed.), *The Reign of Richard II. Essays in Honour of May McKisack*, London, 1971, 108–30.
[35] Cooper, vol. 1, p. 65. [36] Ibid. pp. 41f. [37] Hackett, *Original Statutes*, ch. 7, p. 205.

Some comprehensive material exists to show how a similar arrangement worked in Paris. Here in 1282 the rent commission consisted of two representatives on behalf of house owners and six members of the university, namely four masters of *artes* (one for each nation) plus two theologians. This shows clearly that the accommodation problem was most acute where the younger scholars in the basic faculty of *artes* were concerned. The commission in Paris inspected all rented properties and then negotiated an annual rent street by street, that was entered on a list. The list indicates that all classes of society were renting places out. In the Rue Grande, for example, Theobald the tailor was offered five Parisian pounds a year for his house, which was not described any further, while another house in the same street with six rooms and a garden, belonging to Guillaume de Roseto, was assessed at nine and a half pounds. A house in Rue de la Bûcherie, one belonging to a nephew of the bishop of Cahors, cost 108 sous. In Rue Coupe Guele, Madame Agnes de Gravia offered four rooms, a courtyard, some stables and a big lumber room, in a house that was set at six pounds 14 sous; whereas a house in Rue Sainte Geneviève belonging to a certain Master Remy was estimated at ten pounds, though it had only two rooms, a good cellar, and a little kitchen.[38]

In Paris these assessments seem to have taken place once a year. In Cambridge, on the other hand, the same measure, enforced by a royal decree of 7 February 1266, would take place only one year in five.[39] That valuations were final and without right of appeal, is indicated by a court case in Cambridge in 1292, in which the judge decided that in cases where a householder refused to rent out his house to a student capable of offering surety for the rent, the university had the right to instal the said student in the house regardless of the householder's protest.[40]

Though these surviving assessment lists reveal the supply of rooms and apartments, they give no indication of the density of the student population. This is taken from the evidence, often very incomplete, of the lists which the nations made street by street of the students to whom they had assigned grants of alms. Thus in 1339 the English nation of Paris was supporting Nicholaus ad Latus, Christianus, and his eight comrades, Zindurammus similarly with eight comrades, and Gaufredus de Marec with his five comrades, all of whom lived in

[38] *Chartularium* I, 597–600.   [39] Cooper, vol. I, p. 49.   [40] Ibid. p. 65.

Place Maubert. In the Rue des Anglais (where Peter Arnfast had his house), Nicolaus de Dacia and his four fellows were helped in the same manner, likewise Henricus de Alemania and his two roommates and five other scholars who all seem to have lived singly.[41] However this type of thing seems to have been exceptional. Normally the landlord rented out his house to a particular student who then sub-let the rooms to other scholars. These paid rent for individual rooms to the formal tenant, who was solely responsible to the landlord.

This interpretation is borne out by the oldest statutes of Cambridge, which contain an entire section '*On Lodgings and Rents*' (*De Hospiciis et Pensionibus Domorum*) in which the student formally concluding the tenancy was called the *principal*.[42] He alone was to answer for the rent and any damage to the house occasioned by him or his fellows, so that 'the landlord can have a contract with one man alone and does not need to prosecute a trial with a whole number of opposite parties'. The tenancy started each year on Lady Day (8 September) and the rent fell due on three distinct settling dates. The scholar was expressly forbidden to leave the town before he had paid his rent; if he did, nonetheless, it was his guarantor who had to pay. Finally the householder was forbidden to rent out rooms to any but members of the university; this means that after a while the university assumed the effective right to dispose over more and more houses in the town.

The oldest extant bill for a hospice of this kind comes from about the period 1245 to 1250 in Oxford.[43] It shows five students living together in a house which cost them £2 per year in rent, an annual accommodation expenditure of eight shillings per student. On the other hand, many hospices were quite large and could consist of a house with one, two, or three wings. The most important room was the central 'hall', which was common to all. Here students would eat in fellowship, and here, too, they would hear lectures delivered by the masters belonging to the house or by another teacher. The rooms of medieval houses were normally few, but large. As a rule these were partitioned with simple wooden panelling into small cells for each student, with space for a bed, table, bookcase, and a chest

---

[41] *Chartularium* II, 662. On sub-letting practices, see A. B. Emden, *An Oxford Hall*, Oxford, 1927.
[42] Hackett, *Original Statutes*, ch. 32, pp. 326ff.
[43] See A. B. Emden, Accounts Relating to an Early Oxford House of Scholars, *Oxoniana* 31 (1966), 77–81.

for clothes and other belongings. In the larger hospices the students usually shared the cost of hiring a cook, who would often sleep in the kitchen. There are many cases, too, where the larger hospices had their own chapel with a special dispensation to hold mass.[44]

This communal lifestyle seems to have gone down well with scholars of the middle ages, to judge by the number of hospices known from Oxford and Cambridge, where after a time a score of such 'halls' or 'hostels' appeared. How many there were in Paris is not known, but here the pattern was different right from the early days, in that the first real student colleges were founded here. These differed from the English collectives by being charitable institutions, giving free board and lodging to students in need. The first example was founded as early as 1180 by a rich Englishman by the name of Jocius of London, who acquainted himself on the return leg of a pilgrimage to Jerusalem with the miserable conditions in which many Paris students lived. For this reason he donated to the cathedral chapter the means for a foundation where eighteen poor scholars could get their board and lodging free.[45] This first Collège des Dix-Huit was followed in 1209 by the bigger Collège Saint Honorat, newly established in grounds that a Paris citizen Renoaldus Cherin and his wife Sybilla donated, out of resources that they inherited from the will of a certain Stephanus Berot, his wife Ada and son, Master Stephanus. A canon of the cathedral was installed there as warden, and the diocese reserved the right to replace him if he neglected his office.[46]

From this time onwards there was a flurry of building such student colleges in quick succession, with no fewer than fifty-seven existing in Paris by 1500.[47] Many of them were associated with particular French provinces, in the same way that some of them took students from other countries. The oldest example of the latter type was the Collège de Dace, founded for Danish scholars in 1275 by the Danish canon of Paris, Johannes de Dacia. Following an exchange of property, this moved to a new home on the south side of Montagne Sainte Geneviève, where a plaque still bears witness to its existence. It was never an exceptionally flourishing institution, and only had one alumnus in 1356. Yet there were Danish scholars still seeking

---

[44] On the organisation of the 'halls', see *Oxford Studies Presented to Daniel Callus*, Oxford, 1964, pp. 31–100.
[45] *Chartularium* I, 49f.   [46] Ibid. pp. 68f.
[47] See the list of Paris colleges in Thorndike, appendix II, pp. 433–48.

accommodation in this house in 1424; it was handed over to the
Collège de Laon five years later, which committed itself to offering
shelter to Danish scholars in the Rue Garlande, facing Saint Julien-
le-Pauvre. Of similar style was the Scottish college of about 1325, the
Lombardic college of 1333, and the German college of about 1345.
The Swedes founded an Uppsala College in 1315 that was in use
until 1354, while the small Skara and Linköping colleges seem to
have had an even shorter lifetime. Outwardly these colleges hardly
seem to have differed from the student collectives of England, but of
course they had the advantage of owning their own houses, and were
therefore safe from economic exploitation by private interests.[48]

Wholly different in style was the most famous of the Paris colleges,
the Collège de Sorbonne. This grew so well known in the course of
time that its name became synonymous with the university of Paris
itself. The Sorbonne was founded by an otherwise unexceptional
theologian, Robert de Sorbon, in a house which he bought in 1255 in
Rue Coupe Gueule.[49] Two years later King Louis IX bequeathed
him two more houses in the same street, enabling him to open a
college for twenty theologians, with himself as the director. The first
statutes of the college came out in 1270, according to which
members were to live in fellowship as 'colleagues' (the term 'college'
originally refers to the body of housemates rather than to the house
itself), and were to lead moral and academic lives: *vivere socialiter, et
collegialiter, et moraliter, et scholariter.*[50] The institution rapidly expanded, and a century after it was founded, owned no fewer than
seventy-two houses around the Latin Quarter. From the outset, 'La
Sorbonne' had a character of its own, as it was reserved for
theologians; for scholars, in other words, of one of the advanced
faculties who were no longer freshmen on an equality with students
of *artes*, but were well-established academics often with teaching
commitments of their own, either in the theology faculty or further
down in *artes*. In addition to a director, the house had a purely
academic prior whose job was to assist scholars with their studies.
There was also a rapidly growing library, together with a large aula

---

[48] On the Danish and Swedish colleges, see A. Budinsky, *Die Universität Paris und die Fremden an derselben im Mittelalter*, Berlin, 1876, and A. L. Gabriel, *Skara House at the Mediaeval University of Paris*, Notre Dame, 1960. On the Collège de Dace in particular, see *Chartularium* I, 536 and III, 317, and also the *Liber Procuratorum*, II, 445, and 534.
[49] *Chartularium* I, 349f.
[50] Ibid. 505–14. Cf. P. Glorieux, *Aux origines de la Sorbonne*, vols. I–II, Paris, 1965–6.

for lectures and disputations. These went back to 1267, but reached their final form with a statute only in 1344.[51]

With the Sorbonne, an academic institution of a new type had been founded, one that paid heed to the material, intellectual, and spiritual needs of its members, but without being a monastery. There were no monastic vows, and any member had the freedom to leave when he completed his study, or to stay on if a position in the town made this possible. This is how the Sorbonne became, in a manner of speaking, a centre for teaching and research for advanced studies within a defined subject. It was a model that soon caught on, and after a while the University of Paris was enriched with a large number of similar institutions, none of which, however, could compare in size or reputation with the Sorbonne.

In England this type of college first found a place in Oxford, where Walter de Merton, formerly the government chancellor, donated his goods in Malden, Surrey, to a foundation that founded Merton College in Oxford in 1274. The first Merton statutes clearly show this as an institution for advanced studies, with masters as its proper members or *fellows*; it was no student college founded on a philanthropic basis. The statutes gave the fellows full autonomy, fixed regulations for the election of a director or warden, strongly stressed the importance of higher studies, regulated the division of fellows according to different disciplines and allocated each of them an annual stipend of fifty shillings in addition to board and lodging.[52] Merton soon had its imitators. There was University College (statutes 1280), Balliol (1282), Exeter (1314), Oriel (1326), Queen's (1340), and New College (1380).[53] In Cambridge there was a similar movement, beginning with Peterhouse, which Hugh de Balsham, the bishop of Ely, founded directly on the model of Merton in 1284.[54] Later Clare was built in 1326, King's Hall (1337), Pembroke (1347), Trinity Hall (1350), and Corpus Christi, founded by the people of Cambridge in 1352 on the initiative of two of the town guilds. A priest named Edmund Gonville built Gonville Hall in 1350, which was soon merged with Michael House, built in 1324.[55]

---

[51] *Chartularium* II, 554–7.
[52] See G. C. Brodrick, *Memorials of Merton College*, Oxford, 1885 (with the first statutes on pp. 317–40), and J. R. L. Highfield, *The Early Rolls of Merton College*, Oxford, 1964.
[53] See A. Clark, *The Colleges of Oxford*, London, 2nd edn, 1892; Mallet, vol. I, pp. 83–137, and J. R. L. Highfield, in Catto, pp. 225ff.
[54] T. A. Walker, *Peterhouse*, Cambridge, 1935.
[55] On other Cambridge colleges, see Mullinger, I, 223–57, D. R. Leader, *A History of the*

The material situation

With the colleges, the university of the middle ages became a special kind of institution. Often they have been seen as a sort of monastic society because of the regulated lives of the inhabitants. On the other hand, there is no doubt that the first colleges were founded as purely secular corporations with all the hallmarks of such an institution, and not as religious fellowships. In reality they lacked the monastery's fundamental points. Their aim was study rather than prayer. In the beginning they assumed no responsibility for the religious needs of their members, but assigned them to the general churches of the town. It only gradually became the custom to institute private chapels or hold masses within the walls of the college. This happened in Peterhouse as late as 1388, after this institution had already existed for more than a century. Nor were churchyards associated with the colleges, whose members could not count on staying there to the end of their lives. In opposition to the monastic brotherhoods, the new fellows made no eternal vows on the three 'evangelical' virtues: poverty, chastity, and obedience. Clearly the chastity required of fellows followed naturally from their clerical status. But any obedience to an abbot or prior was replaced by the general corporative requirement to keep statutes and domestic order. Eventually the statutory stipends paid to fellows each year would make the claim of poverty essentially an illusion. Crucial was the fact that a fellow could withdraw from the college at any time, if he wished, without waiting for a dispensation from the church.

To evaluate how important these new masters' colleges were, we must look at their good and bad aspects. It cannot be denied that they helped to raise a hitherto not very prominent social barrier in the university world. With their private capital (usually estates) and their internal self-governing status, they gave their fellows an economic security and standard of living that stood in open contradiction to the conditions in which most ordinary students lived. In due time this way of life could not fail to degenerate into an unconcerned indolence, which did not advance the cause of study or scholarship. On the other hand, the college system also had possibilities hitherto undreamt of for studying in the peace and quiet that are normally indispensable for making great strides forward in

University of Cambridge, Cambridge, 1988, pp. 45–88. The literature on the individual colleges is too large to be mentioned here.

scholarship. From time to time one or another college was able to make its own name as a centre of real stature.

There is hardly any doubt that the great majority of scholars took care of their own daily board and prepared their meals with their own hand, interspersing this with visits to the inns and taverns that seem to have existed in great abundance throughout the university towns. A stock-taking document of September 1311 thus shows no fewer than 199 places in Oxford at this time where beer was served. This means about half the houses of the town; that the tavern-keepers had names such as William le Bocbindere, Walter le Carpenter, Henry le Barber, Nicholas Aurifaber, and Mathilda Scriptor, shows that serving ale – often home-brewed – was a normal sideline for many people of the town.[56] How many of these places also served meals is unknown. On the other hand, we do know that the bigger student collectives sought to make themselves independent by organising meals in common, eventually with the aid of a permanently appointed cook.

Whichever way the catering problem was solved, it is no wonder that it gave rise to daily friction with the town traders, and complaints about the price and quality of victuals were the order of the day. To understand the university's role in these matters, it is worth remembering that late medieval trade did not normally recognise any free competition, and that the price of an item was not directly regulated by the relation between supply and demand. On the contrary, the theory was that each article had a so-called reasonable or 'just' price that was normally fixed by the aldermen of the appropriate guild, who regularly inspected the stalls, controlled the quality of the article, and then told the proprietor and the public at large what the sale-price of the article was. For staple products, however, there were already price-controls in the thirteenth century which the town council operated. A board of council officials would go round undertaking the necessary quality-controls, after which a special chamber of the town court – the assizes – would set the prices. This chamber also had the power to punish tradesmen whose goods were sub-standard, underweight, or unreasonably dear.

In large university towns such as Paris this process seems to have continued independently of the university, that in these cases was a relatively small factor in the economic life of the town. In smaller

---

[56] On Oxford taverns, see Salter, vol. II, pp. 184ff.

towns such as Oxford or Cambridge, however, there is proof that the university made prolonged efforts to influence the price-controls on food. Probably the oldest evidence of this comes from the Cambridge statutes of about 1250, which laid down that the rent commission mentioned earlier, which consisted of the two rectors and two council representatives, should 'also carefully provide that bread and wine and the other necessities of daily life are sold at a reasonable price, with deference to the time of year and the quality of the articles concerned, whether they are sold to members of the university or laity; and that university people and their servants have the right of first choice in all matters of business and above all other buyers'.[57] These royally confirmed statutes gave the university an economic power that the townsfolk no doubt tried to oppose in various ways. Indirect evidence of this comes in the next paragraph, in which the same commission is given the duty of keeping 'a watchful eye on monopolists (*monopolios*), that is to say, on traders entering into private agreements, or conspiring to keep back food and drink, in such a way that in general these wares are not sold to university people below a certain price'.

How little such decrees pleased the town traders appears from the number of royal pronouncements made afterwards in which traders were enjoined and even gradually forced to comply with them. In 1268, for example, it was decreed that all bakers should have their own stamp, with which to stamp their own loaves, so that those who were selling bread under the regulation weight could easily be identified.[58] At the same time penalties were established for brewers and bakers, who were fined on their first offence, had their wares confiscated on the second, and on their third were set in the stocks. The evaluation of bread and ale was set to take place at half-yearly intervals, and was declared invalid unless the chancellor or one of his men were present. In 1293 the king informed the mayor that following a new agreement with the wine exporters of Gascony and their importers in London, a gallon of wine selling for 3 pence in London would not be sold for more than $3\frac{1}{2}$ pence in Cambridge.[59] This measure was reaffirmed in 1351 and 1354, when it was also decided that wine could only be traded in sealed vats with its quantity verified. In 1320 the chancellor and the university com-

---

[57] On the inspection of foodstuffs in Cambridge, see Hackett, *Original Statutes*, cap. 7, p. 205.
[58] Cooper, vol. I, p. 51.   [59] Ibid. pp. 66 and 95.

plained to the king that the business of valuation was not being done in a proper manner. When this dispute was over in 1343, the economic life of the town had been taken almost completely out of the hands of the town government and was subject to university jurisdiction. Not only was it then decreed that each townsman was to be held 'responsible for the food and wine that his family or servants trade either in the town or in its environs', but that all proceedings enacted by university members involving 'loans, gifts, payments, the valuation and letting of houses, the renting, sale or loan of horses or bread or foodstuffs, as well as all other agreements involving personal property in Cambridge and environs ... should be decided by the university chancellor or his representatives'. The town courts were now out of the game, and the university became the dominating power in the city.

Quite a similar development took place in Oxford between 1240 and 1355. Here, too, the dispute ended with the university the total winner, but not before that succession of bloody disturbances discussed in an earlier chapter had taken place. These measures worked as a tightening noose on the business life of the towns, and they gradually created an antagonism between town and university that could only be controlled by constant appeals to the state. And when this happened, the king would nearly always come in on the side of the clerks, which in itself is telling proof of the university's growing power in medieval society. From the university's point of view, on the other hand, it was a matter of trying, understandably, to keep studying expenses down, to prevent higher education from becoming a privilege for the wealthy classes.[60]

Once the student had succeeded in getting a roof over his head and finding something to eat, his next problem of economic relevance lay in obtaining the books he needed for his work. As we saw earlier, nearly all books in the early middle ages were produced in monastic scriptoria; but both the university system itself and the general explosions of knowledge brought with them a huge increase in the demand for books which the monasteries could not, and would not contain. As a result in the thirteenth century there was a surge of widely ramified, secularised book-production, with a whole number of different crafts of parchment-makers, copyists, illuminators, correctors, bookbinders, and booksellers, all depending for

---

[60] On the development in Oxford, see Kibre, pp. 269–309.

their whole existence on an extensive canon of standard works that had been put onto syllabuses as textbooks. The production was especially focussed on and around the university towns, where scholars and teachers had a common interest in bringing this private industry, in terms of pricing and quality, under their control.

One of the first pieces of evidence for an interest in keeping book-prices down comes from Bologna, where the town council decreed in 1227 that textbooks could be imported into the city toll-free along with other personal goods. In the same decree landlords were forbidden to take students' books in pawn for outstanding rent.[61] Toll-immunity for imports of books is also known in Padua in 1444, but here the books could not be exported again without special permission.[62]

In the late middle ages a book could be obtained in various ways; one of them was to have a book copied by one of the practitioners of the skill. This allowed a book to be written and decorated to private specifications, and not least the many brilliantly decorated books of hours and other liturgical literature from these centuries shows how individual book-production continued to be artistic work of high quality. But there is no doubt either that this method of production was the most expensive of all. Table 2 gives an example of the cost of turning out a relatively large book of 200 folio pages in England in the thirteenth century, with individual costs per item.[63] This is nearly half of the 50 shillings that a fellow of Merton College received in allowance for a whole year's personal expenditure. The conclusion is that only a small minority of wealthy students had any chance of obtaining beautiful books in this way.

Table 2

	Shillings	Pence
Parchment	8	8
Copying	9	4
Correction	2	10
Illumination	1	1
Binding	1	5
Total	23	4

[61] Ibid. pp. 12 and 21.   [62] Ibid. p. 76.
[63] This account is quoted from F. Wormald and C. E. Wright, *The English Library before 1700*, London, 1958.

A more accessible solution was to copy the necessary books oneself. Until paper came into general use in the fifteenth century, parchment was required as well as pen and ink, prepared from lambskin or calfskin which could be bought from professional parchment-makers in quires (*pecia*) of normally sixteen pages.[64] In addition a copy or 'exemplar' of the desired book was necessary. If this could not be borrowed from a fellow student, it could still, where standard works were concerned, be had from a bookseller, who to this end would break up the book and hire it out quire for quire on a weekly basis for a deposit.[65] Even this activity in many cases came under the control of the universities, who fixed maximum prices for both the parchment and the exemplars. This happened in Paris in 1291 in an agreement that ensured the interests of buyers by setting up norms for the quality and reasonable pricing of parchments, while one of the ways the sellers' needs were taken care of was to forbid scholars from reselling the parchment themselves.[66] In 1354 the chancellor of Cambridge got jurisdiction in all matters involving booksellers, scribes, bookbinders and illuminators, thus adding a little more to his steadily growing power over the business life of the town.[67]

Finally, if he wished to avoid the time-consuming copying and could afford the expense, a student could buy a ready-made book at one of the booksellers or *stationarii* putting up their stalls in the square of a university town. These traders dealt with mass-produced standard works which were often produced many copies at a time by a whole team of scriveners writing to dictation – a method dating back to ancient Roman times.[68] Normally these booksellers too came under some kind of university control, where in many cases a special committee was set up to assess the price of the books and to see, at the same time, that they were correctly copied and complete. In Paris in 1304 this committee consisted of two masters of theology, one master of medicine, plus rector and proctors; this extremely official character was proof of how seriously the university regarded this service with respect to its scholars. One of the rates set by this

[64] On the *pecia*, see J. Destrez, *La pecia dans les manuscrits universitaires du XIIIe et XIVe siècle*, vols. I–II, Paris, 1935, and Thorndike, p. 259.
[65] On *exemplaria*, see M.-D. Chenu and J. Destrez, Exemplaria universitaires des XIIIe et XIVe siècles, *Scriptorium* 7 (1953), 173ff.
[66] *Chartularium* II, 48–52. [67] Cooper, vol. I, p. 104.
[68] See T. C. Skeat, The Use of Dictation in Ancient Book Production, *Proceedings of the British Academy*, 42 (1956), 179–208.

The material situation

committee was 29 *denarii* for Book I, or 38 *pecia*, of Thomas Aquinas' *Commentary to the Sentences*. The much-used philosophical treatise *De Principiis Rerum* of 14 *pecia* was put at 10 *denarii*, while a commentary on the Gospel of St Matthew of 57 *pecia* was assessed at 4 *solidi* or 48 *denarii*. On average it looks as if the price of a textbook at this time was about $\frac{3}{4}$ *denarius* per quire.[69]

In Paris the book trade was regulated in a statute of 1275, the aim of which was to prevent booksellers from 'putting obstacles in the way of the procuring of those books whose use is of vital importance for scholars, by buying too cheaply and selling too dear, or by thinking up other crafty methods of making the said books more expensive'.[70] The choice of words here shows that they were dealing with the trade of used textbooks. The statute established that when a bookseller had bought a book, he was to put it on sale immediately at a reasonable price, while the name of the salesman and the price the bookseller paid for it were both to be noted down in the book itself. The first mention of a bookseller in Cambridge is a notice of this type in a codex which says 'Memo that I bought this book from John Hackley on the Eve of the Feast of the Apostles Saint Simon and Jude at the house of bookseller William de Newwfylde in the presence of the following witnesses [the names of eight people follow] along with many others.'[71]

Hereby an arrangement was made that offered some guarantee against big profits for booksellers. At the same time booksellers were prevented from keeping books back, thereby contriving an artificial shortage of textbooks with profit-making price-rises as a result. That the salesman should be notified whenever a buyer turned up, indicates that the bookseller effectively only got a simple commission, and one that was not allowed to exceed 4 *denarii* in a pound, that is $1\frac{1}{2}$ per cent, plus a smaller sum *pro rata*. The bookseller had to swear an oath to abide by these decrees. If he exceeded them, he would 'no longer have the freedom to perform the occupation that he formerly practised on behalf of the university'.[72] The fact that people could be made to deal in used books at all under such strict conditions is probably explicable only in terms of the business doing very well.

The last material consideration to be taken into account is the

---

[69] *Chartularium* II, 107.   [70] *Chartularium* I, 532–4.
[71] The memo is printed in Wormald and Wright, *The English Library*, notes 63, 73.
[72] *Chartularium* I, 533.

issue of law and order in the university towns, which again is closely linked with the problem of the student's legal status. As we have seen, the great majority of scholars had clerical status and were thereby taken into the jurisdiction of the ecclesiastical courts. This made it necessary to draw up a precise list of persons who were thus exempted from the normal authority of the town's courts over its citizens. Out of this came the demand for matriculation, on which more will be said in the next chapter. Matriculation was carried out everywhere throughout the thirteenth century. To be entered on a register with one or other teacher, however, offered no direct protection to a member of the university who came up against the police or a crowd of angry townsmen. For this reason it was necessary to have a sign of clerical status that was visible to all.

One such practical sign was the tonsure, the little clean-shaven place on the crown of the head that was the clerk's usual feature. Yet there was also a growing demand for a special type of clothing that won wider acceptance, and that in the later middle ages led in many places to a regular uniform for both scholars and teachers, at any rate in more well-defined circumstances. To begin with, the demand for singularity and uniformity in dress seems to have been imposed on the teachers alone. In the oldest Cambridge statutes of about 1250 there is only a single paragraph stating that university teachers of theology, Canon law, and *artes* should wear a *cappa clausa* or a stole (*pallium*) at general lectures and disputations, and that they should also be decently dressed in this way when they attended funerals.[73] In the statutes for Merton College from 1274 it also says very briefly that those who were selected to be fellows of this house – and as before, this refers to older scholars – 'shall dress as uniformly as possible'.[74] But even in the Toulouse statutes of 1314 there is a long section on dress, containing many good reasons why university folk should go round decently and humbly dressed: too much magnificence in dress was, firstly, condemned by the church fathers; and, secondly, would bar the poor from studying, or make scholars leave their studies prematurely on economic grounds; finally, too much expenditure on clothes would prevent students from buying the necessary books. Therefore the statute puts a fixed price on scholars' garments and prescribes the use of a simple cape to be worn everywhere except on horseback, on journeys, at one's private

[73] Hackett, *Original Statutes*, ch. 5, p. 203.   [74] Brodrick, *Memorials*, p. 382, note 52.

address or up to twenty houses' distance from there. Newly graduated masters and doctors could only wear more distinguished clothes one month after their promotion, after which they were to return to their normal dress.[75] In Paris, on the other hand, a pronouncement from 1339 decrees simply that teachers must be correctly dressed at disputations and other official functions.[76]

This gradual progression towards a uniform dress was probably not the imposition of the more or less puritanical ideas of the past alone, on what was fitting for the clergy. For scholars, this was the price to be paid for not going in fear of night-watchmen, when things were tense between them and the townspeople. Besides, the clerical cape served as identification for the poorest students, if ever they were forced to beg for their living. For townspeople this uniform was no doubt a welcome feature as an immediate indicator of whom not to lay hands on, to avoid the risk of being put before a special ecclesiastical court. It was obviously more than just bourgeois indignation that lay behind the occasional injunctions of the authorities for a certain uniformity in academic dress. In some statutes of Peterhouse in Cambridge from 1342, it is made quite explicit that 'each and every man in this house shal take clerical robes and the tonsure and wear these ... as widely as they are able, not allow their beard or hair to grow against the prohibitions of canon law, nor wear rings on their fingers either for their own vanity's sake or to show off, nor to the bad example and indignation of others'.[77] But only a year later, things went wrong again, with the students of Cambridge

not giving a damn about the tonsure and going about with long hair, which either hung down at the shoulders or was curled and powdered too. They had long beards and looked more like soldiers than clerks in their get-up. They dressed in capes with fur borders and long hanging sleeves that did not cover the elbows. Their fingers were adorned with rings, their shoes were red and blue-checkered with extra long points, and around their waists they wore broad and costly belts with designs on them.[78]

To show a degree of inward independence in outward appearance is clearly not a fashion invented yesterday. But this display of youthful disobedience aroused such consternation that dealing with it on the local level was not enough. At a meeting in London, Archbishop

---

[75] Thorndike, pp. 150ff.   [76] *Chartularium* II, 486.
[77] Mullinger, vol. I, p. 23.   [78] Cooper, vol. I, pp. 94f.

Stratford and eleven other bishops resolved that no scholar would be able even to hope for an academic degree or ecclesiastical office until he had first rectified his attire.

The keeping of law and order around the universities was helped by the general ban on clerks bearing arms. In the middle ages this was a matter of course, but the high number of injunctions relating to this ban, like the number of court cases against scholars who had been mixed up in violence and killing, also shows how hard it was to get the ban enforced. An official proclamation from the Paris episcopal courts says in 1269 that

> constant and persistent complaints have been heard that there are certain clerks and scholars in Paris, together with their servants, who ... under the pretext that they are leading the life of a scholar commit more and more frequently unlawful and criminal acts with confidence in their weapons; to wit, that by day and by night they grievously wound or kill many people, violate women, molest virgins, break into inns, and time after time commit robberies and many other outrages.[79]

The legal protocols show that this was no idle talk. For example, it says much of the danger of life in university towns that of the twenty-nine coroner's inquests recorded in Oxford from 1297 to 1322, no less than thirteen concerned persons who had been killed by members of the university.[80] The Paris proclamation therefore enjoined that any transgression of the ban on bearing arms would lead to excommunication; the same penalty was also established for anyone with knowledge of clerks carrying arms who did not turn them over to the authorities within seven days. It was only on journeys that scholars were allowed to go armed in the same way as all other people; but on their arrival at the university, they had promptly to stack their weapons away at their own address. This proviso undeniably made the whole decree rather pointless, but a general ban on the possession of arms in medieval Europe would have been just as unworkable as in America today.

Throughout the thirteenth century, anyway, there were very few direct orders relating to discipline. Mostly they were aimed at keeping the public peace, as in the case of several prohibitions on holding tournaments or wrestling shows within a certain distance of both Oxford and Cambridge, as these popular events would afterwards give rise to scenes between the hangers-on of different

[79] *Chartularium* I, 481.   [80] See Rait, p. 127.

sporting factions. However, as time went on, the controls on the private lives of scholars and teachers alike tightened; not least because common life in the increasing number of hospices and colleges called for some mutual deference, that would often be expressed in the prohibitions and commands of special statutes. In this way the statutes of Peterhouse from 1342 forbade its fellows to keep either dogs or hunting falcons, 'for if one fellow has leave to keep them in the house, all will keep them, and so there will be a ceaseless barking and howling', and thus no peace to work in.[81] This ban was extended later under King Henry VI to include 'apes, bears, wolves, and harts', as if menageries of this kind were common in colleges of the fifteenth century.[82] That sport was regarded with more scepticism in English universities of the middle ages than it is today can be seen in a Cambridge prohibition of 1410 on playing tennis in the town.[83] This was thought to be a waste of time, whereas a more reasonable ban in Merton College on throwing stones in chapel was probably brought about by a real incident.[84] The same is no doubt true of the comical Heidelberg decree of 1396, which prohibited the catching of the townspeople's pigeons.[85] Nor were more gentle pastimes treated with benevolence. Throwing dice was commonly forbidden to all clerks, and by the same token to all people of the university; and even a game as harmless as chess was sometimes quoted in the statutes as not to be allowed, because it wasted too much time.

In general, the history of universities in the late middle ages shows clearly that the days of the relatively carefree life of a thirteenth-century student were over. Daily student life was now hedged about by numerous regulations, which the student had better learn and live up to, given that they were fixed in statutes and therefore legally binding. And the infringement of such decrees could be punished in many different ways.

The most serious penalty was undoubtedly excommunication, which, as we have just seen, was the result of weapons being used in Paris in 1269. But even in 1210 the University of Paris sought to keep the dangerous books of Aristotle out on pain of excommunication,[86] and this was also the penalty for breaking the first statutes of 1215.[87] There must be some doubt as to how effective this punishment was;

---

[81] Ibid. p. 63, note 80.   [82] Rait, p. 64.   [83] Cooper, vol. 1, p. 152.
[84] Rait, p. 64.   [85] Thorndike, p. 260.   [86] *Chartularium* I, 70.
[87] Ibid. 79.

at any rate, the Papal Penitentiary Alvarus Pelagius of Avignon (who died in 1352) complained that the teachers of Paris were keeping excommunicated students on in their classes, regardless of their exclusion from the church.[88] In other cases of a grave nature, the authorities resorted to prison sentences, but at this point the church seems to have tried to soften the general line. Thus in 1231 Pope Gregory forbade the chancellor of Paris the use of his own university prison; clerks could be only be put into the bishop's prison, and it was asserted that, according to ecclesiastical law, no clerk could be arrested for debt.[89] Normally imprisonment was applied only in cases of serous crime, even if there are many examples where the system was abused. In this way the famous physician and alchemist Arnold of Villanova (died in 1311) complained in 1300 that at the chancellor's instigation he had been put into the jail of the bishop of Paris, for having composed, as a layman, a suspect writing on the imminent coming of Antichrist. This was in spite of his membership of a diplomatic mission from King Jacob II of Aragon to King Philip the Fair of France.[90]

A far more frequent disciplinary measure was exclusion or suspension. In 1252 the English nation at the Paris faculty of *artes* decided that any teacher who failed to hold an examination in the prescribed manner would be suspended from his duties for one month.[91] A hundred years later the price was much higher, in that masters of *artes* in 1355 were threatened with suspension for a whole year from their teaching, college duties, and academic honours, if they failed to lecture in a closely specified way; a slightly earlier statute from 1340 protected new scholars against molestation by threatening their tormentors with the loss of their whole university status from that time forth.[92] In Heidelberg in 1454 a master would be barred from entering the university library for a full year if he lent a book to someone who was not a member of the university.[93]

Yet there is no doubt that fines were the most common punishment for the peccadillos of everyday life. Fines were used especially in the colleges, the statutes of which were full of detailed decrees on what a man could not do without running into a financial penalty. Thus the first statutes of the Sorbonne, as early as in 1274, worked with a standard fine of two litres of wine (in modern measure) to be

[88] Thorndike, pp. 171f. [89] *Chartularium* I, 138.
[90] *Chartularium* II, 86–90; cf. Thorndike, pp. 128ff. [91] *Chartularium* I, 230.
[92] *Chartularium* II, 496 and III, 39. [93] Thorndike, p. 318.

given to the house. This was a punishment for talking too loudly at mealtimes, for starting a meal before Grace or for annoying or molesting the serving staff. Cash fines were inflicted in more serious cases; thus it cost 6 *denarii* to be found entertaining a woman with a meal in a private room, and the same penalty was imposed for leaving the house without permission for one day.[94] Here it was the first day that was most expensive – it cost only one *denarius* per day after that. In 1398 cursing and swearing was punished in Heidelberg with a fine of two pounds' worth of wax for the chapel.[95] In the same place in 1442 it was half a guilder for visiting a gambling den, a whole guilder for going to a brothel; in the last case the man's name was entered on a special list of shame in the university.[96]

[94] *Chartularium* 1, 508.   [95] Thorndike, p. 261.   [96] Ibid. pp. 332f.

CHAPTER 9

The road to degrees

After discussing the student's material welfare in the last chapter, it is time to look at the more 'academic' side of his life, from his qualification for university as a green grammar-school boy, to when six to twelve years later he passed his final examinations. The sources for this part of the history of the universities are rather various, and far less abundant than one could wish. This is because the universities rose up on the foundations of twelfth-century schools which followed an even older tradition of learning, and one that was certainly never committed to paper in the form of syllabuses or examination decrees. By and large where this early period is concerned, therefore, we shall turn to the few autobiographical passages that are found in the writings of Peter Abelard, for example, or of John of Salisbury. Things were no better in the universities just after their foundation. The unwritten tradition reigned in this period too, until conflicts and cases of doubt made well-defined rules necessary, and thereby brought statutes regulating courses of study and examinations into being. In the case of the older universities, this took place about half way through the thirteenth century, where our information comes from documents as important as the oldest statutes of Cambridge and the very detailed regulations that were passed in 1252 and the following years in the faculty of *artes* in Paris, first by the English nation and then by the university as a whole. But these sources only show how the prescribed course of study proceeded. They must be supplemented therefore with a large but haphazard body of material concerning individual cases, as for example the dispensations that were needed when standards could not be maintained.

Once the student had arrived in the university town and had got himself lodgings, his first and most important task was to get himself a teacher. It is not known how this process normally went on, though

The road to degrees

the necessity for it was already stressed in the statutes of Robert de Courçon in 1215, where it says that 'no-one may be a student in Paris without having a specified teacher'.[1] The reason for this is mentioned in the bull of Pope Gregory IX from 1231, in which it is said that 'they who pretend to be students but follow no course of lectures or do not have a teacher, may in no way enjoy the privileges of students'.[2] Since one of the things these privileges consisted of was freedom from all jurisdiction of civil courts, it is easy to understand the importance of knowing precisely who were students and who were not. In addition, it was a general duty of corporations to make a list of their members. This is how the matriculation system came about, and indeed it seems that it went back to even before the time when student corporations were formed, since the job of registering scholars was entrusted everywhere to individual teachers, and not to the nations. The first we hear of this system is a reference in the Cambridge statutes of the middle of the thirteenth century. Here it is said to be improper if a man failed to get a teacher within fifteen days of his arrival in the university, or failed to take the trouble to get his name on his teacher's list within the same period.[3] This decree was made an injunction by the bishop of Ely in 1276.[4]

In Paris the faculty of *artes* introduced a statutory requirement of matriculation in 1289, on the grounds that 'in consideration of the overwhelming number of scholars at our faculty, we do not know the names of many of them and cannot distinguish between those who are good and legitimate, and those who are false and are pretending to study at our faculty so as to enjoy the privileges and freedoms associated with this'. Teachers were therefore obliged by oath to write the names of their own students on a list or *matricula*, and to give information on demand about the diligence and industry of their students. 'Yet bogus students and other hangers-on at the university shall not be inscribed alongside the good ones, but shall be removed as unprofitable from the womb and organisation of the faculty.'[5] Each time a new rector was elected, he would swear an oath that the matriculation decrees would be read out by a sworn beadle in all teachers' classes.

It was mentioned earlier in another connection that there is no evidence of any real entrance or admission tests in medieval

---

[1] *Chartularium* I, 79.   [2] Ibid. 138.   [3] Hackett, *Original Statutes*, ch. 9, pp. 1, 211.
[4] Cooper, vol. I, p. 57.   [5] *Chartularium* II, 35f.

universities. And yet there was an episode in 1369 where a certain grammar-school teacher named John Bonafos of St Germain (at Mende) arrived at Avignon with thirty-one of his pupils to have them 'tested according to the diligence and fitness of each one of them'.[6] The result was that twenty-one were selected to go on to the University of Montpellier (in spite of the fact that at this time Avignon housed a university of its own and the Curia University as well). Of those remaining, some were sent back to grammar school, while some dropped out completely. All of them, however, had their travel expenses paid. This event seems to have been unique, and the particular circumstances are by no means clear. Normally, to be able to begin a course of study it was sufficient to have graduated from a grammar school. Yet this hardly means that all boys leaving school were allowed to start work as students. The individual teacher could not admit everyone who turned up into his care. There would necessarily have to be an interview, and if the applicant showed deficiencies in ability or earnestness it would have been a risk for the teacher to matriculate him, considering that the teacher assumed responsibility not only for the boy's education but also for his good conduct. Yet there seems to have been no mention of any formal entrance examination for all the annual student intake.

There is evidence that incoming scholars in certain cases had to pay a fee to be admitted to his teacher's register. It is no surprise that it was so in Bologna, where according to the statute the expense was 12 *solidi*.[7] The extent to which this custom originally existed in Paris (where teachers were remunerated by the church) may be doubted; but it seems to have penetrated most other places after a while. In the first half of the fourteenth century the Spanish Franciscan Alvarus Pelagius (*c.* 1280–1352), in his social satire *On the Lament of the Church* (*De Planctu Ecclesiae*), ridiculed those teachers who refused to teach poor students without payment, and also those scholars who refused to pay the teacher even if they could afford to do so; however, it is hard to make out whether this was a fee paid before education started or simply a running expense.[8] At the University of Valence in 1490 it was stipulated in accordance with previous regulations that within one month of the university year each wealthy student of noble birth should pay three florins, a less wealthy

[6] Thorndike, p. 249. [7] Rashdall, vol. I, p. 216. [8] Thorndike, pp. 172f.

one two florins, and everyone else one florin, apart from the poor, who were let off the fee altogether.[9]

It is obvious that any student would head straight for the older scholars of his own country when he first arrived, to get advice and tips on how best to settle these formalities. Thereby he would automatically come into contact with the nation to which his countrymen normally belonged, with the result that he would usually get a teacher of this nation as his official guide.[10] That this is how things were done, can be seen in the protocols of the nations that it was the job of the proctor to keep. Thus the English nation in Paris in the beginning of 1340 had a Danish proctor, Henry of Unna, who during his period of office led Nicolaus de Dacia forward to his master's degree, at the same time as one of his other students by the name of Laurentius de Dacia took the introductory bachelor's examination. Two years later the same Nicolaus 'Drukken' de Dacia had got himself promoted to proctor; he led the Norwegian Roland up for his bachelor's examination, at the same time as the Swedish master Suno led up three of his countrymen by the names of Benedict, Petrus Arnoldi, and Petrus Mathiae for the same honour.[11]

While the inscribing of the student with his teacher was without doubt quite an informal affair, his first meeting at close quarters with his fellows, either in the nation or the hospice, could be more dramatic. Here the new boys could only be admitted to the fellowship after a series of rituals.[12] These in the last analysis can be attributed to the need of the strong to humiliate the weak, or to the familiar tendency to have a party at someone else's expense. The justification for it, however, was rather more sly. According to one theory, the student designate was a malignant creature who had to be bodily punished. According to another, he was regarded as dirty and soiled, and therefore had to be washed and scrubbed to remove the unbearable stench that no experienced student could fail to notice whenever a 'fresher' was in the neighbourhood. A third view had the newcomer down as a monster complete with beak, horns, and claws that had to be removed by means of a feigned, but all the

[9] Ibid. p. 365.
[10] See P. Kibre, *The Nations in the Mediaeval Universities*, Cambridge, Mass., 1948; on the Anglican nation in particular, see G. C. Boyce, *The English–German Nation in the University of Paris during the Middle Ages*, Bruges, 1927.
[11] The examples relating to Scandinavian scholars are taken from the *Liber Procuratorum* I, 44 and 60.
[12] On initiation ceremonies, see Rashdall, vol. III, pp. 376f and Rait, pp. 109ff.

same cruelly unpleasant operation. The last view seems to have predominated in the thirteenth century, where the remarkable Latin term, *bejaunus*, used of a new student, appears to be a corruption of the French expression *bec jaune*, 'yellow-beak', one of the newcomer's pretended attributes.

Such initiation ceremonies had been known even in the schools of antiquity. For example, in the preface to his *Digesta*, Justinian forbids older students of law to pull the legs of their new companions.[13] In the middle ages these ceremonies gradually took an unpleasant turn, as they became more and more nasty for the victim personally, and more of a burden to his purse – naturally it was he who had to pay for the drinks that were part of the fun. In the fourteenth century the universities therefore began to intervene. There is a statute from 1340 for the whole University of Paris, which forbids the worst excesses: no-one may receive money from a new student, because he is new, and if anyone hears of a *bejaunus* being molested in any way in word or deed it is his duty to report it to the proctors (of the nations) or to the deans (of the higher faculties), so that the guilty parties may be punished.[14] Two years later it was decided that a pronouncement to this effect would be read aloud at university services.[15] But in these efforts the university met defeat. The need for wine and song had to find expression somewhere, and after a while the *depositio* of the new scholars became an indispensable start to the course; the term comes from *depositio cornuum*, 'deposition of the horns', thus pointing directly to the view that the new boy was a wild animal who had to be rendered harmless. What the authorities could do, on the other hand, was to put a ceiling on the numbers present at the ceremonies, and thus on the related expense, together with a ban on the worst excesses. A statute from Heidelberg in 1466 thus forbade students to 'force a freshman to sing or to cast dirt upon him',[16] while a statute from Valence a little later spoke of the 'superfluous and destructive banquets in which no-one obtains any knowledge, while great scandal results ... in such a way that newly arrived students leave the university immediately, because of the dirty and offensive things that are said or done to them, when they cannot afford to pay so much money'.[17]

Once the preliminaries were over and done with, the course of

---

[13] See the constitution *Omnem* No. 9, published together with the *Digesta*.
[14] *Chartularium* II, 494.   [15] Ibid. 523.   [16] Thorndike, p. 353.
[17] Ibid. pp. 365f.

study could begin. Then as now the university year started after the summer holidays, which were not the same length in all universities, however. Pope Gregory IX established in his *Parens Scientiarum* in 1231 that the summer vacation in Paris should not exceed one month, and that it should preferably be used for non-compulsory teaching.[18] Later the vacation was extended, however, with the faculty of *artes* in the fourteenth century closing down for eight weeks, from the Feast of Peter and Paul on 29 June to the Feast of Saint Louis on 25 August, while the higher faculties took longer to get started; thus doctors of theology and canon law would wait until 14 September.[19] In Bologna, on the other hand, the jurists seem to have been a little more hardworking, and here the university year began on 19 October and ended on 7 September, allowing for a summer holiday of only six weeks.[20] In England there was more freedom. The oldest Cambridge statutes, of about 1250, divide the university year into four quarters, of which the first ran from 9 October to 16 December, the second from 13 January to the Friday before Palm Sunday, the third from the Wednesday after Quasimodo (the first Sunday after Easter) to the Friday before Whitsun, and the last from the Monday after Trinity to 20 July. This gave a long summer holiday of eleven weeks, four weeks' Christmas holiday, nearly three weeks at Easter and ten days around Whitsun – a system that has hardly changed to this day.[21]

This does not mean that teaching ran continuously between holidays. On the contrary, the number of days off was extraordinary. Not only was Sunday naturally kept free, but also a whole number of other church holidays were celebrated wholly or partly free of teaching. On big festivals all lectures were called off. On the lesser ones, the afternoon was kept free, in so far as cursory, that is non-compulsory, teaching alone was allowed. It rested on the beadle or *bidellus* to keep the score of all university holidays with the aid of a special university calendar, and to inform individual scholars of the less well-known holidays; should he neglect to do this, then according to a Paris statute on the work of beadles from the mid-thirteenth century, he could be charged a fine of four *denarii*.[22] Such a Paris University calendar is still preserved from an unknown time after 1325, from which it appears that church holidays allowed for a total

---

[18] *Chartularium* I, 138. [19] *Chartularium* II, 709f. [20] Rashdall, vol. I, p. 219.
[21] Hackett, *Original Statutes*, ch. 3, pp. 201f. [22] *Chartularium* I, 418f.

of seventy-one full free days common to all faculties; of course, some of these could have fallen on a Sunday and so may not have counted. In addition, the individual faculties had extra days off of their own. Students of *artes* had eight such free days extra, the theologians nine, while the jurists knew better about their own comfort, with canon lawyers enjoying thirty-nine days off over and above the total common for the university as a whole.[23] In Bologna, if by some freak chance a week contained no day off, then Thursday was made a holiday.[24]

At the students' University of Bologna, teaching did not start immediately. There, for the jurists, the first three days of the university year following the summer holiday were used for a general meeting of the whole university, where all its statutes were read out, thus allowing the scholars to become familiar with their rights and duties. Furthermore, it was the job of the rectors to see that all special statutes concerning the teachers and their classes, plus the manner of teaching, should be read aloud before all classes when the teaching started. If just one student required it, the rectors would also have to provide for one of the university notaries to read to the class any statute that he thought it was important to know. There was no such hurry to do new scholars this service in the professors' University of Paris. Here the new scholars were first acquainted with their privileges at a public reading of the statutes on All Souls' Day (2 November). To make up for this, the reading was repeated in February; in the university calendar mentioned above, it says: 'Note that on the day when *Esto mihi* is sung (the Sunday before Ash Wednesday), the rector shall preach in the Jacobite Church, and after his sermon a beadle shall read out the privileges of new scholars, and after this comes the real sermon.'[25]

This brings us eventually to the teaching itself, the most suitable manner and method of which were often the subject of the scholarly literature of the middle ages. In the twelfth century the *Didascalion* of Hugo of St Victor was already a much-used pedagogic guide, containing many clever observations on the form of teaching and many strict requirements on the moral position of both teachers and pupils.[26] It stressed the importance of brevity and clarity in presentation. One should start with generally well-known things, so as

---

[23] *Chartularium* II, 709–16. [24] Rashdall, vol. I, p. 219.
[25] *Chartularium* II, 709 and 714. [26] *Didascalion* III, 11; Migne PL 176, 772.

gradually to penetrate deeper into the material and learn to distinguish between essentials and inessentials. In Hugo's view, regular teaching in schools would only bear fruit if it led to independent reflection outside hours, and to a personal engagement with problems that he called *meditatio* and that would supply the scholar lastingly with 'a life full of inward joy and all possible comfort in this vale of sorrows'. Only such *meditatio* could lead to new thoughts and deeper insight. In a modern way of speaking, this was a form of research. But since it could only be achieved with great effort, and was rather personal, the personal ethics of the student were the deciding factor. It was he who had to show self-discipline, lead an ordered life, and not be distracted by irrelevant things. He should also be humble, for no-one may know everything, and be patient too, so as to achieve his aim more quickly, and he was not to form an opinion without first having steeped himself in the subject-matter.

A hundred years later Thomas Aquinas repeated these rules of life to a young novice by the name of John, who had asked him for advice on the best way to study.[27] Otherwise he treated the basic questions of pedagogy in great depth many times in his works, for example, in one *quaestio* 'Utrum unus homo possit alium docere?', 'Whether one man may teach another?', which has an important place in his *Summa Theologica*.[28] At about the same time the encyclopedist Vincent de Beauvais wrote that from a teacher, one 'demands ability and experience in teaching, that is to say, that he has a teaching method. In a lecture four things are required: that it shall be clear, short, relevant, easy to listen to, and correctly measured and balanced.'[29] By clarity he meant that the whole audience should understand all of it, surely no small thing to ask. The brevity would prevent any rambling or irrelevant digressions, but this should not be overdone either, since pupils would then lose the urge to go to the lecture, something that could be offset by an engaging lecture that made them more attentive. By the correct balance, he meant that individual sentences should hang together in a logical way, and should not be reeled off too quickly. These various

---

[27] Thomas Aquinas, *Opuscula*, Turin–Rome, 1954, p. 451.
[28] *Summa Theologica* I^a, q. 117, a 1.
[29] Vincent of Beauvais, *De Eruditione Filiorum Nobilium*, ed. A. Steiner, Cambridge, Mass., 1938; quoted here from E. Schoelen, *Erziehung und Unterricht im Mittelalter*, 2nd edn, Paderborn, 1965, pp. 95f.

basic pedagogic rules seem to have become common property after a while. Thus in a so-called *Prince's Mirror* (a handbook for the training of persons of rank), completed with the title *De Eruditione Principum* by some Dominicans in about 1265,[30] it says that a good teacher must have five properties – a talented mind, good moral conduct, humble knowledge, obligingness, and practical experience of teaching, so that his teaching is clear, brief, useful, agreeable, and measured. Special attention should be focussed on the need for teaching experience; how the medieval universities consciously strove to comply with this, we shall see below.

These more general thoughts on pedagogy and ethics tell us little, however, of the form and method of the teaching itself. Where this is concerned, much has been said and written since then on that 'scholastic method' assumed to be characteristic of the learning of medieval 'scholasticism'.[31] Much of this topic has suffered from being studied from a wrong perspective, in that these questions of methodology were first examined historically by medievalist scholars who were not only exclusively concerned with theology and philosophy, but who also often wished to put their results at the disposal of the so-called 'neo-scholastic' movement, whose heyday was in the Roman Catholic church from about 1880 up to the Second World War.[32] Yet, after a while, since knowledge of the learning and university life of the middle ages has deepened, it has become increasingly clear that the methodological principles of this time cannot be reduced to a simple formula. Henceforth we will try therefore to establish a point of view which is more general and at the same time more down-to-earth. Thus 'scholasticism' will simply be defined without ideological overtones as the sum of scholarly activity in the 'schools' or universities of the late or high middle ages. As one of the consequences, it will no longer be possible to talk of any single scholastic method, seeing that the universities effectively applied different procedures, which, from the methodological point of view, differed widely from one another.

Of the various forms of teaching the new student would meet, one was the lectures, which came in many different kinds. In part they were divided into three different categories according to their

---

[30] Schoelen, *Erziehung*, n. 29, pp. 110f.
[31] The principal work on the early history of the scholastic method is Grabmann.
[32] The Neo-Thomistic movement originated among Catholic philosophers with a strong backing by Leo XIII and later popes, see J. Maritain, *Le docteur angélique*, Paris, n.d., 1930.

importance in the system as a whole; in part, anyhow, the teacher could use two different pedagogic methods. Most important were the *ordinary* lectures, the compulsory bedrock of university teaching. These were given usually by older and more experienced teachers, and comprised the material necessarily belonging to the fixed syllabus of the examination requirements. Normally, therefore, they were given year after year on the same subjects, though the way these were treated might change after a while. Beyond these there were the *extraordinary* lectures, given by less prominent teachers and allowing more variation of theme. Sometimes they came up as a supplement to ordinary lectures; in these cases they were often given a year later as a kind of revision course. But less important subjects, not required for the compulsory examination, were also handled in extraordinary lectures. This state of affairs, in connection with the younger average age of 'extraordinary' teachers, ensured that it was often through this teaching that new subjects or ideas found their way into less formal surroundings, where, so to speak, they could be given a trial run. Finally, there were the so-called *cursory* lectures, which, as the name indicates, were shaped as a hurried march through a subject with no discussion of any depth. Normally these were given by older students, as part of the pedagogic training; it was therefore one of the advantages of the medieval university, that no master could leave it without having pedagogic experience of some kind. The cursory lectures were never compulsory. In many cases they did not much differ from the extraordinary ones, and in Paris, for example, hardly any distinction was made between these two categories.

It is obvious that the cursory teaching had a difficult position in the system as a whole. On one hand, it was not compulsory for scholars who did not need to attend it, and who were quite often tempted to stay away. On the other hand, it was compulsory for potential masters as a requisite part of their education, since they needed to get an audience for themselves. There is also some evidence that it was not at a premium. The Buoncompagni da Signa mentioned earlier thus introduced his new textbook of rhetoric as a commutation of Cicero's treatise on the same, since the latter 'is never the subject of ordinary lectures, but is rather glanced over cursorily or privately on a par with a fable or a "mechanical art" '.[33] Effectively

---

[33] On Buoncompagni, see Thorndike, p. 45.

this teaching went as far as the good will of the scholars studying it. A regulation for the teaching of *artes* in Paris in 1255 says that 'no cursor (i.e. cursory lecturer) may commence a course ... before he has completed the previous one, unless the students wish to listen to him no longer' which puts the situation in a nutshell.[34]

Moreover, non-compulsory teaching was in no way allowed to interfere with the compulsory variety. This caused problems with the timetable, which then as now was a jigsaw which it was hard to get to work properly. Here it is worth remembering first that our present division of the day into equal hours is a modern phenomenon that was accepted long after the mechanical clock came into fashion at the beginning of the fourteenth century. In the middle ages, the day was measured out by the so-called canonical hours, at which the seven daily prayers of the church, or the 'office', were sung in monasteries, cathedrals and college chapels, and also made known to the whole town by bell-ringing. The canonical hours were:

matins, followed by

lauds	at night
prime	at dawn
tierce	at mid-morning
sext	at midday
nones	at mid-afternoon
vespers	at dusk
completorium	at nightfall

It was between *lauds* and *prime* that the first mass of the day was usually said.

The daily work of the university was put into this scheme. Yet this was not easy, due to the structure of the university, which implied that teachers at the basic faculty of *artes* were frequently scholars also at one of the higher faculties. The timetable, therefore, had to be adjusted, so that the teaching they gave did not overlap with the teaching they were supposed to receive. This is the context of a decree in the Cambridge statutes which says that 'no-one may presume to commence a compulsory lecture after the bell begins to ring for *prime*, with the sole exception of the canon lawyers who may give compulsory lectures neither before *prime* nor after the *nones*'.[35] The intention is clearly to reserve the time between *prime* and *nones*

---

[34] *Chartularium* I, 279f, cf. Thorndike, pp. 64–6.
[35] Hackett, *Original Statutes*, ch. 2, 5, p. 201.

for students of law who are also teachers of the *artes* faculty, where by the same token they had to do their teaching before *prime* and after *nones*. This means that the young scholars of *artes* had to get up early in order to attend their compulsory teaching. While their masters went on to study themselves in the middle of the day, they could listen to non-compulsory lectures from the older students who conducted this (cursory) teaching in their own faculty as part of their own education. A statute for the faculty of *artes* in Paris lays down in 1367 that all masters (i.e. fully educated teachers) should start their classes when the Carmelites rang for their first mass; this would remove some earlier confusion, when previously some classes had begun at *prime* in St Jacques, and others at the second mass of the Carmelites – where they should have stopped, according to old custom – with the outcome that teachers could not get to theological lectures, while scholars wasted a large part of the day asleep because there was no teacher, something that brought the whole faculty into disrepute.[36] Other systems were used elsewhere, but the main principle was that ordinary teaching at the faculty of *artes* should coincide with the extraordinary (eventually non-compulsory) teaching at the other schools, and vice versa.

As the etymology of *lectio* – 'reading' – indicates, a lecture was no free discourse on a given subject. It was always based on a textbook or manual from which the teacher read a passage before offering his personal commentary on it. It was left to the scholars to keep notes as aids to their memory; in a time when books were rare and costly, this was in many cases the only chance a student had to get himself a textbook. Yet the pedagogic problems caused by this method are illustrated in a statute which was passed by the Paris faculty of *artes* 10 December 1355, and which seems to describe a real pedagogic experiment:

Two methods have been tried in lectures concerning books on *artes liberales*. The first group of teachers of philosophy [i.e. *artes*] enunciated their words so quickly that while the thought of the audience could well grasp them, the hand could not keep pace. The second group spoke so slowly that the audience managed to write their words down. After careful comparison and examination the first mentioned method was found to be better than the second, for which reason there is general agreement to imitate it in our teaching.[37]

---

[36] *Chartularium* III, 160.   [37] Ibid. 39f, cf. Thorndike, pp. 237f.

The assembled masters, with the rector at their head, therefore decreed that all teachers at the faculty should give both ordinary lectures and extraordinary ones, since 'they speak as if no-one takes notes before them, in the same way as university sermons and commendations are read out, and in the way followed by other faculties in their lectures'.

From the pedagogic point of view, there is scarcely any doubt that this was the correct method. Its manner of presentation was more alive than the soporific dictation favoured by the other method. But it also foresaw protests from scholars who were in this way deprived of the chance to write their own textbooks down in the class. Strong penalties were therefore established for any infringement of this decree. Teachers would have their licence suspended for a year, just as a year's exclusion from the whole course faced 'members of the audience opposing the execution of this our decree by commotion, hissing, alarm, or stone-throwing' – a passage indicating that lecturers in the halls of the middle ages sometimes led a dangerous life. A possibility, nonetheless, was kept open for scholars to have their books dictated, but this could only take place on holidays, when no lectures were given, and only in class and outside the times of university sermons.

When the teacher had chosen the work on which he wished to lecture, in accordance with the syllabuses, he could choose between two different pedagogic methods. Even in the twelfth century the chancellor of Chartres, Gilbert de la Porrée (d. 1154), related that some of his teachers were *recitatores*, confining themselves to a more or less slavish progress through the text, while others might be called *interpretes* or interpreters, for they really made an effort to interpret the text and clear up its obscurities.[38] In the first case the result was just a paraphrase of sorts, such as the commentaries on Aristotle that we know from the following century from the hand of Albertus Magnus, for example. For the teacher, however, who wished to go deeper into the work, there were again two ways of proceeding. He could either expound the content and meaning of the text by simply reading it out – as in *lectio*, 'lesson' – and by linking suitable commentaries with each separate passage. Or, on the basis of the text, he could also formulate a series of crucial problems or *quaestiones* ('questions', the Latin equivalent of the Greek *problemata*), each of which was debated in turn.

[38] On *recitatores* and *interpretes*, see Grabmann, vol. II, p. 421.

As an instance of how the two methods could be applied to the same text, we may look at one of the main works of the study of *artes*, that is, Aristotle's treatise on cosmology *On the Heavens* (*De Caelo*), as it was presented by two different professors.[39] The first of these was Thomas Aquinas, who progressed through the text in the University of Naples in 1272/3 in a course of no less than sixty-five lectures or *lectiones* (though the last five are attributed to Peter de Alvernia). This is also quite an interesting illustration of how even one of the most famous theology teachers of the age was still not thought too good to take his turn at the preliminary *artes* curriculum. The second professor was the Paris Master John Buridanus (d. post 1358), who left fifty-one *quaestiones* on the same work, presumably as a result of many different courses in the period 1328 to 1358.[40]

Thomas chose to give his lectures the form of a general presentation or *expositio* of the whole text. As was customary, he used the first lecture to give a broad introduction to the subject from the point of view of what we would call a philosopher of science, followed by the placing of the work in relation to other texts on natural philosophy which Aristotle wrote.[41] After this the text itself was broached and divided up into sixty-four short extracts, each of which made up the theme of a lecture. The individual *lectio* was introduced with a so-called *divisio textus*, in that the day's extract from Aristotle was further divided into a series of shorter passages, on each of which he would then offer a commentary, with all the thoroughness that the difficulty of the piece demanded – sometimes word for word, sentence by sentence, sometimes in the form of a free discussion of the content, or an explication of the background that would help understanding. A real pearl of this pedagogic style, for example, is the clear and concise presentation of the historical development of Greek astronomy. This is found in association with a brief passage in the text on the movement of the planets. To illustrate the range of such a commentary, we need go no further than the fourth lecture, which dealt with Aristotle's argument that the heavenly bodies were not composed of the conventional four elements, but of a fifth substance called ether. Here Aristotle's text contains about 500

---

[39] This example is based on Thomas Aquinas, *Expositio in Aristotelis libros De caelo et mundo*, ed. R. M. Spinazzi, Turin–Rome, 1952.

[40] *Johannis Buridani Quaestiones super libris quattuor De coelo et mundo*, ed. E. A. Moody, Cambridge, Mass., 1942, Lib. I, q. 1, pp. 3–7.

[41] See above, pp. 4ff, on Aristotle's theory of science and doctrine of abstraction.

words divided into six sections, and yet the corresponding six sections in Thomas' commentary together make up about 2,900 words. The total was thus about 3,400 words, just about the number that can be read at normal speed in an hour. For this reason Thomas was not one of those teachers who gave their scholars time to write down each word from his mouth as he uttered it.

Buridanus, on the other hand, used the *quaestio* method, which gave the lesson a completely different character. First, Aristotle's text was not read out at the beginning of the hour. Consequently there was no *divisio textus* of any kind. Instead Buridanus simply plunges into his *Quaestio prima* or First Problem: *Utrum de mundo debet esse scientia distincta a scientia libri Physicorum?*, or 'Whether there should be any science concerning the universe which differs from the science of physics'. The discussion of this question took up the first hour and therefore was Buridanus' counterpart to Thomas' first lecture, in that it was a theoretical debate on the scientific status of cosmology. What was important was that this debate proceeded according to a prepared outline, as there was first announced a number of reasons to answer the question negatively. In the first four of these *objectiones* it was variously claimed that there was no science on the universe as a whole, and this was based on a conceptual-analytic investigation of the word 'science', as it was used in Aristotle's *Analytica Posteriora*. The fifth and sixth objections claimed, on the other hand, that such a science might indeed exist, if this was identified with Aristotelian physics, which deals with all natural masses and therefore with the heavenly bodies too. Yet Buridanus set out a counter-argument to this view, namely that Aristotle and other philosophers meant something different. This counter-argument – normally, though not here, introduced with the words *Sed contra*, 'But against this' – thus shows not only that these learned men disagreed about the problem, but also that Aristotle seemed to contradict himself.

Both a dialectic and dynamic situation was created thereby, and one can imagine the growing excitement in the lecture theatre as to how the teacher would solve or 'determine' the problem. The solution was normally established with a longer elucidation, which began with the word *Respondeo*, 'I answer'. Here Buridanus went right back to Aristotle's view of science and the doctrine mentioned earlier of the classification of the sciences according to different layers of abstraction within knowledge, reaching the conclusion that cosmology really was a science, but was not a branch of physics in general. Yet the subject was not exhausted. The five original objections needed to be answered or refuted. This proceeded through five corresponding arguments, called *solutiones*, showing the invalidity of the objections in the light of the *respondeo* extract. With that, the lesson was over, and in his next lecture Buridanus could move on to his next problem, which concerned the existence of three spatial dimensions and was discussed along the same logical lines.

There is good reason to compare the two methods of teaching in a little more detail. The simple *expositio* or commentary had certain obvious advantages. It was linked to the text itself, which the scholars thus got to know at first hand. So it was also more fair to the author, whose voice was heard and whose argumentation was developed in the order of presentation that he himself would have wished. If for this reason the basic acquisition of a given text is thought to be the main aim of teaching, this method was to be preferred. But one of its drawbacks that was just as obvious, was that it could be long-drawn-out and tedious if the teacher was not able to keep the attention of the audience by strewing his commentary with inspiring ideas.

The *quaestio* method confronted the teacher far more freely with the text itself, which served here as the source of inspiration when he formulated problems that were exhibited for discussion, and which served in any case as an arsenal for some of the arguments *pro* and *contra* that were cited in the debate. With this it also became possible to refer to other authorities and get hold of new ideas in teaching. This took on a more personal character too, for it was the teacher himself who formulated those questions that he regarded as most important in the material. On the other hand, this increased the danger of arbitrary and subjective treatment of the text, since the author had no chance to defend himself against distortions of his ideas. It cannot be denied, however, that this method was well suited to stimulate an independent mind into thoughts of its own. It consistently operated with opposed points of view that dialectically confronted each other. In addition, it helped to form a general picture of different topics on which there were many different views in circulation. This is because individual opinions could be cleverly worked in as arguments, counter-arguments or solutions, all focussed on the main problem itself. Thus it became possible to add more teaching material to an already fixed syllabus – something teachers have no doubt been doing in all ages – so as to make higher demands on the students. A statute from Cambridge established quite clearly that scholars should not be at a loss to answer any question put to them by their teachers 'in accordance with the way that teachers use to question them, if the form of teaching in the faculty concerned requires *quaestiones*'.[42] This is certainly the reason why in the course of time the *quaestio* method won out over that of the *expositio*, but also why now and again it degenerated into something of a catechism. As a textbook example of what the *quaestio* method could achieve with very extensive and complicated material, we need look no further than the *Summa Theologica* of Thomas Aquinas, in which theology is presented in a wealth of detail, without the thread of the narrative ever being broken; and yet his book looks like an independent handbook that he never used for giving lectures.

Alongside lectures, the universities of the middle ages eagerly cultivated another form of teaching, the *disputatio* or disputation, at which two or more participants went through the material by discussing it with each other. This method too went back to an early stage, even if it was certainly less ancient than the lecture with commentary. In about 1200, an otherwise undistinguished master named Radulphus said that 'to dispute is to introduce an argument that proves or disproves something.[43] In a legitimate disputation of any kind – *disputatio legitima* – there must be a question, an answer, a stated claim, a confirmation, a denial together with arguments and solutions, all of which, God willing, we shall explain together in the proper place according to the teachings of Aristotle.' From this it can be concluded that, even at this time, the disputation had found a permanent form, with a number of elements which by and large were the same as those we know of from the *quaestio* lectures. Even if the *quaestio* lecturer discussed with himself, in a manner of speaking, or with fictitious opponents, whilst the disputation required at least two protagonists, there is still no doubt that the two methods had a common origin, and that it was the lecturers themselves who gradually learnt to make use of the disputation where it was found to be more appropriate than the simple commentary.

On the other hand, the origins of the disputation form cannot yet be said to be clear. We saw earlier how one of the results of the intense cultivation of trivium in schools was a strong technical

---

[42] On the Cambridge statute on the *quaestio*-method, see Mullinger, vol. I, p. 361, note 1.
[43] Radulphus in AD 1200, quoted from Grabmann, vol. II, p. 20.

advance in dialectic. So it is remarkable to find a twelfth-century treatise which says that 'he who teaches through his knowledge of the *artes* is called a dialectician or disputator'.[44] This shows that in part, at least, this method goes back to the teaching of logic in schools, and had in consequence already developed some of its important characteristics on the basis of *logica vetus*, that is, from the few works on logic of Aristotle and Boethius that the schools had at their command before the great wave of translations in the twelfth century. It was also in this tradition of dialectic that Abelard, as we have seen, wrote his theological masterpiece *Sic et Non*, which threw light on problems precisely by putting conflicting points of view up against each other. Another previously mentioned source for this method lay in the teaching of the jurists and moral theologians, whose predilection was to thrash out the *casus* or concrete cases by which questions could be clearly elaborated and dialectical argumentation developed.[45]

However, there is scarcely any doubt that in the quotation above Master Radulphus hits the nail on the head with his reference to 'the teachings of Aristotle', seeing that the various tributaries leading to the method would not have not come together in their final form, if *logica vetus*, thanks to the new translations, had not been augmented with the *logica nova*, 'new logic', directly derived from Aristotle's *Analytica Posteriora* and *Topica*. As we have seen, Buridanus referred to the first of these treatises, and they contained important parts of Aristotle's theory of science, including his doctrine on logico-deductive systems of propositions. The eighth book of *Topica* also gave an illustration of the art of arguing in areas where the syllogistic methods of *Analytica Posteriora* could not suffice. However that may be, it was this method of disputation, more than any other, that came to be identified with what has since been rather simplistically called 'the scholastic method'.

Throughout the university year ordinary disputations were arranged as a compulsory part of teaching in all faculties, and by a teacher who formulated the problems or *quaestiones* to be dealt with and announced them in advance. The exercise was conducted with a so-called *respondens* arguing positively for a particular solution to a problem, while an *opponens* gainsaid him with correspondingly nega-

[44] The quotation on dialecticians is from a manuscript in Vienna, VIN 2486, 45rb; here quoted after *Lexicon für Theologie und Kirche*, vol. VIII, Freiburg i. B., 1963, p. 926.
[45] See G. Makdisi, The Scholastic Method in Medieval Education: An Inquiry into its Origin in Law and Theology, *Speculum* 49 (1974), 640–61.

tive arguments. When this had gone on for a while, or the arguments were just about exhausted, the teacher would intervene and settle or 'determine' the question with a solution or *responsum* of his own, followed by a series of replies or *solutiones* to the objections. This active form of teaching was of great importance. It could be used for two different ends, Thomas Aquinas explained.[46] One aim was 'to remove doubts as to whether the facts of the matter are these' – that is, as they appeared from the formulated questions. Here the disputation was thus a means to create a new understanding, or, as it were, a research method. The other aim, on the other hand, was purely pedagogical, in that for a master a disputation 'does not serve to remove errors but to educate his listeners, so that they may be led to that understanding of the truth which he [i.e. the teacher] has in mind', and which he was therefore presumed to know. It mattered in both cases that the disputations were well-prepared and organised, that the disputants were instructed in advance, and that their disputations perhaps continued in a longer series on the same subject, which would give the teacher a chance to go into a problem deeply without being tied to any textbook. In many cases, the teacher edited such a series, publishing it in a book as *Quaestiones Disputatae*. Three such collections of Thomas Aquinas were *On Truth*, from 1256 to 1259. *On God's Omnipotence*, from 1265 to 1267, and *On Evil*, from 1269 to 1272. It also happened that a series of disputations could be published less authoritatively in the form of notes written down by one of the audience. Such a book would be called a *reportatio*.

The ordinary disputations needed a certain amount of administration, and there were cases when the way they were arranged left something to be wished for. For this reason, in 1344, the masters of the Sorbonne appointed a four-man board with one member from each nation to 'consider how the disputations may be more profitable for the fellows and more honourable for the house'.[47] The board decided to nominate each year a so-called master of students, whose job it would be to formulate the *quaestiones* for the whole year before the university started. These would follow the disposition of Peter the Lombard's *Sentences*, and they would not be identical to the questions of the year before. They were to be written onto a list, which was put up in the chapel, whereafter the respondent and

---

[46] Thomas Aquinas, *Disputationes quodlibetales* IV, q. 9, a 18; cf. Grabmann, vol. II, p. 35.
[47] *Chartularium* II, 554-6.

opponent were both to be advised in person a fortnight before their turn. In order to keep the master of students up to the mark, it was furthermore decided that he would stand in for any disputant who failed to appear. If he defaulted on this arrangement and a week was then missed out, he was to be charged a fine. This, in the custom of the Sorbonne, was a round of wine for the whole college.

While ordinary disputations formed part of the routine teaching, another series of debating exercises was carried out on certain occasions, called *quaestiones quodlibetales*. The correct term would be *quaestiones de quolibet*, or 'questions on whatever'. These were arranged, as we shall see later, especially in Advent and Lent as a branch of examinations. The organiser might announce beforehand that he wanted to dispute certain questions, but otherwise he was obliged to debate any problem that a student from the audience submitted in advance. Such a submission was in written form, in order to give time to prepare or to make some kind of agenda for the proceedings, which could often last from morning to night, since in principle there were no limits on the number of questions. These disputations were well-suited for the discussion of questions that lay outside the range of the normal teaching syllabus, but they often degenerated into an intellectual swordplay where the game was to finish off an unprepared respondent. Therefore it could happen that the proceedings were interrupted for a few days, so as to give him the opportunity to reflect, before he decided to 'determine'; this is why so many *quaestiones quodlibetales* were edited in the past tense.

These edited collections give an interesting insight into the nature of the debating exercises themselves, and they show the liveliness with which problems, often very cunningly phrased, were disputed, and how these could often put the respondent into a precarious position.[48] Thus in 1296 Godefroid de Fontaines (d. post 1303) was faced with the question 'Whether a doctor [i.e. master] of theology can decide a question that pertains to the pope's domain alone.' This would have given him cause to weigh every word of his reply. Henri de Gand (d. 1293) had to take a position on 'Whether a doctor or master who determines would commit a deadly sin by failing to explain a truth which is known to him.' Here there seems to be more than meets the eye. That such theological discussions at times became more entertaining than useful appears from the problem posed for Hervé

---

[48] All these examples are from P. Glorieux, *La littérature-quodlibetique de 1260 à 1320*, Kain, 1925.

Nedellec (d. 1323) by a rather solemn type, on 'Whether a master commits a deadly sin by entertaining curious questions, while overlooking those that are useful for salvation.' The respondent was nonetheless obliged to answer curious questions; and it might be wondered if John Peckham (d. 1292) wished in his heart of hearts in 1270 that he could have declined to answer 'Whether a monster born with two heads shall be baptised as one person or two.' The same was no doubt true of Gerard d'Abbeville, asked in 1269 for his opinion on 'Whether a bishop raised from the dead may return to his office.' That some did not refrain from troubling even the greatest theologians with idiot questions, can be seen with Thomas Aquinas, who had to decide in 1270 the answer to 'Whether it is better for a crusader to die on his outward journey than on the journey home.' At times the exercise would degenerate to asking and solving riddles pure and simple, as in 1277 when Ferrarius Catalaunus was asked 'Whether there is a liturgical prayer in which Amen! is said in the middle.'

It was questions of this kind, more than any other, which brought university teaching in the middle ages into disrepute in later days, when it was forgotten how small the number of foolish questions really was, and how the very best *quaestiones quodlibetales* were serious contributions to the scholarly debate. In a way it was to the credit of the faculties, too, that the disputations were not always deadly serious, but could deal with questions now and again that made the halls echo with laughter. And these were a suitable introduction to the evening festivity that, understandably enough, would often follow the mental gymnastics of a long and tiring day. The popularity of this kind of exercise can be seen from the way it was extended out of formal university teaching into more private arrangements. Disputations were not only arranged for official occasions, but were also held as *collationes*, in individual colleges or in the student collectives which trained their members, if possible, to shine in public functions in this way. Even in their private rooms the students would practise disputation in pairs, in order to learn the material or to rehearse for examinations.

The first examination drew near well into the student's fourth year of study, when he stood on the threshold of being promoted to *baccalaureus*.[49] This word actually means 'garlanded with laurels',

---

[49] On 'bachelor' as a title, see F. L. Ganshof, *Was is das Lehnswesen?*, Darmstadt, 1961, p. 101, where *baccalarii* are equated with *vassi non casato*, or vassals without an estate.

and to this extent has a clear and symbolic meaning; in reality it is just a corruption of late Latin *baccalarius*, which denoted a subordinate person, for example, a vassal of lower rank or a craftsman's apprentice who had not yet become master of his trade. For this reason it was used of older scholars in the university world, who could give masters a hand with the teaching, but had still not taken the master's degree themselves. Perhaps the medieval 'bachelors' can therefore be compared to the student instructors of our days. The bachelor institution seems to have been a very informal arrangement in the beginning that in the given circumstances grew up virtually by itself. Thus there is even a thirteenth-century report of St Richard of Chichester (d. 1253) becoming so clever in his law studies in Bologna, that 'whenever his teacher was held back by illness, he chose Richard above all his other scholars to continue the lectures instead of him'. In other words, Richard had a bachelor's status even before this term was introduced.[50] The term was not used in the Paris statutes of Robert de Courçon of 1215, even though the practice was already taken for granted, with the statutes recognising the right of theology students to hold lessons themselves after five years of study. On the other hand, there is a passage from the oldest statutes of Cambridge, in which 'a master or *bachilarius*' could not hold extraordinary lectures or disputations at times which were fixed for ordinary teaching.[51]

After a while the system became more formalised. Thus it was decreed in Bologna that a scholar might not operate as an assistant teacher without first having obtained permission from one of the rectors of the law faculty, and this permission was only valid for a particular time and syllabus.[52] In the middle of the thirteenth century the institution seems to have been accepted everywhere, also at the youthful faculty of *artes*, where normally a bachelor would be only eighteen or nineteen. Presumably this situation is the reason why a proper bachelor's examination was now introduced in order to stop incompetent scholars from being able to teach. The precise rules are known from a statute passed by the English nation in Paris in 1252,[53] together with a similar statute from 1275, which counted for the whole faculty.[54]

[50] On Richard of Chichester, see Rashdall, vol. I, p. 220, note 4.
[51] See Hackett, *Original Statutes*, ch. 2, 8, p. 201.
[52] On the authorisation of bachelors in Bologna, see Sorbelli, 176–8 and Rashdall, I, 220.
[53] *Chartularium* I, 227–32.   [54] Ibid. 530.

To submit for examination, the potential bachelor had to solicit his teacher for a *schedula* or certificate of having studied in the prescribed way. Thereupon the certificate was to be approved by examiners elected for the year in question, according to rules which will be described below in more detail. When this had been done, a provisional test was held in the period before Christmas. This was called the *responsio*, in that the candidate had to respond or reply to the questions that were put before him. If the outcome were satisfactory, he could go on to the examination proper, which was held in Lent in the form of a public *disputatio*, with the candidate as respondent or *determinator*. The proceedings were therefore defined as *examen determinantium* or just the *determinatio*. The substance of the examination seems nearly everywhere to have been grammar and logic, as the quadrivium subjects were normally left untreated until near the end of the course of study.

If this *determinatio* turned out well, the candidate had the right to call himself *baccalaureus* and to take part in teaching, at the same time as he continued his studies. Normally he would only be trusted with extraordinary or cursory lectures, just as he could only take the chair at disputations in the initial stages until a fully qualified *magister* took charge. Bachelors' teaching worked not only as a relief for permanent teachers, but also as pedagogic training of great importance for scholars who would later become independent teachers themselves. That it was a compulsory part of study was one of the most sympathetic features of teacher training in medieval universities. That bachelors were eager to take part in teaching, can be seen from the frequent injunctions prohibiting them from adjusting the times of their lessons in order to coincide with the compulsory teaching. On the other hand, it could often be a real job to get hold of an audience; for while lessons of this kind were compulsory for the bachelors who taught them, they were voluntary for the scholars who attended. For a bachelor there was therefore nothing for it but to make his teaching so exciting that he could attract his younger fellows in open competition with other bachelors.

Having studied and taught for two more years, the bachelor would eventually have the end of his studies in sight and would be able to prepare himself for the final examination that would gain him the master's degree. The process here took even longer than that of the bachelor's examination, as it appears from the statutes of *artes* in Paris which were cited earlier.[55] First examiners had to be elected. This was a matter of the proctor of the nation first selecting two competent persons who would swear, hand on Bible, with no hidden motives of their own to pick out three masters from their nation whom they knew to be 'strict and competent in examining reliably and inspired with the desire to promote the welfare of the university without allowing themselves to be influenced by petitions or bribes'. Following this, the examiners chosen in this way would themselves swear an oath to examine strictly and correctly, to let only qualified candidates pass, and not to let themselves be swayed by any animosity for a person or group within the nation.

After this, the examiners would take over the governance of the examination process. This was to start with a formal *praesentatio*, at which each individual teacher presented his bachelor student(s) to the examiners, who then made certain as to the candidate's age, length of study, not to mention his dress, and especially ensured that each student had his own particular teacher and had undergone the prescribed course of teaching according to the appropriate syllabus, and had also, in his two years as bachelor, followed disputations with a master and had taken part in them. The candidate was furthermore to certify that he had rented a place for teaching for the whole coming year, and had made a pledge to be respondent in *quaestiones* for the whole of the said year. Finally both he and his teacher were to pay a deposit as surety that they would in no manner try to gain the examiners' favour, but would resign themselves to their decision, so that 'if it happens that a bachelor fails ... he will not come out with sarcastic remarks or complaints or threats or any other nasty cracks aimed at the examiners, neither made by themselves nor by others, because they must assume that the examiners have acted in accordance with their own conscience and good faith, with regard to the honour of the university and the nation'. In 1328 this deposit in the French nation in Paris was the not wholly insignificant sum of 13 *solidi* and 4 *denarii*.[56]

In all, it was this provisional test of such details as we have just seen, that was termed the *examinatio* of the candidate. In reality it was only to ensure that he had undergone his course of study in the ordained manner with a reasonable professional gain. At this stage there was some chance of a dispensation. This could be granted if 'a

---

[55] Ibid. 227.   [56] *Chartularium* II, 307f.

bachelor is found by the examiners to be in possession of the necessary knowledge, but has not submitted himself to the length of study or to the books or lectures ordained'.[57] In this case 'the nation reserves the right to overlook this at its own discretion; but only in cases of this kind may the candidate's teacher make application to the nation about the matter'. It could also be difficult to tell if all conditions had been met, where the candidate had studied in places other than Paris. On this subject, the 1252 statute just says that a bachelor should have studied hard for two years in disputations led by masters of a recognised university. It cannot be clearly made out what this means; but a later statute of about 1280 clears up the uncertainty by requiring candidates to swear an oath to having studied for at least six years in Paris or at another faculty with a minimum of twelve teachers.[58]

When the examination was successfully over, the candidate had the right to present himself to the chancellor with a request for the *licentia*, that is to say, for permission to start work as an independent master. It has already been shown how the issue of the Paris chancellor's position in this matter gave rise to a long struggle that only ended when the faculty took complete control of the whole examination system. The chancellor could now only distribute the *licentia* to those recommended by the faculty as having passed the *examinatio*, no longer to protégés of his own; and he was not allowed to refuse the *licentia* to candidates approved by the faculty. It was also the same for the abbot of St Geneviève, who, as we have seen earlier, had the pope's permission to give the *licentia* to students of *artes*.

After obtaining the *licentia docendi* in this way, however, the candidate was only formally entitled to teach on his own. To exercise this right of occupation – which in any case was reserved for masters in a guild or corporation – he first had to be admitted to the corporation. This naturally required the swearing of a new oath. The oath of the masters of Paris is known from a form of about 1280, and it involved a pledge to respect the laws and privileges of the university, and not to betray its secrets; to be a loyal member of the corporation; to attend the burials of colleagues; to report those who stirred up disorder between the nations; to comply with the ordained times of teaching; together with respecting the scholars' freedom to

---

[57] *Chartularium* 1, 228.   [58] Ibid. 587.

choose whether they sought a *licentia* 'on the island' from the chancellor or 'on the hill' from the abbot.

While the bachelor's examination was held just before Christmas, masters to be would have to wait until just after New Year to obtain the *licentia docendi* and set the remaining formalities in motion, for the concluding ceremonies had to begin at the latest on the Monday after Ash Wednesday. This was the only examination term in the university year, and if the preliminaries had not been carried out, a candidate had to wait until the following year. If all went well, however, the new member of the teachers' guild could eventually show his new worth by using his *licentia docendi* as it was intended, by starting his first ever course of teaching. This official 'start' or *inceptio* did not then take the form of a public inaugural lecture. Instead the common form of disputation was used, which allowed the candidate to 'determine' one or more questions on his own. This process was the final stage of many years' study, and also the beginning of a new life as an academic with responsibility and obligations of one's own. It is no surprise therefore to learn that it was celebrated with complete thoroughness both publicly and in more private circumstances.

In the older statutes there were many rules for the public side of this affair. The disputation form was in any case already well known. But it was almost a matter of course that at this one occasion the disputation would take place with special trappings, and that after a while a ceremonial developed, glimpses of which can be discerned in documents throughout the late middle ages. Sometimes the day started with the candidate being fetched from his dwelling by the faculty beadle and accompanied by a procession of teachers to morning mass, whereupon the disputation started in the place which, as we have seen, he had rented for the whole year. If there were many questions, the process could last into the evening. According to a work by Antoninus, archbishop of Florence from 1446 to 1459, the ceremony at his university ended with the candidate giving a short speech in praise of the faculty, after which a faculty member stood up and recommended him to his colleagues.[59] The new master was then proffered a number of insignia as symbols of his new status; in this ceremony elements can be seen which originated both in the church and the world. He was given 'firstly a

---

[59] Thorndike, p. 309.

closed book, to show that he must keep his knowledge well preserved in his mind ... and not lay it open to those unworthy of it'. This was clearly a symbol of the traditional respect for the secrets of the guild, corresponding to similar symbolic acts in the masters' and apprentices' tests in the craftsmen's guilds. But in the case just mentioned, the symbolism was meaningless, to the extent that the bestowing of knowledge on others was the teachers' guild's only reason for existence. For this reason there was a hasty attempt to restore the balance by secondly presenting the new member with 'an open book, to show that he must be able to teach others and explain things to them. Thirdly he [i.e. the faculty member] will give him a ring, whereby he takes his learning to wife, fourthly a hat in sign of his glory and reward, and fifthly a kiss of peace.'

On top of this, such a day would have been excuse enough for draining a cup or two, and even the earliest statutes mention this private part of the proceedings which the authorities tried to keep on a seemly level. Where Paris was concerned, Robert de Courçon decreed in 1215 that 'at the *principium* [i.e. *inceptio*] of masters and the *responsiones* and *oppositiones* [i.e. bachelor's exams] of boys and youths, no drinking must take place.[60] They may invite a few friends and colleagues, but not very many.' In 1252 the faculty of *artes* gave way a little more to understandable pressure by stipulating that the new master 'may not offer drinks excepting the first and last days on which he determines – unless this takes place with the permission of the rector or proctor of his nation, who can give a dispensation to him according to their own pleasure, yet with consideration of the many different circumstances of which there is mention here'.[61] That these circumstances here were economic is explained by the quite common decrees on the utmost lengths to which a master could go to treat his teacher and friends. There is scarcely any doubt that an exemption was normally sought for and granted, and that the party continued into the small hours. Perhaps this is why the oldest Cambridge statutes were humane enough to give the whole faculty the chance of sleeping it off, by decreeing that 'the day after the *inceptio* all masters, except the inceptor himself, are to refrain wholly and completely from giving lectures, on condition that they have taken part in his feast the evening before, or could have done'.[62] It was perhaps these examination parties in Lent that gave

[60] *Chartularium* I, 79. [61] Ibid. 229. [62] Hackett, *Original Statutes*, ch. 2, 3, p. 199.

rise to the decree that the whole examination process should be concluded before the middle Sunday in Lent.

The concrete and legal outcome of an examination passed in this way was nothing more or less than that the masters' corporation had got a new member who would now be held to its laws for life and would have the right to enjoy its privileges. If the new member stayed in the university and continued to take an active part in teaching, he was called a *magister regens (scholam)*, hence a practising teacher;[63] were he to look for another career, on the other hand, he would become *non regens* and thereby a passive member of the corporation, but without losing his life affiliation to it. This means that in contrast to the title of bachelor, that of master amounted to a real academic degree, that is to say a *gradus* or a 'step' by which the bearer passed into a new social group as the member of a corporation. Once such a degree had been obtained it was for this reason usually inalienable, and there are hardly any examples of a corporation ever striking its members off except in cases of serious crimes. The problem, however, was what the degree could be used for if the master was a *non regens* and had left his original university.

The right to teach everywhere, the *ius ubique docendi*, was the most precious privilege of the medieval university and the basis for a system of education common to 'Christendom' in western Europe as a whole. In the beginning this right seems to have existed more as an unwritten law than a formal institution. As a legal concept it first appears in the statutes of individual universities which required it to be respected for their own masters at other seats of learning too, but which were not always able to overcome the opposition of teachers' corporations elsewhere. Thus the University of Paris complained as late as about 1300 that its masters

> do not find the recognition everywhere to which their education entitles them. For although the university has the privilege that a master or licensed teacher from Paris may 'begin' as a lecturer in Paris as well as elsewhere, there are still areas such as England or Montpellier where this is not respected, and there are also other universities where a master or licensed teacher from Paris is given no access to exercising the functions of master, however great his fame may be.[64]

It is also at this time that the University of Paris tried, as we saw earlier, to define a 'recognised faculty' as one with a minimum of

---

[63] See the definition of *magister regens* in *Chartularium* I, 531f. [64] *Chartularium* II, 182f.

twelve teachers. But it is obvious that it was not in a single university's power to enforce a universal *ius ubique docendi* in the teeth of other well-established teachers' corporations that were engaged in protecting their own members' teaching privileges by excluding others.

The final exercise of the *ius ubique docendi* was therefore limited by the extent to which the power of the local corporations could be bent to the will of a generally recognised higher authority. In practice this could not be anything else but the papacy, after the empire had failed to establish a supreme political structure in Europe. One example of how the papacy tackled the problem is in the privilege that Pope Alexander IV issued in 1255 to the University of Salamanca, which at this time had been in existence for nearly thirty years.[65] Alexander IV was now complaining that 'it sometimes comes to pass that those who have been examined and approved by the University of Salamanca, are not – though they have been found suitable for teaching at any faculty – allowed in any way to teach elsewhere, unless they submit themselves to a new examination at this [i.e. other] faculty'. Consequently the pope decreed that 'after masters and scholars at each of the faculties in Salamanca by means of a regular examination have been found qualified to teach, they are to be able to teach at any university, with the exception alone of Paris and Bologna, in the same faculty through which they have already been examined, without renewed examinations or protests from any area'. Hereby the masters of Salamanca nearly found the status they wished for – nearly, but not quite. The proviso excepting Paris and Bologna shows that the pope was still reluctant, even now, to encroach on the traditional rights of these two oldest and most distinguished universities to decide the composition of their teaching corps themselves.

[65] *Chartularium* I, 291.

CHAPTER 10

Curricula and intellectual trends

Having considered the structural developments of the university, the material welfare of its scholars, courses of study, and examination arrangements, we are now in a position to face the question of the substance of the teaching itself. It is obviously impossible to devote one chapter alone to any discussion of the very detailed history that learning had in the middle ages as a whole. On the other hand, it is necessary to clarify to some extent some of the principal currents in what intellectual development there was as a result of university activity. This is partly to see what the teaching really contained, partly because the debates and disputes on the curriculum often, with historical hindsight, seem to have been the ideological expression of the power struggle which was going on around the university as an institution and which helped to structure it. The most sensible option is to start with the changes in Paris, which provide the clearest illustration of problems that gave rise to equally intense discussion in other places. To understand the main intellectual movement of the day, furthermore, it would be appropriate to turn to the faculty of *artes*, home of both philosophy and a number of basic sciences, and therefore in many ways the trendsetter in hotly contested questions of the greatest moment.[1]

The faculty of the 'liberal arts' had in many ways a unique position in the university. Firstly, it imparted to all scholars a compulsory fundamental education with a concluding degree that was the necessary precondition of entry to all higher studies. The scope of this basic teaching ensured that this faculty, more than any other, suffered from a turmoil in the curriculum and ensuing heated discussions on

---

[1] For this chapter in general, see Gilson, and also his *L'esprit de la philosophie médiévale*, 2nd edn, Paris, 1948; M. Grabmann, *Mittelalterliches Geistesleben*, vols. I–III, Munich, 1926–56; F. Copleston, *A History of Philosophy*, vol. II, London, 1950. The fullest account of medieval science is given in E. Grant, *A Source Book in Medieval Science*, Cambridge, Mass., 1974.

syllabuses and examination requirements. In addition, by the very nature of the affair, this faculty was by far the largest of the university's four main schools. This gave rise to structuring problems, which, as we have already seen, led to the division into the nations, whose leaders eventually came to make up the hard core of the university's central administration. Furthermore, the faculty of *artes*, being the faculty for beginners, had the youngest intake, and became known as a result as the liveliest and most volatile corner of the university. Today it is rather hard to imagine, perhaps, how many of the in-depth debates that will be discussed later in this chapter, those between masters of *artes* on basic questions of a philosophical and scholarly nature, were by and large conducted for the benefit of – and in some cases also over the heads of – small classes of large boys aged between fourteen and twenty, sitting uncomfortably on their straw bundles in the schools of the Rue du Fouarre. That this was so undoubtedly helps to explain the intellectual liveliness within this faculty, where new ideas came naturally to young minds of the most receptive age.

Finally, it is worth remembering that the teachers of the faculty of *artes* were often scholars themselves at one of the higher schools. In Paris the highest place traditionally went to theology, and this ensured that those masters who taught *artes* were very frequently students or bachelors of theology too. Even if the faculties were formally completely independent of each other, this form of personal interdependence meant that the Paris faculty of *artes* in particular could rarely undertake anything that had not been seen by the theologians first. More frequently than elsewhere, therefore, basic teaching in Paris became the subject of theological critiques that could often lead to drastic results in the form of condemnations, prohibitions, and excommunications. And yet the authorities tried repeatedly to ensure the relative autonomy of the subjects involved. When Pope Gregory IX thus restored some order to the university in 1231 after the strike of the two preceding years with his previously discussed bull, the *Parens Scientiarum*, he urged the theologians in particular to 'explore their interests within the faculty to which they belong, and not to appear as philosophers, but to strive to know God ... and only to dispute in the schools on such questions as can be concluded on the basis of theological works and the treatises of the fathers of the church'.[2] In 1272 the masters of *artes*, after long-drawn-

---

[2] *Chartularium* I, 138.

out negotiations on their part between the nations and the Cardinal Legate Simon, agreed that 'no master or bachelor at our faculty shall be so bold as to determine or even dispute any purely theological question such as the Trinity or the Incarnation or similar things, since to do so would be to transgress the boundaries that have been marked out for them, for as the philosopher [i.e. Aristotle] says, it is extremely improper for a non-mathematician to dispute with a mathematician'.[3] This decree was subsequently inserted into the oath of masters of *artes* of about 1280.[4] In practice, however, such measures were undermined in a way that was solely to the advantage of the theologians, whose many extant *quaestiones disputatae* reveal quite clearly their willingness to dispute on questions also of a purely philosophical or scientific nature. No formal objection could be made to any of this, since a bachelor of theology first had to be a master of *artes* and was thus formally qualified to treat topics of the *artes* preserve; whereas no scholar of *artes* could hope to return the favour, as they would not yet have obtained the necessary competence in theology.

In the first analysis the development of what was taught in the faculty of *artes* was affected by the battle of Aristotelianism, in which the faculty became involved right from the start.[5] While there were only a few of Aristotle's writings on logic in Latin translations in the early middle ages, the translators of the twelfth century had made nearly all his works on philosophy and science available in Latin. This large and hitherto unknown material brought about an enormous widening of the thirteenth-century intellectual horizon, and of course began to exercise an irresistible pull on teachers of *artes*, whose previous opportunities of development had been confined to the trivium and quadrivium. In a historical perspective it was clearly just a question of time before Aristotelianism made its influence felt on the universities. However, it would have been quite a serious matter for masters of the past to tackle a philosopher, whose thoughts on the eternity of the world, for example, or on the innate necessity of things, clearly seemed to clash with the belief in the creation of the world in time and the absolute freedom of God.

This can be seen clearly from the episcopal intervention of 1210

---

[3] Ibid. 449.   [4] Ibid. 587.
[5] On Aristotelianism in general, see F. Van Steenberghen, *Aristote en Occident*, Louvain, 1946, and L. Minio-Paluello, Aristotle: Tradition and Influence, in *Dictionary of Scientific Biography*, vol. I, New York, 1970, pp. 267–81.

mentioned earlier against the adherents of the philosophers Amaury de Bene and David de Dinant.[6] This intervention was accompanied by a pronouncement that 'neither the scientific treatises of Aristotle nor the commentaries thereto may be publicly or privately taught in Paris, and this is forbidden on pain of excommunication'. This summary decree should be seen in the light of the statutes of Robert de Courçon in 1215, which command masters of *artes*

to give ordinary, but not cursory lectures on the old and new texts of Aristotle on dialectic.[7] They shall also lecture on both Priscians [i.e. *Institutiones Grammaticae*] or in any case on one of them. They shall not lecture on holidays, except on the philosophers, on either rhetoric, *quadrivium*, Barbarism' [i.e. part of Donatus' Grammar] or ethics, if they wish it themselves, or on the fourth book of *Topica*. They shall not lecture on Aristotle's books on metaphysics or natural philosophy, nor on summaries of them, nor shall they occupy themselves with the teachings of Master David de Dinant or with the heretic Amaury or Mauritius [the Moor?] of Spain.

This first real faculty syllabus shows how even in 1215 Aristotelianism was hardening its grip on teaching. To the works on logic mentioned earlier can now be added the *Analytica Posteriora* as compulsory reading for ordinary lectures. This was a significant step forward. While the *Analytica Priora* contained only the doctrine on syllogisms of formal logic, in the succeeding work it was possible to discern the main elements of Aristotle's theory of understanding and science – empiricism as the basis for all knowledge, the role of reason in the treatment of empirical matter and the eventual presentation of knowledge in logico-deductive systems of definitions, hypotheses (axioms), postulates, and theorems or propositions (derivative statements). Altogether these were new and revolutionary ideas that could have been thrown even further into relief if scholars had been allowed to study Aristotle's *Metaphysics* and *Physics*, works which were, however, constantly blacklisted. On the other hand, parts of Aristotle's practical philosophy, represented in his *Ethica Nicomachea*, were included, even if this was only in the optional lectures held on holidays, where audience numbers were not expected to be high. That the exact sciences in the quadrivium were likewise restricted to this reserved place, shows that the later famous reluctance of the Paris faculty to allow these subjects too much prominence stems from an early date.

[6] *Chartularium* I, 70.   [7] Ibid. 78.

The statutes of Robert de Courçon were only valid for Paris. Therefore the ban on Aristotle's main philosophical works was not yet a sign of any general ecclesiastical policy, but merely a local counter-measure against the university in its fight to free itself from the supremacy of the local church authorities. Nor did the ban, for this reason, have any effect elsewhere, particularly not in the new University of Toulouse (1229) which tried to pull students in by advertising that all Aristotle's works could be freely read.[8] This lasted until the pope tightened the reins here as well in 1245.[9] In any case it was only a question of a ban on the teaching of these works, not the possession or studying of them in private. Of course, the result of this was a roundabout discussion of Aristotle in Paris by which his principal thoughts filtered through the *Analytica Posteriora* into what was taught. So the patently narrow statute of 1215 effectively resulted in an enrichment of compulsory teaching with a welter of new points of view. These would inevitably reveal both the merits of Aristotelianism and the flaws within the traditional system of *artes liberales*.

In real terms, the time-honoured seven 'liberal arts' were an arbitrary conglomerate of widely differing disciplines.[10] The greatest unity there lay within the quadrivium, where the 'pure' subjects of mathematics, that is, arithmetic and geometry, just as the 'applied' subjects music and astronomy, were a survival of the old teaching programme of the Pythagoreans, that was theoretically grounded in the belief that mathematics was both a necessary and a sufficient basis for description of nature. The combination of grammar, dialectic, and rhetoric within the trivium, on the other hand, had its origin in the ancient schools of rhetoric, which had trained lawyers and politicians (in the widest sense of the word) on this basis. From here these subjects had slipped into the school of the early middle ages, which in Italy and Gaul, at least, could be traced back to ancient institutions. As we saw earlier, the grammar schools of Europe even as late as the twelfth century were able to use the seven *artes* as the formal framework for a fruitful education, even if the

---

[8] Ibid. 129–31.
[9] Ibid. 185f, cf. Rashdall, vol. II, p. 164 and C. E. Smith, *The University of Toulouse in the Middle Ages*, Milwaukee, 1958. On similar developments in Oxford, see D. A. Callus, Introduction of Aristotelian Learning to Oxford, *Proceedings of the British Academy* 29 (1944), 229ff.
[10] See P. Delhaye, La place des arts libéraux dans les programmes scolaires du XIIIe siècle, in *Arts libéraux*, pp. 161–73.

faults of the system became more apparent the more the bulk of knowledge and philosophical insight into the problems of the subjects grew.

The obvious faults of the system had already appeared in antiquity, namely the difficulty of adapting new subjects into the old framework. This problem authors such as Geminos (first century BC) and Anatole of Laodicaea (third century AD) had tried to solve, by widening the quadrivium with disciplines such as logistics (numerical methods of arithmetic), geodesy, mechanics, and optics. It was through Euclid, Archimedes, Hero, Ptolemy, and others that these subjects found their present scientific identity. Others tried with less success to place architecture and medicine in the system; the reason this misfired was the practical aims of these subjects, which conflicted with the mainly theoretical character of *artes*. Nor did other new subjects founded by Aristotelians, such as zoology, botany, geology, or mineralogy, succeed in finding a place there, just as little as ancient alchemy did, an art that was certainly too occult to be made into a subject for public education. What was even worse was that the works of Aristotle on ethics, politics, and economy were excluded in spite of their obvious social relevance.

Another rather more telling deficiency of the system was that it lacked any superior metascience that could put the individual subject disciplines into a larger logical and philosophical context, based on some kind of clear theory of knowledge as such. As the only philosophical discipline within the *artes liberales*, dialectic had essentially focussed itself on questions of pure logic, and had neither developed any theory of knowledge nor any general theory of sciences. Such more general questions were usually discussed in the context of theology, therefore, on the basis of the Augustinian view on the object of knowledge as the ideas which were hidden in God but could be revealed in the eternal light with which God illumined the universe. Such a conception made it impossible, among other things, to reach any clear distinction between philosophy and theology. The work of Roscellinus and Abelard, which we saw previously, on the ontological status of general ideas had also revealed how hard it could be in the early period to conduct a philosophical debate without theological overtones that would constantly cause spokesmen of the church to interfere. The first ecclesiastical warnings against Aristotelianism were just such an attempt to combat errors through purely disciplinary measures, and with no philosophical investigation beforehand of the system on which these errors were built.

These and other weaknesses explain how Aristotelianism sooner or later had to win the field. This would come at the moment when its adherents had undertaken this very investigation, when they had borne out the ability of the new philosophy to mend these faults, and deal with important problems that had previously been allowed to lie untouched. This required a comprehensive intellectual effort that was difficult to carry out in the framework of the *artes* faculty, just because this faculty was strongly bound to the tradition of the twelfth-century schools of which it was the heir. In this situation, help came from outside. Ironically it came from the theologians. Their interest in philosophy and formal competence made them natural candidates for working closely with the problems of the *artes* faculty, despite all attempts to stop the demarcating line between them being crossed.

Yet the breakthrough was difficult. On the part of the church, the ban on Aristotle's texts on metaphysics and natural science was still upheld, even in the bull *Parens Scientiarum* of 1231, the decrees of which Pope Innocent IV (1243–1254) also extended in 1245 to cover Toulouse, the place where Aristotle could still be read without reservation.[11] On the part of the university, the situation was complicated by the struggle with the mendicant orders over chairs in the faculty of theology, which was discussed in an earlier chapter, and which was only settled with the bull of Pope Alexander IV *Quasi Lignum Vitae* on 14 April 1255.[12] This bull made it possible to admit the mendicants as teachers in a more harmonious way. But even within this period the faculty of *artes* had taken the decisive step of bringing the formal regulations into line with the facts as they were, regardless of the ill-will of the church. Thus in 1252 the English nation in Paris approved a new arrangement for examinations whereby Aristotle's text *De Anima*, on natural science and psychology, was put on the programme as compulsory reading.[13] On the other hand, Aristotle's *Ethica* is not mentioned here, even though this text had figured on the list in 1215; presumably this means that it was made optional. Nor does the list mention any other philosophical works of Aristotle, though we know that the Franciscan Roger Bacon (1214–1294) had lectured on them earlier in defiance of prevailing decrees.[14]

---

[11] *Chartularium* I, 136–9.   [12] Ibid. 279–85.   [13] Ibid. 227–32.   [14] Ibid. 277ff.

This action on the part of an individual nation should perhaps be taken as a test run, with the aim of drawing a response from the ecclesiastical authorities. When no protest was forthcoming – perhaps because the dispute over the mendicants and Guillaume de St Amour had taken up everyone's attention – the assembled faculty of 19 March 1255 completed the move, approving a new syllabus which is worth quoting in its entirety.[15] For the sake of the general picture little has been changed in the sequence of cited works comprising the reading list for the *licentia docendi* of a potential master of *artes*.

Logic
(a) *Logica vetus*
    Porphyrius' *Isagoge*
    Boethius' *Topica, Divisiones*
    Aristotle's *Praedicamenta*
        De Interpretatione
        De Sophisticis Elenchis
        Topica
        Analytica Priora
(b) *Logica nova*
    Aristotle's *Analytica Posteriora*
    Gilbert de la Porrée's *Liber Sex Principiorum*

Grammar
Priscian's *Institutiones Grammaticae*
Donatus' *Barbarismus*

Philosophy
Aristotle's *Physica*
    Metaphysica

Natural philosophy and science
Aristotle's *De Animalibus*
    De Caelo et Mundo
    De Generatione et Corruptione
    Meteorologica (Books I and IV)
Theophrastus' *De Plantis*

---

[15] See A. G. Little (ed.), *Roger Bacon Essays*, Oxford, 1914, pp. 4ff.

Psychology
Aristotle's *De Anima*
  De Sensu et Sensato
  De Sompno et Vigilio
  De Memoria et Reminiscentia
  De Differentia Spiritus et Animae
  De Morte et Vita

Practical philosophy
Aristotle's *Ethica Nicomachea*

There are various problems in this syllabus, with which we will deal later. The most significant thing about it was that it gave the study of *artes* a content that would hardly be altered for the rest of the middle ages. The first revision of this syllabus was made on 5 June 1366, when on the request of Pope Urban V (1362–1367) and after consultation with the chancellor and a selection of teachers, two cardinals issued new statutes for the whole University of Paris.[16] These only affected the faculty of *artes*, to the extent that Boethius' *De Consolatione Philosophiae* was now put onto the curriculum, while Priscian's Grammar was replaced with the newer works, the *Doctrinale* of Alexander de Villa Dei (of 1199) and the *Graecismus* of Eberhard de Bethune (of 1212). According to a further statement, candidates for the *licentia* had 'heard other mathematical works', but nothing more is said about this. By and large, the same reading list was strengthened by the university reform of Cardinal Guillaume d'Estoutevilles in 1452, with an accompanying invitation to the examiners to place special emphasis on ethics and metaphysics.[17]

With the revolutionising syllabus of 1255, the faculty anticipated the march of events, as the necessary entrenchment of Aristotelianism was still in its infancy. Thus the syllabus intensified the problem of the authority that could be bestowed on a pagan philosopher whose works had now come to dominate studies completely, and whose philosophical tools were slowly becoming more familiar to those who would use them. On the other hand the errors he showed here and there still made people uneasy. For this reason the Aristotelian philosophers faced a hard period of toil, and in their efforts to create an acceptable evaluation of Aristotle they

---

[16] *Chartularium* III, 142–8; cf. Thorndike, pp. 244–7 and Thurot, pp. 51f.
[17] *Chartularium* IV, 713, 734.

came under double fire: partly because certain of their colleagues all too uncritically accepted 'the Philosopher's' opinions *in toto*; partly through rearguard actions from ecclesiastical authorities, whose love for the syllabus of 1255 had never been more than platonic.

The first front was distinguished by the so-called 'Averroists' – a jibe no doubt introduced by Thomas Aquinas – who based their understanding of Aristotle on a threefold set of commentaries written by the Spanish Arab philosopher Averroës (1126–1198), who was often indicated merely as 'the Commentator'.[18] For him Aristotle's teaching was 'the highest truth, since his spirit was the highest point of the human spirit; therefore it is also justly said that he was created and delivered to us by the providence of God, so that we may come to know everything that can possibly be known'. Yet this admiration for Aristotle did not prevent Averroës from striking non-Aristotelian attitudes in his reading of him; thus he was an adherent of a view derived from the Neo-Platonists that the active intellect is numerically one and the same in all people, even if this was irreconcilable with his Islamic faith. Averroës did not try to hide this dilemma when he said that 'With my reason I necessarily conclude that the intellect is one and the same. But in my faith I hold firmly to the opposite view.' Similar difficulties arose in the purely Aristotelian doctrine of the eternity of the universe, time, and matter. This form of intellectual schizophrenia implanted itself in the Paris Averroists, whose leader was Siger de Brabant (d. 1282)[19] and the important Danish linguistic philosopher Boethius de Dacia.[20] It was later known as the doctrine of the double truth, in that it assumes that a proposition can be true in theology and false in philosophy, or vice versa.

The reaction to this unrestrained admiration of Aristotle began as early as 1256, when Albertus Magnus (1193–1280), the German Dominican-Provincial, returned to Paris, where he had got his doctorate in theology in 1245 and had taught until 1248 with Thomas Aquinas (1225–1274) as one of his pupils. With a small text *On the Unity of the Intellect Contrary to Averroës* (*De Unitate Intellectus Contra Averroem*) Albertus weighed in against the central point of Averroism. After his return to Germany, he began from 1258 onwards the long

---

[18] Quoted after Gilson, pp. 360f.
[19] See F. Van Steenberghen, *Siger de Brabant*, vols. I–II, Louvain, 1931–42.
[20] On Boethius de Dacia, see the preface to his writings in *Corpus Philosophorum Danorum*, vols. IV–VI, Copenhagen, 1969–76.

series of Aristotelian paraphrases that were to present a purer Aristotle to his contemporaries. Albertus sketched out his programme in the preface to his version of *The Physics*:

> Our intention in natural science (*scientia naturalis*), so far as is possible for us, is to set the minds of the brethren of our order at rest, those who, for many years now, have encouraged us to draw up for them such a work on physics as could supply them with a complete natural science, and one that could help them to understand the writings of Aristotle correctly... Our intention is to make all the named parts [i.e. of philosophy] – physics, metaphysics and mathematics – intelligible to those who know Latin'.[21]

Later on in *The Physics* Albertus reveals himself to be a by no means uncritical admirer of Aristotle, when he says that 'if Aristotle had been a god, it must be believed that he never made a mistake. But if he is a man, he has quite certainly made mistakes like the rest of us.'[22]

This independent spirit shows that Albertus continued to recognise Augustine as the highest theological authority, to be followed ahead of philosophers in all questions of faith and morality, so far as there was any disagreement between them. But where science and philosophy were concerned, Aristotle was the best guide to be had at that time. The result was a clear distinction between theology and philosophy. This was Albertus' main contribution and pulled the thirteenth century beyond the impasse that the previous Neo-Platonist and Augustinian tendencies had not been able to find their way out of. Theology speaks of God as an object of faith, whereas philosophy can only speak metaphysically of the highest form of existence. Yet though theology could not be derived from philosophy, it could still profit from the arguments of philosophy and natural science that had independent validity in their own domain. Albertus had real scientific interests, and his writings are full of passages revealing his ability to make sharp observations of nature. Not without justice has it been said of him that he was the first thinker to use Christian premises on which to build the possibility of independent science as a legitimate human occupation.

All things considered, it must be said that Albertus' contribution came too late to halt the general course of Aristotelianism in Paris, nor was it sufficiently thorough to cope with the Paris Averroists, among whom Siger de Brabant was teaching in the faculty of *artes*

---

[21] Albertus Magnus, *Physica*, Lib. I, tract. 1, cap. 1.
[22] Ibid. VIII, 1, 14; cf. Gilson, pp. 503–16.

from 1266 onwards. The more systematic bout with Averroism Albertus therefore left to his former pupil Thomas Aquinas. In the critical years, from 1268 to 1272, Thomas returned to Paris, where earlier, between 1252 and 1259, he had written commentaries on *The Sentences* and Boethius' *De Trinitate*, and had completed the important dissertations *De Principiis Naturae* and *De Ente et Essentia*. In between he had written his theological textbook *Summar Contra Gentiles* and some commentaries on Aristotle. Now during his last stay he launched himself into the attack against unquestioning Aristotelianism over a very broad front. Thus in 1269 he persuaded William of Moerbeke, a brother of his order, to start a new translation of all Aristotle's works directly from Greek. This was in order to remove the mistakes that might have crept into the earlier translations from the Arabic. Thomas continued himself to write his series of very thorough and carefully considered commentaries, at the same time as he started work on a great *Summa theologica*, which he just failed to complete before his death in 1274. In between there was time for more anti-Averroist dissertations, the *De Aeternitate Mundi Contra Murmurantes*, the *De Unitate Intellectus Contra Averroistas*, not to mention numerous *Quaestiones disputatae* and *Quodlibetales*. In all these writings there was a clear theological aim; Thomas wished above all to set forth and explore the content of the Christian Revelation, but with particular respect for the right to independent human thought. The belief in the Holy Ghost being the spirit of truth meant for Thomas that 'Everything that is true, comes from the Holy Ghost.' With this he did not mean that the truths of science were due to some form of divine inspiration, or that we can see them in the eternal light, as Augustine said. On the contrary, he meant that a truth must be respected in all conditions, even if uttered from the lips of a pagan philosopher. With this basic principle, Thomas exploded what had formerly been an intellectual ghetto of Christian thought within the confines of Christianity, admitting that all people and ages are potential contributors to the growth of knowledge.

In the question of knowledge Thomas was as much as empiricist as Aristotle: 'Nothing exists in reason which has not come through the senses.'[23] This principle of experience was followed by a theory of science based on Aristotle's doctrine of the gradually progressive

---

[23] In this often-quoted form this famous passage is probably not found in Aquinas, but statements of this type are frequent in his writings, for example, in *Summa Theologiae* I^a, q. 84, a 8, and in the *Quaestio de Veritate* q. 12, a 3, ad 2^m. On Thomas' thought, see E. Gilson,

process of abstraction, one that allowed for a logical classification of rational, theoretical knowledge in physics (natural understanding), mathematics, and metaphysics. In his commentary on Boethius Thomas refined the system himself, with a special class of *scientiae mediae* that described the material universe in the language of mathematics, whereby disciplines (such as optics and mechanics) within mathematical physics might be fitted into the classification in a logical way.

With metaphysics, too, Thomas assumed a basic Aristotelian position: general concepts do not represent ideas in a separate immaterial world inaccessible to the senses, but are abstracted directly from the things we meet in the world of the senses. It is in existing things that forms or essences can be found. For this reason, existence is the fundamental concept in metaphysics and not a simple property of essence, as the whole Platonist tendency had claimed. This volte-face in metaphysics turned everything on its head in the eyes of the traditional thinkers; and Thomas alarmed them even more by rejecting, as a consequence of the first principles of the concept of existence, the proof of God's existence which Anselm of Canterbury had made by insisting on the existence of God as a logical consequence of the very concept of God. For Thomas, at least, there is no way that thought can ever prove the existence of something on the basis of ideas alone.

While Thomas Aquinas thus used Aristotle to clear a path for philosophy which based the independent role of human reason in the development of rational science on the foundation of experience, it was left to him to demonstrate the harmony which in his eyes existed between such a philosophy and theology. This happened with the distinction between a natural and supernatural order. In the natural domain, reason was supreme and unassailable. But 'up there' there was the Three-Personed God Himself whose being lay so concealed from reason that reason could do nothing but discuss Him in purely negative terms; it could say what God is not – not what He is, a state which is only known through the revelation in Christ. Therefore apparently positive statements in philosophical theology were only valid if they were regarded as analogies. The two orders were thus clearly distinguished, but on the other hand not

Le Thomisme, 5th edn, Paris, 1944. On *scientiae mediae*, see J. Gagne, Du quadrivium aux scientiae mediae, *Arts libéraux*, pp. 975–86.

unrelated. Revelation shows God as the creator of the world and its constant upholder; furthermore, Thomas supposed that everywhere in creation there was an innate inclination towards the Creator. Therefore man's salvation lay neither in naturalism, which was wholly given over to the visible world, nor in a purely spiritualistic flight from it, but in a harmonious balance that could only be achieved through God's Grace, 'which qualifies and perfects nature, but does not destroy it'.

Without waiting for the finishing touches to this Thomistic synthesis, however, the ecclesiastical authorities embarked on a new campaign of condemnation which in the first instance was aimed at Averroism, but which brought up such big guns that even moderate Aristotelianism, and in the end some of Thomas' own views, came under fire. This started on 19 January 1263 with a bull from Pope Urban IV (1261–1264), in which he added an injunction to the ban on the Aristotelian texts in the *Parens Scientiarum* of 1231, not so much in the hope of turning the clock right back, as in papal fashion to rally round the decrees of his predecessor.[24] The next move came in 1270, when Bishop Etienne Tempier published in Paris a list of thirteen Averroist theses which he condemned as heretical.[25] The first one comprised the central claim that 'the intellect of all mankind is numerically one and the same'. Of the others, no. 4 presented the basic principle of astrology that 'all that happens down in the sublunary world is governed of necessity by the heavenly bodies'; while no. 12 said in accordance with this that 'human actions are not guided by the providence of God'. It was in the light of this condemnation that we must see the previously cited decision of the masters of *artes* in 1272 to stay out of theological subjects. A new measure was introduced on 18 January 1277, when Pope John XXI (1276–1277) complained to the archbishop about the persistence of the Averroists, demanding an investigation into their affairs.[26] The result was that Tempier issued a new list of no less than 219 statements on 7 March, ascribed to Siger de Brabant, Boethius de Dacia, and others.[27] These were branded as heretical, fallacious, or presumptuous, and under threat of excommunication it was forbidden to teach them in the university. Only eleven days later this measure was extended to England, where the Dominican Robert Kilwardby, in his double capacity as archbishop of Canterbury and

[24] *Chartularium* I, 427f.   [25] Ibid. 486f.   [26] Ibid. 541.   [27] Ibid. 543–55.

chancellor of Oxford, published a similar list of thirty theses, though instead of excommunication he threatened only exclusion from the university.[28]

Tempier's list was an odd document, not least for being knocked together in great haste with no order or design, by a commission whose competence in philosophy was not very striking.[29] It was certainly aimed straight at Averroist views on the unity of the intellect and the material eternity of the universe, matter, and time. In amongst this, however, were some strange theses which fitted in nowhere at all. It is natural to suppose that some of them at least had been gathered in university disputations, perhaps just among the many and often far-fetched *objectiones* against the main thesis but which were not always to be taken seriously. This goes for no. 49, for example, 'that God would not be able to move the heavens in a straight line. The reason is that in this case a vacuum would appear'; or no. 92, which says that 'the heavenly bodies are moved by an inner principle, which is a soul'. The last statement was an ancient Aristotelian conception of the heavenly bodies as animated and thereby alive, an idea the astronomers of the middle ages were already in the process of abandoning.

Yet overall the tendency was clear. It was not so much a matter of a new entry into a scholarly debate, as of a bishop using his teaching authority in a somewhat clumsy way to warn against a philosophy that was coming into conflict with central doctrines on the omnipotence of God and on His freedom, by claiming that things are as they are of necessity. This document in any case achieved greater importance than was normally due to other episcopal interventions into the internal affairs of the universities. The history of both philosophy and science in the next hundred years shows how time after time the 1277 condemnation was brought out as a lever for new ideas and as a weapon against deeply ingrained notions or accepted interpretations which were possibly true, but which were not due to any inner necessity of things – for God could have made the world in a different way. The lively critiques of Aristotle of the later middle

---

[28] Ibid. 558f. Cf. P. Osmund Lewry, in Catto, pp. 419ff.
[29] On such ecclesiastical interventions, see J. Koch, Philosophische and theologische Irrtumslisten von 1270–1329, in *Mélanges Mandonnet*, vol. II, Paris, 1930, pp. 305–29. On the effect of Thomas Aquinas, see E. H. Weber, *La controverse de 1270 à l'Univesité de Paris*, Paris, 1970.

ages were thus directly indebted to the undeniably bombastic salvoes of Etienne Tempier against the Averroists.[30]

After 1277 the nature of the situation changed. Scarcely had Aristotelianism triumphed in the battle of what to teach in the universities, when medieval thought began to fragment into many mutually exclusive schools and tendencies, some of which were very far removed from the synthesis that Thomas Aquinas had tried to build. Closest to the Thomists were the Scotists, whose name was taken from the Scottish Franciscan John Duns Scotus (c. 1265–1308), a teacher in Oxford from 1300 to 1302, and then a teacher in Paris until he died.[31] Just like Thomas Aquinas, Duns Scotus was a philosophical realist, but he was also especially influenced by the condemnation of 1277, in his perpetual stress that philosophers were only capable of drawing conclusions on what was necessary, while theologians might occupy themselves with the freedom of God and man. He was therefore more sceptical than Thomas over the chances of a complete harmony between reason and revelation, and generally regarded will as more basic than understanding. This had important consequences for moral philosophy, and also for science, since the 'laws' of nature appeared as 'contingent' upon the will of God, without any immanent necessity of their own.

A quite different radical tendency was nominalism, revived by an English Franciscan William of Ockham (c. 1290–c. 1350).[32] He taught in Oxford for a short while from 1318 to 1320, and was then summoned to Avignon to defend himself in a trial for heresy, where a number of his views were eventually branded as heretical. Later he took refuge with Emperor Ludwig of Bavaria, with whom he devoted his remaining years to drawing up a series of treatises on ecclesiastical politics in which he attacked the secular power of the papacy. Even earlier, he had made a deliberate attempt to reform the methods and substances of scholasticism on the basis of a clearly theological position marked by the desire to claim the supremacy of

---

[30] See O. Pedersen, The Development of Natural Philosophy 1250–1350, *Classica et Mediaevalia* 14 (1953), 86–155.
[31] See E. Gilson, *Jeans Duns Scotus*, Paris, 1952.
[32] See R. Guelluy, *Philosophie et théologie chez Guillaume d'Ockham*, Louvain–Paris, 1947; G. Leff, *William of Ockham*, Manchester, 1975; S. Moser, *Grundbegriffe der Naturphilosophie bei Wilhelm von Ockham*, Innsbruck, 1932, and the excellent article on Ockham by Paul Vignaux, *Dictionnaire de Théologie Catholique*, vol. XI, Paris, 1933, pp. 748–84. See also J. A. Weisheipl, in Catto, pp. 607ff.

God and the possibility of faith over what philosophers called necessity in the created universe, clearly in the spirit of 1277.

In logic Ockham's most formidable tool was his 'razor', or principle of economy of thought, which states that one should not increase the number of ideas or assumptions without pressing need.[33] Hereby he was in a position to attack the Thomists and Scotists for their introduction of all too complicated hypotheses, as well as of unnecessary distinctions and insubstantial ideas. In his theory of knowledge he acknowledged only one means of proof: an assertion is only true if it is supported by what Ockham called 'immediate experience', or if it followed logically from another such assertion. This immediate experience was a so-called 'intuitive' acceptance of things being what they are. Ockham called this a *cognitio experimentalis* in opposition to the Aristotelians' theory of knowledge as a process of abstraction which, in his eyes, led to the attribution of existence to abstract ideas without their reality being guaranteed through immediate experience. On this basis he rejected philosophical realism, which with the Aristotelians and others bound general concepts to one or other form of extra-mental reality. A general concept was only a sound or a name (*nomen*, hence 'nominalism'), and only so-called 'positive things' had existence outside the mind. Every single thing therefore became something apart, without relation to others: 'Each positive thing outside consciousness is *eo ipso* individual.'[34]

The immediate metaphysical consequence of this was that all relations between things are nothing but empty fabrications of thought. Thereby also the common form of the law of causation fell by the roadside. According to Ockham it is quite possible to talk of a thing A being cause of another thing B (which is thus an effect of A), but only if there is immediate experience that B follows upon A in a situation where all other causes are ruled out. One of the consequences of this is that an effect can easily be taken to derive from different causes, and that any question of there being a necessary context between A and B becomes superfluous.

The appropriate victims of this in natural philosophy were a number of fundamental physical concepts. Even the concept of

---

[33] The economy principle was not invented by Ockham, but has a long history stretching back to natural philosophers of antiquity; see P. Duhem, *Essai sur la notion de théorie physique de Platon à Galilée*, Paris, 1908.

[34] *Quodlibetales* VI, quoted from Vignaux, *Dictionnaire*, pp. 32, 739, n. 69.

motion was too abstract for Ockham to have any independent content apart from the moved body and its starting and finishing positions, which could be immediately experienced. It was also meaningless where Ockham was concerned to regard forces as the cause of movements, the concept of force being far too intangible. Ockham believed that if all such empty ideas and superfluous concepts could be abolished, then it would be possible to deny the concept of necessity, the main philosophical stumbling block towards faith in a free and omnipotent God. In reality Ockham thus wanted to clear a path for theology and revelation, by means of a brutal purgation of metaphysics.

In the course of the fourteenth century nominalism spread through the universities. But while Ockham found general support for his type of logic, his rejection of the concepts of motion and force were too radical to be accepted by natural philosophers. The Paris faculty of *artes* tried to halt the movement in 1340 by sanctioning a not too well-informed protest against Ockham's ideas.[35] Thus in the face of Ockham's critique of general concepts, the masters of Paris claimed that the meaning of words and statements were dependent on the way in which the author and others used them. This is true enough, but it says nothing about the reality of concepts. They went on to defend the distinctions in philosophy as necessary if misunderstandings are to be avoided. That we know things through terms and propositions was finally said to follow from the fact that such terms are applied in place of the material objects to which they refer – but such objects cannot be carried into the halls of the disputations. However, nominalism was not to be stopped in this way, but continued its progress in dialectic as a *via moderna* ('the new direction'), in contrast to traditional realism, which was now known as *via antiqua* ('the old direction').

The dispute between these two tendencies consumed much of the energy of the philosophers of the late middle ages. Normally the university authorities took the side of one party against the other, and it was not everywhere that such a Judgement of Solomon was reached as it was in the solution at Heidelberg. Here in 1452 the rector forced all members of the university to refrain from derogatory remarks about either of the two views represented in the teaching staff. This was followed in 1455 by a statute for the faculty

---

[35] *Chartularium* II, 505ff.

of *artes*, from which it appears that there were now two autonomous courses of study of equal status, in such a way that it was possible, in a manner of speaking, to be master of *artes* both old and new style. These two courses can have had little in common, for a student who wished to change from one to the other would have had to give up the whole of his first syllabus without qualification. This was modified only slightly by a new statute of 1481, whereby lectures on ethics could double for the two courses if an adequate teacher of the subject could not be found for one of them.[36]

In Paris in 1474 King Louis XI made one last attempt to put an end to nominalism, with a decree urging the faculties of *artes* and theology to follow the realists Aristotle, Averroës, Albertus Magnus, St Thomas Aquinas, Aegidius, Alexander of Hales, Duns Scotus, Bonaventura, and others, all mentioned in the same breath without the slightest regard to their mutual differences.[37] Their teachings were said to be more 'useful' than the doctrines presented by more recent doctors such as Ockham, Gregory of Rimini, Buridanus, Pierre d'Ailly, Marsilius of Inghen, Adam Dorp, Albert of Saxony, and other nominalists. But this attempt failed; in 1476 no less than seven books of Ockham's were ready for printing in Paris, and in 1481 the king reversed the decree, after which the masters of Paris produced a long theoretical defence of nominalism, clearly showing that at this time the movement had become irresistible.

After this short and incomplete sketch of some of the main trends of dialectics in the intellectual debate of the later middle ages, we must now look back at the problems that the faculty of *artes* faced relating to the curriculum of 1255. This thoroughly Aristotelian list of books shows better than anything else that the old system of *artes liberales* as a basis and framework for faculty teaching had been changed nearly out of recognition in favour of a new scheme which led, in the course of time, to a new systematisation of the curriculum in the 'three philosophies' – natural, moral, and metaphysical. Above all, it now looks as if the exact sciences within the old quadrivium had been completely dropped. Already in 1215 they had been made cursory, and in 1255 they were not mentioned at all. A list of books or 'exemplars' for copying from 1286 confirms this impression, with not a single mention of a work on arithmetic, geometry, music, or

[36] Thorndike, pp. 346ff. Cf. G. Ritter, *Via antiqua und via moderna auf den deutschen Universitäten des XV. Jahrhunderts*, Heidelberg, 1922.
[37] Thorndike, pp. 355–60.

astronomy in the real sense of the word.[38] Even Aristotle's *De Caelo* is missing from this list, though it had been entered onto the curriculum.

It would be natural to conclude that the scholars of *artes* in Paris neglected the whole of the exact part of *artes liberales*, if it were not for our knowledge that a change around 1230 enabled the exact sciences to be consolidated as a crucial element of university teaching. This was essentially due to the work of one individual man, the Englishman John de Sacrobosco or John of Holywood, of whom we hardly know more than that he wrote three concise textbooks which, in the next two or three hundred years, would be used in practically every university in Europe.[39] One of them was an *Algorismus*, containing an exposition of arithmetic based on the application of an Indian system of numbering which, via the Arabs, had now arrived in Europe and was gradually displacing the Roman system. Another book was the famous *Tractatus de Sphaera*, which gave a brief and clear introduction to astronomy, with the main emphasis on the phenomena resulting from the apparent daily rotation of the heavens: the rising and setting of the stars, the division of the earth into geographical zones, and much besides; the theoretical section on planetary movement, on the other hand, was quite short and failed to cover more than the basic principles of the circular motion of the sun and moon, and the explanation of solar and lunar eclipses. Both treatises were together the basis for Sacrobosco's third textbook *Compotus*, which gave a careful account of problems relating to time-reckoning and the calendar.

After Sacrobosco's time Paris became a centre for astronomy capable of attracting researchers from many lands. In about 1260 the Italian Campanus de Novara (d. 1296) could be found here, as the author of a comprehensive work on planetary theory of a high mathematical standard; here he also described the construction and use of an instrument for rapid mechanical calculation of planetary positions.[40] Towards the end of the century, the leading astronomer in Paris was Guillaume de Saint Cloud,[41] followed by the Dane

---

[38] *Chartularium* I, 644–9; cf. P. Kibre, The Quadrivium in the Thirteenth-Century Universities, *Arts libéraux*, pp. 175–91.

[39] See the preface to L. Thorndike, *The Sphere of Sacrobosco and its Commentators*, Chicago, 1949, and O. Pedersen, In Quest of Sacrobosco, *Journal of the History of Astronomy* 16 (1985), 175–221.

[40] See G. J. Toomer, *Campanus of Novara and Medieval Planetary Theory*, Madison, 1971, and his article on Campanus, in *Dictionary of Scientific Biography*, vol. III, New York, 1971, pp. 23–9.

[41] On Guillaume de St Cloud, see P. Duhem, *Le Système du Monde*, vol. IV, Paris, 1916, pp. 10–31.

Peter Nightingale or Petrus Philomena de Dacia (d. post 1303), who came to Paris from Bologna in 1292, and who in the same year published his new calendar, which was generally used over much of Europe for the next 150 years.[42] In 1293 he continued with a large dissertation on a strongly simplified version of Campanus' calculating instrument. This treatise was succeeded a few years later by a similar description of a calculating machine for predicting lunar eclipses. And yet none of these names was ever entered into the annals of the faculty of *artes*. The astronomers named above must therefore have been *magistri non regentes*, or researchers without teaching duties, who found the Paris milieu sufficiently inspiring for purely scientific work. This is an unusual case of how the divide between teaching and research could sometimes open up even in the middle ages.[43]

There is other evidence, too, that the exact sciences were pursued despite the official silence of the Paris faculty. Even in the thirteenth century there had been great progress in optics. This was due, among others, to Robert Grosseteste of Oxford (1175–1253),[44] his pupil the Franciscan Roger Bacon in Paris (*c.* 1215–1294), the Silesian Vitello, and the German Dietrich of Freiburg (d. *c.* 1310). One of the things now being achieved was a clear understanding of lenses, and towards the end of the century spectacles were invented, with an importance for daily life and science that can hardly be overestimated.[45]

After 1325 a new tendency began to emerge among the fellows of Merton College, Oxford.[46] Generally they were interested in describing physical phenomena in mathematical terms, and with this in

---

[42] On Peter Nightingale, see above, ch. 5, note 38. Cf. O. Pedersen, Petrus Philomena de Dacia, A Problem of Identity, *Cahiers de l'Institut du Moyen-Age Grec et Latin* 19, Copenhagen, 1976.

[43] See e.g. O. Pedersen, Du quadrivium à la physique, in J. Koch (ed.), *Artes Liberales*, Leiden, 1959, pp. 107–23, and Gagne, Du quadrivium.

[44] See A. C. Crombie, *Robert Grosseteste and the Origins of Experimental Science 1100–1700*, Oxford, 1953, and D. A. Callus (ed.), *Robert Grosseteste, Scholar and Bishop*, Oxford, 1955.

[45] On medieval optics, see D. Lindberg, Lines of Influence in Thirteenth-Century Optics, *Speculum* 46 (1971), 66–83, and D. Lindberg, *Studies in the History of Medieval Optics*, London, 1983.

[46] On the Merton school, see M. Clagett, *The Science of Mechanics in the Middle Ages*, Madison, 1959; J. E. Murdoch, The Rise and Development of the Application of Mathematics in Fourteenth-Century Philosophy and Theology, in *Arts libéraux*, pp. 215ff. Cf. C. Wilson, *William Heytesbury: Medieval Logic and the Rise of Mathematical Physics*, Madison, 1956. The existence of a 'school' in the proper sense is contested by E. Sylla, Medieval Quantification of Qualities: The Merton 'School', *Archive for History of Exact Science* 8 (1971–2), 9–39.

mind they developed new methods of theoretical importance. The *Treatise on Proportions* (*Tractus de Proportionibus*) of 1328, written by Thomas Bradwardine (d. 1349), thus contained a new dynamic relation between the force by which a body is moved and the velocity it achieves. This was formulated with the aid of a highly advanced theory of mathematical proportions. In his *Regulae Solvendi Sophismata* of 1335, Bradwardine's colleague William Heytesbury (d. *c.* 1370) was working on the mathematical description of the concept of velocity, a subject which also engaged another colleague of Bradwardine's, Richard Swineshead or Suiseth (fl. mid-fourteenth century). The result was an important kinetic relation for uniformly accelerated movements, the precise form of which shows how far the mathematicians of Merton had come in comparison with the vague way in which Aristotelian philosophers treated problems of motion.

Swineshead produced a special form of speculative mathematical physics, the so-called *calculationes*, in his voluminous *Liber Calculationum*, by which he became known as 'the Calculator'. In this, with numerous examples from many different areas, he showed how a hypothesis in physics could be formulated as a precise mathematic relation between a number of variables which were indicated with letters. Each variable was then given a numerical value, which certainly did not derive from quantitative experiments which no-one at that time knew how to set up correctly, but which was selected with a sound sense of what could be considered possible. If the result thus produced appeared to be absurd – again evaluated on the basis of sound reason – the hypothesis was then dropped. With such *calculationes* it was possible in some cases to eliminate a false hypothesis, even if the method did not make it possible to prove an hypothesis true; it is worth noting that even Galileo much later made occasional use of *calculationes*, and Leibniz advocated a new edition of Swineshead's book.

In the second half of the fourteenth century this movement spread to Paris, where Nicole Oresme (d. 1382 as bishop of Lisieux) invented a graphic method of delineating continuously variable quantities.[47] It was this method that Galileo would use later in his exploration of the laws of free fall, while Oresme himself established how many of the assertions peculiar to Aristotelian physics could be

---

[47] O. Pedersen, *Nicole Oresme og hans naturfilosofiske System*, Copenhagen, 1956; cf. M. Clagett, Oresme, in *DSB*, vol. x, pp. 223–30.

refuted by simple mathematical arguments. But even if Oresme was a well-known figure in the university, his work was too advanced to be put straight into the *artes* syllabus. The revised syllabus of 1366 indeed was a little more positive about the quadrivium than the reading list of 1255, requiring masters of *artes* to have attended one hundred hours of lectures in astronomy and mathematics – though undeniably this is not much for six years. A note in one of the manuscripts explains that 'this is interpreted by the faculty in such a way that it is enough to have heard one book on mathematics read such as [Sacrobosco's] *Tractatus de Sphaera*, and to be engaged in hearing another book read in the honourable hope of hearing it to the end'. In this way after a delay of more than a century, Sacrobosco's main work was eventually named in an unofficial commentary to the curriculum. Perhaps this reveals more than many other examples how little the masters of Paris felt it necessary to disseminate the results of the research that they were so busy producing. Here it should be added that after a while, many of the new ideas found their way into the commentaries on Aristotle that were the normal outcome of lectures. This goes for John Buridanus' great commentary on *De Caelo* which was mentioned earlier, in which the theory of the absolute immobility of the earth was made the object of criticism; just as in the commentary on the *Physics* written by Albert of Saxony (d. 1390), which contains the same precise mathematical hypotheses on free fall as those later discussed by Galileo. On the other hand, the most revolutionary new ideas of the age – Oresme's assumption of the infinity of space (deriving from Thomas Bradwardine) and his careful discussion of the possible daily rotation of the earth – only appeared in a French commentary to *De Caelo* which Oresme had produced for the pleasure of none other than King Charles V.

How small the importance of the mathematical subjects was in the formal curriculum can be seen in a number of dispensations. In 1340 a Swedish master Suno, or Sven, sought and won the faculty's permission to organise a course of astronomy on Sacrobosco's *Sphaera*, in his own house and on holidays, in such a way that he neither imposed on the faculty's own places nor disturbed the routine ordinary teaching. In 1382 John of Austria was allowed on the same terms to lecture on Euclid's geometry, and in 1427 it was a Finn by the name of Jacob Peter Roodh who gained status as *magister regens*, though he only gave extraordinary lectures at midday at the

Carmelites on *Theorica Planetarum* (planetary theory).[48] Geometry and astronomy clearly had very low status in the faculty's judgement. Perhaps it was to make amends for this that two lectureships, set up in 1378 at the Collège de Maître Gervais and financed by the king, were devoted to mathematics and astronomy. Considering that Pope Gregory XI (1370–1378) had appointed Nicole Oresme to reform this college as early as 1374, one could be excused for thinking that Oresme had engineered this development himself to strengthen his own favourite subject.

Elsewhere there was less reluctance to update the curriculum. This was the case, of course, especially in new and less hidebound universities. One example of this is the syllabus for Vienna in 1389,[49] which required of a candidate for the bachelor's degree, besides the works we have already seen, that he had attended lectures on

Tractatus de Sphaera (of Sacrobosco)
Algorismus (of Sacrobosco)
Euclid's 'First Book' or one similar
A book on rhetoric,

while the curriculum for the master's degree contained in addition, among other works.

Theorica Planetarum (an anonymous standard work on planetary theory)
Five books of Euclid
Perspectiva Communis (a work on optics by John Peckham)
A *Tractatus de Proportionibus*
A *Tractatus de Latitudinibus Formarum*
A book on music
A book on arithmetic.

This reading list, which was due no doubt to the reformer of this university Heinrich von Langenstein (d. 1397), clearly shows the effort that had been made to incorporate the new mathematics from Oxford and Paris into a curriculum which was probably as up-to-date as could be managed.

For the sake of brevity it is not expedient to go into the history of the exact sciences in more detail. It is only reasonable to say something about music. Normally the subject of music was a part of

---

[48] On Suno, John of Austria, Jecob Peter Roodh, and the two lectureships at the Collège de Maître Gervais, see Thurot, p. 81.

[49] Rashdall, vol. II, p. 243 note 1; cf. J. von Aschbach, *Geschichte der Wiener Universität*, Vienna, 1865, pp. 91ff. Cf. the corresponding syllabus for Erfurt in Thorndike, pp. 296f.

quadrivium and thus a purely mathematical discipline concerned with the theory of numerical proportions in musical intervals. This was usually taught with Boethius' classical textbook as a base, and by applying a highly developed terminology of the mathematical doctrine of proportions as an instrument. There was no question of any link between this very abstract study and practical musical performance in the middle ages. Practical teaching in music took place outside the universities in cathedral and monastery choirs, while the college statutes are full of prohibitions against any performance of music that might break the peace. All the more reason, therefore, to note the few instances of the universities' allowing practical music on the programme; this was already the case when King Alfonso X regulated conditions in Salamanca. There was a university organist and a music professor here right from the start. A *rotula* from 1355 mentions a total of two *magistri in musica*. As a result, Salamanca was able to confer degrees in theoretical and performed music, and one of the fathers of the new art of music, Bartolomeo Ramos de Pareja, received his education here.[50] Yet this was an exception in the whole middle ages, where nothing apart from this is heard of degrees in music until Cambridge in 1464 and Oxford in 1507.[51]

From the exact sciences we can now turn to the old trivium, which was also radically rearranged by the syllabus of 1255. This appeared above all in the strong upsurge of dialectic, which succeeded the introduction of Aristotle's works in their entirety. On the other hand, rhetoric seems to have been dropped completely, after having languished as an optional subject since 1215. This is confirmed by the list of books from 1286 mentioned earlier, in which not one work on rhetoric can be found. The subject had obviously lost the interest of the faculty in Paris, and this is probably connected to the lack of any civil law faculty in Paris, or of any advocates in the common laws of the land who might have been trained there. In any case it was different in the lawyers' university of Bologna, where the art of eloquence had constantly been highly regarded.

The memorable events of 1215 have already been mentioned, when the word *universitas* was used for the first time of the assembly of teachers and scholars before whom the orator Buoncompagni da Signa read out his new work, later entitled *Rhetorica Antiqua*. The

[50] Rashdall, vol. II, p. 81.   [51] Rashdall, vol. III, p. 160.

same work was otherwise read out in its entirety in 1226, in Padua, to teachers and scholars in the presence of the chancellor and the papal legate. A *Rhetorica Novissima* of the same industrious author was also first offered to the university of Bologna with a reading in the cathedral in 1235.[52] This work was provided with a long preface in which Buoncompagni justified his reasons for writing a new book in the subject. One of his reasons was, as we saw earlier, that scholars were tired of reading Cicero and had reduced him to the optional lectures. Another reason was that 'scholars of Canon and civil law do not have much profit in the liberal arts, unless through public speeches', that is to say, through exercises in rhetoric. Generally in most places, however, the subject seems to have been in decline, until the humanist movement later restored interest in it.

If we finally consider the evidence of the syllabuses on grammar, the changes here seem to have been minimal. But even in this field, we can observe, just as in the quadrivium, an important development in scholarly research in the subject, though this did not leave many traces behind in the official programmes.[53] Not the least example of this was the theoretical philosophy of language which the Danish master of Paris Martin de Dacia (d. 1304) helped to pioneer at the end of the thirteenth century.[54] The aim was to look for a general or universal grammar underlying all forms, rules, and vocabulary of concrete language. These efforts, which have sometimes been viewed as the prototype of modern linguistics, barely flourished for half a century before they were finished off by nominalism.

This interest in linguistic problems and the structural aspect of language was scarcely unconnected with the movement that sought to widen, in the same period, the linguistic horizons of the medieval university. The impulse behind this, in the first instance, came from the Christian mission that was gradually bringing the military actions of the Crusades against Islam to a peaceful conclusion. Not least did the Dominicans prefer winning with the word to bearing down with the sword, and also the Franciscan missionaries gained notoriety by going the whole way to China as early as in the

---

[52] Thorndike, pp. 41ff.
[53] On the philosophy of language in the middle ages, see J. Pinborg, *Die Entwicklung der Sprachtheorie im Mittelalter*, Münster, 1967.
[54] On Martinus de Dacia, see H. Roos, *Die Modi Significandi des Martinus de Dacia*, Copenhagen–Münster, 1952.

thirteenth century. Naturally these Europeans met great language difficulties in the east, and it was not long after the mendicant orders entered the universities that they saw a chance to use them to improve their members' deficient skills. So it appears from a circular letter, which the Dominican-General Humbert (1254-1263) sent in 1256 to all members of the order who 'have now grown in number over the whole world, and also include brethren who have made up their minds to leave their own people and set out into barbaric tribes, and sweat over the learning of a foreign language so as to spread the name of Our Lord Jesus Christ'.[55] In particular, Humbert mentioned the mission in Georgia, now in its eighth year, and the brethren who had studied Arabic among the Saracens in Spain, and had made great progress in this language.

A dozen years later the problems encountered by the missionaries induced the Franciscan Roger Bacon to conceive a great plan for the evangelisation of the whole world.[56] This would be done with a new programme of scholarship that would reform philosophy on an experimental and experiential basis and at the same time cultivate the many languages spoken by heathens the world over. A third of his great *Opus Maius* from 1266 to 1268 was wholly given over to language, emphasising the special need for knowledge of Greek, Hebrew, and Arabic. Roger Bacon himself left us with a complete Greek grammar – the first ever written in Latin for the use of scholars in the west. He also completed a smaller Hebrew grammar, whereas there is no doubt that his knowledge of Arabic was modest. A more competent attempt to introduce the study of Arabic into Christendom was made by one of the most universal men of learning in the middle ages, the Majorcan Ramon Lull (*c.* 1232–*c.* 1315), who was brought up to speak and write Arabic just as well as his mother tongue, while he published in both Latin and Catalan.[57] Even as a layman, he realised the need for better language training for missionaries, and in 1276, with the support of King Jacob II of Majorca and Pope John XXI (Peter the Spaniard), he founded an Arabic college in Miramar. This effort died out after 1292, however, whereas other Spanish schools of Arabic lasted longer. Ramon Lull made persistent attempts to get the universities to give these studies

---
[55] *Chartularium* I, 327ff.
[56] See S. Easton, *Roger Bacon and his Search for a Universal Science*, Oxford, 1952.
[57] See J. N. Hillgarth, *Ramon Lull and Lullism in Fourteenth Century France*, Oxford, 1971; cf. Sarton, vol. II, pp. 900ff.

a more secure status, with a series of memoranda to the church on this matter, such as the *Petitio Raymundi* addressed to Pope Celestine V (drawn up in Naples in 1294), and the *Petitio in Concilio Generali*, written for the ecumenical council of Vienne in 1311/12.

The last request bore fruit, to the extent that the Vienne council passed a decree that from that time forth there should be teaching in Hebrew, Greek, Arabic, and Chaldaean (formerly Syrian) in five specially chosen universities: the University of the Curia, Paris, Oxford, Bologna, and Salamanca.[58] Taken together, these places were assumed to cover the need for oriental philology in Europe. In each university there would be two lecturers in each of the named languages, and these were also to undertake translations from their own respective languages into Latin. The missionary motive was expressly mentioned – it was a matter of evangelising the world beyond Christendom.

It is hard to say how far this decree was carried out in real life, except in the University of the Curia, where teachers are known to have been appointed, and the money for their salaries raised; if they did more, there is no record of it.[59] In 1320 the synod of Canterbury, in order to comply with this decree, decided to introduce a tax from all benefices of one farthing in the pound for the salary of a Jewish convert teaching Hebrew in Oxford. However, the consequences were easiest to see in Paris, where the teaching of Hebrew can be traced up to 1430, in which year the French nation recommended an application for teachers' stipends in Greek, Hebrew, and Chaldaean.[60]

It was the modern European languages, on the other hand, which were cold-shouldered. Because of the pressure to read Latin in the universities, these failed to find their way into the curriculum. Yet there are two examples of the universities' showing some interest in the vernaculars. In one, it was the growth of interest in what might be described as the mission within Christendom that was responsible, when in 1266 the theological Collège de Sorbonne received a gift of 500 Paris pounds from Archbishop Nicholas of Tournai in Flanders, to be used for the maintenance of five Flemish scholars of theology in such a way that henceforth Flanders might be supplied with well-educated priests.[61] This is evidence of an interest in

[58] *Chartularium* I, 154. [59] Rashdall, vol. II, pp. 30f.
[60] *Chartularium* IV, 505. [61] *Chartularium* I, 460.

spreading the gospel in the mother tongue, but not of any accompanying study in the Flemish language.

On the other hand, there were some interesting developments in England, brought on by a somewhat unique situation, namely, the fact that not one, but two foreign languages each had their part to play in public life: Latin, which here as elsewhere in Europe was the language of learning and at the same time the linguistic basis of Canon law; and French, which ever since the Norman Conquest in 1066 had predominated in the court and among the largely French nobility. As a result of this, French was used for many centuries as the language of the royal law-courts, even though a steadily shrinking number of people could actually understand it. This created a need for proficiency in French that the universities could not or would not supply. Yet there is evidence that in fourteenth-century Oxford, in any case, there were teachers offering instruction in 'the art of writing in, composing documents in or speaking in the Gallic language' – teachers, in other words, of the dominant legal language. This teaching went on outside the university, though with its agreement.[62] Teachers of French thus had to swear an oath to respect the university statutes; in addition, they had to pay a joint indemnity of 13 shillings and 4 pence to masters of *artes*, which may mean perhaps that scholars of *artes* had official permission to take French as an option, so to speak, at the expense of another subject within their faculty. Finally there was a decree that scholars of French should attend faculty teaching in those subjects closest to French, that is to say, in grammar and rhetoric. This is certainly the only case in the middle ages of regular teaching in a modern language which was coordinated with genuine university teaching.[63] After a while the position of French became untenable, however, and a statute of 1362 established that English should henceforth be the language of the law-courts, while records should be kept in Latin. To reinforce this decisive innovation, the chancellor the following year took the unusual step of opening parliament with an oration in English. That English legal language to this day is full of curious

---

[62] On the teaching of French in Oxford, see Rashdall, vol. III, p. 162. On legal language in England, see M. McKisack, *The Fourteenth Century*, Oxford, 1959, pp. 524f, and W. Stubbs, *The Constitutional History of England*, vol. II, Oxford, 1877, pp. 414f.

[63] See in general B. Bischoff, The Study of Foreign Languages in the Middle Ages, *Speculum* 36 (1961), 209–24.

words and phrases from medieval French is proof that no language deeply rooted in tradition lets itself be easily changed by legislation.

Surveying the changes within the faculty of *artes* we notice, firstly, the great upheaval brought about by the intrusion of Aristotelianism in the thirteenth century. The contents of the *artes* were marked by the main works of Aristotelian philosophy to such an extent that non-Aristotelian topics (for example the subjects of the *quadrivium*) apparently disappeared from view. Neither syllabuses nor booklists devoted much attention to them. But we have also seen how false this picture is, and that in practice a lively series of changes was taking place in some of the exact sciences. So we may conclude that official syllabuses are a poor guide when it comes to establishing what masters of *artes* were actually engaged on. A much clearer indication of this is the works they left behind, even if it is not always easy to see how far their new ideas had any place in their teaching, or how far they simply represented research done privately with results that were bound to reach the lecterns sooner or later. The school of astronomy in Paris in the second half of the thirteenth century, for example, seems to have been occupied essentially with research, without being further associated with the university.

Another characteristic feature of the syllabuses was their rigidity. In Paris the curriculum of 1255 changed only slightly in the next two hundred years. It is also significant that each time such a change took place, it did so as a result of initiatives from outside. It had to be papal legates reforming a university that in the fourteenth century and later seemed to have no more inclination to renew itself from within. The statutes and privileges were too precious to be tampered with, lest rights already obtained were lost, chief among them being the right of the universities to govern themselves. To this extent their inactivity was understandable. But as far as any progress was concerned, it was positively detrimental that statutes relating to teaching defined its substance not only in general terms, by naming the subjects on which lectures would be given, but also in particulars, by naming the books to be used. This gave the system a rigidity which made it difficult to modernise textbook material, forcing teachers to disseminate new ideas in the framework of well-known texts. This was why the strong criticism of Aristotle in the fourteenth century, for example, was produced in commentaries (to *Physica* and *De Caelo*) which sometimes have little more than a title in common with Aristotle. The history of scholarship has often misconstrued the intellectual life of the later middle ages by taking these works at face value, which has resulted in portraits of university teaching as the slavish unspirited parroting of 'the Philosopher's' opinions. Had these works been read beyond their titles, however, the picture would have been more varied.

All things considered, perhaps the greatest cause for amazement is how the pressure for renewal was able to get the profound results it did, broadening horizons, for example, in the philosophy of language and applied mathematics. On the other hand, we should note that there were always important areas lying outside the university's line of vision. Thus it is surprising how history was continually neglected despite the fact that the late middle ages were particularly rich in historical writers. The story was somewhat similar in literature, which, as far as Latin poetry was concerned in this period, seems to have followed rhetoric out into the cold, while the steadily growing use of the vernacular in literary productions was never enough to rouse scholastic interest. This can hardly be explained solely in terms of the dominant role of Latin as the international language of learning. The reason is rather that the university had come into being and developed in response to a concrete social need for teachers, physicians, lawyers, and theologians with a high level of training. Society as such had no official use for historians or poets. One thing supporting this view is the fact that the universities only began to concern themselves with other languages to help the mission in the east which, although in the hands of the Dominican and Franciscan orders, was presented as a beneficial duty for a Christendom as a whole which still, justly or unjustly, felt itself threatened by Islam. Also, in this respect, the key to understanding the development of the university is its role in medieval society.

Index of names

A. EARLY PERIOD

Abbo of Fleury 86
Abbo of St Germain 90
Abelard (eighth century) 77
Abelard (twelfth century) 110, 112f, 130, 132, 134f, 137, 145, 147, 242, 259
Absalon 132f
Accursius 127
Ada Berot 226
Adam Dorp 289
Adam Elyot 185
Adam Parvipontius 131
Adamnan 45, 51
Adelard of Bath 119f, 123
Aegidius 289
Aelbert 48, 74f
Aethelwald 8of
Agapitus 39
Agnes de Gravia 224
Agobard of Lyons 84
A'h-Mose 3
Aidan 45
Akhtoy 4
Alaric 34, 55
Albert the Great 180, 254, 280ff, 289
Albert of Saxony 289, 293
Alcuin 48ff, 74–7, 84, 89, 122
Aldhelm 49ff
Alexander the Great 13, 16
Alexander III 124, 128, 147ff, 216
Alexander IV 164, 178–81, 191, 200, 270, 277
Alexander of Hales 175, 289
Alexander Neckham 190
Alexander of Villa Dei 279
Alfanus of Salerno 123
Alfonso VI 120
Alfonso VIII 162
Alfonso X 295
Alfred the Great 1, 42, 79, 81
Algers of Liège 127

Alvarus Pelagius 240, 244
Amalarius 112
Amaury de Bene 166, 274
Ambrose, St 54, 58f, 112
Amenemhed III 3
Amenemopes 5
Anatole of Laodicaea 276
Anders Sunesøn 106, 133f
Andreas Copernicus 219
Angilbert 77
Anselm of Canterbury 110f, 283
Anselm of Laon 134
Anselm of Milan 86
Anthony, St 58
Antoninus of Florence 267
Antony 19
Apollonius 118
Arcadius 34
Archimedes 42, 120, 276
Archytas 8f
Aristotle 8f, 12–17, 22, 24, 42, 106, 109, 118, 120, 125, 167, 171, 101, 239, 254–9, 273–82, 289f, 293, 295, 300
Arnobius 58
Arnold of Villanova 240
Asclepius 7
Asser of Lund 81
Athanasius, St 58
Atto of Vercelli 125
Augustine, St 54, 56f, 60–5, 95, 112, 135, 281f
Augustine of Canterbury 46f
Augustus 24, 26
Averroës 118, 280, 289
Avicenna 118, 125

Baldwin 165
Bangulf 72
Bartolomeo Ramos 295
Basil 58f
Bede 46, 48–50, 52f, 57ff, 74, 81, 85, 98, 112
Benedict IX 216f

Index of names

Benedict XII 223
Benedict Biscop 47f, 58
Benedict of Nurcia 41, 43, 83
Benedict from Sweden 245
Bernard of Chartres 129
Bernard of Clairvaux 98f, 103, 112, 124
Bernard Guidonis 181
Bernard de Insulis 217
Bernard of Pavia 128
Bernard Silvestris 129
Berno of Cluny 97
al-Biruni 118
Blanca of Castilla 172, 222
Boethius 8, 38, 42f, 52, 59, 64f, 81, 84, 106f, 121, 259, 278f, 282f, 295
Boethius de Dacia 71
Bonaventura 136, 181, 289
Boniface 71
Brahe, Tycho 85
Bulgarus 127
Buoncompagni da Signa 144, 251, 295f
Buridanus 255–9, 289, 293

Caedmon 82
Caesar 17, 19
Callimachus 18
Campanus of Novara 290f
Canute, King 93, 98, 104
Carcalla 25
Carloman 68, 71
Cassian 58
Cassiodor 38–43, 50ff, 58, 63f, 73, 76
Cato 21, 215
Celestine V, 298
Ceolfrid 48
Charlemagne 23, 68–77, 79f, 82f, 86f, 90f, 93f, 119, 123, 147
Charles the Bald 87
Charles Martel 68, 70, 82
Charles V, King 211, 293
Chlodoveg 34, 46, 56
Christian of Ribe 216
Christianus 224
Chrysostomus 58
Cicero 7, 20f, 25, 41, 59, 62, 65, 107, 109, 206, 251
Claudius 23
Clement III 142
Clement IV 198f
Clement VI 217f
Cleopatra 19
Columba 45
Columbanus 44–7
Constantine of Fleury 107
Constantine the Great 25, 31, 33

Constantinus Africanus 123
Copernicus, Nicolaus 18
Cynewulf 82
Cyprian 58

Dagobert 46, 56
David de Dinant 274
Demetrius of Phaleron 16
Desiderius 74
Dicuil 85
Didier of Vienne 64
Dietrich of Freiberg 291
Diocletian 25, 31, 33
Dionysius Areopagites 84
Dionysius Exiguus 52
Dioscorides 23
Dominicus 194
Dominicus Gundissalinus 115, 120
Donatus 41, 64, 108, 174, 215, 278
Duns Scotus, Johannes 286, 289

Eadmer 110
Eberhard de Bethune 279
Edmund 80
Edmund Gonville 228
Edward III, King 185
Edwin 45
Egbert 48
Einhard 77f, 88, 90
Eleanor 219
Eratosthenes 18
Erigena, Johannes Scotus 84f, 89, 91, 166
Eskil of Lund 106, 132
Ethelbert 46
Etienne Tempier 284ff
Etienne de Tournai 113, 130, 217
Euclid 18, 120, 276, 293f
Eudemus 14
Eudoxus 7
Eugenius II 79, 125
Eusebius 58

al-Farabi 117
Ferrarius Catalaunus 262
Finnian 44
Francis of Assisi 116, 174
Freculf of Lisieux 89
Fredegarius 52
Fredegise of Tours 84
Frederic II 162, 206
Frederic Barbarossa 128, 139f, 147
Frontinus 24
Fulbert of Chartres 128
Fulcher of Chartres 96
Fulques de Deuil 132

Index of names

Gaius 26f
Galen of Pergamon 23, 123
Galerius 31
Galileo 292f
Gaufredus de Marec 224
Geminus 276
Genseric 34
Gerard d'Abbeville 262
Gerardo de Borgo San Donnino 178
Gerard of Cremona 120f, 125
Gerbert of Aurillac 106–9, 119, 122, 128
Germanus 58
Gilbert de la Porrée 129, 254, 278
Gildas 44, 58
Giraldus Cambrensis 113
Godefroid de Fontaines 261
Gottschalk 89
Gratian, canonist 127f, 147
Gratian, Emperor 32
Gregory the Great 46, 51, 58, 63f, 76, 81, 112
Gregory VII 96, 99, 112, 136
Gregory IX 169, 172, 174, 240, 243, 247, 272
Gregory XI 294
Gregory of Nazianzus 58
Gregory of Nyssa 84
Gregory of Rimini 289
Gregory of Tours 38, 51, 57f
Grimbold 81
Guala Bichierus 151, 165
Guido of Arezzo 86
Guillaume d'Auvergne 176
Guillaume de Champeaux 130, 134, 137
Guillaume de Conches 129
Guillaume d'Estouteville 279
Guillaume de Roseto 224
Guillaume de St Amour 178f, 278
Guillaume de St Cloud 290
Guillaume de St Thierry 129
Guillermus de Insulis 197
Gunnar of Viborg 106

Hadrian, Emperor 19, 26
Hadrian I, 69, 86
Hadrian, monk 47, 49
Harun al-Rashid 119
Heinrich von Langenstein 294
Heiric d'Auxerre 83f
Heiric of Friaul 87
Heloïse 110, 134, 145
Henri de Gand 161
Henricus de Alemania 225
Henry IV, Emperor 96
Henry V, Emperor 127
Henry II, King 102, 152f
Henry III, King 160, 172, 183, 223

Henry VI, King 239
Henry the Barber 230
Henry of Blois 105
Henry of Gamtofte 217
Henry, schoolmaster 105
Henry of Unna 245
Heracleides 85
Herman of Bury 104
Herman the Lame 119
Hero of Alexandria 18, 276
Hervaeus of Troyes 168f
Hervé Nédellec 262
Hieronymus, see Jermome, St
Hilary 58
Hincmar of Rheims 87ff
Hippocrates 7
Hoger of Verden 86
Homer 18
Homer of Ribe 106
Honoratus 40
Honorius 34
Honorius III 161, 165, 171, 173f, 192f, 217
Horace 23, 50, 109
Hrabanus Maurus 77f, 82f, 85, 89, 108f
Hucbald of St Amand 86
Hugo de Alberico 127
Hugo de Balsham 183, 228
Hugo Capet 82
Hugo de St Cher 176
Hugo of St Victor 115f, 131, 248f
Hugo de Seghuin 217
Hugolin Conti 174
Humbert 179f, 297

Ibn Khaldoun 68
Ibn Roshd, see Averroës
Ibn-Sina, see Avicenna
Innocent III, 150f, 159f, 164, 166ff, 177, 193, 217
Innocent IV 177, 191, 217, 222, 277
Irnerius 127
Isidore of Seville 52ff, 58, 65
Isocrates 7
Ivo of Chartres 111, 127

Jacob II of Aragon 240, 297
Jacob of Auxerre 112
Jacob Peter Roodh 293
Jacob da Porta Ravennate 127
Jean de Meung 42
Jeremiah 5
Jerome, St 19, 32, 58, 64, 76, 112
Jocius of London 226
Johannes Cancellarius 167ff, 193
Johannes Cassianus 40

Index of names 305

Johannes de Dacia 226
Johannes de Firdanza, *see* Bonaventura
Johannes de Rupella 176
John XXI 284, 297
John XXII 218
John, King 102, 159f
John, novice 249
John of Austria 293
John Bassianus 142
John Bonafos 244
John Buridanus, *see* Buridanus
John de Cella 150
John Duns Scotus, *see* Duns Scotus
John Hackley 235
John Peckham 262, 294
John de Sacrobosco 290, 293f
John of Salisbury 96, 109, 129, 131, 146, 152f, 242
John the Saxon 81
John of Stratford 238
John Tzetzes 10
John Wyclif 183
Jonas of Bobbio 44
Jonas of Orleans 87
Jordanus of Saxony 175
Josephus 58
Justinian 36f, 87, 126ff, 246
Juvenal 50

Ketil of Viborg, St 106
al-Khwarizmi 120
al-Kindi 117
Konrad of Hirsau 109

Lactantius 58
Lanfranc 125
Laurentius de Dacia 245
Leibniz 292
Lenthenius 49
Leo the Great 33
Leo II 69, 95
Licinius 25, 31f
Lothar 82, 125
Louis IV 123
Louis IX, St 172, 222, 227
Louis XI 289
Louis the German 82
Louis the Pious 82, 90
Lucas Watzelrode 218
Lucullus 20
Ludwig of Bavaria 286

al-Mahmun 117
Maidulf 49
Margaret of Flanders 222

Marsilius of Inghen 289
Martianus Capella 24, 85
Martin IV 195, 198, 202, 273
Martin of Braga 51
Martin de Dacia 296
Martin of Tours 40
Martinus of Bologna 127
Mathaeus de Arginis 197
Matthaeus de Scotia 165
Matthew Paris 150, 160, 172
Mathilda Scriptor 230
Maximus the Confessor 84
Michael III 95
Mohammed 67

Ne-Ma'et-Re 3
Nero 23
Nicholas I 95
Nicholas of Salerno 124
Nicholas of Tournai 298
Nicholaus ad Latus 224
Nichomachus 16
Nicolaus de Dacia 225, 245
Nicole Oresme 292f
Nithard 90
Nothelm 52
Notker Balbulus 83, 97
Notker Labeo 42

Oddo de Carnoto 197
Oddo de Polengeio 197
Odo of Cluny 106
Odo of Paris 82, 130, 150, 165f
Odoacer 34
Oresme, *see* Nicole Oresme
Origenes 58
Osmund 104
Oswin 47
Otto II 106f
Otto Morena 139

Pandolfo 160
Pascal III 147
Pascasius Radbertus 89, 112
Patrick, St 44
Paul of Aquileia 74, 87
Paul, jurist 26, 36
Paulus Diaconus 74, 76, 85
Paulus Orosius 81
Peder Arnfast 220, 225
Peder of Odense 216
Peder Sunesøn 132
Peder Vognsen 106
Pelagius II 63
Pepi 4

Index of names

Pepin 82, 87
Peter Abelard, *see* Abelard
Peter de Alvernia 255
Peter Anchamaro 143
Peter Calo 180
Peter Cantor 130
Peter Comestor 130
Peter Damianus 112
Peter the Lombard 111, 130, 152, 180, 195, 260
Peter Nightingale, *see* Petrus Philomena de Dacia
Peter Pisanus 73f
Peter of Poitiers 130
Peter the Venerable 112, 135
Petrus Arnoldi 245
Petrus Cornubiensis 197
Petrus Lemovicensis 197
Petrus Mathiae 245
Petrus Philomena de Dacia 143, 291
Philippe II 158, 160, 172, 191
Philippe III 220
Philippe IV the Fair 222, 240
Philippe de Thori 196, 199
Pierre d'Ailly 289
Pierre de Corbeil 165f
Pierre Dubois 214
Pierre de Nemours 166
Pierre de Paris 168
Pippin the Short 68
Plato 1, 9–15, 17, 22f, 36, 42, 72, 77
Pliny 54, 58, 152
Plotinus 30
Porphyry 8, 42, 106, 278
Prepositinus 168
Priscian 274, 278f
Prosper of Aquitaine 58, 112
Ptolemy 8, 18, 42, 118, 121, 276
Ptolemy I Soter 16, 19
Pythagoreans 8–11, 23

Quintilian 21
Quintus Mucius Scaevola 26

Radolphus 258f
Rahere 124
Rahevin 139
Ramon Lull 297
Ratramnus of Corbie 89
Regino of Prüm 86, 89
Remigius of Auxerre 84f, 112
Remigius of Trier 107
Renoaldus Cherin 226
Richard of Chichester 263
Richard of Devizes 153
Richard of St Victor 131

Richard Swineshead 292
Richer 106f
Richer de St Remi 90
Robert of Boulogne 222
Robert I Capet 97
Robert of Champagne 98
Robert de Courçon 151, 167, 170, 191, 221, 243, 263, 268, 274f
Robert of Cricklade 152f
Robert Grosseteste 190, 219, 291
Robert Kilwardby 284
Robert Pullen 152
Robert de Sorbon 227
Robert de Winchelis 197
Rodrigo of Spain 67
Roger Bacon 175, 277, 291, 297
Roger Fugardi 124
Roland Bandinelli, *see* Alexander III
Roland, theologian 175
Roland, scholar 245
Rollo 93
Romolus Augustulus 34
Roscellinus 109f, 276
Rufinus 58

Sabinus Masurius 26
Salvius Julianus 26
Samson of Bury 104
Saxo Grammaticus 133
Scipio 20
Sedulius Scotus 83
Seneca 109
Servatus Lupus 83
Siger de Brabant 280f, 284
Simon de Brie, *see* Martin IV
Simon de Messemy 220
Sisebut 54
Smaragdus of St Mihiel 87
Socrates 7, 9, 11
Solomon 174
Statius 107
Stephan II 68
Stephan Cancellarius 199
Stephanus Berot 226
Stephen Harding 98
Stephen Langton 130
Suiseth, *see* Richard Swineshead
Sulla 20
Suno 245
Suno of Sweden 293
Sybilla Cherin 226
Sylvester II, *see* Gerbert of Aurillac

Terence 50
Thegan 90

Index of names

Theobald of Paris 216
Theobald, tailor 224
Theobaldus Stampensis 152
Theodore the Greek 47, 49
Theodoric 34, 38f
Theodosius I 32f
Theodosius II 27
Theodulf of Orleans 75, 77, 80, 88
Theophilus 58
Theophrast 14, 17, 278
Thierry, King 46
Thierry of Chartres 129
Thomas Aquinas 42, 120, 136, 180f, 200f, 207, 235, 249, 255f, 258, 260, 280, 282–6, 289
Thomas Becket 146, 153
Thomas Bradwardine 292f
Thomas de Chanteloup 219
Thomas of Ireland 40
Thomas, *praepositus* 158
Tiberius Coruncanius 26
Tobias of Rochester 49

Ulpian 26, 36f
Urban IV 181, 198, 284
Urban V 279

Valdemar 133
Varro 19, 23, 41
Venantius Fortunatus 51
Vespasian 19
Victorinus 106
Villard de Honnecourt 114
Vincent de Beauvais 249
Virgil 50, 59, 109
Vitellian 47
Vitello 291
Vitruvius 24

Walafrid Strabo 85f, 90
Walter the Carpenter 230
Walter of Henley 100
Walter Map 160
Walter de Merton 228
Walter Teutonicus 176
Widukind 69
William Bateman 220
William the Bocbindere 230
William Heytesbury 292
William of Moerbeke 120, 282
William de Newwfylde 235
William of Ockham 286–9
Willibrord 71, 74
Wynfrith, *see* Boniface

Zeno 36

Zindurammus 224

B. MODERN AUTHORS

Aigrain, R. 44, 221
Albright, W. F. 2
Alföldi, A. 32
Ali, J. 118
Altaner, B. 29
Anawati, M. M. 117
Aschbach, J. von 294
Archibald, R. C. 3
Aston, T. H. 219

Baldwin, M. W. 128, 148
Baynes, N. H. 32
Beddie, J. S. 59
Binding, C. 114
Bischoff, B. 299
Blair, P. H. 48
Bloch, M. 94
Boissonnade, P. 101
Bonnaud, B. 42
Bonnet, S. F. 21
Boserup, J. 133
Boyce, G. C. 245
Branner, R. 43
Brodrick, G. C. 228, 236
Brown, P. 59
Browne, G. F. 49, 81
Brunet, A. 109
Brunner, O. 94
Budge, E. Wallis 2
Budinsky, A. 227
Burkert, W. 8

Callus, D. 205, 275, 291
Caplan, H. 109
Cappuyns, M. 84
Carolsfeld, L. S. von 27
Carra de Vaux, B. 117
Carus-Wilson, M. 103
Catto, J. I. 152, 205, 219, 228, 285f
Chase, A. B. 3
Chenu, M. D. 116, 234
Chesterton, G. K. 180
Christensen, T. C. 31
Chydenius, J. 88
Clagett, M. 18, 291f
Clark, A. 228
Clerval, A. 128
Cobban, A. B. 122
Colbourn, R. 94
Cooper, C. H. 160, 183, 220, 223f, 231, 234, 237, 239, 243

Index of names

Copleston, F. 180
Cowdreay, H. E. J. 97
Coyne, G. V. 53
Crombie, A. C. 119, 291
Cumont, F. 30f

Daniel, N. 67
Davis, R. 58
Dawson, C. 67
Deanesley, M. 47, 92
Dehnert, E. J. 65
Delauny, P. 124
Delhaye, P. 92, 275
Denifle, H. 122, 126, 130, 133, 139, 141f, 144, 162, 164, 197
Destrez, J. 234
Dickinson, J. 129
Diels, H. 8
D'Irsay, S. 122
Donnel, T. R. O. 108
Du Boulay, F. R. H. 223
Duckett, F. S. 75
Dufeil, M. M. 179
Duhem, P. 85, 287, 290
Dühring, I. 13

Easton, S. 297
Ebbesen, S. 133
Emden, A. B. 205, 225
Endres, J. A. 112
English, B. 59
Erman, A. 2
Espenberger, J. N. 111

Faith, R. 219
Falco, G. 88
Fellner, S. 78
Fliche, A. 99
Forbes, R. J. 103
Fournier, P. 53, 57, 86
Fraser, P. M. 17

Gabriel, A. L. 227
Gagne, J. 283, 291
Gallen, J. 283, 291
Ganshof, F. L. 94
Gardet, L. 117
Garmondsway, G. N. 81
Garner, H. N. 99
Gascoigne, C. J. B. 75
Ghellinck, J. de 111
Gille, B. 103
Gilson, E. 40, 59, 84, 104, 111, 135, 166, 175, 180, 271, 280, 282, 286
Gilson, M. T. 108

Gimpel, J. 103
Glorieux, P. 227, 261
Gougard, L. 44
Grabmann, M. 250, 254, 258, 260, 271
Grane, L. 111
Grant, E. 271
Gratien, O. 174
Gruner, O. C. 125
Guelley, R. 286
Guenée, B. 89

Hackett, M. B. 183, 205f, 209, 223, 225, 231, 236, 243, 247, 252, 263, 268
Hall, A. R. 103
Harrison, F. 105
Harvey, B. F. 223
Haskins, C. H. 109, 121, 153, 206
Hazeltine, D. D. 127
Heer, F. 148
Hendley, B. P. 129
Highfield, J. R. L. 228
Hillgarth, J. N. 297
Höd, L. 111
Holmes, U. T. 109
Honoré, A. 37
Hoskin, M. A. 53
Hussey, J. M. 34

Inge, W. R. 30

Jaeger, W. 6, 13
Jedin, H. 67, 97
Jenks, E. 55
Jensen, P. J. 30
Jolowicz, H. F. 25, 37
Jones, A. H. M. 29
Jones, C. W. 53
Jones, L. W. 41, 43
Jørgensen, J. 174

Kibre, P. 140, 142, 145, 188, 210, 219, 222, 232, 245, 290
Kirk, G. S. 8
Knowles, D. 47, 97, 99, 174
Koch, H. 106
Koch, J. 285, 291
Koepler, H. 139
Kraft, H. 32
Kramers, S. N. 4
Kranz, W. 8
Kristeller, P. O. 123

Lacroix, B. 89
Laistner, M. L. W. 57

Index of names

Landgraf, A. H. 111
Lange, H. O. 2
Langosch, K. 77
Lattin, H. Pratt 107
Lawn, B. 122
Leach, A. E. 49, 80, 104f
Leader, D. R. 183, 228
Le Bras, G. 57, 86, 128
Leclerq, J. 59
Leff, G. 286
Le Goff, J. 101
Leo XIII 250
Lewry, O. 285
Lindberg, D. 291
Little, A. G. 278
Lloyd, G. E. R. 13
Lot, F. 29
Luscombe, D. 110, 135

Macdonald, A. R. 125
McGary, D. D. 129
Machabey, A. 86
McKeon, R. 109
McKisack, M. 299
Maitland, F. W. 102
Maitre, L. 80
Makdisi, G. 259
Mallet, C. E. 152f, 159f, 206, 228
Mandonnet, P. 174
Manitius, M. 67, 92
Maritain, J. 250
Marrou, H. I. 2, 6, 59
Marshall, E. 152
Mathon, G. 84
Meyer-Steineg, T. 123
Michaud-Quantin, O. 145
Mieli, A. 117
Minio-Paluello, L. 42, 273
Momigliano, A. 41
Mommsen, Th. 27
Moody, E. A. 255
Moore, N. 124
Mortensen, L. B. 133
Mortet, V. 24
Moser, S. 286
Muckle, J. T. 119
Mullinger, J. Bass 222, 228, 237, 258
Muntz, P. 139
Murdoch, J. E. 291

Neugebauer, O. 3
Niels, F. 97
Nitze, W. A. 109
Nussbaum, N. 114
Nyrop, C. 113

Ogilvy, J. D. A. 59
O'Leary, D. L. 117
Olsen, B. Munk 109
Orme, N. 92
Oschinsky, D. 100
Ostrogorsky, G. A. 34

Pacaut, M. 148
Palmer, R. B. 48
Paré, G. 109
Parent, J. M. 128
Parsons, E. A. 17
Pedersen, O. 18, 53, 143, 286, 290ff
Pegues, F. 218
Petersen, F. Saaby 143
Picavet, F. 109
Pinborg, J. 296
Pirenne, H. 35, 68, 101
Portalié, A. 59
Post, G. 148, 151
Prümmer, D. 181

Rait, R. S. 238f, 245
Rand, E. K. 42
Rashdall, H. 122–7, 133, 139, 141f, 144f, 147, 150–4, 159–62, 169, 172, 177, 182, 186, 190, 199, 202, 204ff, 208, 212, 214, 219, 244f, 247f, 263, 275, 294f, 298f
Raven, J. E. 8f
Reynolds, R. L. 215
Riche, P. 92
Ridder-Symoens, H. de 122
Ritter, G. 289
Rodger, A. 37
Roesdahl, E. 81
Rogers, J. E. Thorold 186
Roos, H. 296
Rupp, J. 95

Sabatier, P. 174
Salter, H. E. 160, 186, 230
Sanford, E. M. 109
Sarton, G. 18, 24, 85, 119, 297
Savigny, F. K. 126f
Schiefer, Th. 71
Schoelen, E. 249f
Schultz, F. 27
Sezgin, F. 117
Shirley-Price, L. 46
Sikes, J. G. 135
Singer, Ch. 103
Skeat, T. C. 234
Smail, W. H. 21
Smith, C. E. 275
Sorbelli, A. 126, 142, 161, 263

Southern, R. W. 92, 152, 159, 205
Spinazzi, R. M. 255
Stahl, W. H. 23
Steiner, A. 249
Stenton, F. M. 81
Stephenson, C. 102
Stubbs, W. 299
Sudhoff, K. 120, 123
Sylla, E. 291

Tarn, W. 18
Taylor, A. E. 9
Taylor, Ch. 148
Taylor, L. R. 30
Theurkauf, G. 55
Thomas, P. G. 81
Thompson, A. Hamilton 48, 57
Thorndike, L. 144, 153, 214, 216, 226, 234, 237, 239ff, 244, 246, 251ff, 267, 279, 289f, 294, 296
Thurot, C. 279, 294
Toomer, G. J. 290
Treitinger, O. 38
Tremblay, P. 109
Touilier, A. 130, 136
Tureau, D. 78

Ullmann, W. 55, 57, 87f, 140

Van der Baer, P. A. 88
Van Steenberghen, F. 273, 280
Vicaire, M. M. 174
Vignaux, P. 286f
Vinogradoff, P. 34
Vleeschauwer, H. J. de 17, 19
Vyver, A. van de 119

Waddell, H. 136f, 146
Walker, T. A. 228
Wallach, L. 75
Waltzing, J. P. 27
Ward, P. L. 87
Watt, D. E. R. 218
Weber, E. H. 285
Wedel-Jarlsberg, E. 174
Weisheipl, J. A. 180, 286
White, L. 70, 100, 103
Whitelock, D. 81
Williams, J. R. 107
Williams, T. J. 103
Wilson, C. 291
Wise, J. E. 59
Wormald, F. 233, 235

Printed in the United States
143457LV00003B/35/P